CHAUCER TRADITIONS

Chaucer was perceived as the father of English poetry, and his works gave rise to a diversity of traditions of both creative response and critical commentary, to subsequent 'Chaucerian' authors, and to a body of comment about his writings, one of the longest continuous critical traditions in vernacular European literature. This book is the first to describe Chaucer's literary influence across a wide range of writers and periods. It takes as its theme the *variety* of responses to Chaucer or 'Chaucer traditions', and addresses topics of special interest arising from the effects Chaucer's work had on subsequent writers in the three centuries leading up to Dryden. Each essay focusses on a certain writer or literary tradition (Gower, Hoccleve, Skelton, late medieval romance, early Tudor song, Shakespeare, Dryden, and so on), discussing these in the context of Chaucer's work and its influence.

The result is an important collection of essays by prominent Chaucer scholars, which will be of interest to all teachers and students of Chaucer, as well as to scholars of poetry in later periods.

CHAUCER TRADITIONS
Studies in Honour of Derek Brewer

Edited by

RUTH MORSE

and

BARRY WINDEATT

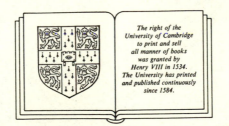

The right of the
University of Cambridge
to print and sell
all manner of books
was granted by
Henry VIII in 1534.
The University has printed
and published continuously
since 1584.

CAMBRIDGE UNIVERSITY PRESS

CAMBRIDGE

NEW YORK PORT CHESTER

MELBOURNE SYDNEY

Published by the Press Syndicate of the University of Cambridge
The Pitt Building, Trumpington Street, Cambridge CB2 IRP
40 West 20th Street, New York, NY 10011, USA
10 Stamford Road, Oakleigh, Melbourne 3166, Australia

First published 1990

Printed in Great Britain by the University Press, Cambridge

British Library cataloguing in publication data

Chaucer traditions: studies in honour of Derek Brewer.
1. poetry in English, Chaucer, Geoffrey
I. Morse, Ruth II. Windeatt, B. A. (Barry A.) III. Brewer, Derek.
821'.1

Library of Congress cataloguing in publication data

Chaucer traditions: studies in honour of Derek Brewer/edited by
Ruth Morse and Barry Windeatt.
p. cm.
1. Chaucer, Geoffrey, d. 1400 – Criticism and interpretation.
2. Chaucer, Geoffrey, d. 1400 – Influence. 3. English poetry – Middle
English, 1100–1500 – History and criticism. 4. Scottish poetry –
To 1700 – History and criticism. 5. Brewer, Derek.
I. Morse, Ruth. II, Windeatt, B. A. (Barry A.). III, Brewer, Derek.

ISBN 0 521 35247 9

Contents

Contributors

RICHARD AXTON, Christ's College, Cambridge
ANNA BALDWIN, University of York
RICHARD BEADLE, St John's College, Cambridge
PIERO BOITANI, University of Rome
J. A. BURROW, University of Bristol
HELEN COOPER, University College, Oxford
DOUGLAS GRAY, Lady Margaret Hall, Oxford
THOMAS J. HEFFERNAN, University of Tennessee
JILL MANN, Girton College, Cambridge
RUTH MORSE, Fitzwilliam College, Cambridge
CHARLES MUSCATINE, University of California, Berkeley
DEREK PEARSALL, Harvard University
JOHN SCATTERGOOD, Trinity College, Dublin
A. C. SPEARING, University of Virginia
JOHN STEVENS, Magdalene College, Cambridge
TOSHIYUKI TAKAMIYA, Keio University
BARRY WINDEATT, Emmanuel College, Cambridge

Preface

For Derek Brewer

The essays in this volume have been contributed by colleagues, friends and former pupils in honour of Derek Brewer in the year of his retirement, and as an affectionate tribute to his achievements in the study of medieval literature and especially of Chaucer.

Derek Brewer was educated at Magdalen College, Oxford, where he was taught by C. S. Lewis and J. A. W. Bennett, and took up his first appointment as a lecturer in English at Birmingham University in 1949. From 1956 to 1958 he lectured at Keio University in Tokyo, returning to Birmingham until 1965, when he was appointed a lecturer in the Faculty of English in the University of Cambridge, and elected a Fellow of Emmanuel College. A Readership in Medieval English followed in 1976, and Derek Brewer was elected Master of Emmanuel College in 1977, and Professor of Medieval English in 1983.

The list of his published writings which closes this volume bears witness to the range and energy of Derek Brewer's interests: his critical interpretation of Chaucer, successively revised and extended; his concern for the editing of medieval texts; his curiosity to see Chaucer's life and work in the context of its times; a stream of important articles on aspects of Chaucer as a narrative poet and in relation to traditions, now assembled in two volumes of collected essays; and, in addition, a range of contributions on other medieval literature (notably on Malory and romance), and on the history of response to Chaucer's work.

The present collection of essays takes as its theme this variety of responses to Chaucer or 'Chaucer traditions', and aims to address topics of especial interest within the field of Chaucer's influence on subsequent writers until the end of the seventeenth century. In assembling this collection the editors have been grateful for that good will abundantly shown by the contributors, a good will which flows from our shared regard and affection for Derek Brewer. It is a rare modern scholar who has done so much for his subject, both through his own work and through what he has encouraged and enabled others to do. These essays are offered in tribute to a modern Chaucerian, most generous of teachers, and an unfailing friend.

RUTH MORSE   BARRY WINDEATT

Note on the text

The text of Chaucer used throughout for quotation and reference is *The Riverside Chaucer*, ed. Larry Benson (Boston, 1987; Oxford, 1988), except where reference is specifically made to editions of Chaucer before 1700.

Abbreviations

EETS   *Early English Text Society*
PMLA   *Publications of the Modern Language Association*

1

Chaucer traditions

BARRY WINDEATT

The works of Chaucer gave rise to a diversity of traditions of both creative response and critical commentary, to subsequent 'Chaucerian' authors, and to a body of comment about Chaucer's writings, one of the longest continuous critical traditions in vernacular European literature.[1] It was Chaucer who began it. For Chaucer was both the first English author to conceive of his writings as a whole oeuvre and the first so clearly to have thought of his works as having a posterity. In the two *Prologues* to the *Legend of Good Women* (F, 417ff., G, 405ff.), the Introduction to the *Man of Law's Tale* (II, 46–76), and in the *Retractions* at the close of the *Canterbury Tales* (x, 1081–92), Chaucer lists his writings – in recollecting, 'collects' them – as an assembled corpus of individual work. At the close of *Troilus and Criseyde* he envisages a future for his writing in relation to the past, when he bids his poem follow in the footsteps of the ancient poets, but also worries about textual transmission and future interpretation. This collection of essays on 'Chaucer traditions' is devoted to topics in the first three centuries of imitation and re-creation by subsequent authors, a period brought to a close by those verse translations or modernizations of Chaucer by Dryden in his *Fables Ancient and Modern* (1700), which register how understanding of Chaucer's language has changed, just as Dryden's Preface to the *Fables* marks a transition in critical interpretation of Chaucer.

Earliest responses to Chaucer's works by other writers date from the 1380s and 1390s and in themselves suggest the variousness of the stimulus offered by Chaucer's writings. The most important contemporary English author who shows an awareness of Chaucer is John Gower, and Richard Axton has written ('Gower – Chaucer's heir?') about the nature of the literary commerce which flowed between these two late fourteenth-century poets. Such early responses may offer valuable pointers to what aspects of Chaucer's works were then prized. The contemporary French poet Eustache Deschamps praises Chaucer in a poem (*c.* 1385) which opens with this stanza:

> O Socratès plains de philosophie,
> Seneque en meurs, Auglius en pratique,
> Ovides grans en ta poëterie,
> Briés en parler, saiges en rhetorique,
> Aigles treshaulz, qui par ta theorique
> Enlumines le regne d'Eneas,
> L'Isle aux Geans, ceuls de Bruth, et qu'i as
> Semé les fleurs et planté le rosier
> Aux ignorans de la langue Pandras,
> Grant translateur, noble Geoffrey Chaucier ... [2]

and while a French poet will naturally attach significance to Chaucer's translation of the *Roman de la Rose* into English for those ignorant of the French language ('et planté le rosier ...'), the English *Romaunt* was indeed an important part of early conceptions of Chaucer as a poet of the experience of love, as well as a poet 'full of philosophy', 'a Seneca in morality', and 'wise in rhetoric'.

Chaucer the learned, moral and philosophical poet is a continuous theme in comment by subsequent writers, and in Thomas Usk's prose *Testament of Love* (?1387) – heavily influenced by Chaucer's *Troilus* and *Boece* – the allegorical figure of Love recommends a reading of *Troilus* in terms which underline the contribution of Chaucer's translation of the *De Consolatione Philosophiae* of Boethius in forming this conception of him as a 'philosophical poet'. To the author's question as to how God's foreknowledge may be reconciled with free will, Love replies:

> Myne owne trewe servaunt, the noble philosophical poete in Englissh, whiche evermore him besieth and travayleth right sore my name to encrese (wherfore al that willen me good owe to do him worship and reverence bothe; trewly, his better ne his pere in scole of my rules coude I never fynde) – he (quod she), in a tretis that he made of my servant Troilus, hath this mater touched, and at the ful this question assoyled. Certaynly, his noble sayinges can I not amende; in goodnes of gentil manliche speche, without any maner of nycetè of storiers imaginacion, in witte and in good reson of sentence he passeth al other makers. In the boke of Troilus, the answere to thy question mayst thou lerne ... [3]

That the claim made for Chaucer as both philosophical poet and poet of love may surprise some modern readers does not lessen the seriousness with which this contemporary claim for Chaucer is made, and made in terms which also acknowledge something special in Chaucer's language and in the comparison between his narratives and those of conventional tellers of stories. In so recognizing the example set by Chaucer's narrative technique, Usk anticipates how subsequent Chaucerian writers will draw on the narratorial models available in Chaucer's recasting of dream poem and romance forms,[4] just as Gower's tribute to Chaucer as the composer of love lyrics (see below, p. 29) is the earliest acknowledgement in a long tradition of much greater response to the short poems of Chaucer than they have more recently enjoyed.[5] In the *Moral Balade* of Henry Scogan (c. 1361–1407) esteem for Chaucer's short poems, for his language, and for his achievement as a moral, philosophical poet come together. The Scogan to whom Chaucer addresses his *L'Envoy de Chaucer à Scogan* is presumably the courtier who was tutor to the sons of Henry IV and supposedly sent the princes a poem of 189 lines, which recommends virtue, refers to the discussion of *gentilesse* in the *Wife of Bath's Tale* and quotes within itself the whole of Chaucer's poem *Gentilesse*, in a way that is editing and anthologizing Chaucer as a source of morally instructive poetry while commending his language ('My mayster Chaucer ... That in his langage was so curious ...' 65–6).[6]

Scogan was a courtier while Usk was a minor London official (possibly known personally to Chaucer), and the nature of Chaucer's circle and early readers had consequences for the traditions of his poetry.[7] Of a younger generation but also a London official and apparently known to Chaucer, Thomas Hoccleve (*c.* 1368–1426) – about whom John Burrow writes in his 'Hoccleve and Chaucer' – was Clerk to the Privy Seal and, with Lydgate, one of the first important English successors to Chaucer. By far the most prolific of fifteenth-century English poets, it is John Lydgate (*c.* 1370 – *c.* 1451) whose own view of Chaucer is long influential on subsequent opinion, and Derek Pearsall contributes in his essay on 'Chaucer and Lydgate' an assessment of the relation between the poetry of Chaucer and that of a disciple who responded so voluminously to the range of Chaucer's poems, and whose name is soon included in what becomes a traditional view of Chaucer, Gower and Lydgate as the three figures who stand at the beginning of English poetry.[8]

Lydgate's praise of Chaucer is so frequent and so insistent, and Lydgate's own writings achieved such wide circulation, that it is he who establishes the terms of praise in the fifteenth century. His is already a retrospect. He is not Chaucer's pupil, never enjoyed Chaucer's personal acquaintance and instruction, and presents as oral tradition a reminiscence of Chaucer's kind dealing with those situations in which the poet is asked to comment on the works of others (see p. 57). Indeed, some of Lydgate's most ringing praise of Chaucer comes in the context of laments that Chaucer is removed by death:

> Chaucer is deed that had suche a name
> Of fayre makyng that [was] without wene
> > (*The Flower of Courtesy*, st. 34; *CH*, p. 45)

> And eke my maister Chauser is ygrave
> The noble Rethor, poete of Brytayne
> That worthy was the laurer to haue
> Of poetrye, and the palme atteyne
> That made firste, to distille and rayne
> The golde dewe dropes of speche and eloquence
> Into our tunge, thurgh his excellence

> And fonde the floures, firste of Retoryke
> Oure Rude speche, only to enlumyne
> That in our tunge was neuere noon hym like ...
> > (*The Life of Our Lady*, 1628–37; *CH*, p. 46)

> Noble Galfride, poete of Breteyne,
> Amonge oure englisch þat made first to reyne
> þe gold dewe-dropis of rethorik so fyne,
> Oure rude langage only tenlwmyne . . .
> (*Troy Book*, ıı, 4697–700; *CH*, p. 47)

From these and comparable passages a number of patterns emerge which are to prove influential in the evaluation of Chaucer.

First of all – for it still governs any popular conception of English literary history to this day – is the notion that Chaucer is the first. What Chaucer did he did first, and not only first but best: 'þer is no makyng to his equipolent', as Lydgate comments in the *Troy Book* (ıı, 4712), while casting himself as gleaning in Chaucer's works much as Chaucer had cast himself as gleaning in old books in the *Prologue* to the *Legend*. Lydgate's eulogies establish Chaucer's achievement as unique, and Lydgate's professions of modesty continue to insist that Chaucer is inimitable even as the poems containing such professions represent continual reinterpretation of Chaucer's subjects and idioms.

For Lydgate – as in the passages just quoted – the primacy of Chaucer is founded on what he sees Chaucer's poems achieving with the English language: it is Chaucer 'That made firste, to distille and rayne / The golde dewe dropes of speche and eloquence / Into our tunge . . .' This notion of Chaucer's 'golden' eloquence and rhetoric which 'gilds' the English language – the root of what has become known as the 'aureate style' in fifteenth-century poetic diction – also carries with it the assumption that before Chaucer wrote in it so transformingly 'our rude langage' had little worth:

> For he owre englishe gilt with his sawes
> Rude and boistous firste be olde dawes
> þat was ful fer from al perfeccioun
> And but of litel reputacioun
> Til þat he cam and þoruȝ his poetrie
> Gan oure tonge firste to magnifie
> And adourne it with his elloquence . . .
> (*Troy Book*, ııı, 4237–43; *CH*, p. 48)

> My maistir Chaucer dede his besynesse,
> And in his daies hath so weel hym born,
> Out off our tunge tauoiden al reudnesse,
> And to refourme it with coloure of suetnesse . . .
> (*Fall of Princes*, Prol. 275–8; *CH*, p. 53)

> And ffor memoyre off that poete,
> Wyth al hys rethorykes swete,
> That was the ffyrste in any age
> That amendede our langage . . .
> (*Pilgrimage of the Life of Man*, 19773–6; *CH*, p. 51)

Such an evaluation of Chaucer represents his achievement as having a fundamental value for all who wrote after him in English. It is Chaucer who is understood to have created the means and the medium for poetry in English and – in a way that has great implication for those who read and write after Chaucer – his achievements in English are represented as magnifying, adorning and sweetening English poetic diction. The subsequent influence of Lydgate's insistent praise of what he understood as Chaucer's achievement is shown by the way that Lydgate's description of Chaucer ('Off oure language he was the lodesterre', *Fall of Princes*, Prol. 252) is approvingly quoted in the introductory epistle by 'E.K.' (Edward Kirke) to *The Shepherd's Calendar* (1579) and in Beaumont's prefatory letter in Speght's edition of Chaucer (1598).

But there were other legacies too from Lydgate's way of representing Chaucer. If Chaucer's listings of his own works suggest that he thought of his writing as a corpus, the very comprehensiveness with which Lydgate attempted so many of his poems on Chaucerian models reinforced the idea of Chaucer's works as a canon, and one with a posterity both in itself and in its progeny. This is also so of Lydgate's readiness to list and refer to Chaucer's works, while in his copious praise there is room to pass on a sense of Chaucer's variety, not only 'ful pitous tragedies' but also 'his fresh comedies' (*Fall of Princes*, Prol. 246–8), for Lydgate shows some sense of the gaiety that there is in Chaucer, as does the anonymous author of the prologue to *The Tale of Beryn* (*c.* 1410) which imagines Chaucer's pilgrims arriving at Canterbury.[9] In the fifteenth-century manuscript anthologies which include selected *Canterbury Tales*, however, it is the moral and courtly pieces which are copied rather than the fabliaux.[10] The unfinished and open-ended framework of the *Canterbury Tales* pilgrimage was an invitation not only to fifteenth-century scribal editors of the manuscripts,[11] but also to Lydgate, who in his *Siege of Thebes* imagines the pilgrims' tale-telling on the journey home. In a passage praising the *Canterbury Tales* in his own Canterbury Tale, this most diffuse of writers is among the earliest to praise Chaucer's pregnant pithiness:

> Be rehersaile / of his Sugrid mouth
> Of eche thyng / keping in substaunce
> The sentence hool / with-oute variaunce
> Voyding the Chaf / sothly for so seyn,
> Enlumynyng / þe trewe piked greyn
> Be crafty writinge / of his sawes swete... (52–7)

So much praise of Chaucer's inimitable qualities by his professed imitator leaves an uncertain space for Lydgate himself to move in, and when in the *Siege of Thebes* Lydgate imagines himself joining Chaucer's pilgrims on their return journey to London, the only pilgrim who seems to be absent is Chaucer himself.[12] But then – as Lydgate's poetry at its most self-conscious moments had so often lamented – the poet Chaucer was dead. Whatever anxiety of influence there was in Lydgate's relation as a poet to Chaucer, his view of Chaucer as the laureate poet in English, comparable to Petrarch and drawing on the spring guarded by the Muses (*Troy Book*, III, 553–5, 4546ff.), sows the seed which is later to grow in the sixteenth-century view of Chaucer as a writer whose qualities and place in English letters may be defined in relation to classical models.

In his own way Hoccleve comparably praises and understands Chaucer's achievement. In his *Regement of Princes* (*c.* 1412) Hoccleve presents himself as personally acquainted with his 'maister' Chaucer – whose portrait Hoccleve has had included in the manuscript in order to perpetuate Chaucer's memory[13] – and casts himself as the dilatory and unprofitable pupil of a kindly would-be teacher (see p. 54). At the beginning of a long tradition of such praise Hoccleve commends both Chaucer's eloquence and his learning:

> O maister deere and fadir reverent
> Mi maister Chaucer, flour of eloquence,
> Mirour of fructuous entendement,
> O vniuersal fadir in science... (1961–4; *CH*, pp. 62–3)

Hoccleve is also an early example of praise – taken further in the sixteenth century – which sets Chaucer alongside classical authors: in rhetoric no English writer was ever so like Cicero, and

> Also who was hier in philosophie
> To Aristotle in our tonge but thow.
> The steppes of Virgile in poesie
> Thow filwedist eeke, men wot wel ynow (*CH*, p. 63)

while Hoccleve's hailing of Chaucer as 'The firste fyndere of oure faire langage' shares with Lydgate a conception of Chaucer as the originator of a language for poetry in English.

Fifteenth-century praise of Chaucer continues to laud his achievements in style and diction. John Walton, a canon of Oseney Abbey, in his verse translation of Boethius' *Consolation* (1410) calls Chaucer 'floure of rethoryk / In englisshe tong & excellent poete' (33–4), acknowledging that Chaucer's achievements are not to be matched ('This wot I wel no þing may I do lyk', 35; *CH*, p. 61), as he introduces his translation of a work Chaucer had already translated.[14] At the close of *The Kingis Quair* (*c.* 1425) the dream poem is commended to Gower and Chaucer:

> Vnto [th']inpnis of my maisteris dere,
> Gowere and Chaucere, that on the steppis satt
> Of rethorike quhill thai were lyvand here,
> Superlatiue as poetis laureate
> In moralitee and eloquence ornate,
> I recommend my buk in lynis sevin. (1373–8)[15]

In John Metham's poem *Amoryus and Cleopes* (1448–9), influenced by *Troilus*, he commends that mastery of a natural versification by Chaucer ('... that longe dyd endure / In practyk off rymyng: qwerffore proffoundely / With many prouerbys hys bokys he rymyd naturally', 2189–91),[16] while John

Shirley commends (*c.* 1450) 'þe laureal and moste famous poete þat euer was to-fore him as in þemvelisshing of oure rude moders englisshe tonge' (*CH*, p. 66).

With Chaucer established as an *auctor*, English poets could for the first time look back in that tradition-conscious way that was necessary for a sense of the seriousness, the dignity, the worthiness of their own literary culture. Reference to Chaucer as *auctor* could be a claim for poetic identity in the sense in which Englishness competed not only with the classical past but also with the continental vernaculars. No poet needed to have read Chaucer in order to use him in this way.

But that poets read Chaucer, read him with extraordinary attention, and loved him, is clear in many different ways, which the essays in this book touch on at numerous points. That Chaucer – however much he himself may have worried over them, even, at the end of his life, repudiated them – nevertheless established *in English* secular story-types, secular literary genres, and numerous 'characters', was a legitimating action for his successors. The very incompleteness of his poems encouraged his imitators to do what he had done. That they sometimes seem to have misunderstood what he did was one of the forces which we might think of as creative misinterpretation, resulting in new works which stem from old ones and add to the stock of literary types in their turn. Though most of Chaucer's imitators wrote poetry inferior to his, their efforts nevertheless forged a literary culture in which, for example, a narrating persona within varieties of fictions could be taken for granted. As many of the essays in this collection point out, that persona was particularly useful for handling questions about women and the risks of love. That Chaucer was thought to have been their advocate was a way in to a succession of difficult arguments and attitudes.

It was above all, however, for the richness of Chaucer's English styles that his followers treasured him, treasured as a rich thesaurus of registers, of techniques of rhyme and rhythm, of syntactic adventurousness that had enriched the possibilities of English expression. For poet after poet, the education of long and deep study of Chaucer's poetry created a verbal reservoir which became a kind of lexicon. The accomplished English lyrics associated with Charles d'Orléans will in places draw closely on the language and contexts of Chaucer's poems, so as to present the lover's sorrows in the accents of the *Book of the Duchess*:

For whoso seeth me first on morwe
May seyn he hath met with sorwe,
For y am sorwe, and sorwe ys y.
Allas! and I wol tel the why:
My song ys turned to pleynynge,
And al my laughtre to wepynge,
My glade thoghtes to hevynesse;
In travayle ys myn ydelnesse
And eke my reste; my wele is woo,
My good ys harm, and evermoo
In wrathe ys turned my pleynge
And my delyt into sorwynge.
Myn hele ys turned into seknesse,
In drede ys al my sykernesse . . .

(*BD*, 595–608)

For alle my ioy is turnyd to hevynes
Myn ese in harme my wele in woo
Mi hope in drede in dowt my sikirnes
And my delite in sorow loo
My hele seeknes / and ovirmoo
As euery thing that shulde me plese
I-turned is god helpe me soo
In his amverse to my disese

For who with sorowe list aqueyntid be
As come to me and spille no ferthir wey
For sorow is y and y am he
For euery ioy in me is goon away

(5848–59)[17]

or the pains of absence in reminiscences of Book v of *Troilus*:

Fro thennesforth he rideth up and down,
And every thyng com hym to remembraunce
As he rood forby places of the town
In which he whilom hadde al his plesaunce.
'Lo, yonder saugh ich last my lady daunce;
And in that temple, with hire eyen cleere,
Me kaughte first my righte lady dere.

'And yonder have I herd ful lustyly
My dere herte laugh; and yonder pleye
Sauch ich hire ones ek ful blisfully.
And yonder ones to me gan she seye,
'Now goode swete, love me wel, I preye';
And yond so goodly gan she me biholde,
That to the deth myn herte is to hire holde.

'And at that corner, in the yonder hous,
Herde I myn alderlevest lady deere
So wommanly, with vois melodious,
Syngen so wel, so goodly, and so cleere,
That in my soule yet me thynketh ich here
The blisful sown; and in that yonder place
My lady first me took unto hire grace . . .'

(v, 561–81)

. . . For when me happith here or there to go
And thenke that yondir lo my lady dere
Gaf me this word/or made me suche a chere
And aundir herde y hir so swetely syng
And in this chambre led y hir daunsyng

In yondir bayne so se y hir alle nakid
And this and that y sawe hir yondir worche
Here y fond hir slepe/and yondir wakid
And in this wyndow pleide we at the lorche
And from this stayre y lad hir to þe chirche
And bi the way this tale y to hir tolde
And here she gaf me lo þis ryng of gold

And there at post and piler did she play
And so y first my loue vnto hir tolde
And there aferd she start fro me away
And with this word she made myn hert to
    bold
And with this word allas she made me cold
And yondir sigh y hir this resoun write
And here y baste hir fayre round pappis
    white

In suche a towre also y sigh hir last
And yet wel more a thousand thoughtis mo

(4822–42)

   Through the language of Chaucer's love poems the feelings of succeeding
generations of courtly and would-be courtly lovers might be lent a voice, and
in its advice on improving reading a *Book of Curtesye* printed by Caxton
recommends reading Chaucer as an example of eloquence, clarity, and
concision ('O fader and founder of ornate eloquence'), while also expressing
perhaps the earliest appreciation of Chaucer's lifelike vividness of representation:

Redith his werkis / ful of plesaunce
Clere in sentence / in langage excellent
Briefly to wryte/ suche was his suffysaunce
What euer to saye / he toke in his entente

His langage was so fayr and pertynente
It semeth vnto mannys heerynge
Not only the worde / but verely the thynge... (*CH*, p. 72)

In his various prologues and epilogues to his editions of Chaucer Caxton echoes Lydgate in order to draw together some of the strands in this body of praise.[18] In his epilogue to his edition of Chaucer's *Boece* (1478) he repeats with emphasis the view of Chaucer as 'the worshipful fader & first foundeur & enbelissher of ornate eloquence in our englissh ... enbelissher in making the sayd langage ornate & fayr' (*CH*, p. 75) and includes a Latin epitaph of Chaucer by the Italian Humanist scholar Surigo. In the epilogue to the *House of Fame* (1483) it is Chaucer's pregnant concision which Caxton praises by echoing Chaucer's own praise of the Clerk of Oxford ('For he wrytteth no voyde wordes / but alle hys mater is ful of hye and quycke sentence / ... For of hym alle other haue borowed syth and taken / in alle theyr wel sayeng and wrytyng', *CH*, p. 75). It is in the prologue to his second printing of the *Canterbury Tales* (1484) that Caxton draws together the accumulated Lydgatean estimates of Chaucer, echoed by others, praising the learning of Chaucer, whose transformation of English diction from its prior rude state makes him deserve the title of laureate, and repeating Lydgate's praise in *The Siege of Thebes* of the 'pyked grayn' of Chaucer's 'sentence':

> ... That noble & grete philosopher Gefferey chaucer the whiche for his ornate wrytyng in our tongue may wel haue the name of a laureate poete / For to fore that he by hys labour enbelysshyd / ornated / and made faire our englisshe / in thys Royame was had rude speche & Incongrue ... He comprehended hys maters in short / quyck and hye sentences / eschewyng prolyxyte / castyng away the chaf of superfluyte / and shewyng the pyked grayn of sentence / vtteryd by crafty and sugred eloquence. (*CH*, p. 76)

It was not until twenty and thirty years after these comments by Caxton that William Dunbar (*c*. 1460 – *c*. 1530) and Gavin Douglas (*c*. 1475–1522) wrote their famous praise of Chaucer's rhetorical eloquence, which represents the flamboyant culmination of fifteenth-century eulogies of Chaucer's diction by two of those post-Chaucerian poets who most established an independence for themselves in their drawing on the Chaucerian inheritance.[19] In his dream poem *The Goldyn Targe* (*c*. 1503) Dunbar addresses Chaucer before proceeding to praise Gower and Lydgate:

> O reverend Chaucere, rose of rethoris all,
> As in oure tong ane flour imperiall
>   That raise in Britane, evir quho redis rycht,
> Thou beris of makaris the tryumph riall;
> Thy fresch anamalit termes celicall
>   This mater coud illumynit have full brycht:
>   Was thou noucht of oure Inglisch all the lycht,
> Surmounting eviry tong terrestriall
>   Alls fer as Mayes morow dois mydnycht? (253–61)[20]

Although two of Dunbar's other poems – his *Tretis of the Tua Mariit Wemen and the Wedo* and *Sir Thomas Norny* – are written with telling recollections of the *Wife of Bath's Prologue* and *Sir Thopas* respectively, the use by Dunbar, Henryson, and other Scottish writers, of the thematic and stylistic legacy of Chaucer is independent and innovative, as Douglas Gray illustrates ('Some Chaucerian themes in Scottish writers'). Presented as what the poet found when turning from Chaucer's *Troilus* to another book about Criseyde, Robert Henryson's *Testament of Cresseid* differentiates itself in part through an interpretation of the classical gods distinct from that of Chaucer, as Jill Mann shows ('The planetary gods in Chaucer and Henryson'). Like Dunbar, Gavin Douglas in the first prologue in his *Eneados* (1513) also praises Chaucer's eloquence with his own eloquence ('Hevynly trumpat, orlege and reguler, / In eloquens balmy, cundyt and dyall ...'; see p. 114). Yet it is also Douglas who in praising Chaucer distances himself from Chaucer's approach to classical literature by pointing out that Chaucer's account of the story of Dido and Aeneas is a misreading of Virgil, although understandable in a poet so sympathetic to women ('My mastir Chauser gretly Virgill offendit ... / For he was evir – God wait – all womanis frend', 1, 410, 449). How Douglas represents his own standing towards Chaucer is discussed by Ruth Morse ('Gavin Douglas: "Off Eloquence the flowand balmy strand"'), and like Douglas in his *Palice of Honour* the English poet John Skelton (1460–1529) is responding to the example of Chaucer's *House of Fame* in his *Garlande of Laurell*, about which John Scattergood writes ('Skelton's *Garlande of Laurell* and the Chaucerian Tradition'). In *Phyllyp Sparowe* Skelton – who always shows a keen sense of Chaucer's humour – praises Chaucer's diction and singles out its distinctive concision and clarity, yet evidently sees the need to protest against a contemporary tendency to feel that Chaucer's language is growing obscure:

> There is no Englysh voyd,
> At those dayes moch commended;
> And now men wold have amended
> His Englyssh whereat they barke
> And mar all they warke;
> Chaucer, that famus clerke,
> His termes were not darke,
> But plesaunt, easy and playne;
> Ne worde he wrote in vayne...   (795–803)[21]

Not so obscure, however, as to prevent the dramatist John Heywood setting on stage in his play *The Pardoner and the Frere* (1533) the figure of a pardoner whose speech includes a transposition of the monologue of Chaucer's Pardoner in the Prologue to his Tale.

Satire on clerical abuses is also the theme of the *Plowman's Tale*, which is printed along with Chaucer's works and other 'apocryphal' Chaucerian texts in Thynne's edition of Chaucer (1532), and Thomas J. Heffernan has written about the developing conception of the Chaucer canon and especially its inclusion of apocryphal material which might enable Chaucer to be seen as something of a proto-Protestant ('Aspects of the Chaucerian apocrypha: animadversions on William Thynne's edition of the *Plowman's Tale*'). Thynne's edition influences sixteenth-century conceptions of Chaucer by affecting impressions of what Chaucer wrote, of both a religious and courtly kind. The appearance of the earliest printed editions of Chaucer only confirms the tradition of Chaucer's poems as a school for courtier poets. John Stevens has written about one of the early Tudor songbooks – the 'Fayrfax Manuscript', British Library MS Add. 5465 – which presents a manuscript miscellany of lyric poems in a Chaucerian tradition ('Chaucerian metre and early Tudor songs'). But the later 'Devonshire Manuscript' (British Library MS Add. 17492) of *c.* 1530–40 was apparently composed with a knowledge of Chaucer in Thynne's edition,[22] and contains some poems which are comprised of excerpted lyric passages from *Troilus*,[23] removed from their original context to form free-standing courtly lyric poems.[24] The Devonshire Manuscript also contains many poems by Sir Thomas Wyatt (d. 1542), whose knowledge of Chaucerian traditions is perhaps one reason for the terms in which Surrey eulogized him after his death, the first English poet deemed to have surpassed Chaucer ('A hand that taught what might be sayd in ryme; / That reft Chaucer the glory of his wit . . .').[25] As late as 1553 Thomas Wilson – discussing in his *Arte of Rhetorique* the need for plain English speech – can comment that 'the fine Courtier wil talke nothyng but Chaucer' (*CH*, p. 103), and in his copy of Thynne such a courtier would find both Chaucer's works and such 'Chaucerian' writings as Clanvowe's *The Cuckoo and the Nightingale*, Usk's *Testament of Love*, the *Assembly of Ladies*, and the translation by Sir Richard Roos of *La Belle Dame sans Merci*. As late as *c.* 1535 the sophisticatedly Chaucerian vision-poem *The Court of Love* is being composed in response to this particular side of the Chaucer tradition, and then itself incorporated into that tradition when included in Stow's edition of Chaucer (1561), while in Speght's edition (1598, 1602) the courtly Chaucerian apocrypha of dream and vision poems is swelled by inclusion of *The Flower and the Leaf* and *The Isle of Ladies* (or *Chaucer's Dream*, see p. 64).[26]

The generous praise of Chaucer's achievements by Sir Brian Tuke – in the dedication to Henry VIII which he provided for Thynne's much-read edition of Chaucer – shows astute appreciation of Chaucer, while acknowledging in a new way Chaucer's antiquity. Tuke voices traditional praise of Chaucer's 'excellent lernyng in all kyndes of doctrynes and sciences', while Thynne's commendable editorial efforts enable him to commend 'suche perfectyon in metre'. Tuke also echoes familiar praise of the fittingness and sweetness of Chaucer's diction ('suche frutefulnesse in wordes / wel accordynge to the mater and purpose / so swete and plesaunt sentences'), but proceeds to articulate a fuller appreciation than hitherto of Chaucer's grasp as a narrative poet:

The composycion so adapted / suche fresshnesse of inuencion / compendyous-
nesse in narration / suche sensyble and open style / lackyng neither maieste ne
mediocrite couenable in disposycion / and suche sharpnesse or quycknesse in
conclusyon...   (*CH*, p. 88)

From praising such achievements, however, Tuke goes on to enhance that
praise by emphasizing how Chaucer almost miraculously overcame the
disadvantage of living when he did:

It is moche to be marueyled / howe in his tyme / whan doutlesse all good letters
were layde a slepe throughout the worlde ... suche an excellent poete in our
tonge / shulde as it were (nature repugnyng) spryng and aryse...   (p. 88)

This is a contextualization of Chaucer which recurs in sixteenth-century
comments. By 1555 Chaucer's achievements are commended because 'so
farre was the grosenesse and barbarousnesse of that age from the vnderstand-
inge of so deuyne a wryter' (*CH*, p. 104), and in 1589 Thomas Nashe values
Chaucer the more because he 'liued vnder the tirranie of ignorance' (*CH*,
p. 128). But the most eloquent expression of this Elizabethan view of
Chaucer's relation to his age is in Sir Philip Sidney's *An Apologie for Poetrie*
(written *c.* 1581?):

Chaucer, vndoubtedly did excellently in hys *Troylus* and *Cresseid*; of whom, truly I
know not, whether to meruaile more, either that he in that mistie time, could see
so clearly, or that wee in this cleare age, walke so stumblingly after him. Yet
had he great wants, fitte to be forgiuen, in so reuerent antiquity... [27]

By the same token, when sixteenth-century writers conceive of a literature
in English the antiquity of Chaucer gives him a role comparable to that of the
earliest figures in Greek and Roman literature. Sidney grants that Chaucer
and Gower fulfil this role, and Roger Ascham also calls him 'our Englishe
Homer', setting Chaucer alongside Sophocles and Euripides in moral
comment, and with Thucydides and Homer in describing not only outward
appearance but 'the inward disposition of the mynde' (*CH*, pp. 100–1). But
the poet Barnaby Googe by remarking in 1565 that Chaucer 'liueth in like
estimation with vs as did olde *Ennius* wyth the Latines' (*CH*, p. 106) voices a
sense of Chaucer's remote antiquity by likening him to the early Latin poet
Ennius.

With this growing sense of Chaucer's antiquity there are increasingly
decided comments on the antiquity of his language. William Webbe's *A
Discourse of Englishe Poetrie* (1586) comments on Chaucer: 'The manner of hys
stile may seeme blunte and course to many fine English eares at these dayes'
(*CH*, p. 125), and in his prefatory epistle to Speght's edition of Chaucer
(1598) Francis Beaumont acknowledges a common objection 'that many of
his wordes (as it were with ouerlong lying) are growne too hard and
vnpleasant' (*CH*, p. 136). For Spenser, however, in *The Faerie Queene* Chaucer

is 'Dan Chaucer, well of English vndefiled' (IV, 2, 32), and Chaucer had already appeared as the figure of Tityrus in *The Shepherd's Calendar* ('The God of shepheards Tityrus is dead, / Who taught me homely, as I can, to make'), with a preface by 'E.K.' itself a tissue of reminiscences of Chaucer. In the *Mutabilitie Cantos* 'old' Chaucer is again for Spenser an unpolluted well and ultimate source of poetic diction (' ... old *Dan Geffrey* – in whose gentle spright / The pure well head of Poesie did dwell ...' VII, 7, ix). Spenser's relation to Chaucer's language is characterized by Beaumont in his epistle in the Speght edition:

> But yet so pure were *Chaucers* wordes in his owne daies, as *Lidgate* that learned man calleth him *The Loadstarre of the English language*: and so good they are in our daies, as Maister *Spencer*, following the counsaile of *Tullie in de Oratore*, for reuiuing of antient wordes, hath adorned his owne stile with that beauty and grauitie, which *Tully* speakes of: and his much frequenting of *Chaucers* antient speeches causeth many to allow farre better of him, then otherwise they would ...

But Beaumont lists two common objections to Chaucer's language: not only that it has become difficult through antiquity, but also that 'hee is somewhat too broad in some of his speeches'. The impropriety of Chaucer's language and of his tales is an issue raised in the sixteenth century: earlier readers evidently took Chaucer's advice to turn the leaf or not, but the power of a broad-speaking character like the Wife of Bath to prompt the writing of new broadness is part of a Chaucer tradition in merry tales and broadside ballads, as Helen Cooper has shown ('The shape-shiftings of the Wife of Bath, 1395–1670'). After the appearance of *The Cobler of Caunterburie* (1590)[28] the dramatist Robert Greene in his *Greene's Vision* (1592) denies authorship of the *Cobler* but imagines himself visited by the shades of Chaucer and Gower who debate about the moral aims and effects of writing and each tells a tale – Chaucer's is predictably a fabliau. Greene represents his 'Chaucer' as dismissing Gower's moralizing approach and arguing that a writer may still improve and correct through delight. Greene's is an attempt to assert the moral worth of Chaucer's works while acknowledging his mirth and bawdy. This is not so far removed from part of the marginalia written (*c.* 1600) in his copy of Speght's Chaucer by Spenser's friend Gabriel Harvey (commending 'the varietie both of matter, & manner, that delightes with proffit, & proffittes with delight. Thowgh I could haue wisshed better choice of sum arguments, and sum subiects of more importance', *CH*, p. 123). Beaumont's own shrewd defence of Chaucer's broadness is on the principle of decorum ('How much had hee swarued from Decorum, if hee had made his Miller, his Cooke, and his Carpenter, to haue told such honest and good tales, as hee made his Knight, his Squire, his Lawyer, and his Scholler tell?' *CH*, p. 137). It is also Beaumont – writing in the heyday of the Elizabethan theatre – who comments most acutely on the power of Chaucer's poems to make real their world to the imaginations of their readers:

One gifte hee hath aboue other Authours, and that is, by the excellencie of his descriptions to possesse his Readers with a stronger imagination of seeing that done before their eyes, which they reade, than any other that euer writ in any tongue...   (pp. 138–9)

In addition to the work of Shakespeare, at least thirteen plays based on works by Chaucer were apparently written between 1558 and 1625: more may have been written and not recorded, while out of the thirteen seven are lost and the degree of Chaucer's influence cannot be determined.[29] (In a more diffused way, evidence of a knowledge of Chaucer's work has been detected in Lyly, Peele, Day, Marston, Jonson, Middleton and Beaumont, but especially in Chapman, Dekker and Fletcher).[30] Of the thirteen 'Chaucerian' plays, three were apparently based in some way on *Troilus*, three on the *Clerk's Tale*, and two on the *Knight's Tale*, in addition to single plays based on the *Man of Law's Tale*, and *Physician's Tale*, the *Melibee*, the *Wife of Bath's Tale*, and the *Franklin's Tale*. Such evident interest in *Troilus*, the *Knight's Tale* and the *Clerk's Tale* is a pattern also reflected in Shakespeare's reading of Chaucer in his *Troilus and Cressida*, *The Winter's Tale*, and *The Two Noble Kinsmen*, on which he worked with Fletcher.[31] In his essay ('Transformations of the *Knight's Tale*') Piero Boitani has written about *The Two Noble Kinsmen*, while Anna Baldwin has discussed sixteenth-century perceptions of the Griselda story ('From the *Clerk's Tale* to *The Winter's Tale*'). Shakespeare's reading of Chaucer has also been detected through various echoes in *A Midsummer Night's Dream* of *Sir Thopas*, the *Legend* of Thisbe, the *Knight's Tale* and the *Merchant's Tale*, and in parallels between *Troilus and Criseyde* and *Romeo and Juliet* and between the characters of the Wife of Bath and Falstaff.[32]

An exceptional clustering of five plays with Chaucer sources in the years 1599–1602 (including Shakespeare's *Troilus and Cressida*) may indeed reflect the appearance of Speght's edition in 1598, the first to appear for nearly forty years. Among these plays *Sir Giles Goosecap* (1602) – by George Chapman, the translator of Homer – reveals an appreciative reading of Chaucer's *Troilus* through realizing the dramatic potential of the scenes of dialogue in the first three books of the *Troilus*, especially those involving Criseyde and Pandarus, which Chapman 'translates' into a contemporary setting, with many echoes of phrasing and dramatic situation.[33] In the same year that Speght's edition appeared with Beaumont's preface Chapman had written of Chaucer's language as a standard which authorizes what is 'true English', and had recycled the traditional view of Chaucer as an originator of language ('*Chaucer* – by whom we will needes authorise our true english – had more newe wordes for his time then any man needes to deuise now ...' *CH*, p. 140). Already, however, a contemporary antiquary Richard Verstegan, who had studied Anglo-Saxon at Oxford, anticipates a more historical understanding of Chaucer's place in the development of English: '*Chaucer* ... is of some called the first illuminator of the English toung: of their opinion I am not (though I reuerence *Chaucer* as an excellent poet for his tyme). He was indeed a great

mingler of English with French ...' (*CH*, p. 145). That the Speght edition of
Chaucer was the first to attempt a glossary ('The old and obscure words of
Chaucer explaned') is a telling indication of how Chaucer's language was
regarded at the beginning of the seventeenth century, and by 1622 Henry
Peacham must exhort the readership of his *The Compleat Gentleman* to over-
look the language ('the stile for the antiquitie, may distast you') because
Chaucer is to be accounted part of an English gentleman's reading ('In
briefe, account him among the best of your English bookes in your librarie',
CH, p.149). This is the context for some gentlemanly 'translations' of the
Troilus in the earlier seventeenth century: a translation of the first three
books into English verse by Jonathan Sidnam (*c.* 1630),[34] and a translation
into Latin verse with commentary by Sir Francis Kinaston (1635), about
which Richard Beadle has written ('The Virtuoso's *Troilus*'). The title page of
Sidnam's paraphrase, which declines to follow Criseyde into the infidelity of
Books IV and V, introduces itself as 'For the satisfaction of those / Who either
cannot, or will not, take ye paines to vnderstand / The Excellent Authors /Farr
more Exquisite, and significant Expressions / Though now growen obsolete,
and / out of vse' (*CH*, p. 152). A prefatory poem in the Kinaston edition
catches the contemporary sense that – unless translated – linguistic change will
make Chaucer's text incomprehensible ('Thus the Translation will become /
Th'Originall, while that growes dumbe ...' *CH*, p. 153).

It says much for response to Chaucer in the seventeenth century that the
longest gap between editions in the history of Chaucer editing occurs in the
gap between Speght's edition of 1602 and its reprint in a consciously antiquarian black-letter edition in 1687. Yet in the 1660s Samuel Pepys – who
owned some Chaucer manuscripts and a Caxton *Canterbury Tales* as well as
Speght's 1602 edition – shows in his diary his affection for Chaucer's works:
when he notes how the *Troilus* line about engravers needing sunlight (III,
1462) is not actually the view of an engraver known to him, he reveals how
he values Chaucer's poetry so as to carry it with him in a way that tests it
against experience (*CH*, p. 154-5). Pepys also suggested to Dryden that he
translate the portrait of the Parson from the *General Prologue* published in the
Fables Ancient and Modern (1700), which included Dryden's modernizations of
the *Knight's Tale*, the *Wife of Bath's Tale*, the *Nun's Priest's Tale*, and *The Flower
and the Leaf*, together with various tales from Ovid and Boccaccio. It is the
increasing remoteness of Chaucer's language which Dryden sets out to overcome by his verse modernizations, and in his Preface Dryden repeats and
develops some of the customary praise of Chaucer's contribution to the
development of English:

[Boccaccio] and *Chaucer*, among other Things, had this in common, that they
refin'd their Mother-Tongues...; [Chaucer] first adorn'd and amplified our
barren Tongue from the *Provencall*...; From *Chaucer* the Purity of the *English*
Tongue began ...   (*CH*, pp. 161–2)[35]

In his modernizations Dryden claims to have 'added somewhat of my own where I thought my Author was deficient, and had not given his Thoughts their true Lustre, for want of Words in the Beginning of our Language'. But the language of Chaucer has by now become not only quaint but a positive barrier to understanding. Not unlike Kinaston's translating Chaucer out of an antiquated language into the timeless medium of Latin, Dryden presents himself as concerned to bring out a comparison between Ovid and Chaucer which he thinks is to Chaucer's advantage, by presenting both Ovid and Chaucer in modern English verse. The wheel has come full circle from Deschamps's praise of Chaucer as 'Ovides grans en ta poëterie'. But language is one area in which Dryden does not claim equality between Ovid and Chaucer, the former writing 'when the *Roman* Tongue was in its Meridian; *Chaucer*, in the Dawning of our Language'. In metre and versification Dryden also makes allowance generously for Chaucer's position early in the development of English poetry, and in the context of what Dryden could know of Chaucer's metre in the available editions there is nothing condescending in his characterization ('There is the rude Sweetness of a *Scotch* Tune in it, which is natural and pleasing, though not perfect', p. 165).

Other than in language and versification, Dryden compares Chaucer favourably against Ovid:

> Both of them were well-bred, well-natur'd ... Both of them were knowing in Astronomy ... Both writ with wonderful Facility and Clearness; neither were great Inventors ... Both of them built on the Inventions of other Men; yet since *Chaucer* had something of his own, as *The Wife of Bath's Tale*, *The Cock and the Fox*, which I have translated, and some others, I may justly give our Countryman the Precedence in that Part; since I can remember nothing of *Ovid* which was wholly his ...   (*CH*, p. 162)

It is this (mis)conception of the originality of Chaucer which governs Dryden's choice of the tales he translates, and in his essay ('Rewriting romance: Chaucer's and Dryden's *Wife of Bath's Tale*') A. C. Spearing discusses the relation between Dryden's version and the original which he imagined to be one of Chaucer's most independent works. As with the *Wife of Bath's Tale*, so too Dryden stresses what he sees as the originality of the *Knight's Tale* which he modernized in his *Palamon and Arcite*, discussed by Piero Boitani in his essay ('Transformations of the *Knight's Tale*'). An allusion in the *Decameron* to Palamon and Arcite disappoints Dryden in his earlier hope that the story was original to Chaucer without informing him of the actual source (see below, p. 185), but Dryden stoutly rescues what he can ('the Name of its Author being wholly lost, *Chaucer* is now become an Original') for the sake of a poem which he sets in the most exalted company:

> I prefer in our Countryman, far above all his other Stories, the Noble Poem of *Palamon* and *Arcite*, which is of the *Epique* kind, and perhaps not much inferiour to the *Ilias* or the *Aeneis*: the Story is more pleasing than either of them, the Manners as perfect, the Diction as poetical, the Learning as deep and various; and the Disposition full as artful.   (*CH*, p. 171)

If Dryden's modernizations are justified by the antiquity of Chaucer's language, Dryden's evaluation of Chaucer is far from that of an antiquary, and the whole thrust of his commendation of Chaucer in his Preface is to recognize a worth in Chaucer which is timeless, quite beyond the attractions of quaintness and an accumulating patina of age:

> In the first place, as he is the Father of *English* Poetry, so I hold him in the same Degree of Veneration as the *Grecians* held *Homer*, or the *Romans Virgil*: He is a perpetual Fountain of good Sense; learn'd in all Sciences; and, therefore speaks properly on all Subjects: As he knew what to say, so he knows also when to leave off ... *Chaucer* follow'd Nature every where, but was never so bold to go beyond her ... He must have been a Man of a most wonderful comprehensive Nature ... 'Tis sufficient to say according to the Proverb, that here is God's Plenty. We have our Fore-fathers and Great Grand-dames all before us, as they were in *Chaucer*'s Days; their general Characters are still remaining in Mankind, and even in *England*, though they are call'd by other Names ...   (*CH*, pp. 164–7)

This series of generous recognitions of Chaucer's achievements makes an apt close, for it represents a climactic and transitional moment in the traditions of response to Chaucer, who is now established at the beginning of English literary history, both as an ancient author and also as an irresistibly vivid and valuable poet. As the translator of 'The Character of a Good Parson; Imitated from Chaucer, and Inlarg'd', Dryden may aptly be seen as himself near the beginning of any history of that modern criticism of Chaucer which has burgeoned so variously in the present and which Charles Muscatine discusses ('Chaucer's religion and the Chaucer religion'), in a coda to the present studies of some 'Chaucer traditions'.

NOTES

1 Cf. Derek Brewer's essay 'Images of Chaucer 1386–1900', in D. S. Brewer (ed.), *Chaucer and Chaucerians* (London, 1966), pp. 240–70, and the 'Introduction' (pp. 1–29) in Derek Brewer (ed.), *Chaucer: the Critical Heritage*, 2 vols. (London, 1978), vol. I (hereafter *CH*). See also C. F. E. Spurgeon, *Five Hundred Years of Chaucer Criticism and Allusion*, 3 vols. (Cambridge, 1925).

2 *Oeuvres*, ed. le marquis de Saint-Hilaire and G. Raynaud, Société des anciens textes français, 11 vols. (Paris, 1878–1904), II, 138–9; for text and translation, see *CH*, pp. 39–42.

3 For the *Testament of Love* and other Chaucer 'Apocrypha', see W. W. Skeat (ed.), *Chaucerian and Other Pieces* (Oxford, 1897).

4 Cf. A. C. Spearing, *Medieval Dream-Poetry* (Cambridge, 1976), ch. 4 ('The Chaucerian Tradition').

5 See Denton Fox, 'Chaucer's Influence on Fifteenth-Century Poetry', in *Companion to Chaucer Studies*, ed. Beryl Rowland (Toronto, 1968), pp. 385–402; Derek Pearsall, *Old and Middle English Poetry* (London, 1977), pp. 212ff. ('Fifteenth-Century Courtly Tradition'). Cf. E. P. Hammond (ed.), *English Verse between Chaucer and Surrey* (Durham, N.C., 1927).

6 *Chaucerian and Other Pieces*, pp. 237–44. See R. T. Lenaghan, 'Chaucer's *Envoy to Scogan*: The Uses of Literary Conventions', *Chaucer Review*, 10 (1975), 46–61, and

M. N. Hallmundsson, 'Chaucer's Circle: Henry Scogan and His Friends', in *Medievalia et Humanistica*, 10 (1981), 129–39.

7 Cf. Paul Strohm, 'Chaucer's Fifteenth-Century Audience and the Narrowing of the "Chaucer Tradition" ', *Studies in the Age of Chaucer*, 4 (1982), 3–32.

8 Cf. Derek Pearsall, 'The English Chaucerians', in *Chaucer and Chaucerians*, pp. 201–39; Derek Pearsall, *John Lydgate* (London, 1970); W. F. Schirmer (tr. A. E. Kemp), *John Lydgate: A Study of the Culture of the Fifteenth Century* (London, 1961).

9 *The Tale of Beryn*, ed. F. J. Furnivall and W. G. Stone, *EETS*, e.s. 105 (London, 1909). One copy of this tale survives in the Northumberland MS of the *Canterbury Tales*, inserted after the *Canon's Yeoman's Tale* as the first tale of the return journey, told by the Merchant. The main narrative thread of the prologue describing the pilgrims' stay at Canterbury is a racy fabliau-type escapade, in which the Pardoner is tricked in his hopes of sleeping with Kit, the attractive Tapster, who greets him so promisingly ('She halid hym in-to the tapstry, þere hir bed was makid: / "Lo, Here I ligg" (quod she) "my selff al nyȝt al nakid / With outen mannys company, syn my love was dede ... " ', 27–9).

10 Cf. Daniel S. Silvia, 'Some Fifteenth-Century Manuscripts of the *Canterbury Tales*', in *Chaucer and Middle English Studies in Honor of Rossell Hope Robbins*, ed. Beryl Rowland (London, 1974), pp. 153–61. The inventory of English books belonging to Sir John Paston II includes an anthology of pieces by Chaucer, Lydgate and Roos, and other pieces: 'Item, a blak Boke with *the Legende off Lad[ies, la Belle Dame] saunce Mercye, the Parlement off Byrd[es, the Temple of] Glasse, Palatyse and Scitacus, the Me[ditations of ...] the Grene Knyght ... ' (*CH*, p. 71). On various extant manuscript evidence of tastes and interests in Chaucer, see Paul Strohm, 'Jean of Angoulême: A Fifteenth-Century Reader of Chaucer', *Neuphilologishce Mitteilungen*, 72 (1971), 69–76; Lee Patterson, *Negotiating the Past: The Historical Understanding of Medieval Literature* (Madison, 1987), ch. 4 ('Ambiguity and Interpretation: A Fifteenth-Century Reading of *Troilus and Criseyde*'); B. A. Windeatt, 'The Scribes as Chaucer's Early Critics', *Studies in the Age of Chaucer*, 1 (1979), 119–41. For an older survey, see Aage Brusendorff, *The Chaucer Tradition* (Oxford, 1925).

11 Cf. Larry Benson, 'The Order of the *Canterbury Tales*', *Studies in the Age of Chaucer*, 3 (1981), 77–120; Derek Pearsall, *The Canterbury Tales* (London, 1985), ch. 1; A. I. Doyle, 'The production of the *Canterbury Tales* and the *Confessio Amantis* in the early Fifteenth Century', in *Medieval Scribes, Manuscripts and Libraries: Essays Presented to N. R. Ker*, eds. M. B. Parkes and Andrew G. Watson (London, 1978), pp. 163–210.

12 See A. C. Spearing, *Medieval to Renaissance in English Poetry* (Cambridge, 1985), ch. 3 ('The Chaucerian Tradition'), especially the sections on 'Lydgate's Canterbury Tale' and 'Father Chaucer' (pp. 66–110).

13 Cf. James H. McGregor, 'The Iconography of Chaucer in Hoccleve's *De Regimine Principum* and in the *Troilus* Frontispiece', *Chaucer Review*, 11 (1976–77), 338–50.

14 *Boethius De Consolatione Philosophiae*, translated by John Walton, ed. M. Science, *EETS*, o.s. 170 (London, 1927).

15 *The Kingis Quair*, ed. J. Norton-Smith (Oxford, 1971). See Gregory Kratzmann, *Anglo-Scottish Literary Relations 1430–1550* (Cambridge, 1980), ch. 2 ('*The Kingis Quair* and English Poetry').

16 *The Works of John Metham*, ed. H. Craig, *EETS*, o.s. 132 (London, 1916).

17 *The English Poems of Charles of Orleans*, ed. R. Steele and M. Day, *EETS*, o.s. 215, 220 (London, 1941, 1946; repr. 1970). For some 'Chaucerian' poems attributed to the Duke of Suffolk, see H. N. McCracken, 'An English Friend of Charles of Orleans', *PMLA*, 26 (1911), 142–80.

18 See N. F. Blake, 'Caxton and Chaucer', *Leeds Studies in English*, n.s. 1 (1967), 19–36, and also his *Caxton's Own Prose* (London, 1973).

19 See Denton Fox, 'The Scottish Chaucerians', in *Chaucer and Chaucerians*, pp. 164–200; Gregory Kratzmann, *Anglo-Scottish Literary Relations 1430–1550* (Cambridge, 1980); R. D. S. Jack (ed.), *The History of Scottish Literature, Vol. 1, Origins to 1660 (Mediaeval and Renaissance)* (Aberdeen, 1988); I. S. Ross, *William Dunbar* (Leiden, 1981); Douglas Gray, *Robert Henryson* (Leiden, 1980); Priscilla Bawcutt, *Gavin Douglas: A Critical Study* (Edinburgh, 1976); A. C. Spearing, *Medieval to Renaissance*, ch. 5 ('Henryson and Dunbar'); Denton Fox, 'Middle Scots Poets and Patrons', in V. J. Scattergood and J. W. Sherborne (eds.), *English Court Culture in the Later Middle Ages* (London, 1983), pp. 109–27.

20 *The Poems of William Dunbar*, ed. J. Kinsley (Oxford, 1979).

21 *John Skelton: The Complete English Poems*, ed. John Scattergood (New Haven and London, 1983). See A. C. Spearing, *Medieval to Renaissance in English Poetry*, ch. 6 ('Skelton and Hawes'), especially section 2 ('Skelton and Chaucer'). For Stephen Hawes (*c.* 1475–1525), see *The Pastime of Pleasure*, ed. W. E. Mead, *EETS*, o.s. 173 (London, 1928), *Stephen Hawes: The Minor Poems*, ed. F. W. Gluck and A. B. Morgan, *EETS*, o.s. 271 (London, 1974), and A. S. G. Edwards, *Stephen Hawes* (London, 1983).

22 R. Harrier, 'A Printed Source for the Devonshire Manuscript', *Review of English Studies*, n.s. 11 (1960), 54.

23 See Kenneth Muir, 'Unpublished Poems in the Devonshire MS.', *Proc. Leeds Phil. and Lit. Soc., Lit. and Hist. Sect.*, VI. iv (1947), and Ethel Seaton, 'The Devonshire Manuscript and its Medieval Fragments', *Review of English Studies*, n.s. 7 (1956), 55–6. Poems have been cannibalized from *Anelida*, Hoccleve's *Letter of Cupid*, and *La Belle Dame sans Merci* of Sir Richard Roos. Five 'poems' (Muir's poems nos. 50–54) comprise excerpts from Book II of *Troilus* (ll. 337–51, 778–84, 785–91, 855–61), while Muir's poem 14 is made up entirely of excerpts from Book IV arranged as a continuous 'new' poem (IV, 13–14, 288–308, 323–9; three stanzas of Troilus' lament at Criseyde's departure and his subsequent address to lovers, introduced by two lines of fearfulness from the proem).

24 Cf. John Stevens, *Music and Poetry in the Early Tudor Court* (London, 1961), ch. 10 ('The Courtly Makers from Chaucer to Wyatt'):

> It is no accident, and certainly no anomaly, that *The Devonshire MS* includes several 'poems' which are simply excerpts from Chaucer – from *Troilus and Criseyde* and *Anelida and Arcite*. The lovers . . . utter their hearts to one another in the very words of the great poet of love, who had a word for everything they felt – Chaucer. Who can doubt that to this group of courtiers and their ladies Chaucer was, above all, the Articulate Lover, the 'well of eloquence', the master of the language of the heart? To read the *Knight's Tale* or *Anelida and Arcite* was a sentimental education . . . It did not always happen that the courtly 'maker' *lifted* his poems out of Chaucer. But with very few exceptions it can be said that he *wrote* them out of Chaucer. In particular he wrote them out of *Troilus and Criseyde*, the great poem in which he could study and find how 'most felingly' to speak of love . . .   (p. 213)

25 Emrys Jones (ed.), *Henry Howard Earl of Surrey: Poems* (Oxford, 1964), p. 27. See Helen Cooper, 'Wyatt and Chaucer: A Re-Appraisal', *Leeds Studies in English*, n.s. 13 (1982), 104–23. For Wyatt's echoes of Chaucer, see the Commentary in *Collected Poems of Sir Thomas Wyatt*, ed. Kenneth Muir and Patricia Thomson (Liverpool,

1969), *passim*, and for the background more generally, cf. H. A. Mason, *Humanism and Poetry in the Early Tudor Period* (London, 1959), Patricia Thomson, *Sir Thomas Wyatt and his Background* (London, 1964), and Raymond Southall, *The Courtly Maker* (Oxford, 1964). On Surrey, see A. C. Spearing, *Medieval to Renaissance*, ch. 7 ('Wyatt and Surrey').

26 See *La Belle Dame* and *The Court of Love* in Skeat, *Chaucerian and Other Pieces*; V. J. Scattergood (ed.), *The Works of Sir John Clanvowe* (Cambridge, 1975), D. A. Pearsall (ed.), *The Floure and the Leafe and The Assembly of Ladies* (London, 1962); Anthony Jenkins (ed.), *The Isle of Ladies, or The Ile of Pleasaunce* (New York, 1980). On the sixteenth-century editions of Chaucer, see Eleanor Prescott Hammond, *Chaucer: A Bibliographical Manual* (New York, 1908), and Paul G. Ruggiers (ed.), *Editing Chaucer: The Great Tradition* (Oklahoma, 1984).

27 *CH*, p. 120; cf. Geoffrey Shepherd (ed.), *Sir Philip Sidney: An Apology for Poetry, or The Defence of Poesy* (London, 1965), p. 133.

28 The *Cobler* is a collection of six *novelle* set in the frame of an imagined journey by water from Billingsgate to Gravesend. See Geoffrey Creigh and Jane Belfield (eds.), *The Cobler of Caunterburie and Tarltons Newes out of Purgatorie* (Leiden, 1987): 'Although unable to imitate Chaucer's verse, the author of *The Cobler* appears to have had a sufficiently close familiarity with *The Canterbury Tales* to make creative use of the detail. He also appears to have had a detailed grasp of Chaucer's sense of structure, and his imitation of Chaucer's narrative method and of the framework of *The Canterbury Tales* is imaginative' (p. 12).

29 See Ann Thompson, *Shakespeare's Chaucer: A Study in Literary Origins* (Liverpool, 1978), ch. 2 ('The Use of Chaucer by Dramatists other than Shakespeare, 1558–1625').

30 For Fletcher's *Women Pleas'd*, see below (Helen Cooper, 'The Shape-Shiftings of the Wife of Bath'), pp. 173–5.

31 See Thompson, *Shakespeare's Chaucer*, chs. 3–5, and references to previous studies therein, especially of the much-studied relation between Chaucer's *Troilus* and Shakespeare's *Troilus and Cressida*. Cf. also E. Talbot Donaldson, *The Swan at the Well: Shakespeare Reading Chaucer* (New Haven and London, 1985), chs. 3–5, and Piero Boitani (ed.), *The European Tragedy of Troilus* (Oxford, 1989).

32 See Donaldson, *The Swan at the Well*, chs. 1, 2 and 6.

33 See Thompson, *Shakespeare's Chaucer*, pp. 35–44.

34 See H. G. Wright (ed.), *A Seventeenth-Century Modernisation of the First Three Books of Chaucer's 'Troilus and Criseyde'*, 'The Cooper Monographs' (Bern, 1960), edited from British Library MS Add. 29494.

35 For the Preface, see also *The Poems of John Dryden*, ed. J. Kinsley, vol. IV (Oxford, 1958).

2

Gower – Chaucer's heir?

RICHARD AXTON

The idea of Gower as Chaucer's heir looks at first unpromising. It seems that Gower was the older and that, although he outlived Chaucer and the century by eight years, by then he was blind and poetically inactive. 'Chaucer's master', as Dr Johnson called him, has usually been counted as creditor and Chaucer as debtor in scholarly reckonings of the literary commerce between them. Gower appears older and also older-fashioned in liking long allegorical complaint poems and in choosing French and Latin for his first and second great works. When he turned to English narrative verse at the age of about fifty, it was to octosyllabic couplets – the form used by Chaucer in his earliest poem, the *Book of the Duchess*, and in the *Roman de la Rose*.[1] The typical differences in language and metre between the two poets make it hard to trace possible allusions from one to the other. For, if poetic allusion to the words of another poet depends on the text of the earlier work already being established and familiarly resonant, then the case of Chaucer and Gower is problematic. As co-workers in the newly-delved field of authorial poetry in English, it is doubtful that either could assume that the words of any text of the other's making would be recognized in quotation.[2] Yet the poets allude to each other's work and appear to be mutually indebted. Beyond this there lies a much larger area of common land where the stories, themes and forms of their works coincide. Thus the question proposed – of Gower's debt to Chaucer – needs to be considered in the larger context of their influence on one another.

Gower's late turning to English in order to 'speke ... of love' must rate as the most significant evidence of Chaucer's influence on him. In this sense, *Confessio Amantis* may be seen as paying back the trust expressed by Chaucer's dedication of *Troilus* to his 'moral' friend (*TC*, v, 1856–9). The attribute 'moral' points to Gower's fame in about 1385 as arising from his expertise in 'expounding the precepts of ethical conduct'.[3] In turn, 'moral Gower' seems to have considered love particularly as Chaucer's field of poetic expertise. This is evident from the terms of his reciprocation, for at the end of *Confessio*

Amantis (in 'first recension') Venus sends word through the poet Gower to her
'disciple' Chaucer, urging that,

> he which is myne owne clerk,
> Do make his testament of love,
> As thou hast do this schrifte above,
> So that mī Court it mai recorde.[4]   (*CA*, VIII, 2954–7*)

It sounds natural for the ageing lawyer to invite his friend to match his own
poetic *testament* and *recorde* it in Venus' *court*. The metaphorical use of legal
language has often been noted as a feature of the Ricardian period, yet with
Chaucer and Gower there is more particular point to the allusion. Theirs is a
relationship caught and held for posterity in the tangles of the law.

Sixteenth-century biographical tradition, which gentrified the literary pair,
gave Chaucer a share in Gower's legal education. Thomas Speght says in his
'Life' of Chaucer (1598):

> It seemeth that both these learned men were of the inner Temple: for not many
> yeeres since, Master Buckley did see a Recorde in the same house, where Geoff-
> rey Chaucer was fined two shillings for beating a Franciscan fryer in Fleet-
> streete.[5]

Gower says of himself in his *Mirour de l'Omme* (21772–4) that he is not a cleric
but has donned 'la raye mance', i.e. the striped robe that was the distinctive
dress of serjeants-at-law and of certain court officials.[6] Though Chaucer need
not have been a student at the Temple to have taken part in the street brawl
for which he is commended by his Protestant editor, most scholars have
thought it likely that part of his education took place at the Inn.[7] The first
evidence of the very existence of the Temple in the time of Richard II as
'England's third university' comes from Chaucer's own account of the
Manciple 'of a temple', who was 'wise in byynge of vitaille' and who

> Of maistres hadde he mo than thries ten,
> That weren of law expert and curious,
> Of which ther were a duszeyne in that hous
> Worthy to been stywardes of rente and lond
> Of any lord that is in Engelond.   (*CT*, I, 576–80)

A legal connection crops up in the summer of 1378, when Chaucer was sent to
Lombardy on the King's business and made Gower his attorney.[8] Finally,
Chaucer's plainest allusion to the poetry of Gower is made through the mouth
of the Man of Law (*CT*, II, 77–89), a figure identified with Gower by some
scholars.[9] The law thus loosely fences Chaucer and Gower in an area of shared
experience, a common ground lying between Chaucer's field of love and
Gower's field of ethics.

Clearly Chaucer and Gower read many of the same books. Thematic
parallels in their writings have been well explored by Gower's biographer
John Fisher. While never insisting that a single word or phrase constitutes a

deliberate echo, Fisher rests his case that Gower was Chaucer's senior and 'mentor' on the anthropologists' notion of 'stimulus diffusion'; Gower is seen as a think-tank, 'a sort of conscience to his brilliant but volatile friend, encouraging him both by precept and example to turn from visions of courtly love to social criticism'.[10] From the *Mirour de l'Omme*, written in the impersonal and encyclopedic tradition of French *plainte*, Gower turned to more pointed political advice in Latin, disguising his own opinions, often in allegorical form, as *Vox clamantis, vox populi*. For *Confessio Amantis*, the third of his great poetic works, he chose the English language; he recast his social and political concerns in terms of the behaviour of individuals acting under the influence of love; and he developed his powers as story-teller. Chaucer, in contrast, apparently began with dream visions of love, modelled on the French court poets, then turned to Italian and classical narratives and, finally, to social satire.

If there is truth in this general outline of paths crossing, then the literary relationship of Chaucer and Gower may be seen as mutual attraction and responsiveness. Verbal evidence for such a symbiosis is often inconclusive: it is possible that Chaucer 'got some ideas' for *Troilus* from the *Mirour de l'Omme* (which was finished by 1378), yet, however suggestive the parallels are, the French octosyllabics do not seem to have exercised *textual* force on the composition of Chaucer's poem.[11]

This distinction between ideas and texts works in both directions. In the course of his writing Gower refers seven times to the story of Troilus. Yet none of these allusions betrays any distant verbal sense of Chaucer's working of the story. Sometimes it seems as if Chaucer is recalling a motif from Gower: 'And sche which mai the hertes bynde / In loves cause and ek unbinde' (*CA*, VIII, 2811–12) *may* recall Troilus' prayer (*TC*, III, 1766). Again, Gower's 'In [love] ther can noman him reule, / For loves lawe is out of reule' (*CA*, I, 17–18) may hark back to the *Knight's Tale*: 'Who shal yeve a lovere any lawe?' (*CT*, I(A), 1164). But this, as Arcite admits, is 'olde clerkes sawe'. Both poets are rooted in the proverbial. Phrases which might look like borrowings often turn out to be commonplaces. Moreover, the poets have a common schoolmaster in Ovid:

> Ovide ek seith that love to parforne
> Stant in the hond of Venus the goddesse,
> Bot whan sche takth hir conseil with Satorne,
> Ther is no grace, and in that time, I gesse,
> Began mi love ...   (*CA*, VIII, 2273–7; cf. *CT*, I(A), 1328)

A modern reader might want to hear an echo of the *Knight's Tale* but Gower's more natural allusion is to the classic of their common schooling. There was hardly yet time in 1390 for Chaucer to have acquired Ovid's canonical status.

Ovid stands behind both poets as *the* medieval authority on love and as mediator of classical legends.[12] He may be seen as a sort of broker in the

relationship between Chaucer and Gower, a third party in whose presence
poetic intercourse can take place. Standing at the convergence of their paths,
he held out a fabulous wealth of story which had never before been turned into
English. Composition of *Confessio Amantis*, of the *Legend of Good Women* and of
Canterbury Tales must have proceeded in large part simultaneously, involving
the two poets in telling substantial narratives of the same eleven Ovidian
heroines and three other non-Ovidian tales.[13]

The best evidence for mutual exchange between Chaucer and Gower is, of
course, the similarity in the general conception of the *Legend of Good Women*
and *Confessio Amantis*. There is the matter of royal command: Gower (in the
unrevised Prologue), rowing upon the Thames, 'under the town of new Troy',
is summoned aboard the royal barge and bade to 'doon his business' and
make a book of 'some newe thing'. Chaucer, in his (unrevised) Prologue,
compliments Queen Anne as the 'day's eye' and is commanded by Alcestis,
impeccably wifely Queen of Love, to write a legendary of love's martyrs,

> And whan this book is maad, give it the quene,
> On my behalf, at Eltham or at Sheene.   (*LGW*, F, 496–7)

In each work, some of the same French sources are used to create a dream
vision of a delightful 'grene' or May meadow, with a King and Queen of Love;
these are familiar presiding deities from the world of courtly 'game', with its
enigmatic cult of the flower and the leaf, rather than classical deities. The
lovers who throng their garden scene are Ovidian heroines and heroes and the
majority of guests are the same in both parties. In both scenes Alcestis is
picked out and her authoritative matrimonial presence casts a questioning
light on the unstable – often tragic – lives of the lovers around her. This
courtly and bookish vision is not accepted at its own valuation, but is seen
within the larger frame of human society.[14] In both works the figure of the
poet is presented with humorous detachment; he is chastised by the deity of
love, and intercession is made to the queen of love. Gower confesses his 'sins'
and receives shrift. Chaucer is given a penance to perform. Both works have a
'religious' framework for a collection of amorous stories gleaned largely from
Ovid.

In this shared enterprise, the difficulties of establishing a firm chronology of
composition seem insuperable. The fact that Chaucer's dream and appraisal
of his own writing comes in his Prologue, setting in motion his martyrology,
while Gower's comes towards the end of his final book, *may* mean that Gower
borrowed the idea of his dream vision from Chaucer; yet even if he did, the
conclusion of *Confessio* does not appear improvised, but, rather, as beautifully
integrated in his dramatic structure.[15]

Chaucer's example may most have helped Gower to find an English voice
and in cultivating a sophisticated attitude towards both his reader and his
subject matter. In comparison to Chaucer's, Gower's voice sounds mild, thin,
impersonal. In *Vox Clamantis* he claims only to say 'what is in the air'. Refer-

ences to himself are confined to naming himself in dedications and to a colourless narrative 'I'. In the Prologue to Book I he includes a pedantic riddle spelling out his own name. The prologues to Books II and III express fear of detraction and disclaim any authorial responsibility for the opinions in the book: 'I speak only as the people do'.[16]

But in Book I of *Confessio* Gower relaxes, to find a more intimate and conversational voice:

> Forthi the Stile of my writinges
> Fro this day forth I thenke change
> And speke of thing is noght so strange,
> Which every kinde hath upon honde,
> And whereupon the world mot stonde . . .   (*CA*, I, 8–12)

The explicit intention to 'speke of thing is noght so strange', to find a theme which touches 'every kinde' and 'any man', 'And that is love, of which I mene / To trete . . .' may best be understood as a response to royal suggestion that Gower come down from his ivory tower. In the discarded prologue Gower carefully projects his self-esteem by distinguishing 'royal heste' from 'jangling tunges', and suggests that 'To make a bok after his [King Richard's] heste' is to write in

> such a maner wise
> Which may be wisdom to the wise
> And pley to hem that lust to pleye   (*CA*, Pr. 83–5)

Tentative as this is, these look like the first steps into a territory of writing-as-entertainment ('pleye') that was already occupied by Chaucer.

It has been argued that Gower learned from the French poets, particularly in Machaut and Froissart, to develop the persona of the *petis servans* of the god of love, the quizzical, self-deprecating 'amant couart'.[17] By combining this received stereotype with the persona of *senex amans* he generates a wintry pathos that is also humorous and elusive. Critical disagreement about the age of Amans, inconsistencies in his dramatic presentation, together with the contradictory pictorial evidence in the manuscripts, all suggest how difficult it is to interpret Gower's autobiographical mode.[18]

Granted the guiding spirits of the French poets, is it not also the case that Chaucer's presence hovers here? The light, self-mocking humour of the non-playing spectator of the game of love is like Chaucer, though the underlying sense of pathos and helplessness is different from Chaucer's images of aged sexuality (in, for example, the Wife of Bath or the Reeve). Gower also includes a formal signal of the Chaucerian debt. Advised by Genius that it is time to withdraw from the blind world of love and to live under the law of reason, Amans makes a last bid for pity, composes a letter to Venus, which Genius agrees to deliver. The supplication (*CA*, VIII, 2217–300) consists of twelve seven-line stanzas in rhyme royal. This shift from the informal, 'spoken' short lines into the higher epistolary register, which

Chaucer had developed in *Troilus*, anticipates Gower's memorial image of the famous lovers themselves.

From this point in Book VIII possible allusions to Chaucer suggest themselves with increasing frequency. In his perplexity and despondency in love Amans thinks of Pan, 'which is the god of kinde'. Chaucer had found the same correspondent to look over the 'sorwe' and 'hevy thoght' of the Black Knight:

> For he had wel nygh lost hys mynde,
> Thogh Pan, that men clepe god of kynde,
> Were for hys sorwes never so wroth.   (*BD*, 511–13)

Amans' proverbially wry judgement,

> For evere I wrastle and evere I am behind   (*CA*, VIII, 2241)

recalls not Pan but Pandarus:

> 'How ferforth be ye put in loves daunce?'
> 'By God,' quod he, 'I hoppe alwey byhynde!' (*TC*, II, 1106–7)

Having despatched Genius with his supplication, Amans is left waiting

> And I bod in the place stille,
> And was there bot a litel while
> Noght full the montance of a Mile,
> Whan I beheild and sodeinly
> I sih wher Venus stod me by.
> So as I myhte, under a tre
> To grounde I fell upon mi kne,
> And preide hire forto do me grace: (*CA*, VIII, 2310–17)

Curious here is the index of time: it is Genius who walks away, Amans who stays 'noght full the montance of a Mile'. There is nothing remarkable about the idiomatic use of walking distance to indicate time, except that this is the only occasion in his writing that Gower uses the word 'montance'. In the corresponding scene in the *Legend of Good Women* (where a company of nineteen ladies kneels upon the green and the poet kneels with them, in honour of the King and Queen of Love), Chaucer observes:

> Ne nat a word was spoken in the place
> The mountance of a furlong wey of space.   (*LGW*, F, 306–7)

The goddess now admonishes Gower by name, ' "Now John" quod sche . . .' and proceeds to enumerate his complaints against Nature. How far Gower has come from the elaborate pedantic self-naming of *Vox Clamantis* towards the idiom of Chaucer!

> 'Geffrey, thou wost ryght wel this,
> That every kyndely thyng that is
> Hath a kyndely stede . . .'
>   (*HF*, 729–31)

Venus finds no pleasure in the figure of the aged poet:

> For loves lust and lockes hore
> In chambre acorden neveremore,
> And thogh thou feigne a yong corage,
> It scheweth wel be the visage
> That olde grisel is no fole:
> There ben fulmanye yeres stole
> With thee and with suche othre mo,
> That outward feignen youthe so
> And ben withinne of pore assay. (*CA*, VIII, 2403–11)

Is Chaucer included in that knowing phrase, 'such othre mo'? 'Old Grisel' is of course proverbial, but it is a phrase which comes to Chaucer's lips in his more complex and humorous essay in the same vein – the *Envoy to Scogan*:

> Now certes, frend, I dreede of thyn unhap,
>   Lest for thy gilt the wreche of Love procede
> On alle hem that ben hoor and rounde of shap,
>   That ben so lykly folk in love to spede,
>   Than shal we for oure labour han no mede;
> But wel I wot, thow wolt answere and say:
> 'Lo, olde Grisel lyst to ryme and playe!' (29–35)

These lines were probably written around 1393, but the vein is one that Chaucer had begun to explore much earlier, in the banter of the Eagle in the *House of Fame* and in the badinage of Pandarus. It is not altogether surprising, then, that the green garden of love with its garlanded routs, 'Some of the lef, some of the flour' (*CA*, VIII, 2468) for which Chaucer expresses such poetic indifference (in the unrevised, 'courtly' text, *LGW*, F, 188–93) contains also strains of rougher music. Gower's 'piping and melodie' include also,

> such a soun
> Of bombard and of clarion
> With Cornemuse and Schallemele, (*CA*, VIII, 2481–3)

– instruments that make up the 'lowde mynstralcies' in the House of Fame ('In cornemuse and shalemys', 'In trumpe, beme, and clarion', *HF*, 1218–40).

Like Chaucer, Gower casts himself as an outsider viewing the young people as they 'springe and dance', 'laghe and pleie'. He is also, like Chaucer, bemused by 'tidings' in the House of Fame, an eavesdropper; he draws attention to the physical distance which separates him from the origin of the sounds he hears, placing a question mark over the faithfulness of his own recording of such 'matiere':

> And overthis I understood,
> So as myn Ere it myhte areche,
> The moste matiere of her speche
> Was al of knyhthod and of Armes,
> And what it is to ligge in armes
> With love, whanne it is achieved. (*CA*, VIII, 2494–9)

The gentle and well-worn word-play upon the achievements of knighthood (night-hood?) recalls Chaucer as outsider in the Hall of Fame, listening to the confused voices of the world for something to make poetry out of.

So, when Gower comes to review the world's famous lovers and to make his own testament of love, revealing at last the face of John Gower, the aged poet behind the youthful lover he had feigned, the shadow of Chaucer is already falling over his page. Yet, in celebrating the most famous of Chaucer's lovers, Gower reveals how different is his own kind of poetry from Chaucer's. Among the company that Gower sees (or seems to see: 'Me thoghte that I sih') in his bemused state are Troilus and Criseide. The figures are abstract, devoid of detail, and betray no debt to Chaucer's mnemonic portraits (*TC*, v, 799–840). At first sight, Gower's Criseide appears to stand between her two lovers. But whether Diomede is presented to the reader's view or not is unclear. The focus on Troilus is anything but static and monumental; even as we watch, the play of emotions across his face reveals the pain of his story as he resists the knowledge of Criseide's infidelity. Like so many of Gower's Ovidian heroes, he is seen experiencing change, caught in the process of metamorphosis:

> And Troilus stod with Criseide,
> Bot evere among, althogh he pleide,
> Be semblant he was hevy chiered,
> For Diomede, as him was liered,
> Cleymeith to be his parconer.   (*CA*, VIII, 2531–5)

Gower's company of noble wives and lovers is neither strictly a review of the protagonists of tales he has told nor an entirely random list chosen from within the Ovidian canon. It seems, rather, to contain recollections of stories which formed part of the common enterprise with Chaucer. The ghost of Chaucer may perhaps be sensed in Gower's vision of

> the wofull queene
> Cleopatras, which in a Cave
> With Serpentz hath hirself begrave,   (*CA*, VIII, 2572–4)

where he seems to recall the death of Cleopatra as it occurs in Chaucer's telling, uniquely:

> Among the serpents in the pit she sterte
> And there she ches to have hire buryinge.   (*LGW*, F, 697–8)

Similarly when Gower recollects Thisbe – Chaucer's next in order. Like Ovid, Chaucer keeps his urgent narrative teetering on the edge of comedy, assigning the cause of the tragedy to Pyramus' tardiness: 'But al to long, allas, at hom was he.' In Gower's five-line recapitulation, we hear Thisbe complain, 'Wo worthe alle slow!'[19] So Gower moves through his gallery of Ovidian memories, to the four chaste wives, while Elde 'cam a softe pas', creeping up almost unnoticed and casting a chill shadow over the bright spring scene. In a series of perfectly paced shifts of mood and temperature, Gower shapes his 'quiet close'.[20]

Repentant, shriven, chastened by his apprehension of Elde and by Venus' reasonable reminders of the course of Nature, Gower is turned back towards the proper – and earlier – subjects of his bookish concerns:

> Mi Sone, be wel war therfore
> And kep the sentence of my lore
> And tarie thou mi court nomore,
> Bot go ther vertu moral duelleth,
> Wher ben thi bokes, as men telleth,
> Which of long time thou hast write   (*CA*, VIII, 2922–7)

as if he has been trespassing all along.

Venus' admonition of her doting clerk is a timely reminder that Gower's English voice is not confined to the plaintive strain of the first person Lover. In this final address, Venus adopts the form of speech that Genius has taken towards his recalcitrant pupil, 'Mi Sone'. The formula is both priestly and Solomonic. The dialogic device of the confession has allowed Gower to create two voices for his English poetry, one mild and complaining, deferential, courtly, the sound of the *amant couart*; the other fatherly, a steady, admonishing voice of moral authority with ready access to bookish and proverbial wisdom – the voice of Solomon to his son. This voice of parental authority is one that echoes in Chaucer's verse only once – in the *Manciple's Tale*.

Gower's advice to Chaucer is – playfully distanced through Venus and the fiction in which she appears – to think on his end and make his poetic reckoning:

> And gret wel chaucer whan ye mete,
> As mi disiple and mi poete:
> For in the floures of his youthe
> In sondri wise, as he wel couthe,
> Of Ditees and of songes glade,
> The whiche he for mi sake made,
> The lond fulfild is overal:
> Wherof to him in special
> Above alle othre I am most holde.
> For thi now in hise daies olde
> Thow schalt him telle this message,
> That he upon his latere age,
> To sette an end of alle his werk,
> As he which is myn own clerk,
> Do make his testament of love,
> As thou hast do thi schrifte above,
> So that mi Court it mai recorde.   (*CA*, VIII, 2941–57*)

The salutation of Chaucer, though it was later omitted,[21] is no spontaneous afterthought; it rises, rather, to the playful surface from a current flowing deep and almost transparent within the stream of Gower's own verse.

Whether or not as a result of this banter, Chaucer clearly attended to both tasks. His detailed listing of his works – in the Prologues to the *Legend* and to the *Man of Law's Tale* and, finally, in the *Retraccions*, is specific and tendentious where Gower is merely general in his appreciation of Chaucer's 'ditees and … songes glade'. Interestingly, Chaucer's revision of the Prologue (where F makes nothing of the poet's age), between mention of the 'Romauns of the Rose' and 'the bok How that Crisseyde Troylus forsok', adds:

> And thynkest in thy wit, that is ful col,
> That he nys but a verray propre fol
> That loveth paramours, to hard and hote.
> Wel wot I thereby thow begynnest dote
> As olde foles, whan here spiryt fayleth;
> Thanne blame they folk, and wite nat what hem ayleth.
>
> (*LGW*, G, 258–63)

It is as if he now follows Gower's lead, confessing that they grow old together.

Though Chaucer probably rewrote his Prologue after the death of Queen Anne in 1394 (three or four years after Gower finished the *Confessio*) he did not 'finish' the *Legend*, presumably because he found the *Canterbury Tales* more exciting. He found there the greatest possible freedom as story-teller, a framework hospitable not only to 'wicked women' left over from Ovid (the story of Phebus' wife and the crow), but even to a further reviewing of his own poetic production. In the substantial Introduction to the *Man of Law's Tale* he draws up a list of Ovidian work-in-progress, which turns – almost inevitably – from humorous advertisement of what he has achieved to repudiation of what he has left alone. Scholars are almost unanimous in seeing here an allusion to Gower's work, but there is disagreement about Chaucer's tone. Did he really find Gower's stories of incestuous Canacee and of Apollonius 'horrible' and 'unkynde abhomynacions'? It seems he did. Gower's most celebrated story (the tale of *Pericles*) is one which Chaucer makes a great fuss about *not* telling.

In spite of all the shared poetic interests, at heart the two poets are very different. The murky and dangerous material that they found in Ovid's *Metamorphoses* brought quite different poetic responses from them. This is plainest in those tales where they both confront sex and violence and the magic of metamorphosis. Gower's sense of man's creatureliness – rather than his beastliness – enables him to render wonderfully the love-making of Ceyx and Alcyone, even as they are changing to sea-birds (*CA*, IV, 3106–12): clearly such a scene could have had no part in the decorous consolations offered by the *Book of the Duchess*. Ever sceptical of all forms of magic, Chaucer systematically avoided metamorphosis wherever he could or (as in the *Wife of Bath's Tale* and *Manciple's Tale*) made it merely perfunctory. By contrast, Gower is intimate with Ovid's sense of man as 'Semibovemque virum, semivirumque bovem'. The savage tale of the rape of Philomela (*Metamorphoses*, VI, 424–605) brings out most strongly these temperamental differ-

ences; Gower's success and Chaucer's self-confessed repudiation of the story
shed a good deal of light on the Introduction to the *Man of Law's Tale*.

In the simplest terms, Gower is able to retell the whole story, dreadful as it
is, while Chaucer must omit for the purpose of his *Legend* the atrocious revenge
of the 'good' women so wronged by Tereus, and seems often to be averting his
eyes from the events he does tell. Gower is closer to Ovid in his fascination,
which is neither morbid nor prurient, with the vision of man as half-beast. In
the psychology of his *Confessio Amantis*, Rape is classed as a branch of Avarice,
a violent extortion which stems from loss of reason. To this extent Gower (like
Chrestien before him) thinks of Tereus' rape of his wife's young sister as
within Nature, though against 'kynde' because unreasonable. Gower's Tereus
acts in a rage of self-forgetting and

> Foryat he was a wedded man,
> And in a rage on hire he ran,
> Riht as a wolf which takth his preie,
> And sche began to crie and preie,
> 'O fader ...'   (*CA*, v, 5631–5)

The violence of the verbal play here anticipates metamorphosis at the climax
of the story.[22] It is because Tereus' act is seen as within the laws of nature
(though not of reason), that the conclusion of the tale in lyrical evocation of
the changing seasons is not felt to be incongruous. The violence of the story
subsides as 'the wodes and the greves / Ben heled al with grene leves' (v,
5965–6), to hide the pain and shame of Philomene's wounded form.

Chaucer's considered response to the story comes in his Prologue to
Philomene, written, he says, after composing the narrative. For him, the story
has no redeeming qualities and most critics have seen him as making a mess of
telling it. His fussy, sympathetic, narratorial voice intrudes as if to shield the
violence of the events he must relate, even assuring the heroine that help is at
hand, when patently it is not so. The tone seems uneasy, embarrassed, finally
dismissive. He cuts the story short with never a hint of metamorphosis ('The
remenaunt is no charge for to telle'); instead, there is only a startlingly lame
moral, 'be war of men'. Yet Chaucer almost redeems the botched telling with
the pained and sombre prologue. The words he speaks in his own person take
up the last cry of Philomene before her tongue is cut out, 'Help me, God in
hevene.' It is, however, the Christian God he addresses, the Author of Nature,
'Thow yevere of the formes, that hast wrought / This fayre world' (*LGW*,
2228ff.).

Not content with asking – more directly, perhaps, than anywhere else in his
work – where evil originates in creation, Chaucer turns in his anguish from
reflection upon God's responsibility as author of nature to his own, secondary,
authorial responsibility: merely to retell Ovid's story seems to be to pollute the
world. The tendency of modern moral thought favours Gower's reading of
violent sexual crime rather than Chaucer's, preferring the idea of beastly

human nature to the more disconcerting idea of evil. Yet the sincerity and pain of Chaucer's indignation seem to me undeniable and the seriousness of his sense of authorial responsibility is not anything a modern reader can lightly dismiss. The Prologue is like a cry of betrayal, betrayal of the author Chaucer by his story-master Ovid; its seriousness provides a point of view from which to gauge the tone of the Man of Law, when he distinguishes the stories of Ovid's lovers told by Chaucer from those of his friend and rival John Gower.

In the Introduction of the *Man of Law's Tale* Chaucer starts a new fragment, and takes stock of his own – and Gower's – part in the Ovidian enterprise. Chaucer has had enough of his large volume, 'Cleped the Seintes Legende of Cupide':

> For he hath told of loveris up and doun
> No more than Ovide made of mencion.   (54–5)

But at least he has not written of incest ('Canacee,/That loved hir owene brother synfully'), nor of incestuous rape (King Antiochus). Chaucer would never write of such things, says the Man of Law with complacent piety:

> He nolde nevere write in none of his sermons
> Of swiche unkynde abhomynacions.   (87–8)

Who writes sermons – Chaucer or Gower? Chaucer's own work is more moral, he claims. The tone is bantering, but the attitude seems consistent with the heavy-weight philosophical reaction to the story of Philomene.

Chaucer completes the self-reflexive joke by having his Man of Law propose to speak in prose, because

> Me were looth be likned doutelees
> To Muses that men clepe Pierides –
> Methamorphosios woot what I mene.   (91–3)

A wink here – for those of Chaucer's audience that know – hints that the author of Metamorphosis or, more likely, Gower will understand the allusion. In referring to the nine daughters of Pierus transformed into magpies for presuming to compete with the Muses, there lurks an idea which Chaucer will brilliantly expand in his *Manciple's Tale*.

Before turning to that final riposte to Gower, it is worth pondering some strategic implications of Chaucer's response. As Chaucer developed his plan for the *Canterbury Tales* rivalry with Gower certainly played a part; it may help to explain two notorious changes of Chaucer's mind. In the first, the Man of Law, promising a tale in prose, delivers up a tripartite poem in 'high-style' rhyme royal, ostentatiously pious, adorned with homiletic tropes and astrological flourishes. Twice he hints that 'other men' have told the story differently. That Chaucer has in mind here to outdo Gower's tale of Constance in Book II of *Confessio Amantis* is now maintained by a majority of scholars. There are nine passages in Chaucer that suggest precise verbal recollection of Gower.[23] Problematic too is the connection of the Prologue proper (in rhyme royal) with the Man of Law. Based on part of *De miseria condicionis humane* by Innocent III, its wry-sounding dispraise of poverty is offered to 'riche marchauntz', who are commended for their wealth and jovially greeted, 'At Cristemasse myrie may ye daunce.' In conclusion, the Man of Law, claiming otherwise to be 'of tales desolaat', attributes his effort to 'a marchaunt, goon is many a yeere'. The text registers a number of changes of direction. Since the prose tale of *Melibee* would seem to fit the Man of Law very well – even to his legalistic idiom[24] – and constitutes an essay on political morality in a genre more frequented by Gower than Chaucer, there is a tantalizing coherence in the puzzles presented. The identity – or association – of Gower with the Man of Law repeatedly suggests itself, and Chaucer's change of plan appears at least partly to have been a response to the publication of Gower's *Confessio*. This likelihood is strengthened by consideration of the second crux, involving the *Wife of Bath's* and *Shipman's Tales*. For Chaucer's decision to sever the fabliau from its knowing female teller (vestigially present in 'we sely women' of the Shipman's speech) and develop richer possibilities for the Wife, led him to the folk-tale which Gower had treated as the Tale of Florent (*CA*, I, 141ff.). Here, characteristically, he made fun of the magic and played down the climactic metamorphosis. In two instances where Chaucer changed his plan while imperfectly adjusting the dramatic framework of the *Canterbury Tales* the shift may be viewed as part of his creative response to Gower.

Chaucer's final response to Gower is another tonally complex piece: the *Manciple's Tale*. It seems to develop out of a seed in the Man of Law's Introduction and it is taken from the *Metamorphoses*. Ovid's fable of 'How the crow became black' reached both Gower and Chaucer through the *Ovide moralisé*, where it is explained as a warning against slander.[25] *Ovide moralisé* takes a sympathetic and courtly view of adultery and blames the lady's slanderers. In the *Confessio Amantis (CA*, III, 768ff.) Gower retells the story as an exemplum of Cheste (backbiting), and a warning against fault-finding and not keeping counsel. As is usual in the *Confessio*, the moral is explicitly stated by the priest confessor; its proverbial nature is reinforced by the usual Solomonic form of address to the penitent.[26]

> Mi sone, be thou war ther by,
> And holde thi tunge stille close.   (*CA*, III, 768–9)

Again, at the end,

> My son, be thou non of tho,
> To jangle the telle tales so.   (831–2)

Chaucer's harsher version is, characteristically, self-reflexive. For him the essence of the sour little story lies in an English pun: the tell-tale bird is a teller of tales. The most important thing about Chaucer's crow is not (as Ovid has it) its beautiful plumage, but its voice. The crow is Apollo's bird (as white as his traditional sweet-singing swan) and Phebus Apollo is the god of poetry:

> Now hadde this Phebus in his hous a crowe
> Which in a cage he fostred many a day,
> And taughte it speken, as men teche a jay.
> Whit was this crowe as is a snow whit swan
> And countrefete the speche of every man
> He koude, whan he sholde telle a tale.   (IX(H), 130–5)

The syntax is ambiguous here. Who originates tales, a man or the crow? The crow is a mimic, but does he counterfeit the speech of a man-telling-a-tale or does he counterfeit the speech of the right sort of man when he (the crow) wants to tell a tale? Does the poet report or does he make up his fictions?

For Chaucer the story is not really about Coronis' adultery, but about social and linguistic decorum: How do you tell a man (or a god of poetry) that he is a cuckold? The tale becomes a reflection on how to tell a tale. Hence the relevance of the Manciple's long digression on whether to call a man's mistress his lady or his wench or his lemman. The crow's problem is how to tell his master that he is abused. First he tries a traditional voice, one unpleasing to the married ear:

> And whan that hoom was come Phebus, the lord,
> This crowe sang, 'Cokkow, Cokkow, Cokkow!'
> 'What, bryd!' quod Phebus, 'What song syngestow?'   (IX(H), 242–4)

But the courtly Phebus cannot understand, 'Allas, what song is this?' So the crow lets him have it more rhetorically:

> 'By God', quod he, 'I synge nat amys.
> Phebus', quod he, 'For al thy worthynesse,
> For al thy beautee and thy gentilesse,
> For al thy song and al thy mynstralcye,
> For al thy waityng, blered is thyn ye
> With oon of litel reputacioun,
> Noght worth to thee, as in comparisoun,
> The montance of a gnat, so moot I thryve!
> For on thy bed thy wyf I saugh hym swyve.'   (IX(H),248–56)

The polite crescendo of qualifying clauses winds to a climax on the vulgar word. In the 'brode' speech register of Chaucer's *fabliau* tellers the word passes without notice. Here it is all the more shocking for the Manciple's squeamish digression on linguistic decorum. It is a shock that Gower would have registered; for all modernity of his moral thinking, his choice of words is always delicate and the word 'swyve' does not occur once in his entire writing.[27]

Phebus understands the message and slays his wife, instantly regretting it. More significantly, the god of poetry now destroys his musical instruments:

> For sorwe of which be brak his minstralcie,
> Both harpe and lute and gyterne and sautrie. (ix(h), 267–8)

Phebus however convinces himself that he has been rash and that the crow has been lying, so 'out at dore hym slong', commending him to the devil. Such is the reward for telling the truth.

Granted that Chaucer turns the Ovidian tale into a reflection on poetry and truth-telling, why need it refer to Gower? From Chaucer's perspective, Gower was – after the completion of *Confessio Amantis* – preeminently the provider of morals for stories from Ovid. Moreover, Chaucer's choice of the Manciple to tell this story was not fortuitous. The *Manciple's Prologue and Tale* form the ninth fragment and – though we cannot know Chaucer's final intention – are generally thought to precede the *Parson's Tale*. They offer the last secular view of the world that the pilgrimage allows. The sardonic little bird-fable is preceded by some of the nastiest horseplay in the pilgrimage (wine has rendered the Cook 'sow drunk' and incapable of speech, the Manciple's sanctimonious denunciation of the poor sot incurs the Host's professional rebuke and the 'penance' of a tale). It will be recalled that the Manciple had been represented in the *General Prologue* as in charge of buying provisions for 'a Temple'. He is one of the very few figures in the *General Prologue* for whom no literary model in the estates satire tradition has been found.[28] This makes it likelier that the Manciple owes his presence in the *Canterbury Tales* to Chaucer's recollection of the Inner Temple, an experience of law and business which, I have suggested, he shared with Gower. The Manciple, then, can be seen in this literary exchange as inhabiting that 'common ground'.

So far as this relationship is inscribed in the writings of the two poets, we have Gower's image of Chaucer as 'Venus clerk' – a view which Chaucer readily elaborates in the Prologue to the *Man of Law's Tale* – but we have two Chaucerian images of Gower. One is formal, even reverent – the 'moral Gower' entrusted to 'correct' *Troilus*. The other, a teller of immoral tales, 'abhominations', in contrast to Chaucer's 'sermons'. It is the good faith of Gower as moralist that is in question here, and his resourceful credulity in always being able to draw a patent moral from the murky stuff of classical fable.

The Manciple's tale is very short, only 250 lines, and much of this taken up with moralizing digressions. The last fifty lines are devoted to pointing the moral that true wisdom lies in silence:

> Daun Salomon as wise clerkes seyn
> Techeth a man to kepen his tonge wel. (ix(h), 314–15)

The proverbial admonition is repeated twenty-two times in these fifty lines and there is a pungent irony in the uncontrollable tell-tale preaching the virtues of silence.

Chaucer seems to be doing two things here: he is parodying the proverbial tale, since no other explanation of the too-muchness of the moralizing seems to me possible.[29] He is also, through his cacophony of voices, parodying the work of his friend Gower. Not content with the Manciple's proverbial excess, Chaucer introduces a further-off-stage character in the voice of the Manciple's mother, who is quoted for the final forty-three clamorous lines of the tale. From this parental tongue rattles a volly of Solomonic wisdom directed at 'My son'; the formula is the one which Gower has worked to death:

> My sone, thenk on the crowe, a Goddes name!
> My sone, keep wel thy tonge, and keep thy freend.
> A wickked tonge is worse than a feend.
> My sone, thy tonge sholdestow restreyne
> At alle tymes ...
> ... The first vertue, sone, if thou wold leere,
> Is to restreyne and kepe wel thy tonge.   (IX(H), 318–33)

What a thankless task, Chaucer seems to say, as he focusses his last sardonic image of the poet as scarecrow, what a thankless task to be an *auctour*.

> My sone, be war, and be noon auctour newe
> Of tidynges, wheither they been false or trewe.
> Wherso thou come, amonges hye or lowe,
> Kepe wel thy tonge, and thenk upon the crowe.   (IX(H), 359–62)

The final reflection on the tell-tale art of tale-telling links two words that had become thematically charged through Chaucer's recurrent use of them: *auctour* and *tidings*. An auctour is a poet, a moral authority. 'Am I an auctour?' Chaucer humorously asks. Tidings are what Chaucer had searched for in the journey to the House of Fame.[30] Tidings are what you make poetry out of, but they are also the report of those events. When the Man of Law addressed the unnamed merchants as 'fadres of tidynges' and ascribed the origin of his tale to a merchant, Chaucer was confirming his own use of the word from the *House of Fame*; he was also acknowledging his debt for a story which 'father' Gower had already told.

Chaucer's reflections on his art are bleak and black in the *Manciple's Tale*: no matter whether you make everything up or are a mere rapporteur (the ambiguity in the function of the Crow), you will have little thanks for telling the truth. The bitter proverbial wisdom mocking Gower mocks Chaucer too, typically and, pointedly, in the last of his fictional tales before Canterbury. If Chaucer's mockery of Gower seems a little ungrateful in view of a lifelong debt to his 'mentor' then it is also worth remembering that so far as writing in English is concerned, Chaucer was the master and Gower his poetic son.

NOTES

1 Gower's choice of metre is discussed by Bruce Harbert, 'Lessons from the Great Clerk: Ovid and John Gower', *Ovid Renewed*, ed. Charles Martindale (Cambridge, 1988), p. 87.

2 The same general problem is encountered in judging whether or not Chaucer is

quoting himself; even regular decasyllabic lines appearing almost verbatim in *Troilus* and the prose *Melibee* are best explained in genesis and function as proverbial. See Carleton Brown, 'The Man of Law's Headlink and the Prologue of the *Canterbury Tales*', *Studies in Philology*, 34 (1937), 8–35.

3 Derek Pearsall, 'The Gower Tradition', in A.J. Minnis (ed.), *Gower's 'Confessio Amantis': Responses and Reassessments* (Cambridge: D. S. Brewer, 1983), p. 179–97, 180.

4 Quotations from *CA* are from *The English Works of John Gower*, ed. G. C. Macaulay, 2 vols. (Oxford: *EETS*, 1900).

5 *Chaucer Life Records*, ed. Martin M. Crow and Clair C. Olson (Oxford, 1966), p. 12n.

6 Cited by D. S. Brewer, *Chaucer and His World*, 3rd edn (London, 1978), p. 83.

7 *Riverside Chaucer*, p. xviii. The educational function of the Temple in Chaucer's time – denied by J. A. Hornsby, *Chaucer and the Law* (Norman, Oklahoma, 1988), p. 20 – is established beyond doubt by Samuel E. Thorne and J. H. Baker, *Readings and Moots at the Inns of Court in the Fifteenth Century*, vol. II (London, Selden Society, 1989), pp. xxv–xxxv.

8 *Chaucer Life Records*, p. 54 and n.

9 Others have argued for Ralph Strode. 'Philosophical Strode', who disputed with Wyclif in his youth and who shared with Gower the dedication of *Troilus*, became a common sergeant and was pleader-at-law during the period 1374–86 when he was a close neighbour of Chaucer's in Aldgate.

10 John H. Fisher, *John Gower* (New York and London, 1964), p. 207.

11 For instance, *MO*, 25–32 (*Complete Works: The French Works*, ed., G. C. Macaulay, Oxford, 1899), where Chaucer, if he had looked only at the first page, would have read how a man's heart's desire would pass like a dream, ending in sorrow, as all secular love returns in the end to nothing.

12 Chaucer names Ovid eighteen times (also thrice as 'Naso' and, possibly – see below p. 32 – once as 'Metamorphosios'). In *CA* Gower refers specifically to Ovid twenty-two times. In an elegant recent discussion of 'Chaucer and Ovid' (*Ovid Renewed*, pp. 71–81), Helen Cooper claims, 'Chaucer makes more extensive use of him than of any other Roman poet, Virgil included' (p. 72), and argues that Ovid was the *auctor* who taught Chaucer not to accept *auctoritas* on trust.

13 The stories of Cleopatra, Philomela, Alcestis, Lucrece, Thisbe, Phyllis, Ariadne, Hypsipyle, Medea, Dido are told in *CA* and *LGW*; the story of Phebus' crow is told in *CA* and *McpT*, and of Alcyone in *CA* and *BD*. All but the last three appear in the Man of Law's list (*Riverside Chaucer*, p. 855); of those in the same list, Deianira, Hermione, Hero, Helen, Laodomia, Penelope, Briseis have their stories told in *CA*, while Hypermnestra is in *LGW*. In addition, the stories of Constance, Virginia, and Florent (*WBT*) are told in both *CA* and *CT*.

14 See, for instance, Fisher, ch. 4 and Elizabeth Porter, 'Gower's Ethical Microcosm and Political Macrocosm' in *Responses and Reassessments*, ed. Minnis, pp. 135–62. *LGW* F, 366–408, G, 346–94 ('tirayntz of Lumbardye') show one of Chaucer's rare passages of political philosophy. A number of commentators have seen in this speech a serious lecture on the duties of a king addressed to Richard II by Anne in the person of Alceste. This uncharacteristic touch suggests a motive of rivalry with Gower (see Robinson, p. 845). The philosopher of F381 seems to be Aristotle, whose advice to Alexander on the subject of kings in cited by Gower in *CA*, VII, 2149ff. The rhyme 'philosophre ... gold in cofre' is repeated in Introduction to *MLT*, II, *25ff.*

15 This point is well made by John Burrow, 'The Portrayal of Amans in *Confessio Amantis*', in *Responses and Reassessments*, ed. Minnis, pp. 5–24.

16 The Prologue to *Confessio Amantis* promises to complain of the same concerns as in both the earlier two works: the state of England, the corruption of the church, the nobles, the commons. Indeed, 'Gower seems about to rewrite *Vox Clamantis* in English', Porter, p. 142.

17 Burrow, pp. 5–15. Bruce Harbert suggests *Tristia* and Ovid's other exile poems as sources of 'the persona Gower creates for himself at the end of the *Confessio*'.

18 Burrow, pp. 11–12; Jeremy Griffiths, '*Confessio Amantis*: The poem and its pictures', in *Responses and Reassessments*, ed. Minnis, p. 174–5.

19 The versions of Pyramus by both poets are discussed by Norman Callan, 'Thyn Owne Book: A Note on Chaucer, Gower, and Ovid', *Review of English Studies*, 22 (1946), 269–81: 'to anyone making a comparison of the first fifty lines it must appear that Gower, far from working from a general recollection [of Ovid], is following Chaucer', whereas Chaucer wrote 'from a recent perusal of Ovid'. Callan draws attention to *LGW*, 706ff. and *CA*, III, 1332ff.

20 C. S. Lewis, *The Allegory of Love* (Oxford, 1936), p. 218.

21 Reasons for Gower's excision of the gracious compliment may have been purely technical. The 'recension' manuscripts may date from after Chaucer's death, so there is no need to suppose a falling out between the friends, as elaborated by Fisher. (See particularly P. Nicholson, 'Poet and Scribe of the MSS of Gower's *Confessio Amantis*', in *Editorial Problems in Later Middle English Literature*, ed. D. Pearsall (Cambridge: D. S. Brewer), pp. 130–42.) Since Gower also cut the praise of King Richard in the Prologue, excision may have been to protect Chaucer, a royal favourite.

22 Gower releases murderous possibilities in the most intimate words, as when Tereus, having bound the *arms* of his victim, '*clippeth* also faste / Her tunge'. The force of Gower's renderings of metamorphosis is well discussed by Christopher Ricks, 'Metamorphosis in Other Words', in *The Force of Poetry* (Oxford, 1984), pp. 1–33.

23 *Riverside Chaucer*, p. 857.

24 Carleton Brown, 'The Man of Law's Headlink', pp. 17–18.

25 Chaucer's indebtedness to *Ovide moralisé* is not proven. See D. C. Baker, ed. *The Manciple's Tale*, Variorum Chaucer, vol. 2, part 10 (Norman, Oklahoma, 1984), 4–11; and Cooper, 'Chaucer and Ovid', p. 79.

26 Cf. the Sloane MS 2593 song, 'Kepe thy tunge, thy tunge, thy tunge' and Pandarus' advice to Troilus: 'That firste vertu is to kepe tonge' (*TC*, III, 294).

27 *A Concordance to John Gower's 'Confessio Amantis'*, ed. J. D. Pickles and J. L. Dawson (Cambridge: D. S. Brewer, 1987).

28 Jill Mann, *Chaucer and Medieval Estates Satire* (Cambridge, 1973), p. 174.

29 See R. Hazleton, *Journal of English and Germanic Philology*, 62 (1963), 1–31. For other interpretations of the tale see *Riverside Chaucer*, p. 952 and A. C. Spearing, 'The *CT* IV: Exemplum and Fable', in *The Cambridge Chaucer Companion*, ed. P. Boitani and Jill Mann (Cambridge, 1986), pp. 172–5.

30 Out of thirty-eight occurrences of the word, twenty-two are in that poem.

3

Chaucer and Lydgate

DEREK PEARSALL

John Lydgate was considered to be a very important poet in his own day and for at least a century afterwards: he received many commissions to write poems from patrons in all walks of life; his poetry was widely admired and imitated; he is frequently alluded to, usually in conjunction with Gower and Chaucer, as one of the founding fathers of English poetry; there are many manuscripts of his works. In more recent times he has been more or less universally contemned and become the butt of every jibe, especially for his prolixity and the great bulk of his writing. He now appears like a great whale helplessly beached on the shore of reputation. The tide has gone out, or elsewhere. Nature was resting, and Lydgate was born. What really happened?

The difference of opinion, so stark and apparently inexplicable, is a challenge, and various explanations have been offered, usually involving extremely derogatory estimates of the good sense of Lydgate's fifteenth-century admirers, or else unlikely suggestions as to the merit of his verses. In taking up the challenge, again, one would not want to become embroiled in further debate about whether Lydgate's poetry is any good. There is no need for a debate: it is not very good. It is often dull, especially in long stretches, and it usually comes in long stretches. It is hard work to read, and the most skilful reader, however optimistic he is about Lydgate's versification, will stumble every few lines. But it is not as bad as it is often made out to be, and sympathetic readers, from Thomas Gray to Rosemary Woolf, have found things to admire.[1] What one might better do, instead of seeking an absolute judgement on the value of Lydgate's poetry, is to make the contrary opinions part of the subject matter of enquiry, build the observer into the experiment, so to speak. What we find when we do so is that the differences of opinion are not so hopelessly inexplicable. Indeed, they are susceptible of an explanation that may appear hopelessly simple-minded: it is all Chaucer's fault. What Lydgate did was to absorb Chaucer to the official taste of the fifteenth century, by praising and imitating him in ways that were acceptable to that taste. To borrow a word that Geoffrey Shepherd applied to the subject, he 'encapsulated' Chaucer so that he could be digested without discomfort to the established system, much as a nurse will get a child who has swallowed a sharp-pointed object to eat a sticky bun, so as to ease its passage through the digestive tract. Chaucer is the sharp-pointed object; Lydgate is the sticky bun. Modern readers, by contrast, need no mediator, and they are offended by Lydgate because he lacks almost everything they admire in Chaucer. How could Lydgate not suffer when judged by a taste shaped by admiration of such a poet? (Gower has suffered similarly, and more unfairly.) There is something quite touchingly ironic in the fact that it was Lydgate who helped to make the way broad for Chaucer's poetry to be accessible to later readers, particularly by ensuring that the language of the poetry was more widely and serviceably current, and that it is Lydgate who is trampled underfoot in the flood of admirers who flock to the older poet.

Some things are of course more difficult to explain than others in this Chaucerian 'reconfiguration' of Lydgate. The Monk of Bury's versification, for instance, is not readily to be seen as anything but a mistake. The frequency of lines which lack an unstressed syllable at the beginning, or at the caesura, or indeed at any one point in the line, makes for awkwardness, and certainly does not inspire confidence in Lydgate's ear or in any historical explanation of his prosody that would suggest he had one. Loss of sounded final -e, often cited as an important factor in the breakdown of the Chaucerian pentameter in the fifteenth century, does not seem to be relevant to Lydgate, who uses final -e in much the same way as Chaucer.[2] Nor do his own comments help much. On several occasions his apologies for his metre, as well as implying that there are more important things for a poet to think about, seem to suggest that he thought that English verse was quantitative:

> And trouþ of metre I sette also a-syde ...
> I toke non hede nouþer of schort nor long,
> But to þe trouþe, and lefte coryouste
> Boþe of makyng and of metre be.[3]

It may be that 'long and short' refer to stressed and unstressed syllables, as the *OED* suggests, but it is probably best to assume that Lydgate is speaking in a conventional way, and entirely abstractly, about 'metre'. In *The Flower of Courtesy* he seems to put forward a quite different view, perhaps echoing, in a similarly conventional way, Chaucer's prayer that no one 'mysmetre' his *Troilus* (v, 1796). Lydgate expresses his fear

> Leste out of lose any worde asterte
> In this metre to make it seme lame.[4]

With Chaucer in mind, one would think that this refers to scribal carelessness, but, given Lydgate's overwhelming and understandable addiction to the modesty-topos, it seems that it might refer to his own.

Comparison of lines that Lydgate copies from Chaucer, where metre often suffers because of the loss of some little word or of final -e, does not make it clear whether the loss is due to Lydgate or to his scribes. The following lines, for instance, occur in Lydgate's attempt to imitate and improve upon Chaucer's portrait of Criseyde (*Troilus*, v, 806–26) in his *Troy Book* (ii, 4736–62):

> þer-to of schap, of face, and of chere
> (*Troy Book*, ii, 4738)

Cf. Therto of shap, of face, and ek of cheere
(*Troilus*, v, 807)

> [And] Saue hir browes Ioyn[e]den y-fere
> (*Troy Book*, ii, 4748)

Cf. And save hire browes joyneden yfeere
(*Troilus*, v, 813)

> þe best norissched eke þat myȝt[e] be
> (*Troy Book*, ii, 4757)

Cf. The best ynorisshed ek that myghte be
(*Troilus*, v, 821)

(Bergen, incidentally, offers no manuscript source for his emendations.) Here is another line, copied or remembered from the description of Emelye in the *Knight's Tale*, and destroyed:

> þat whilom was frescher for to sene
> þan þe lillye on his stalke grene
> (*Troy Book*, ii, 3921–2)

Cf. That Emelye, that fairer was to sene
Than is the lylie upon his stalke grene
(*Knight's Tale*, i, 1035–6)

The metrical defects are such as are commonly created by characteristic kinds of scribal omission, but the difference in scribal practice between the best Lydgate manuscripts and the best Chaucer manuscripts suggests that the problem is not one of scribal carelessness, but one of deliberate, inveterate, systematic practice on Lydgate's part.

It was Chaucer who provided him with the model for his practice and particularly for his frequent use of 'headless' and 'broken-backed' (or 'Lydgate') lines, that is, lines technically deficient of an unstressed syllable at line-beginning or caesura. Such lines are a good deal more common in even the best manuscripts of Chaucer than in modern critical editions of Chaucer, and it is clear that Chaucer allows himself more freedom in the handling of the pentameter than his modern editors are prepared to allow him, though of course it is a freedom that is defined by rhythmical, rhetorical and syntactical constraints and contexts. What Lydgate seems to have done is to elevate occasional variant lines into types of line and to use them systematically and indiscriminately, without Chaucer's subtle sense of semantic context or verse-flow.[5] The span of his metrical attention does not seem to have extended beyond the line, which fits well with what we know and can imagine of his mechanical activities as a versifier and translator. The consequences are disastrous, not so much for the individual line as for the flow of the verse-paragraph, which is continually broken by aggressive variants which have no rhetorical point. It is an odd proceeding, and not one that is generally characteristic of fifteenth-century Chaucerian verse, whatever that verse may suffer from other kinds of prosodic vertigo.[6] It is the product, however, not of incompetence or drivelling idiocy, but of a rigid and systematic imitation of Chaucer, and an attempt to improve upon his practice by doing what he did, not better but more. No one in the fifteenth century seems to have complained, and in the surrounding chaos his lines may have seemed models of metrical purity, especially when compared with the unspeakable verse of his contemporary John Metham, or lines like these from a spurious late continuation of Lydgate's *Life of St Alban*:

> Yet I can not knowe what parte they shulde haue
> For kynge Offa founde nothyng but the bones in his graue.
>
> (Appendix B, stanza 35)

Lydgate's lines at least always fitted neatly in the double-column format of big manuscripts such as those of the *Troy Book* and the *Fall of Princes*.

The peculiar sentence-structure of Lydgate's verse may likewise seem difficult to explain in terms of an imitation of Chaucer such as I have suggested. The looseness of his syntax is notorious, particularly the way in which sentences straggle on in a profusion of hanging participial phrases and absolute constructions. *Guy of Warwick*, traditionally but rather arbitrarily regarded as Lydgate's worst poem, has been said to begin with a sentence where not only the predicate is wanting, but the subject as well.[7] Yet all the syntactical licences characteristic of Lydgate have a precedent in Chaucer, and his syntax is often deliberately archaic and 'poetic' in imitation of Chaucer,[8] whatever added incentive to afflatus he may have received from the example of professional and legal writing in Latin and French. Lydgate seizes on a syntactical usage practised by Chaucer as an occasional licence – unattached participial phrases or absolute constructions, unidiomatic inversion of auxiliary and verb or verb and object-pronoun, use of *as he that* for 'who' or of *for* as a non-subordinating conjunction – and employs it with systematic frequency, as if it were a mark in itself of poeticness. He has also ambitions to emulate Chaucer's mastery of larger syntactical patterns, the most notorious example being the opening of the Prologue to the *Siege of Thebes*, where his model is the first sentence of the *General Prologue* to the *Canterbury Tales*. Chaucer sustains his reader with nonchalant ease over a firmly controlled eighteen lines ('Whan ... Whan ... Thanne ...'); Lydgate, without ever completely losing control, multiplies temporal clauses, appositional and participial phrases, relative clauses, and has his reader staggering with exhaustion at line 66, still waiting for the main clause (which never comes). Again, it is not a matter of drooling incompetence but of systematic practice in the attempt at fulfilment of an inflated ambition. What Chaucer did well, and for the first time in English poetry, in securing control over long and complex poetic utterances, Lydgate must do better. He seems to have been doing what his admirers wanted: Benedict Burgh, the continuator of the translation of the *Secrees of Old Philisoffres* left unfinished at Lydgate's death, has no hesitation in imitating the tortured syntax of his master, even though he himself could write a plain and sensible English verse (in his paraphrase of Cato's *Distichs*) when he was not trying to 'clymben over so heigh a style' (*Squire's Tale*, v, 106). Skelton was the first to smoke Lydgate out: 'It is dyffuse to fynde/The sentence of his mynde', he says, mildly enough, of Lydgate, in *Phyllyp Sparowe* (806–7).

Imitation by Lydgate of particular passages in Chaucer demonstrates a similar concern to strengthen and consolidate Chaucer's stylistic achievement, an ambition that is only superficially at odds with the tone of humility he adopts towards Chaucer in his many passages of adulation. There is no anxiety in his imitation of Chaucer, no sense of labouring feebly in his master's footsteps, content to bask in a reflected glory. To Lydgate, as to Dryden, in his Preface to the *Fables*, Chaucer may well have seemed to lack 'the modern art of fortifying', and Lydgate is as happy as Dryden to supply what is lacking in a way of ornate diction and rhetorical figuration. Here is Chaucer describing the Friar, in his simple fashion.

> His eyen twynkled in his heed aryght,
> As doon the sterres in the frosty
> nyght.   (*Gen. Prol.*, i, 267–8)

This is what happens to those two lines in Lydgate's description of Lady Fortune in the *Fall of Princes*:

> Whos brennyng eyen sparklyng of ther
> liht
> As doon sterris the frosti wyntres
> niht.   (*Fall of Princes*, vi, 27–8)

No matter that the syntax is shaken loose by the substitution of participle (*sparklyng*) for finite verb, or that the second line stumbles: what is important is the amplification (*wyntres* as well as *frosti*) and the added ornament of language (*brennyng* as well as *sparklyng*). We might complain that *brennyng* eyes do not 'sparkle', that *brennyng* is not appropriate to stars, that *wyntres* is superfluous, but we should be complaining about what the fifteenth century would have praised Lydgate for, certainly what Lydgate praised Chaucer for, luxuriance of vocabulary and surface decoration:

> Noble Galfride, poete of Breteyne,
> Amonge oure englisch þat made first to reyne
> þe gold dewe-dropis of rethorik so fyne,
> Oure rude language only t'enlwmyne.   (*Troy Book*, ii, 4697–4700)

Lydgate's is not a servile imitation of Chaucer, but a *de luxe* version of Chaucer, obviously meant to be thought of as an improvement.

Sometimes the strain of imagining how such a thing could ever have been thought lessens momentarily. The elaborate spring-description at the beginning of *The Complaint of the Black Knight* is a *cento* of reminiscences of Chaucer:

> In May when Flora, the fressh[e] lusty quene,
> The soyle hath clad in grene, rede and white,
> And Phebus gan to shede his stremes shene
> Amyd the Bole wyth al the bemes bryght ...
>
> The dewe also lyk syluer in shynyng
> Vpon the leves as eny bavme suete
> Til firy Tytan with hys persaunt hete
> Had dried vp the lusty lycour nyw
> Vpon the herbes in [the] grene mede ...   (1–4, 26–30)

The opening lines recall *Troilus*:

> In May, that moder is of monthes glade,
> That fresshe floures, blew and white and rede,
> Ben quike agayn, that wynter dede made,
> And ful of bawme is fletyng every mede;
> Whan Phebus doth his bryghte bemes sprede,
> Right in the white Bole ...   (II, 50–5)

The later lines challenge comparison with Chaucer's imitation of Dante in the *Knight's Tale*:

> And firy Phebus riseth up so bright
> That al the orient laugheth of the light,
> And with his stremes dryeth in the greves
> The silver dropes hangynge on the leves.   (I, 1493–6)

Lydgate extends the range of mythological reference, amplifies the image of 'silver dropes', gives Phoebus 'stremes shene' as well as 'bemes bryght', adds more luxurious nomenclature for 'dewe'. What is important is amplification, elaboration, reduplication: two words must never be allowed to do the work that four might do equally well. What is even more important is the heightening of colour, the emphasis on verbal decoration, the literary allusiveness, the sense of poeticness, of the textuality of the text. This was true of Chaucer too, of course: he was no outsider to these traditions of medieval rhetoric. But here those stylistic traditions are in their purest form, without any of the adulteration that might come from the intrusion of individual imagination or direct reference to experiential reality. Indeed, the very nature of the relationship between words and the reality they purport to represent comes to seem unimportant by comparison with the increase in verbal abundance, of *florida verborum venustas*.[9] Lydgate picks up *licour* from the third line of the *General Prologue*, where it has its normal referential meaning, 'sap', and uses it, in 'lusty lycour', simply as a decorative synonym for 'dew'.

So too with 'baume suete', taken from *Troilus*, II, 53, and used as another synonym for 'dew', despite the fact that the word, even in figuratively extended uses, must have reference to sweetness of scent. Words of precise referentiality thus lose their fullness of sense and become elements in the pattern of surface decoration. The 'aureate' style has essentially to do with this emphasis on the surface textures of words, and is appropriately expressed in imagery of painting and jewels.

Fifteenth-century readers would have seen no cause to do anything other than congratulate Lydgate on achieving exactly what he set out to do. They would have been delighted too by his constant acknowledgements of his rudeness, his lack of 'colours', of 'rethorikes swete', of poetic cunning and craft,[10] recognizing the decorum of self-display in the modesty of self-deprecation. Many of these admissions of poetic incompetence are associated with eulogies of Chaucer, and it is perhaps no accident that Lydgate will often proceed from his adulation of Chaucer and the acknowledgement that none can 'counterfete / His gaye style' to the demonstration that he can not only do what Chaucer did but do it better, or, as I have said, more.[11] Rhetorical figures that Chaucer uses in a discreet and restrained manner, or even, with the licence of a dramatic or ironic context, in an indiscreet and unrestrained manner, are detached from context, amplified, inflated, and become objects of admiration almost in their own right. The anaphora which Chaucer exploited to such powerful effect in the closing stanzas of *Troilus* ('Swich fyn ...', 'Lo here ...'), and which to some extent even in Chaucer seems rhetorically over-emphatic, is returned to again and again by Lydgate, who clearly had no sense that one could have too much of a good thing.[12] *Occupatio*, the refusal to narrate or describe, always has a point in Chaucer in relation to larger patterns of meaning within the story, as in the *Knight's Tale* or the *Squire's Tale*; in Lydgate, it is one of a number of *topoi* which are used to enhance the sense of the indescribability or inexpressibility of something, and in so doing to deflect attention from the object of reference to the manner in which it is being referred to. The subject is style. The antithesis of hot and cold which is part of the oxymoron of love, and which is briefly alluded to by Chaucer in his version of Petrarch in the *Canticus Troili*,

> For hete of cold, for cold of hete, I dye   (*Troilus*, I, 420)

is expanded by Lydgate, in the *Complaint of the Black Knight*, into a stanza and more of contrarieties:

> Now hote as fire, now colde as asshes dede,
> Now hote for cold, now cold for hete ageyn,
> Now colde as ise, now as coles rede
> For hete I bren; and thus betwexe tweyn
> I possed am and al forcast in peyn;
> So that myn hete, pleynly as I fele,
> Of grevous colde ys cause everydele.   (232–8)

In other poems, such as *Troilus* or the *Romaunt of the Rose* (4703–56), the metaphors of paradox correspond to a wealth of perception, of 'matter'; in Lydgate, they correspond to nothing. The impression of copiousness derives solely from the elevation of a formal structure into a figure of thought. Lydgate has achieved the full ambition of the medieval rhetorician: art without matter. As Derek Brewer puts it, 'Lydgate is the sort of writer who gives rhetoric a bad name.'[13]

Examples of Lydgate's systematic habit of adopting Chaucer's techniques and re-medievalizing them could be multiplied. The idealizing, generalizing, non-specifying tendency of medieval rhetorical description is certainly present in Chaucer, and could not be better exemplified than in the first introduction of Criseyde:

> She nas nat with the leste of hire stature,
> But alle hire lymes so wel answerynge
> Weren to womanhod, that creature
> Was nevere lasse mannyssh in semynge.   (*Troilus*, I, 281–4)

Within the context of the story it is the *idea* of Criseyde's womanliness that is important here, so that Troilus, falling in love with her, will appear sufficiently idealistic. Elsewhere Chaucer will vary the pattern of the *descriptio feminae*, embedding it in dialogue and reminiscence (in the *Book of the Duchess*) in order to give vividness and immediacy, or exploring the opportunities of the low style for a different kind of description (in the *Miller's Tale*). But the immediate and the individual are of no interest to Lydgate: the idealizing and non-specifying are meat and drink to him, and he would have felt that he had betrayed the high cause of poetry if his audience could have detected, in one of his descriptions, any straying into the specific:

> But first yf I shal make mencyon
> Of his persone and pleynly him discrive,
> He was, in soth, without excepcion,
> To speke of manhod oon the best o[n] lyve.
> Ther may no man ayein[es] trouthe stryve,
> For of his time and of his age also
> He proued was there men shuld haue ado. (*Black Knight*, 155–61)

Another technique, again picked up and improved upon from Chaucer, is based on synonymy, where the satisfaction is in admiring the wealth of language that says nothing – 'Let it be varied but always the same', as Geoffrey of Vinsauf advises.[14]

> He was þe Rote and stok of cheualrie,
> And of knyȝthod verray souereyn flour,
> þe sowrs and welle of worschip and honour;
> And of manhod, I dar it wel expresse,
> Example and merour ...   (*Troy Book*, II, 244–8)

A particularly neat example, very self-conscious in its varying of synonymous terms, is to be found in the *Fall of Princes*:

Welle of worshep, conduit of al noblesse . . .
Hedspryng of honour, of largesse cheef
    cisterne,
Merour of manhod, of noblesse the lanterne.

(Fall, VIII, 2853, 2855–6)

This is not mere prolixity: the taste and the ambition must be recognized, even relished. It would be singularly pointless to criticize Lydgate for lacking what he has spent the resources of a laborious art in trying to avoid.

But Chaucer not only gave Lydgate his language, his verse-forms and his poetic style, and with that the urge to refine and elaborate them into a high medieval art. It could also be argued that Lydgate's career, poem by poem, is a determined effort to emulate and surpass Chaucer in each of the major poetic genres that Chaucer had attempted. The most striking example is the *Troy Book*, his major poem, which he takes up, at the behest of the Prince of Wales in 1412, as a self-conscious and deliberate attempt to define and consolidate the new status of English as a literary language by tackling the greatest epic story of antiquity. Lydgate builds on Chaucer, but also presses consciously beyond Chaucer, annexing large new territories to literary English. Chaucer uses a vernacular source for his *Troilus* (though he claims a Latin one) and tells only an episode from the Troy-story; Lydgate takes a Latin source, a true 'auctoritee', and tells the whole story, expanding enormously on everything – the moralizing, the invocations and apostrophes, the learned digressions – that contributes to the story's *sentence*. Systematically, in fact, and in accord with the best medieval theory and practice, Lydgate empties the story of everything but *sentence* and in so doing restores it to that world of stable truths which fiction always threatens to subvert.[15]

Chaucer treats his story of *Troilus* seriously as a story, giving to his representation of people's lives and feelings a degree of autonomy, and seeking the meaning of the story in that representation and his commentary upon it. In so doing, he contradicted, though implicitly and incompletely, the traditional medieval assumption that fictions are exemplary, and exist to demonstrate truths outside themselves. Lydgate does not understand that there could be any other assumption. Chaucer is interested in Boccaccio's *Il Filostrato* as a story, but for Lydgate Guido's *Historia Destructionis Troiae* is a text. It is immovable, it has authority, it is 'true', but it exists not for the sake of its own truth but for the truth that can be drawn from it. It may be history, but it has no autonomous historical existence or importance, and Lydgate's medieval purpose is to demonstrate how history is transcended in the interests of truth, so that Hector, Achilles and the rest may take their place in the universal hierarchies. Lydgate may have begun the poem to please Henry and to keep alive the memory of ancient chivalry, but Troy has little meaning for him until he is drawn in Book IV to contemplate its fall, the great tragedy of pagan times. It is in this that the moral commentary, up till this point largely factitious and indiscriminate, finds at last its centre, in the contemplation of the inexorability of Fate, the mutability of Fortune, and the transitoriness of worldly bliss. Within a narrative context of ruin, destruction and loss, Lydgate comes to grips finally with a significance in the story which is profoundly meaningful to him, namely its profound meaninglessness. What Chaucer acknowledges ruefully in a few stanzas at the end of the *Troilus* concerning 'thise wrecched worldes appetites' (v, 1851) becomes for Lydgate the whole manner in which the story is contained within a Christian understanding.

Lydgate's prime interest in stories is thus in destroying them as imagined realities so as to reveal more clearly the hidden truth that is the justification for their existence. Where such a truth is not immediately to hand, the lived experience of story must be hypostatized into essences so that the reader is not distracted. The parting of Troilus and Criseyde, so intensely lived through by the reader of Chaucer as a uniquely sad and painful event in a continuum of such unique events, is transformed by Lydgate into a static tableau in which the lovers seem forever frozen in their postures of grief:

> For she ne myȝt nat a worde speke,
> And he was redy with deth to be wreke
> Vp-on hym silfe, his nakid swerd beside;
> And she ful ofte gan to grounde glide
> Out of his armys, as she fel a-swowne,
> And he hym silf gan in teris drowne.   (III, 4171–6)

The key words are 'ful ofte': Criseyde's repeated swoons are made to seem mechanically prompted, like an animated waxworks display.

Even where Chaucer offers an almost irresistible invitation to think again about the story, or just to begin thinking about it *as* a story, Lydgate seems unaware of any temptation. The extraordinary skill and depth of Chaucer's exploration of Criseyde's predicament, as a woman, in a land at war, leaves him unmoved, and he reabsorbs Criseyde into the conventional stereotypes of medieval anti-feminism. To the suggestion that Criseyde was false to Troilus because she took pity on Diomede, which Chaucer entertains with rueful regret (*Troilus*, v, 1048–50), Lydgate responds with spitting malice:

> Loo! what pite is in wommanhede,
> What mercy eke and benygne routhe,
> þat newly can al her olde trouthe
> Of nature late slyppe a-syde
> Raþer þanne þei shulde se abide
> Any man in meschef for hir sake!
> þe change is nat so redy for to make
> In Lombard Strete of crowne nor doket –
> Al paie is good, be so þe prente be set:
> Her lettre of change doth no man abide!
> So þat þe wynde be redy and þe tyde,
> Passage is ay, who-so list to passe.   (IV, 2148–59)

This is skilfully and wittily done, of course, in its own genre, and Lydgate is perfectly at home with the conventional anti-feminism of Guido, whose attacks on women he expands with relish, at the same time assuring us that he himself is outraged by Guido's opinions. The irony of his disclaimers is commendably straight-faced, as in the comment he makes at the end of a long diatribe against the fickleness of Helen and Criseyde:

> For ʒif wommen be double naturelly,
> Why shulde men leyn on hem þe blame?   (III, 4408–9)

Elsewhere too he has witty asides, as on Helen's recovery from her grief for Paris,

> And ʒit she roos aʒeyn fro deth to lyve,
> Only by grace ...   (IV, 3700–1)

or on Clytemnestra's taking of Aegisthus as her lover,

> Suche drede hadde she for to lyn allone.   (V, 1109)

In responding thus vividly to Guido's mechanical anti-feminism ('tamquam varia et mutabilis, sicut est proprium mulierum', Guido says, of Criseyde,[16] not anticipating much debate on the matter), and in closing his eyes to the complexities which modern readers have found in Chaucer's account of Criseyde, Lydgate may seem to have acted strangely. Yet what he did was entirely in accord with fifteenth-century taste, as it may be judged from readers' marks and comments in the margins of *Troy Book* manuscripts, where the passages concerning women (along with passages of direct moralization) are the ones most frequently singled out for attention.[17] Did Lydgate learn *anything* from Chaucer, other than ambition? Can an age understand anything other than what it is preconditioned to understand?

The answer to the second question must be 'Yes – but with difficulty', and there are some signs of understanding in another of Lydgate's Chaucerian imitations, *The Siege of Thebes*. The whole poem is framed as a Canterbury tale, with a Prologue in which Lydgate the monk meets the pilgrims as they leave Canterbury and is cajoled by the Host into telling this tale. The Prologue is not badly done: Lydgate has learnt something from Chaucer about comic self-presentation, and the Host's language has a certain colloquial liveliness. But everything tends to slip back into the stereotypes of caricature from which Chaucer had rescued character-description, and the other pilgrims are blurred and out of focus. Lydgate hardly seems to remember which is which:

> And ek also with his pylled nolle
> The pardowner, beerdlees al his Chyn,
> Glasy-Eyed and face of Cherubyn,
> Tellyng a tale to angre with the frere.   (32–5)

There are reminiscences here, inextricably confused, of the miller of the *Reeve's Tale* and the Summoner as well as the Pardoner. It is odd that Lydgate should not have remembered the *General Prologue* better, or looked things up, but we must reckon with the possibility that the attachment of detail to the individual pilgrim was less important to Lydgate than the compendious accumulation of detail for its own sake. The main point of interest, though, is not whether Lydgate has done well what he has done, but that he should have done it at all, given that the playful if elephantine comedy he engages in here is so alien to the moralizing poetics of his age. Such a close imitation of Chaucer, on his own ground, argues further an extraordinary confidence on Lydgate's part.

The fiction that the tale is being told on the road from Canterbury to London is kept up by Lydgate with more literal realism than Chaucer ever admitted, which says something of the fifteenth-century response to the dramatic framework of the *Canterbury Tales*.[18] There are references to the progress of the journey as he tells the tale: he explains early that he must hasten on with his story, since it is going to take up seven miles of their journey (320–4), and he makes a pause between the first and second parts as the pilgrims descend into Blean Vale and pass the village of Boughton-on-the Blee. He notes the time as 9 a.m.,

> The same hour all the hoole Route
> Of the pylgrymes rydyng round aboute,
> In my tale whan I gan procede.   (1057–9)

There is some curiosity expressed at times concerning the paucity of such reference in Chaucer to the literal reality of the roadside tale-telling, but the fact that Lydgate does something that Chaucer does not do is usually taken as *a priori* evidence that Chaucer knew what he was doing, or, in this case, not doing. Perhaps Chaucer recognized intuitively how far the illusion of the roadside drama might be pressed, and saw that to press it further would be to substitute a trivializing literalism for the grand illusion of the story-telling.

Later in his tale, as he approaches the episode in which Theseus intervenes on behalf of the Theban widows, Lydgate alludes to the previous telling of this part of the story:

> ȝif ȝe remembre, ȝe han herde it to forn
> Wel rehersyd at Depforth in the vale
> In the bygynnyng of the knyghtys tale.   (4522–4)

Dramatic considerations inhibit the eulogy of Chaucer which would normally follow; instead Lydgate proceeds to a rehearsal of the story as told by Chaucer, borrowing some lines, adding others, in a manner quite unabashed. He no doubt thought these three lines:

> And how this Duke with-oute more abood,
> The same day toward Thebes rood,
> Ful like in soth a worthy conqueror   (4533–5)

an improvement on Chaucer's one:

> Thus rit this duc, thus rit this conqueror.   (1, 981)

To show further that he is not to be outdone, he borrows and improves material from Chaucer's description of Arcite's funeral in his account of the obsequies at Thebes (4565–79), even to the extent of adopting Chaucer's figure of *occupatio* (*Knight's Tale*, I, 2919–66) for the whole of his account of the latter part of the story.

A third example of Lydgate's ambitious attempt to build an English poetic tradition by 'fortifying' preliminary structures thrown up by Chaucer is the *Fall of Princes*, in which he brings to conclusion an enormous encyclopaedic collection of framed narratives. The immediate model is the *Monk's Tale*, which is unfinished when it is interrupted by the Knight, but the *Fall* is Lydgate's answer too to Chaucer's other two unfinished collections of framed narratives, the *Legend of Good Women* and the *Canterbury Tales*. Whatever else it may be, the *Fall* is finished, and at 36,365 lines that represents itself something of an achievement.

The *Fall of Princes* does, systematically and comprehensively, what the medieval poet was above all supposed to do, that is, to teach Christian virtue by multiplying examples of the mutability of Fortune to those who put their trust in the world. The reservoir of *exempla* is inexhaustible, and the opportunity of drawing the correct moral impossible to miss. Lydgate expands on what he finds in his immediate source, the French translation and amplification by Laurent de Premierfait of Boccaccio's *De Casibus Illustrium Virorum*, and adds moralizing envoys, at the earnest instigation of his patron, Humphrey of Gloucester, that proved to be particularly to the taste of fifteenth-century readers.[19] Like those readers, Lydgate believes that stories exist principally or even solely to exemplify truths already known, from Christian revelation, to be true. In this, Lydgate and his readers stand in sharp contrast to Chaucer, whose endeavour, in a poem like the *Nun's Priest's Tale*, was to question the nature of the relationship between a story and its 'moral' and everywhere to explore the possibilities of autonomous fiction, of stories that might have their own access to 'truth'. In the *Legend of Good Women* and the *Monk's Tale* Chaucer experimented with non-narrative frameworks for collections of stories, but found himself imperfectly engaged with the stories, presumably because the 'point' of each story was already dictated by the frame. He was content to leave a question-mark hanging over the *Legend*, but with the *Monk's Tale* he included the defect of form within the meaning of the Tale by the dramatic attribution to the Monk, to whom such miscellaneous and patchwork erudition may have seemed appropriate. In fact Chaucer's portrait of his monk in the Prologue to his Tale, with his 'celle' full of 'tragedies', is an eerie premonition of Lydgate, whose well-stocked monastic library and naïve encyclopaedic habit of mind led him in the same direction, and whose longest work is a gigantic amplification of the same theme. Chaucer is not making fun of the Monk, but he is suggesting the limitations of a view of life in which all stories exemplify the same truth and he sharpens that suggestion by having the *Monk's Tale* interrupted by the Knight, whose own

Tale has some claim to a more sophisticated vision of the tragedy of human existence. Chaucer's implied criticism of the form of the *Monk's Tale* is of course a prophetic criticism of Lydgate's *Fall of Princes*. The *Canterbury Tales* was Chaucer's answer to the problem of form; Lydgate, as usual, was aware of no problem.

It would be possible to extend the present argument, and to suggest further examples of a pattern in Lydgate's career in which he uses academic rhetoric to fortify and improve upon successive Chaucerian models: the *Complaint of the Black Knight* upon the *Book of the Duchess*, the *Temple of Glass* upon the *House of Fame*, the translation called *Reason and Sensuality*, with its pictorial allegory, garden, and analysis of different kinds of love, upon the *Parliament of Fowls*, the richly aureate Marian poems upon the *ABC* and the *Invocacio ad Mariam* at the beginning of the *Prioress's Tale*, the elaborately rhetoricated saints' legends and that extraordinary stylistic *tour de force*, the *Fabula Duorum Mercatorum*, upon the *Man of Law's Tale*. The 'improvement' is generally of the kind that assumes two lines are better than one, and three lines better still, but the pattern is interesting, especially in the light of Lydgate's frequent and fulsome tributes to Chaucer.

NOTES

1 Thomas Gray in his essay 'On the Poems of Lydgate', and Rosemary Woolf in *The English Religious Lyric in the Middle Ages* (Oxford, 1968), e.g., pp. 198–202.

2 See Charlotte F. Babcock, 'Metrical Use of Inflexional -e in Middle English, with Particular Reference to Chaucer and Lydgate', *PMLA*, 29 (1914), 59–92.

3 *Troy Book*, ed. H. Bergen, *EETS*, e.s. 97, 103, 106, 126 (1906–20), III, 181, 184–6. Cf. v, 3484; *Life of Saint Alban and Saint Amphibal*, ed. J. E. van der Westhuizen (Leiden, 1974), 102. Other poems by Lydgate are cited from the following editions: *The Siege of Thebes*, ed. A. Erdmann and E. Ekwall, *EETS*, e.s. 108, 125 (1911, 1920); *The Fall of Princes*, ed. H. Bergen *EETS*, e.s. 121–4 (1918–19); *The Flower of Courtesy*, in *The Minor Poems of John Lydgate*, Part II, ed. H. N. MacCracken, *EETS*, o.s. 192 (1934), pp. 410–18; *The Legend of Saint Margaret*, in *Minor Poems*, Part I, *EETS*, e.s. 107 (1911), pp. 173–92; *Secrees of Old Philisoffres*, ed. R. Steele, *EETS*, e.s. 66 (1894); *The Complaint of the Black Knight* ('A Complaynt of a Loveres Lyfe') and *The Temple of Glass*, in John Lydgate, *Poems*, ed. J. Norton-Smith (Oxford, 1966), pp. 47–66, 67–112.

4 *Flower of Courtesy*, 234–5. *OED* glosses *out of lose* as 'to one's disprayse'.

5 This is essentially the explanation offered by Eleanor P. Hammond, 'The 9-Syllabled Pentameter Line in Some Post-Chaucerian Manuscripts', *Modern Philology*, 23 (1925–6), 129–52; also Hammond (ed.), *English Verse between Chaucer and Surrey* (Durham, N. Carolina, 1927), pp. 17–24, 83–6.

6 For a lively description of the 'sheer chaos' of fifteenth-century versification, see G. Saintsbury, *History of English Prosody*, 3 vols. (London, 1908), I, 218–45.

7 The statement is attributed to Zupitza by J. Schick in his edition of Lydgate's *Temple of Glas*, *EETS*, e.s. 60 (1891), Introduction, p. cxxxvi.

8 See A. Courmont, *Studies on Lydgate's Syntax in the Temple of Glass* (Paris, 1912).

9 E. F. Jacob, 'Florida Verborum Venustas', *Bulletin of the John Rylands Library*, 17 (1933), 264–90.

10 *Flower of Courtesy*, 178, 101; *Legend of St Margaret*, 3; *Temple of Glass*, 538; *Secrees*, 337; *Fall of Princes*, I, 229–34, 435–69; *Troy Book*, Prol. 28–35, I, 3090, II, 4701–35, III, 540–64, IV, 7096–7, V, 3466–533.

11 *Flower of Courtesy*, 239–10. Cf. *Troy Book* II, 4677–718. In the latter passage Lydgate explains that there is no need to describe at length the sorrow of Troilus and Criseyde since it has been done by 'my maister Chaucer' so much better than he could do it; but he does it, and at length.

12 E.g. *Troy Book*, III, 4224–5, IV, 3210; *Black Knight*, 400–6; *Thebes*, 4628–30; *Fall*, II, 1856–9.

13 *English Gothic Literature* (London, 1983), p. 131.

14 *Poetria Nova*, 225 ('varius sis et tamen idem'), in E. Faral (ed.), *Les Arts poétiques du XIIe et du XIIIe siècle* (Paris, 1924), p. 204.

15 See J. Gellrich. *The Idea of the Book in the Middle Ages* (Ithaca, NY, 1985). For an interesting account of some of the borders 'where the exemplary and the imitative meet', see T. Silverstein, 'Allegory and literary form', *PMLA*, 82 (1967), 28–32.

16 Guide delle Colonne, *Historia Destructionis Troiae*, ed. N. E. Griffin (Cambridge, Mass., 1936), p. 198.

17 See Bergen (ed.), *Troy Book*, Introduction, pp. 24ff.

18 The Prologue to the *Tale of Beryn*, another 'Canterbury tale', is a vivid example of such a response, as is the placement of the pilgrim portraits in the Ellesmere Manuscript at the head of the tale allotted to the pilgrim.

19 See A. S. G. Edwards, 'Selections from Lydgate's *Fall of Princes*: A Checklist', *The Library*, 26 (1971), 337—42; 'The influence of Lydgate's *Fall of Princes c.* 1440–1559: A Survey', *Mediaeval Studies*, 39 (1977), 424–39.

4

Hoccleve and Chaucer

J. A. BURROW

Some twelve years after Chaucer's death, Thomas Hoccleve paid tribute to the eloquence, wisdom, and piety of his predecessor in three passages of *The Regement of Princes*.[1] Hoccleve's admiration, he claims, is based upon personal acquaintance; for when, in the *Regement* prologue, he first reveals his name to the old almsman, the latter's immediate reaction is to identify him as one of those people who knew Chaucer:

> 'Hoccleve, sone?' 'Iwis, fadir, þat same.'
> 'Sone, I have herd or this men speke of þe;
> þou were aqueynted with Caucher, pardee –
> God have his soule best of any wyght!' (1865–8)

Later, Hoccleve recalls how Chaucer was accustomed to help him with 'consail and reed':

> 'Mi dere maistir – God his soule quyte! –
> And fadir Chaucer fayn wolde han me taght;
> But I was dul, and lerned lite or naght.' (2077–9)

The apology for dullness is conventional enough; but there are no good reasons to doubt that Hoccleve had, towards the end of the previous century, sat at Chaucer's feet and received from him some kind of instruction in the art of English poetry.[2]

Given this association, it is not surprising that certain of Hoccleve's own poems should have been attracted into the Chaucerian orbit during the fifteenth and sixteenth centuries. Like Chaucer, Hoccleve 'wroot ful many a lyne' in praise of the Virgin Mary (*Regement*, 4987), and two of his eight Marian poems proved capable of being mistaken for the master's. The Miracle of the Virgin which he wrote in imitation of the *Prioress's Tale* found a place in one manuscript of the *Canterbury Tales*, introduced there in a spurious prologue as the *Plowman's Tale*;[3] and one of his Marian lyrics, having been attributed to Chaucer by two Scottish scribes, was accepted as his by

54

Victorian editors – even, to begin with, by Furnivall and the Chaucer Society.[4] One of Chaucer's other voices is to be heard in the *Letter of Cupid*, for here Hoccleve followed his master in adapting the courtly matter of Cupid from the French: the god Cupid writes a letter to his loyal servants offering a defence of women against false lovers and slanderers of the sex (he mentions Ovid and Jean de Meun). It is clear that Hoccleve had Chaucer's *Legend of Good Women* in mind here, for Cupid refers to 'our legende of martirs'.[5] In later life, Hoccleve was to report that some ladies took offence at the *Letter*, presumably because it quoted the opposition anti-feminist case at too great length; but the poem won a secure place in that select group of courtly pieces, many of them by Chaucer himself (including the *Legend*), which circulated in fifteenth- and sixteenth-century copies. It appears in three manuscripts of the so-called Oxford group, in one of Shirley's manuscripts, in a Scottish 'Chaucerian' collection, in the Findern anthology, and in two major six-teenth-century volumes, the Bannatyne and Devonshire manuscripts.[6] The poem was printed by Thynne in his 1532 Chaucer, and it continued to appear in later 'Chaucers' up to and including Urry's in 1721.[7]

If all Hoccleve's poems were like his Marian pieces or the *Letter of Cupid*, he might be remembered only as a technically proficient Chaucer clone; but his actual body of work creates a very different impression. Hoccleve's claim to attention in his own right rests mainly upon *The Regement of Princes*, the so-called *Series*, and the *Male Regle*; and these works, taken together with some of the epistolary ballades, witness to a mind quite unlike that of his master. The essential, and undoubtedly damaging, difference is that Hoccleve had very little imagination – if by that one understands a capacity and desire to dwell in imaginary worlds, or at least to transgress the limits of one's own immediate experience:

> He had as much imagination
>   As a pint-pot; – he never could
> Fancy another situation
> From which to dart his contemplation,
>   Than that wherein he stood.[8]

Chaucer is supreme among English poets in his ability to 'fancy another situation': even in such a short piece as the *Prioress's Tale* he manages to conjure up a whole little world of people and places – the school, the street, the Jewish quarter, the boy and his schoolmate, the mother – and also to persuade many readers that it is seen from that other situation which the fancied Prioress occupies. By contrast, Hoccleve's Miracle of the Virgin lacks imaginative body. His story of the miraculous origin of Our Lady's Psalter is competently told; but it leaves (if my own experience is to be trusted) only the faintest imprint of its outlines upon the memory. Hoccleve's best imagined narratives concern encounters between himself and another – the old almsman in the *Regement* prologue and the friend in the *Series*. These scenes display the poet's undoubted skill at rendering dialogue in verse; but he can hardly be said here to get outside the 'situation wherein he stood', for the energy of the scenes is drawn most from precisely that situation, which is the chief subject of the conversation in both. The friend has opinions but no character; and the almsman is a far fainter presence than Wordsworth's corresponding creation, the old leechgatherer, let alone the old man in the *Pardoner's Tale*.[9] Both the *Regement* and the *Series*, it is true, also incorporate a variety of subsidiary narratives set in imagined worlds (fictive or not) quite remote from the real worlds, private and public, of Hoccleve's own experience – the two *Gesta Romanorum* stories in the *Series* and the numerous moral *exempla* in the *Regement* – but even the best of these 'goodly tales', the story of John of Canace (*Regement*, 4180–354), remains firmly subordinated to its non-imaginary context and occasion.

Yet if Hoccleve cannot hold a candle to his master as a poet of imaginary worlds, he has his own distinctive strength as a poet of the non-imaginary worlds of public and private life. He does best, in fact, what Chaucer hardly does at all. Chaucer rarely addresses himself to the public affairs of the day, either in general or in particular (witness his passing reference to the Peasants' Revolt), and he only once permits more than a glimpse of his private circumstances – and that in a fantastically imaginary context.[10] The private and public worlds displayed in the *Chaucer Life-Records* bear little or no relation to the worlds we inhabit as readers of his poems. By contrast, the 'Appendix of Hoccleve Documents, copied from the Record Office by Mr R. E. G. Kirk' in Furnivall's edition of the Minor Poems takes one directly into the world of the poems themselves.[11] 'Thomas Hoccleve, unus clericorum nostrorum de officio privati sigilli nostri', is recognizably the author of the *Series*, the *Male Regle*, and the *Regement*, living in a state of anxious dependency upon the favour of the great and the uncertain grant of his annuity.

The Hoccleve who writes on public themes has attracted rather little attention recently: the righteous indignation of his attack on Lollardy in the *Address to Sir John Oldcastle* has repelled most readers, and Furnivall's 1897 edition of the *Regement* has yet to be replaced by a critical and annotated edition in modern times.[12] Yet the *Regement*, which survives in no less than forty-three manuscripts, was far and away Hoccleve's most successful poem in its day, and it must presumably again occupy a central place in any future account of his achievement. Recent studies have shown more interest in that other unChaucerian Hoccleve, the poet of the home and the office, the pub and the club. This is the Hoccleve whom Derek Brewer justly characterizes as 'amusing but undignified'.[13] If Chaucer may be considered an example of the 'negative capability' of which Keats spoke, this Hoccleve can only represent, by contrast, the egotistical ridiculous. Like Pandarus, Hoccleve 'japes at himself', and his japes expose him to ridicule in a way that Chaucer's more guarded self-depreciations rarely if ever do.[14] Yet this peculiar mixture of clowning and complaint is neither pointless nor artless: Hoccleve is at once bringing himself to the attention of those upon whom his livelihood depended and at the same time discovering his own distinctive way of writing poems. Both the *Male Regle* and also, in its much more ambitious fashion, the *Series* represent something new in English poetry – nothing less, in the latter case, than a long poem in which the poet himself plays the leading role.[15]

Hoccleve and Chaucer hardly resembled each other in temperament, and most of Hoccleve's poems, as I have suggested, are of a kind quite different from his predecessor's. Yet it remains evident that he could not have written them in the way he does – not even the least Chaucerian of them – had Chaucer not lived. The example of *Troilus*, the *Canterbury Tales*, and the shorter poems might well have been enough, even if Hoccleve had not been 'aqueynted with Caucher'; but it is tempting to suppose that the master's 'consail and reed' played a significant part in forming the younger poet's awareness of the disciplines of English verse. Lydgate (who does not claim to have known Chaucer) records that Chaucer 'said alway the best' when called upon to comment on other people's poems:

> My maister Chaucer, þat founde ful many spot,
> Hym liste nat pinche nor gruche at every blot,
> Nor meve hym silf to parturbe his rest
> (I have herde telle) but seide alweie þe best.[16]

This interesting piece of anecdotal evidence confirms the impression given by his poems, that Chaucer was not one to speak of the innermost secrets of his art. Perhaps, like some more recent poets, he preferred to confine discussion to technical matters and so minimize any perturbation of his rest. Yet the poet who in the *House of Fame* feared for the error of a single syllable in his verses (line 1098) and who in *Troilus* prayed that they should not be 'mismetred' by scribes (v, 1796) was not one to speak lightly about technical matters; and it may be conjectured that his discussions with Hoccleve were quite earnestly concerned with the duty of composing lines and stanzas of verse according to the dictates of the 'art poetical'.

Hoccleve's sense of responsibility to that art as it was practised by his master finds its clearest expression, characteristically, in an apologetic request for correction:

> If þat I in my wrytynge foleye,
> As I do ofte, I can it nat withseye,
> Meetrynge amis, or speke unfittyngly,
> Or nat by iust peys my sentences weye,
> And nat to the ordre of endytyng obeye,
> And my colours sette ofte sythe awry,
> With al myn herte wole I buxumly
> It to amende and to correcte him preye;
> For undir his correccioun stande y.[17]

Like Chaucer's coinage 'mysmetre', Hoccleve's 'meetrynge amis' must refer (though not exclusively) to the matter of syllable count. In a recent essay,

Judith Jefferson has demonstrated the scrupulosity of Hoccleve's attention to
this matter, as displayed in his own autograph copies. These copies show, for
instance, that Hoccleve consistently employed variant forms of words in order
to ensure that his lines should not 'fayle in a sillable'. Chaucer would certainly
have approved.[18] After referring to this matter, in the stanza quoted,
Hoccleve goes on to invoke the standard rhetorical doctrines of *decorum*
('speke unfittyngly'), *dispositio* ('the ordre of endytyng'), and *colores* ('my
colours'). Like Chaucer's similar apologies, Hoccleve's imply a claim – a
claim to be at least aspiring to meet the high standards of premeditated art set
by the Latin *artes poetriae*. The ideal was expressed by Geoffrey of Vinsauf in a
passage which both Hoccleve and Chaucer rendered into English. Here is
Hoccleve's version:

> 'Thow woost wel, who shal an hous edifie
> Gooth nat therto withoute avisament
> If he be wys, for with his mental ye
> First is it seen, pourposid, cast and ment,
> How it shal wroght been, elles al is shent.'[19]

But the most interesting of Hoccleve's apologies concerns the possibility
that he may on occasion 'nat by iust peys my sentences weye'. The ideal of
artistic premeditation or 'avisament' evidently requires that a poet's thoughts
or ideas should be weighed out 'by just measure'.[20] I guess that Hoccleve had
in mind here, among other things, his experience in writing the kind of
stanzaic verse that he learned from Chaucer. In the majority of his works,
Hoccleve employs long ballade stanzas, most often rhyme royal but sometimes eight- or nine-line stanzas.[21] The composition of these requires that the
mind or 'mental ye' should see in advance how they are to turn out – the shape
of the syntax of each, and the development of its thought. In particular, the
principle of 'iust peys' requires that the thought should be weighed out so
prudently that the stanza does not, as it were, run out of matter in its closing
lines. One of the pleasures of reading Hoccleve is to see how well, on the
whole, he succeeded in mastering this art – controlling the syntax and sense of
the whole stanza with a firm hand. Here, for instance, is his stanzaic
amplification of an ancient commonplace:

> 'How fair thyng or how precious it be
> þat in the world is, it is lyk a flour,
> To whom nature yeven hath beautee
> Of fressh heewe and of ful plesant colour,
> With soote smellynge also and odour;
> But as soone as it is bicomen drye,
> Farwel colour, and the smel gynneth dye.'   (*Dialogue*, 267–73)

In this rhyme-royal stanza, the first five lines are devoted to comparing the
beauty and value of earthly things to the colour and scent of a flower. The
fourth and fifth lines depart from the concise manner of the first three to

indulge in what may seem merely slack synonymy: 'heewe ... colour', 'smellynge ... odour'; but the final couplet, which concerns the dying flower, makes this expansiveness meaningful by setting against it the bald manner, without variation or epithet, in which the last line recapitulates the flower's colour and smell:

> But as soone as it is bicomen drye,
> Farwel colour, and the smel gynneth dye.

Hoccleve's style of writing is in some ways unlike Chaucer's. Although he is just as careful about the syllable count, his rhythms seem more uncertain; and his English tends more to the plain and to the colloquial than Chaucer's does. There are, as several critics have noticed, far fewer verbal echoes of Chaucer than one would expect to find in the work of an immediate follower.[22] Yet Hoccleve's debt to Chaucer, and especially to rhyme-royal Chaucer, was immense. One way of measuring it is to compare his version of the miracle of Our Lady's Psalter with the version in the Auchinleck Manuscript – taking the latter (perhaps a little unfairly) to represent the state of English verse as Chaucer found it. Here are the two openings of the story:

> Auchinleck: A riche man was while
> þat loved no gile;
> He loved holi chirche.
> Bisiden him a mile
> An abbay of Seyn Gile
> His eldren dede wirche.

> Hoccleve: Ther was whilom, as þat seith the scripture,
> In France a ryche man and a worthy,
> That God and holy chirche to honure
> And plese enforced he him bisily;
> And unto Crystes modir specially
> þat noble lady, þat blissid virgyne,
> For to worsshipe he dide his might and payne.[23]

Hoccleve's stanza of rhyme royal is by no means one of his best; but it does represent, by contrast with his predecessor's tail rhyme, that enhanced awareness of the ample potentialities of English verse which Hoccleve was among the first to learn from Chaucer.

NOTES

1 *The Regement of Princes*, ed. F. J. Furnivall, *EETS*, e.s. 72 (1897), 1958–74, 2077–107, 4978–5012. Citations throughout are from the *EETS* editions of Hoccleve's works, but with some altered punctuation.
2 Doubts are expressed by Jerome Mitchell, *Thomas Hoccleve: A Study in Early Fifteenth-Century English Poetic* (Urbana, Ill., 1968), 115–18, and in his essay, 'Hoccleve's Tribute to Chaucer', in A. Esch (ed.), *Chaucer und Seine Zeit: Symposion für Walter F. Schirmer* (Tübingen, 1968), 275–83. For arguments to the contrary, see J. A. Burrow, 'Autobiographical Poetry in the Middle Ages: The Case of Thomas Hoccleve', *Proceedings of the British Academy*, 68 (1982), 397–8.

3 Christ Church, Oxford, MS 152. Like Chaucer, Hoccleve prefaces the miracle narrative with a Marian prologue: items VI and VII in *The Minor Poems II*, ed. I. Gollancz, *EETS*, e.s. 73 (1897), reissued with *The Minor Poems I*, ed. F. J. Furnivall, *EETS*, e.s. 61 (1892), in one volume revised by J. Mitchell and A. I. Doyle (1970).

4 *Minor Poems I*, item x. The two manuscripts are Bodleian MS Arch. Selden B. 24 and National Library of Scotland MS Adv. 18, 2, 8. On the career of this poem as 'Chaucer's "Mother of God"' in the nineteenth century, see E. P. Hammond, *Chaucer: A Bibliographical Manual* (New York, 1908), 438–9, and *Minor Poems I*, xxxix–xl. It may be noted that both Chaucer and Hoccleve translated Marian poems of Deguileville: Chaucer from *Le Pelerinage de la Vie Humaine* ('An ABC'), Hoccleve from *Le Pelerinage de l'Ame* (*Regement*, xxxvii–xlv).

5 Line 316, not in the French of Christine de Pisan. The best discussion of the *Letter* is by John V. Fleming, 'Hoccleve's "Letter of Cupid" and the "Quarrel" over the *Roman de la Rose*', *Medium Aevum*, 40 (1971), 21–40. Fleming notes that Hoccleve's later defence of the poem (*Dialogue*, 745–84) may be seen as his 'adaptation of that elegant fiction spun by Chaucer in the *Prologue* to the *Legend of Good Women*'.

6 Bodleian MSS Fairfax 16, Tanner 346, and Bodley 638; Trinity College, Cambridge, MS R. 3, 20; Bodleian MS Arch. Selden B, 24; Cambridge University Library MS Ff. 1, 6; National Library of Scotland MS Adv. 1, 1, 6 and British Library MS Add. 17492. The *Letter* is also found with Chaucer's *Troilus* in Durham University Library MS Cosin v, ii, 13. There are two other MS copies: Huntington Library MS HM. 744 (Hoccleve's holograph) and Bodleian MS Digby 181.

7 Hammond, *Chaucer*, pp. 434–6.

8 Shelley on Wordsworth, *Peter Bell the Third*, 298–302.

9 Comparison between the *Regement* prologue and the *Pardoner's Tale* is suggested by M. C. Seymour (ed.), *Selections from Hoccleve* (Oxford, 1981), xxiii.

10 *Nun's Priest's Tale*, VII, 3396; *House of Fame*, 614–60. Even in *Melibee* Chaucer addresses public affairs obliquely within a fictional context. It is Hoccleve, not Chaucer, who refers to Edward III and John of Gaunt by name (*Regement*, 2556, 512). Yet Hoccleve defers to Chaucer on a matter of public policy (the holding of council meetings on holy days): Chaucer, he says, makes this kind of point better than I can (*Regement*, 4978–81). Chaucer's surviving works offer no obvious 'caas semblable'.

11 *Minor Poems I*, li–lxx, with additions on pp. lxxi–lxxii.

12 A new edition is in preparation by David Greetham and others.

13 D. S. Brewer (ed.), *Chaucer and Chaucerians: Critical Studies in Middle English Literature* (London, 1966), 28.

14 Pandarus 'gan at hymself to jape faste' (*Troilus*, II, 1164). Chaucer's own style of japing is best sampled in the *Envoy to Scogan*.

15 J. A. Burrow, 'Hoccleve's *Series*: Experience and Books', in R. F. Yeager (ed.), *Fifteenth-Century Studies: Recent Essays* (Hamden, Conn., 1984), 259–73.

16 Lydgate, *Troy Book*, ed. H. Bergen, *EETS*, e.s. 97, 103, 106, 126 (1906–20), v, 3521–4.

17 'Balade to my gracious Lord of York', *Minor Poems I*, item IX, lines 46–54.

18 Judith A. Jefferson, 'The Hoccleve Holographs and Hoccleve's Metrical Practice', in Derek Pearsall (ed.), *Manuscripts and Texts* (Cambridge, 1987), 95–109. Jefferson's discussion of final -*e* in the Hoccleve holographs incidentally throws light on the still sometimes disputed question of final -*e* in Chaucer, for she shows beyond doubt that -*e* is syllabic in the disciple. Can it have been otherwise in the master?

19 *Dialogue*, 638–42. The holograph adds parts of Geoffrey's Latin in the margin: 'Si quis habet fundare domum, non currit ad actum' and 'Impetuosa manus, &c' (*Poetria Nova*, 43–4). Compare *Troilus*, I, 1065–9. J. Mitchell, *Thomas Hoccleve*, 119–20, rightly notes that Hoccleve's version is independent of Chaucer's.

20 'Peyse' (glossed 'id est pondus') appears in a similar context in Lydgate's *Reson and Sensuallyte*, ed. E. Sieper, *EETS*, e.s. 84 (1901), line 1666.

21 See the excellent discussion of Hoccleve's relation to Chaucer in M. R. Pryor, 'Thomas Hoccleve's Series: An Edition of MS Durham Cosin v, iii, 9' (unpublished Ph.D. thesis, University of California, Los Angeles, 1968), pp. 52–3. Hoccleve uses the term 'balade' for what we would now call a rhyme-royal stanza in *Dialogue*, 551.

22 Thus Pryor, 'Thomas Hoccleve's Series', 38–44, Mitchell, *Thomas Hoccleve*, 118–22, Seymour, *Selections*, xxi–xxvii. Echoes do occur, of course. Thus, the *Regement* occasionally echoes Chaucer's shorter poems: 'þis olde dotyd Grisel' (401, cf. *Scogan*, 35); 'Pyte, I trowe, is beried' (882, cf. *Pity*, 14); 'it sore me agaste / To bynde me, where I was at my large' (1454–5, cf. *Bukton*, 11–12); 'Suffiseth to your good' (5375, cf. *Truth*, 2). See also A. C. Spearing, *Medieval to Renaissance in English Poetry* (Cambridge, 1985), 114–17.

23 Auchinleck MS f. 259ʳᵇ, corresponding to lines 19–24 in the Digby text edited by C. Horstmann, *Altenglische Legenden: Neue Folge* (Heilbronn, 1881), p. 220; *Minor Poems II*, item VII, lines 1–7.

5

Chaucer and fifteenth-century romance:
Partonope of Blois

BARRY WINDEATT

> Men speken of romances of prys,
> Of Horn child and of Ypotys,
> Of Beves and sir Gy,
> Of sir Lybeux and Pleyndamour –
>
> (*Sir Thopas*, VII, 897–900)

What are the lessons that could be learned from Chaucer by any post-Chaucerian writer of romance in England, granted the way that Chaucer's poems show both his indebtedness to the English romances yet also his transcendence of conventional romance?[1] One answer to this question is provided, not by those usually termed English and Scottish Chaucerians, but by the writing of an anonymous English 'Chaucerian', evidently steeped in a knowledge of Chaucer's poems but never naming the author he echoes so frequently. This English Chaucerian is the fifteenth-century translator from the French original of an English version of the romance of *Partonope of Blois*.[2] Like Chaucer he is a freely creative translator, and – as with Chaucer's own silence about Boccaccio – a translating poet who does not acknowledge by name one of his principal inspirations. The direct influence of Chaucer in the *Partonope* translation manifests itself in many close verbal echoes of Chaucer's poems, usually confined to remembered phrases or single lines, and drawn from a range of Chaucer's works.[3] But the volume and detail of such allusion to Chaucer in this post-Chaucerian writer points also to resemblances to Chaucer's poems in technique and approach, even where close verbal indebtedness may not be so apparent in the romance, the story of which may be outlined as follows:

> Partonope, lost while hunting a magic boar, is conveyed by a magic ship to a wonderful yet apparently deserted city and its castle, where he is served a sumptuous meal by unseen hands and guided by torches to a magnificent bed. In the following scene Partonope becomes the lover of an unseen maiden, Melior, empress of Byzantium, who tells him that although they will continue to spend nights together he must not try to see her until two and a half years have passed, after which they will be married. After one year Melior agrees to his return to France, to see his mother and to help his uncle the king in his wars. During this and a later visit Partonope's mother – who fears the unseen mistress is a fiendish delusion – tries unsuccessfully to induce him to abandon Melior but does persuade him to return with a magic lantern. With this lantern he succeeds for an instant

in beholding Melior's beauty, but in so doing breaks their agreement and destroys her magic powers. Her trust in him is betrayed; she banishes him from her; and in a lengthy period of despair Partonope lives in the forest and goes nearly mad for grief and self-reproach. Despite his breaking of trust Melior is still loyal to Partonope and suffers grievously, for her lords will now force her to marry. A tournament is arranged for her hand, and at this Partonope at last wins back his love, and the romance ends with their wedding night.[4]

'This may wel be rym dogerel?' and such a romance is apparently very unlike what Chaucer's own treatments of romance suggest that he would have taken seriously. Here is another tale of a chivalrous knight and his 'elf-queene', written after *Sir Thopas*. Here is the reiterative, loose but patterned plot of romance with alarums and excursions, on which the unfinished nature of the *Squire's Tale* has seemed so eloquent a comment. But in translating his French original the poet of the English *Partonope* shows that as the author of a romance he has learned from Chaucer at several levels, not only translating into Chaucerian diction but also developing some characteristic devices and emphases of Chaucer's writing. In not every case is the outcome necessarily 'like' Chaucer, but the underlying resemblance is there, and the difference is in deploying Chaucerian techniques in very non-Chaucerian material, which only reflects the force of Chaucer's example. What follows is an account of the Chaucerian features in a post-Chaucerian English translator of romance, looking especially at narratorial technique, at presentation of the lovers and their meetings, and at the lessons learned from the diction of Chaucer's poems in *Partonope of Blois*.

I

What more potent model of narratorial technique could there be for fifteenth-century writers than Chaucer's handling of the narrative 'I'? It is the example of Chaucer which repeatedly serves as a model for presenting the figure of the poet in his works. When Sir Richard Roos sets about translating into English verse Alain Chartier's *La Belle Dame sans Merci* he adds his own brief introduction (1–28) in gracefully Chaucerian vein: the task of translation has been set him as a kind of penance, and the author presents himself as awaking preoccupied ('Half in a dreme, not fully wel awaked') and wandering into a verdant flowery valley where he is emboldened to begin his task.[5] When it comes to concluding, Roos similarly adds his own envoy along Chaucerian lines ('Go, litel book! god sende thee good passage!' 829ff.), so that in both beginning and ending his work this fifteenth-century English translator expresses himself by remembering something of the persona of Chaucer as the author inside his works. The vision and dream poems which become associated with the Chaucerian apocrypha reflect a comparable response to the Chaucerian persona, but the best of such poems show a realization that the Chaucerian narrator needs to be imagined afresh in each new poem.[6] In *The Cuckoo and the Nightingale* or *The Kingis Quair* both poets see the potential in

Chaucer's narratorial device, but develop their narrators to suit the demands of their poems, as in the vivacious dream poem now called *The Isle of Ladies*, but long known as *Chaucer's Dream*. Here is one of the liveliest of 'Chaucerian' narrators: a wistfully unsuccessful lover who in dream follows both his own fortunes in love and those of a knightly but timorous hero in a realm ruled by ladies. (The scene in which the knight faints when asked to explain what he wants from the queen he loves, and the ensuing reactions of lover and lady, are a tissue of recollections from the third book of *Troilus and Criseyde*.)[7] Both the dreamer and those within his dream amuse themselves by reading romances (973–8), and the events inside the dream form so unusually full and connected a story as to give the whole narrative the effect of a woman-centred lay or romance mediated obliquely through the often wryly humorous frame of a post-Chaucerian narrator figure.[8]

In the romance of *Partonope* the English translator shows a sense of narratorial technique which also suggests a lesson remembered and adapted from Chaucer. First signs come as early as the poet's preface to his romance, in the claims that he makes for his subject when beginning the tale with commendation of the role of old books in the preservation of our knowledge of the past:

> For ne had bokes ben wryten in prose
> And eke in ryme, of them þat be-fore vs were,
> We shulde haue lytelle luste to lere . . .   (5–7)
> Ther-fore be wrytinge of olde storyes
> Ys now broghte to owre memories
> The olde law and eke the newe . . .   (10–12)

If there is no special recollection here in *Partonope* of Chaucer's vocabulary in the *Prologue* to the *Legend of Good Women* ('And yf that olde bokes were aweye, / Yloren were of remembraunce the keye', F, 25–6), the emphasis on the role of human memory and old books at the very start of both works – the self-consciousness about writing in relation to tradition – suggests that the romance translator's ideas about the role and ambition of writing have been educated by his reading of Chaucer's own passages about reading and writing, especially since he shows a recollection later in his preface of another Chaucer passage which reflects on a literary question. The French original had made a conventional reference to St Paul, but in rendering this into English the translator apparently echoes the end of the *Nun's Priest's Tale* ('For Seint Paul seith that al that writen is, / To oure doctrine it is ywrite, ywis . . .' VII, 3441–2) in arguing for the morally educative role of stories ('That alle þat euer ys y-wrytte / In boke we owe welle to wytte, / That alle to vs ys goode doctryne', 32–4). Taken together, these Chaucerian allusions in the preface to the English *Partonope* suggest that it is the poet's awareness of the way Chaucer's poems ask questions about poetry which has educated him to be self-conscious about his own role as the translator of a romance.[9]

It is this awareness of Chaucer's example which surfaces at points in *Partonope* where the poet most explicitly refers to his task, casting himself in the role of merest translator, in terms that echo the self-presentation of the poet persona in the proem to Book II of *Troilus*. In the second proem Chaucer had characterized the activity of the poet as limited to translation and versification into English:

> Forwhi to every lovere I me excuse,
> That of no sentement I this endite,
> But out of Latyn in my tonge it write... (*TC*, II, 12–14)

Nor is the *Partonope*-poet writing out of 'sentement', out of any personal feeling or experience which enables him to write a tale about lovers from within the knowledge of love. In his own way, he has absorbed the lessons of the second proem to *Troilus*, and its stratagems reappear in some of the ways he develops his self-conscious narrative technique. The *Partonope*-poet declares, conventionally enough, that he has been commanded to make the present translation from French to English, although his capacities are altogether too dull to do justice in translation to the merits of his source ('... yt to paynte / In Engelysche tunngge y saye for me / My wyttys alle to dullet bee', 2344–6). Then, in a clear echo of the *Troilus* proem (perhaps fused with a trace of the poet as reluctant learner in the *House of Fame*) the poet goes on:

> He tellyth hys tale of sentament,
> I vnder-stonde noȝth hys entent,
> Ne wolle ne besy me to lere... (2347–9)

and after this self-dramatization as translator and outsider to love he announces his intention of picking up his narrative thread again ('Therefore strayȝthte to the matere / I wylle go of Partonope', 2350–1) in an echo of the words with which the narrator of *Troilus* takes up his narrative at the end of the first proem ('For now wil I gon streght to my matere', I, 53). Chaucer has given him phrase and stance.

The *Troilus* proems give the *Partonope*-poet the model of a narratorial persona concerned with literary questions which he develops as part of his own self-characterization as an outsider to love. In the guise of a mere translator, the persona of the poet in *Troilus* declines to accept the blame for any shortcomings in his text ('Wherfore I nyl have neither thank ne blame / Of al this werk... / Disblameth me if any word be lame, / For as myn auctour seyde, so sey I', II, 15–18). This *Troilus* stratagem evidently lodges in the memory of the *Partonope*-poet. In Partonope's sufferings and separation from his beloved Melior after his betrayal of her, the hero is cheered and cared for by Melior's sister Urake and another lady, Persevis, both of whom feel sexually attracted to him. When Persevis comes near to forgetting her chastity, the narrator abruptly intervenes to stress that he is not to blame for his subject matter:

> Thus seith myn auctour after whome I write.
> Blame not me: I moste endite
> As nye after hym as euer I may,
> Be it soþe or less I can not say... (7742–5)

The disinclination to accept blame and the emphasis on mere faithful translation of a source echo the *Troilus* proem, while uncertainty over the source's truthfulness is a characteristic embellishment in a Chaucerian mode. In rehearsing what the source relates of female desire, there is evidently a recollection of how the *Troilus* narrative approaches the problem of describing Criseyde's inward state after her first sight of Troilus ('And what she thoughte somwhat shal I write, / As to myn auctour listeth for t'endite', II, 699–700). But it is apparent that this *Partonope* passage fuses together several different contexts in Chaucer's works where questions of literary representation are raised. Here the translator of the English romance has combined echoes of *Troilus* with the disclaimer in the *General Prologue* ('Whoso shal telle a tale after a man, / He moot reherce as ny as evere he kan', 731–2) and the disclaimer in the Prologue to the *Miller's Tale* ('Blameth nat me if that ye chese amys', I, 3181), where the narrating voice argues that he should not be blamed for honestly representing what was said and done on the pilgrimage, even if that involves repeating morally questionable material.

It is in the narration of his romance that the English translator of *Partonope* vigorously develops that distinctive lesson of Chaucer's narrative technique, a technique which in itself raises questions about the nature and processes of literature. This the translator evidently recognizes and in *Partonope* aspects of the Chaucerian narrator persona are repeated in a post-Chaucerian voice. With the model of Chaucer's dream poems and *Troilus* before him, the translator develops a strand already present in his French source in order to dramatize the narrator modestly and rather comically as an outsider to love, or at least the unsuccessful lover of a lady who will not favour him.[10] Stemming from this characterization is a development of the Chaucerian device of address to an audience of lovers, and also a tender narratorial interest in the plight and difficulties of his women characters.

It is after narrating one of Partonope's happy nights with his secret love Melior that the poet-persona exclaims on his own removedness from such experience, and thus his inability to write from experience. The expression of his distress and predicament are written out of a recollection of the *Troilus*:

> Where-fore me thynkyth myn herte-bloode
> Fulle offte tyme away doth mylte.
> I fare thenne as y ne felte
> Gode ner hylle, but lye ynne a trawnce.
> Thys hathe ffortune caȝthte me ynne a chanse
> Vppon hys dyce thatt neuer wylle turne.
> Thus muste y euer yn wo soiorne.
> Butte playnely excusyth me,
> I am noȝth in thus in-firmyte.
> God schelde me euer fro that mischaunce
> To hoppe so ferre ynne loue-ys dawnce...   (2324–34)

This echoes Troilus' anguish ('The blody teris from his herte melte', III, 1445) and misery ('... joie nor penaunce / He feleth non, but lith forth in a traunce', IV, 342–3). In his complaint on his fortune there is a recollection of *Troilus* ('And after that thise dees torned on chaunces, / So was he outher glad or seyde "Allas!"' II, 1347–8), and his sojourning in woe looks back to Troilus' early feelings in love ('Al feyneth he in lust that he sojorneth', I, 326). The narrator's final prayer echoes the self-deprecating jest of Pandarus in describing to Criseyde his own poor rate of success in love (' "How ferforth be ye put in loves daunce?" / "By God," quod he, "I hoppe alwey byhynde!"' II, 1106–7).

These half-submerged Chaucerian echoes mark narratorial technique at frequent points. After comparing Partonope with his own faithful but unrewarded service in love ('Yette frome her seruyse shall I not swerue ...' 4469), the English translator apologizes for mentioning his own sufferings in a passage that recollects the sufferings of Troilus. In the poet's mind as he characterizes his remoteness from his love there seems to be Chaucer's early description of Troilus ('By nyght or day, for wisdom or folye, / His herte, which that is his brestez ye, / Was ay on hire ...' I, 452–3), for the *Partonope*-poet apologizes for his compulsion to talk of his love with a backward glance to the phrasing of *Troilus*, albeit modified by his own homely vigour:

> For of suche mater speke moste I,
> Whether hyt be wysdome or ffoly.
> For þer þe sore ys, þe fynger woll be,
> And where thy loue ys, þyne ey ys to se ...   (4478–81)

When Partonope is being tricked into betraying his lady the narrator intervenes to protest that he could never be brought to do such a thing himself (5269ff.), and this intervention seems to trigger other Chaucerian associations in the translator's mind: behind Partonope's deluded delight in his new love ('Fresshe and lusty ys Partonope; / For in hys armes hys loue haþe he', 5274–5) lies the *Franklin's Tale* ('O blisful artow now, thou Dorigen, / That hast thy lusty housbonde in thyne armes, / The fresshe knyght, the worthy man of armes', V, 1090–2). And later, when the narrator intervenes to declare that he will not repeat his source's description of Melior's sister, he concludes the interpolation by describing her ('... one off the ffayreste / That was on lyue, and þer-to þe goodelyste', 6184–5) in terms that recall language used by Criseyde ('I am oon the faireste, out of drede, / And goodlieste', II, 746–7).

Among the most Chaucerian aspects of the self-dramatization of the *Partonope*-poet is his addressing of his audience as if they were an audience of lovers ('Yow loveres axe I now this questioun', *KnT*, I, 1347). When Partonope and Melior first find themselves in bed, the poet turns to his audience with a question about Melior ('What say ye loueres, was hyt not thys / A gentylle herte of here þys was?' 1231–2). When Partonope thinks he has lost his lady the narrator comments 'Euery trew louer on hym ought to rewe'

(11507), and the poet gives some advice to lovers on perseverance ('Therfore I counseylle now euery lovere', 12106ff.). The *Partonope*-poet can make a play of assuming that his audience share his own expectations of lovers ('He is a lover, what wole ye more?' 9654), and will ask rhetorical questions of his audience which seem to have learned a lesson from Chaucer's poems in framing invitations to the reader to reflect upon what is suffered by the characters of the romance, and especially its heroines ('But who trow ye sighed now so sore / As did þis queen, faire Meliore?' 10671–2), or the difficulty in imagining such suffering ('Lorde, what herte couthe now devise / The grete sorowe þat hath Meliore?' 11735–6). In the Chaucerian manner the English *Partonope* projects an audience sympathetic to its romance about the trials and sufferings in love of lovers and ladies.

Like Chaucer, the *Partonope*-poet addresses himself specifically to ladies in his audience, as when he defers to them in their understanding of the heroine:

> She stonte in doute, and þus her spirites bene,
> As I suppose, in grete troublenesse.
> Ye ladies þat haue loue, ye knowe, I gesse...   (10678–80)

There are Chaucerian undertones to his sympathetic understanding of the predicaments of women in his romance narrative ('Alle here lyffe she myghte welle rewe / Vppon hyr-selfe, *and eche man haue rowthe*, / That euer so fayre on for here trowþe / Falssely shulde deseyued be / Off here lofe in eny degre', 1237–41), all the more so in the way his regard for the *trowþe* of his women characters coexists with a wry narratorial manner which can comment drily on the heroine's ability to dissemble her feelings ('Thus wele and better can ladies do ...' 12105). When Melior shows her favour for her lover at the tournament the poet steps in to dismiss those men who spread tales about women:

> Therfore all men þat be so light of tonge –
> That as a grete bell þat longe is ronge
> Noyse her lesynges – God gife hem grace
> Not amonge ladies to dwell any space...   (10137–40)

Here is not only a backwards glance to the anticipations of her notoriety by Chaucer's Criseyde ('Thorughout the world my belle shal be ronge' v, 1062), but also – as elsewhere in the poet's protective interventions on behalf of women – the legacy of those impish prayers and animadversions on men's betrayal of women at the close of the *Troilus* ('God yeve hem sorwe, amen! / That with hir grete wit and subtilte / Bytraise yow ... / Beth war of men....' v, 1781ff.).

II

If we now turn to the episode of the first meeting and lovemaking of Partonope and Melior, the 'Chaucerianism' of the fifteenth-century English translator of

Partonope of Blois comes even more clearly into focus as he reads and rewrites the original romance in the light of his knowledge of Chaucer's poems. Lost while hunting, transported by a magic ship to a marvellous city where all is done by unseen hands, Partonope is brought to lie in a rich bed where he is joined by the young maiden queen of the city, who does not realize a man is there until she happens to touch him in the bed. The outline of what follows is comparable in both French and English versions: the lady orders Partonope to leave but, too exhausted and too apprehensive of her retainers, he asks her for mercy; his initial attempts to embrace her are repulsed, but eventually he is successful, and both the hero and the heroine lose their virginity.

The French romance offered a delicate and intimate scene, and the English translator realizes to the full the original's potential for comedy and for the depiction of the lovers' feelings, in ways that evidently draw on the model of the consummation scene in Book III of the *Troilus*. The whole scene in the English romance is presented with a delicate humour and an eye for detail. As Partonope hears the lady coming towards his bed ('And hys herte fulle nere quappynge', 1180), he is as nervous as Troilus awaiting Criseyde's arrival at their first meeting ('And, Lord, so that his herte gan to quappe, / Heryng hire come ...' III, 57–8). Once the lady has slipped under the covers both lie absolutely still, he petrified with fear and she as yet unaware of the young man in her bed. Despite the fact that she has not yet happened to touch that young man, the English translator 'improves' his source with a lengthy interpolation which shares with its reader the woman's predicament ('... all here plesaunce was hym to haue / To here husbande, and so to saue / Here worshyppe ... / For she wyth-owten varyauns / Purposyd euer to ben hys ...' 1222ff.). It is here that the *Partonope*-translator characteristically turns to address an imagined audience of lovers in the Chaucerian manner, and focusses on the theme of his story as one of *trouthe* and the tribulations of women ('What say ye loueres, was hyt not thys / A gentylle herte...? / But here-after she fownde hym vntrewe ...' 1231ff.). This is even followed by an invocation to Venus (that this woman should not suffer for her *trouthe*), in what seems to combine a recollection of some of Chaucer's classical machinery with a version of his sympathy for the position of women:

> But to þat lady I clepe and calle
> That Venus ys called, goddas of loue ...
> Brynge þys lady to here desyre ...
> þat she here-after fele no smerte
> For here trowþe, ne for here kyndenes...   (1245ff.)

With further insight into the womanly predicament of a 'lady', the English translator goes on to invent an internal monologue in which his heroine lies awake much of the night, worrying how she can show the desire she feels for this man lying beside her without his thinking her too forward ('And parauenture þynke þat I / Off a-nother wolle be wonne / As lyghtely ...' 1267–9).

Our doughty hero of romance is meanwhile in some terror lest he be lying beside some 'Illusione / Off þe deuylle', and in the French text the necessary discovery is endearingly effected when the heroine happens to stretch out in bed and touches Partonope with her foot:

> La damoisele atant s'estent
> Et o son pie le tousel sent,
> Et quant l'a sentu, si tressaut,
> Escria soi et nient trop haut:
> 'Comment' fait ele, 'qui es tu?
> Qui t'a en mon lit enbattu?'   (1143–8)

The translator of the English *Partonope* approaches this turning point with flurries of narratorial deliberation and bookishness which look back to Chaucer's handling of the consummation scene in *Troilus*. The lovers in *Partonope* are made so fearful and reflective that the poet draws his audience into a kind of complicity in 'devising' their union ('Lette se nowe ho can beste deuyse / þes tweyne to make a-quentyd to be', 1287–8). When Troilus at long last takes Criseyde in his arms, the narrator comically steels himself to follow his source without further delay ('Though that I tarie a yer, somtyme I moot, / After myn auctour, tellen hire gladnesse', III, 1195–6). It is hard to believe that this moment was not at the back of the *Partonope*-translator's mind when he contemplates the comic impasse created in his romance by the fears of both lovers, and comparably prolongs the uncertainty while at the same time declaring he must make an end of it in accord with his source ('Off alle þys fere make we a fyne ... / Ther-fore fully I me purpose / After myn auctor to make an ende ...' 1292, 1295–6). Now comes that turning point in which the heroine first touches the man in her bed and then cries out. But in the English romance the report of both these intimate actions is interpolated – in a distinctly Chaucerian manner – with a commentary acknowledging the poet's authorities:

> Thys fayre lady þat was so hende,
> Streyghte forþe here legge, and happed to ffele,
> *Trewly þe ffrenshe boke seyeth þe hele*
> Off þys wofulle Partonope.
> 'Owte! allas þen!' sayde she,
> And In a maner gan to crye,
> *For sothe I wolle not lye,*
> *Myne auctor seyethe hyt was not lowde ...*   (1297–1304)

When shortly afterwards in the same scene the lady takes pity on Partonope with a trembling heart ('Here herte wyth-in her body fferde / Lyke as þe leffe dothe on a tre', 1484–5), it seems that both moments in *Partonope* have been composed by a poet who has carried with him and made part of his own imagination Chaucer's art in presenting the possession of Criseyde:

Criseyde, which that felte hire thus itake –
As writen clerkes in hire bokes olde –
Right as an aspes leef she gan to quake ...			(III, 1198–1200)

From his French original the *Partonope*-poet derives his hero's plea to the lady
– reminiscent of the *Troilus* – for a mercy which will save him from death, but
it is the English translator who highlights the idea of a mutual asking of
forgiveness between the lovers ('Sho porposed her to aske mercy / Off hym þat
fayne wolde mercy haue', 1506–7), in a scene that seems to remember the
moment of reversal when Criseyde moves from forgiving Troilus to asking
forgiveness for herself:

And she answerde, 'Of gilt misericorde ...'
'And now,' quod she, 'that I have don yow smerte,
Foryeve it me, myn owene swete herte'			(III, 1177, 1182–3)

And just as Criseyde's surrender is related by the narrator to womanly
behaviour more largely ('For love of God, take every womman heede / To
werken thus ...' III, 1224–5), so too in the English *Partonope* the translator
seems to remember something of the narratorial approach of *Troilus* before
developing his own themes of womanly qualities and *trouthe*:

Nowe me þynketh, so Gode me saue,
Sho owte of very homanhede
Off hys desese to take grette hede ...			(1508–10)
Ther ys in erthe no-þynge so kynde
As be þys wymmen, ther as þey fynde
Here serwandes trewe and stydfaste ...			(1513–15)

   This is a reading of romance in the light of a knowledge of Chaucer, but a
knowledge that shows itself through verbal echoes translated into a confident
handling of parallel situations and feelings. Some of the gesture of *Troilus* Book
III ('And therwithal hire arm over hym she leyde', 1128; '... hire streghte
bak and softe ... He gan to stroke ...' 1247ff.), together with the example of
Chaucer's Troilus and his innocence –

That what to don, for joie unnethe he wiste ...			(1253)
That where his spirit was, for joie he nyste ...			(1351)

– has been drawn together into the *Partonope*-translator's emphasis on the
unknowing innocence of the pair of lovers in his romance:

Ouer here hys arme he gan to laye,
Thys ys soþe as I yowe saye.
So softe, so clene she was to fele
þat where he was he wyste not welle.
Plesaunce had hym ouer-come
þat all hys wyttes were fro hym nome.
Whan þys lady hys honde can fele,
Whatte to done sho wotte not welle ...			(1535–42)

The ensuing description of Partonope's physical possession of Melior follows the French text, and as such leaves rather less to the imagination than Chaucer's evocation in *Troilus* of the sweet woodbine twisting its tendrils about the tree ('And her legges sho gan to knytte, / And wyth hys knees he gan hem on-shote', 1565–6). Yet the English translator's summing up of this scene ('Thus Entergamynyd they I-wys. / Suche game a-fore he neuer a-sayde', 1572–3) once again looks back to *Troilus* through its association of such experience with 'assaying' (cf. *TC*, III, 1219–20), and the apparent coinage of a verb for intercourse (*entergamynyd*: no other instance is known to the *Middle English Dictionary*), which perhaps builds on the model of some of Chaucer's diction in *Troilus* (e.g. 'And pleyinge entrechaungeden hire rynges', III, 1368). In Melior's words of acceptance to her lover ('Ryghte welcome be ye, my herte dere, / My hertes Ioy, myn erthely make', 1710–11) there sounds Criseyde's acceptance of Troilus ('Welcome, my knyght, my pees, my suffisaunce,' III, 1309), just as her thankfulness 'þat I be-sette my loue In so goode a place' (1864) is a recollection of the encouragement given by Pandarus to Troilus about Criseyde ('That thow biset art in so good a place', I, 905).

This scene of first love – which comes early and unearned to the romance hero – establishes strongly the joy of what Partonope has once possessed, betrayed and lost, and must then earn anew. As such, its bliss is echoed again when Partonope and Melior are reunited at the close of the romance, but both scenes would resemble each other less pointedly if they were not framed by the *Partonope*-poet's Chaucerian pose of exclusion from love, and with that his combination of tenderness and humour about the experience of romance. In the *Wife of Bath's Tale*, when the knight sees his fairy mistress transformed into a beauty, he embraces her ('His herte bathed in a bath of blisse', III, 1253), and this blissful climax to the romance told by the Wife is evidently in the *Partonope*-translator's mind when he describes his hero's first happiness ('... he may bathe ynne so hye a blysse', 2305), and the lovers' reunion much later ('þus in endlesse blisse baþed thei be, / The good hertes of þes lovers two ...' 12137–8). Here at the very conclusion of the whole romance, where the lovers – reunited and married after long separation – are brought to bed together, the poet presents their happiness as a heaven from which he is excluded, and which he hence cannot write about, although like the *Troilus* narrator ('And write hire wo ...' *TC*, I, 49) he can write of lovers' care. In the last lines of the romance the poet prays to the god of love to allow his servants to attain the same bliss in love that Partonope and Melior achieved, in which may be heard a faint echo of the prayers to the god of love and to Venus in Chaucer's *Troilus* proems. And this is another reminder that the location of Chaucerian lessons needs also to be taken into account. As the narrator learned from Chaucer's proems how to introduce his narrative and himself within it, so at the end of the romance – in the presentation of the translator as outside the experience of successful love and so unable to describe it – there is a sense of a lesson learned and modified from the characterization of the poet figure in the third book of Chaucer's *Troilus*:

Of hire delit, or joies oon the leeste,
Were impossible to my wit to seye;
But juggeth ye that han ben at the feste
Of swich gladnesse, if that hem liste pleye...
And lat hem in this hevene blisse dwelle,
That is so heigh that al ne kan I telle
(III, 1310ff.)

Ya, who can tell þo Ioies now
That they bene In? forsoþe not I.
But þe sorowe and þe care full truly
That longeth to love, þat can I tell.
Thei are in heven, and now I in hell...
(12139–43)
...And how þat nyght her life they ledde
And in what Ioy then they be.
But this may not be declared for me,
Ne what her Ioy was, ne her delite,
For I was neuer yite in þat plite... (12185–9)

III

If a developed narratorial persona and a comic sense suggest comparisons with the example of Chaucer, it is evident that the English translator of *Partonope* is also a 'Chaucerian' in the way that a familiarity with the diction of Chaucer's poems gives him an idiom through which he can translate and extend his original romance, when the first love scenes of Partonope and Melior are followed by betrayal and separation. The received story of the Partonope romance follows a traditional romance pattern of trial and testing for both hero and heroine. Melior places all her trust in Partonope ('In yow fully ys alle my truste', 5559) in terms that recall Criseyde's trust in Troilus ('Gramercy, for on that is al my trist', III, 1305), and after betraying Melior Partonope condemns himself ('Off trowþe for euer ys loste my name', 6095) in an echo of the way Criseyde's betrayal is regretted ('...for now is clene ago / My name of trouthe in love, for everemo', v, 1055). But because Partonope's betrayal of the queen exposes her to the anger of her lords, who will now force her to marry, the heroine – in her continuing love for the man who betrayed her trust – is also placed in a position of testing and trial. Although the romance is ostensibly about Partonope, the poet hence focusses with sympathetic understanding throughout on the trials of his heroine. Granted that the translator is evidently steeped in a reading of Chaucer's poems, there are many tokens in *Partonope* that it is Chaucer who has educated the poet's concern for the difficulties of women and who has provided an idiom in which the translator can realize some of the implications of his romance.

The poet draws on Chaucer's language to refine his presentation of both hero and heroine. In an account of Partonope's qualities ('And heven[ly] ytte was hym to see, / So ȝonge, so fresche, so welle be-sene', 3772–3) there is an echo of how Criseyde first sees Troilus ('So fressh, so yong, so weldy semed he, / It was an heven upon hym for to see', II, 636–7), just as the heavenly qualities associated with Melior ('Men seide she was an hevenly þing. / It were Impossible, thei seide, þrugh nature / Might be brought forþe such a creature,' 11461–3) recall those identified with Criseyde ('...As doth an hevenyssh perfit creature, / That down were sent in scornynge of nature', I,

104–5). If romance presents a superlative world, then a fifteenth-century romance translator could draw on Chaucer's poems for an idiom which enables him in this way to present his characters with more lustre. Chaucerian accents intensify the expression of feelings and values as these arise in his romance. Behind the voice of the betrayed heroine of *Partonope* there are often echoes loud or soft of the voices in Chaucer's *Legend of Good Women*. In Melior's pleadings for her lover's loyalty ('And lokyth alle-way thatt ȝe be trewe / To me and chancheth for no newe . . . ' 2393–4) there sounds an echo of Lucretia's story ('I telle hyt for she was of love so trewe, / Ne in hir wille she chaunged for no newe', *LGW*, 1874–5), just as there are also echoes of Dido and Medea.[11] When the heroine faints for distress at her betrayal it is the English translator who criticizes his hero's speechlessness ('Me þynkethe þys was not gouerned manly', 6007), has his heroine complain to God about the plight of women in a vein recalling the *Legend of Good Women*:

> Why sufferyste þou euer wommanys þoghte
> Wyth mannys loue encombred to be,
> Or tryste here worde? for well by me
> Eche woman may ensampell take . . .   (6013–16)

and presents her womenfolk's reproaches to Melior ('And þes wemmen had well I-ronge / Here belle, wyche was heuy to here', 6139–40) with what seems another echo of the fate anticipated by Criseyde ('Thorughout the world my belle shal be ronge! / And wommen moost wol haten me of alle', v, 1062–3).

Yet in *Partonope* the translator's awareness of the sum of Chaucer's poems means that, as he works at improving the effects of his source, his memory may also draw on Chaucerian accents regardless of their original context. In the moment when Melior realizes Partonope has betrayed her, the English translator adds to his version the pathetic detail that the woman gives her lover one piteous look before swooning ('On hym she caste a pytuos eye, / And sowned wyth a dedely chere', 5867–8) which fuses recollections both of the moment when Troilus parts from Criseyde outside Troy ('And caste his eye upon hire pitously', v, 79) and of the Theban widow fainting before Theseus ('Whan she hadde swowned with a deedly cheere', *KnT*, I, 913). His memory sometimes combines or disperses elements from the Chaucer lines he recalls in order to enhance the presentation of his romance heroine and her predicaments. Arcite's self-description as a lover –

> Love hath his firy dart so brennyngly
> Ystiked thurgh my trewe, careful herte
> That shapen was my deeth erst than my sherte . . .   (I, 1564–6)

– resurfaces in two different contexts in the English *Partonope*. One Chaucer line becomes the climactic final line of the English heroine's first confession to Partonope of her love for him, which she phrases in fatalistic terms ('I se þat hyt ys the ordynauns / Off gode of loue, howe sore me smerte. / Hyt was me shape or then my serke', 1714–16), while the other Chaucer lines do not emerge until a much later account of the tenacity of love in the betrayed heroine ('The fyres darte of love so smerte / So þrilled hadde hir meke herte ...' 9118–19). In a comparable process of poetic memory the translator of *Partonope* may combine various Chaucer contexts together to produce a tissue of Chaucerian ideas. Recollections of Arcite arguing with Palamon in the *Knight's Tale* ('Wostow nat wel the olde clerkes sawe / That "who shal yeve a lovere any lawe?"', 1163–4) and some of the imagery of *Troilus* ('That al this world ne myghte hire love unbynde', iv, 675) are mingled when Melior defends her love to her sister:

> Therfore þis is a full olde sawe:
> Who may give to a lovere lawe?
> For þough reasone wolde make a lovere se
> That all his foly, yite can not he
> The wofull bondes wele vnbynde ...   (8709–13)

It is the model of Chaucer's poems which has given the translator a vein of expression in English in which his romance characters can voice their distress and their values, in which they can talk about and analyse their love.

Such recollections of Arcite's proverbial or fatalistic idiom in the *Knight's Tale* ('shapen was my deeth'; 'olde clerkes sawe') are characteristic more largely of a tendency to translate *Partonope* not simply into English but into a Chaucerian idiom as a way of extending its implications, and the English translation is invested with an alertness to the workings of Fortune and the passing of time articulated through recollection of Chaucer's poems. It is from the *Knight's Tale* ('Wel hath Fortune yturned thee the dys ... / Now up, now doun, as boket in a welle', i, 1238, 1533) that the poet draws some of that language through which he adds reflections on the misfortunes befalling the lovers in his romance after their early joy is lost ('Lo, thus ffortune can turne hur dyse / Nowe vp, nowe downe; here whele ys vnstabelle', 4389–90). A sense of destiny and 'aventure' is filtered into the translation from memories of Chaucer, as is an occasional sense of the workings of fame.[12] A memorable description of dawn in the *Knight's Tale* ('And firy Phebus riseth up so bright / That al the orient laugheth of the light', i, 1493–4) is indeed remembered and woven into the translation of *Partonope* ('Se þe sonne he[r] bemus sprede In so bryghte / þat all þe chamber was laughynge lyghte', 1931–2). But this is only the more noticeable of a tissue of absorbed Chaucerian descriptions of time passing which have been worked into the translation, just as the self-conscious taste in the English *Partonope* for proverbial expressions ('Ther-fore me seythe an olde sawe', 3316; 'Yite an olde proverbe seide is all day', 7981; 'Therfore þis proverbe is seide full truly', 10883) probably reflects an attempt to follow Chaucer's example not only by using the same proverbs but by associating narrative with a commentary of proverbial wisdom.[13]

As with the language of fortune, of time and of proverbial wisdom, so too with that Chaucerian idiolect of *routhe*, *trouthe* and *gentilesse* into which the translator renders the actions and reactions of the characters in his post-

Chaucerian romance. The gentle falcon's trust in her lover in the *Squire's Tale* ('That semed welle of alle gentillesse', v, 505) expresses the values Melior hopes to find in Partonope ('Loo yender goþe the welle of gentylnes', 1857), and this is true of scene after scene in *Partonope*, where compassion and constancy are the ideals the characters seek and express. In such scenes the sensibility and worth of the women characters expecially has been refined through the example of Chaucer's romances and his 'legends' of good women.[14] Yet there are also shifts of tone, as when the English translator – in a passage interpolated into the source (1761–83) – makes his romance hero warn his lady against jealousy through an indecorous exemplum of a distinctly *fabliau* kind: an unjustly jealous husband, persuaded that his neighbour is cuckolding him, is convinced of his foolish belief by a delusive and bathetic dream ('He þo3te he sawe hys ney3bore drawe owte hys swerde, / And fulle hys scawbarte he þo3te þat he pyssed ...', 1772–3).

What does the occurrence of Chaucer allusion in *Partonope* suggest about the nature of the translator's access to Chaucer's poems? For the most part, the allusions point to a poetic memory freely moving about within a familiarity with the phrasing, manner and thematic emphases of Chaucer's poems, although in a context like this description of the final tournament the Chaucerian echoes from the *Knight's Tale* suggest either that the English translator of *Partonope* did sometimes turn to a copy of Chaucer's text, or that he shows a remarkable capacity to recall the fine texture of Chaucerian idiom in this climactic knightly action of his romance:[15]

...This Palamon	
In his fightyng were a wood leon ...	Now as wode bores or lyons two
As wilde bores gonne they to smyte ...	Partonope and þe soudan gan go
(*KnT*, I, 1655–8)	(11120–1)
In goon the speres ful sadly in arrest;	In gone þe speres sadly vnder þe arme ...
In gooth the sharpe spore into the syde.	The good hors men now fiersly they ride,
Ther seen men who kan juste and who kan	Through hauberke gothe þe spere into þe
ryde ...	syde,
(2602–4)	Oute with swerdes a-boute helmes rounde ...
	(11130–4)
Out goon the swerdes as the silver brighte,	
The helmes they tohewen and toshrede ...	
(2608–9)	
He thurgh the body is hurt and sithen take,	And for wery of fight some are I-take
Maugree his heed, and broght unto the stake	And magre her hede ben ladde to þe stake
(2617–18)	(11142–3)
Som tyme an ende ther is of every dede.	Ye wote wele of all þing moste be an ende,
For er the sonne unto the reste wente ...	The Day is nye ydo, þe sonne doþe faste
(2636–7)	wende (11144–5)

IV

Where was there to go in English romance after Chaucer? In his *Sir Thomas Norny* Dunbar alludes to *Sir Thopas* in burlesquing a court jester, and in his *The Douty Duke of Albany* Skelton exults over an unsuccessful Scottish incursion into England through some reference to the hasty retreat beaten by Chaucer's Thopas ('But hyde the, Sir Topias ...' 287).[16] In these two short poems the character of Chaucer's absurd romance hero has become a type, and the comment in a poem of Wyatt's ('[I am not he that can] ... / Praysse Syr Thopas for a noble tale, / And skorne the story that the knyght tolld ...')[17] is one of a number showing that the parodic ineptitude of Chaucer's poem was appreciated as a burlesque of romance. Yet from *Troilus* to *Thopas* there is a secret at the heart of Chaucer's uses of romance, which is his ability – for all his shimmering irony and ambiguity – to retain something of its essential allure. It is this which enables Spenser to gaze past the burlesque and draw upon *Sir Thopas* for elements of romance in *The Faerie Queene*.[18]

In *Partonope of Blois* the interest of this fifteenth-century romance translator lies in how he uses what he has learned, for here is a post-Chaucerian writer who draws on and applies a wide knowledge of Chaucer's poetry. Unlike some of the other Chaucerians, he is not setting out to rewrite Chaucer's works, or to pursue an extended imitation of Chaucer's narratives in any of the genres Chaucer chose. Nor does he invoke Chaucer's authority as a model in language or form, and he is therefore not avowedly or self-consciously a Chaucerian, locating himself for his reader in relation to an acknowledged literary model or master. But then, the translator of *Partonope* is drawing on his familiarity with the sum of Chaucer's poems in texture and technique in order to create an English version of a literary form – the romance – with which Chaucer's own relationship is always ambiguous. As Derek Brewer has shown,[19] Chaucer owed a great deal in his diction and narrative technique to the English popular romances, and yet he combined a style overlapping the accents of popular romance with a mixed, elusive attitude to the characteristic subject-matter of romance, a Chaucerian mixture of sympathy and irony. To post-Chaucerians Chaucer's romances were hence a legacy difficult to inherit undivided. Like Chaucer in some of his romances, the *Partonope*-poet creates an English romance through freely adaptive translation, and in writing after Chaucer – whose style had united the plain, homely stength of popular romance narrative with diction and syntax of more spacious amplitude – the *Partonope*-poet is able to translate into an idiom which reflects both aspects of the style Chaucer had evolved and accepts some of the consequences of the mixture. The plot of *Partonope* – despite the translator's extension of that narratorial archness already present in the French – remained one that Chaucer would probably have regarded with amused impatience. But it is too easy with hindsight to conclude that there was nowhere to go in romance after Chaucer. Both in the sympathetic realization of romance characters' typical feelings and predicaments, and in a narratorial commentary, the *Partonope*-translator tries to apply the lessons in sympathy and irony learned from the model available in Chaucer. Not surprisingly, the sympathy and the wryness now exist less in that balance of mutual commentary which is Chaucer's highest art: the translator has divided the inheritance and applied its resources eclectically, as he had to if he were to write a romance like *Partonope*. The English *Partonope* is very different than Chaucer would have left it, even though it is as it is in large part because of Chaucer's example: a romance full of reminiscence of Chaucer yet like no Chaucer work as a whole, by a fifteenth-century translator who reads romance in the light of what romance had meant to Chaucer, and who as such deserves to be counted among the English Chaucerians.

NOTES

1 Cf. D. S. Brewer, 'The Relationship of Chaucer to the English and European Traditions', in D. S. Brewer (ed.), *Chaucer and Chaucerians* (London, 1966).

2 Cf. *The Middle-English Versions of Partonope of Blois*, ed. A. Trampe Bödtker, *EETS*, e.s. 109 (London, 1912). This edition is based on the longest and most complete MS (British Library MS Add. 35288); there are four other fifteenth-century MSS of this couplet version, and a fragment in stanzas. Composition of the romance may be dated to the second quarter of the fifteenth century. For the twelfth-century French romance, see *Partonopeu de Blois*, ed. J. Gildea, o.s.a., 2 vols. (Villanova, Pa., 1967–8), and for an account, A. Fourrier, *Le courant réaliste dans le roman courtois en France au Moyen Age* (Paris, 1960), i, pp. 318–83. The extant French MSS apparently do not represent the immediate source of the English version which, although faithful to the order and content of the French story, is not simply a translation.

3 Cf. B. J. Whiting, 'A Fifteenth-Century English Chaucerian: The Translator of *Partonope of Blois*', *Mediaeval Studies*, 7 (1945), 40–54; R. M. Smith, 'Two Chaucer Notes . . . ', *Modern Language Notes*, 51 (1936), 314; J. Parr, 'Chaucer and *Partonope of Blois*', *Modern Language Notes*, 60 (1945), 486–7; Lillian M. McCobb, 'The English *Partonope of Blois*, its French Source, and Chaucer's *Knight's Tale*', *Chaucer Review*, 11 (1976–7), 369–72.

4 The romance of Partonope and Melior represents a medieval transformation of the Cupid and Psyche story, beginning with features resembling some Breton lays, and developing in some overlap with romances like those of Yvain and of 'The Fair Unknown', *Lybeaus Desconus*, or 'sir Lybeux' as Chaucer calls it in *Sir Thopas*.

5 Cf. W. W. Skeat (ed.), *Chaucerian and Other Pieces* (Oxford, 1897), pp. 299ff. At l. 29 Roos begins to follow Chartier's poem; cf. J. C. Laidlaw (ed.), *The Poetical Works of Alain Chartier* (Cambridge, 1974), p. 332.

6 See A. C. Spearing, *Medieval Dream-Poetry* (Cambridge, 1976), ch. 4 ('The Chaucerian Tradition'), pp. 176–87.

7 Cf. *The Isle of Ladies, or the Ile of Pleasaunce*, ed. Anthony Jenkins (New York, 1980):

> . . . Awacke, for shame!
> What will ye do? Is this good game? . . .   (545–6)

> 'Yf he dye here, lost is my name.
> How shall I pleye this perilous game? . . . '   (561–2)

> All was for nawght, for still as stone
> He laye, and worde spake he none . . .   (583–4)

> 'Mercy' twies he cried faste . . .   (588)

> 'Ffor, in good faythe, I ment but well . . . '   (647)

> And him vpdressed for to knele
> The quene avisinge wonder well.
> But as he rosse, he over-threwe . . .   (663–5)

> ... she did her paine
> Him to recover from the paine ...   (679–80)

8 In the magic apples and the island bounded by glass the poet of *The Isle of Ladies* toys with motifs from Arthurian legend, while the denouement shares motifs with the Marie de France *lai* of *Eliduc*.

9 As Derek Pearsall puts it: 'What distinguishes the English poem is the quality of its literary self-consciousness', in his 'The English romance in the fifteenth century', *Essays and Studies*, 29 (1976), 56–83.

10 For instances of the English translator's development of narratorial interventions in his French source, see the following:

   (1) 2310ff. (French, 1871ff.) Telling of Partonope's joy in love upsets the narrator, unsuccessful in love himself ('Alas, thus story schendyth me. / For alle my loue canne y haue no3thte').

   (2) 4453ff. (3423ff.) 'Lowe, thys can loue wyth-owte ffayle ...'

   (3) 6759ff. (5503ff.) Elaboration of the French author's condemnation of clerks' misrepresentation of women.

   (4) 7635ff. (6261ff.) The relation between beauty and chastity ...

   (5) 8669ff. (7119ff.) The poet pities unhappy ladies.

   (6) 9664ff. (8057ff.) Ladies are nowadays grown too chaste and religious to have mercy on their lovers ...

   (7) 10121ff. (8397ff.) 'Though a lady for þe best a þing do, / Men haue such Ioy to lye so, / They wole it turne all for þe worste ...' But a verbose description in the French original of the appearance of Melior's sister (4879–922) is replaced with some narratorial flourish 'That Idell mater I forsoke' (6171) and with a mock-indignant *occupatio*: every one knows a lady of high degree will be attired in the best manner ('Whatte nedes to speke of hur forehedde, / Off hur nose, hur mowþe, hyrre lyppes redde, / Off hur shappe, or of hur armes smalle? / Off þys and more, a ryghte grette tale / Myne auctor makethe ...', 6178–82). Pearsall remarks on 'the distance travelled from popular romance in this quasi-courtly poem' (p. 68).

11 Cf. *Partonope*, 1877, 5885, and *LGW*, 1361, 1662–3.

12 This Eolus gan hit so blowe   For þorowe þe worlde þys fowle ffame
    That thrugh the world hyt was yknowe   Was so dryffe and forth I-blowe;
       ...   (*HF*, 1769–70)   Thorowe alle londys hyt was knowe ...
                                                                      (*Partonope*, 179–81)

13 'There-fore me seythe an olde sawe: 'But who may bet bigile, yf hym lyste,
    He to home a man dothe tryste,   Than he on whom men weneth best to triste?'
    Euer may dyseue hym beste ...'   (3316–8)   (*TC*, v, 1266–7)

    'Yite an olde proverbe seide is all day: 'A fool may ek a wis man ofte gide ...'
    Of a fole a wyse man may   (*TC*, I, 630)
    Take witte, þis is with-outen drede ...'   'For wyse ben by foles harm chastised ...'
                              (7981–3)   (*TC*, III, 329)

14 A lady whose husband holds Partonope prisoner feels pity and agrees to release him so that he may attend the tournament for Melior's hand, trusting that he will keep faith and return in time to save her from her husband's wrath. She exacts no oath from Partonope and her womanly pity is seen as the highest test of his *trouthe* ('His hye trouþe now wole she prove', 9371). The lady's solemn language ('My life, my dethe lieth all in you', 9349) converges with the language of commitment in *Troilus* ('My lif, my deth, hol in thyn hond I leye', I, 1053), although the poet has some wry reservations ('But I can not wele sey where she / Hath wisely done, or as elles a fole', 9351–2). The resolution redounds to the honour of women, for when

Partonope freely returns to resume his imprisonment the lady releases him with a
ringing speech ('God forbede þat cruelte or vengeaunce / In any woman founde
shall be; / A foule illusion it were to se, / For in hem moste euer be mercy and
rouþe', 11277–80).

15 Partonope's uncle, the king of France, is praised (480–2) in terms echoing the
portrait of the Knight in the *General Prologue* (43–5), while in the adjudication of the
tournament for Melior's hand Partonope is also praised in the same terms as the
Knight:

At many a noble armee hadde he be.	In many a mortall battaille haþe he be.
At mortal batailles hadde he been fiftene,	In listes often eke fought haþe he,
And foughten for oure feith at	And euer of his Enemeyce þe better haþ
Tramyssene	hadde ... (11858–60)
In lystes thries, and ay slayn his foo ...	
(I, 60–3)	

16 See J. A. Burrow, '*Sir Thopas* in the sixteenth century', in *Middle English Studies
Presented to Norman Davis in Honour of his Seventieth Birthday*, ed. Douglas Gray and
E. G. Stanley (Oxford, 1983), pp. 69–91.

17 Kenneth Muir and Patricia Thomson (eds.), *Collected Poems of Sir Thomas Wyatt*
(Liverpool, 1969), p. 89.

18 In the Preface to the *Fables*, Dryden comments: '*Spencer* more than once insinuates,
that the Soul of *Chaucer* was transfus'd into his Body; and that he was begotten by
him Two Hundred years after his Decease. *Milton* has acknowledg'd to me that
Spencer was his Original' (*CH*, p. 160). Milton's reference in *Il Penseroso* to 'him that
left half-told / The story of Cambuscan bold' (109ff.) may suggest that he did not
see the way Chaucer leaves the *Squire's Tale* as itself a comment on that kind of
romance.

19 Cf. 'The Relationship of Chaucer to the English and European Traditions'.

6

Some Chaucerian themes in Scottish writers

DOUGLAS GRAY

The title of 'Scottish Chaucerians', which used to be applied to a number of the Scottish poets of the fifteenth and early sixteenth centuries, seems now to be almost defunct, and deservedly so, since it always did more harm than good, not only because it suggested an exaggerated degree of dependence, but also because by focussing attention on what is simply one strand – although an important one – in the Scottish literary tradition it distracted attention from the extraordinary variety of that tradition. Even though the ravages of time have left the surviving evidence in fragments, enough remains to show that the literature was far more extensive and varied than the conventional procession of 'Chaucerian' makars – King James, Henryson, Dunbar and Douglas – might suggest.

There is certainly no doubt that the presence and influence of Chaucer was an important one, especially for those two fifteenth-century poets who seem most deeply and most interestingly involved with his work, King James and Robert Henryson – though their treatment of him is distinctive and original. It is a pity, however, that much of the discussion of Chaucer's influence on the later writers of Scotland has tended to regard it as predominantly or exclusively 'rhetorical' or stylistic in nature. Again, there is here a basic truth which is being exaggerated – like their English counterparts, Scottish writers do praise Chaucer's verbal skills and his role in the adornment of the poetic vernacular. He is said to have sat (with Gower) 'on the steppis ... of rethorike'; he is praised for his 'gudelie termis' and his 'joly veirs', and for his 'fresch anamalit termes celical'.[1] And, of course, there are conscious and unconscious echoes of and allusions to Chaucerian phrases. But the influence of Chaucer can be seen over a much wider area, for example on genre – most obviously perhaps in the popularity of the dream vision – or on narrative technique – in Henryson's developed use of the 'narrator' in his *Fables*, which is highly unusual in that 'kind', and certainly owes much to his reading of Chaucer; it is likely too that Henryson's skilful handling of narrative tempo in the *Fables*, and his use of 'digression', or the oblique way he will move a story

81

forward by 'matter collateral', or the blending of earnest and game, or the occasional sudden shift of register also reflect his careful reading of Chaucer.

However, it is yet another aspect that I wish to consider briefly in this study, that of Chaucer's ideas and themes. He was a poet fascinated by ideas, 'un grand poète philosophique',[2] and in his writings ideas are both stated and discussed and enacted dramatically in narrative. This is too large a field to plough; I shall simply make a few general remarks about a number of inter-connected themes, and then discuss one of them in rather greater detail. Inevitably, such a discussion must move beyond the narrow confines of 'influence': in some cases we can see writers grappling with a specifically Chaucerian formulation of a favourite idea or theme, in others themselves taking part in a continuing discussion, as Chaucer himself had done earlier; this will allow us not only to see Chaucer in a Scottish milieu, but also afford a glimpse of the context of medieval ideas in which he worked.

Since then there has been a good deal of discussion of the most influential and the most complex of Chaucerian 'ideas' – love – I will only mention it here. At the end of the period we find Douglas worrying over Chaucer's treatment of Dido; earlier we find Henryson grappling with the difficult story of Cresseid. The vehemently pro-feminist *Quare of Jelusy* (?c. 1424–88) echoes words and concerns in Chaucer.[3] Where King James in *The Kingis Quair* tends to soften the sharp paradoxes of Chaucer's views of love, Henryson on the other hand intensifies them. Outside the more obviously 'Chaucerian' tradi-tion, the medieval statements and celebration of the extremes continue – fab-liaux and merry tales treat passion and attempts to thwart it with some esprit; romances continue to portray noble *fin'amour*. And in the moralizing *The Spek-takle of Luf* (translated, it says, from Latin in 1492), an old knight gives examples 'by the quhilk men suld eschew the delectatioun of luf' – Eve, Dalilah, Helen, Jocasta, and Cresseid (in what is often taken to be an allusion to Henryson's version of the story: 'how quyte Cresseid hir trew luffar Troye-lus his lang service in luf, quhen scho forsuk him for Dyomeid, and thare efter went common amang the Grekis, and syd deid in great myssere and pane').[4]

But, as in Chaucer, love is not seen as existing in isolation. Henryson's Cresseid laments that she 'clam upon the fickill quheill sa hie'; his Orpheus 'wyth inwart lufe replete' loses his Eurydice, and comes to feel the sharp con-trarieties of Love – 'bitter and suete, cruel and merciable' – but 'the lowe of luf' and its power is formidable and seems irresistible – 'quhare lufe gois, on forse turnis the ee' – just as Chaucer saw it as part of the 'law of kind'; his Troilus is 'nobill' and shows 'knichtlie pietie'. These various spiritual or cos-mological powers or human qualities are associated, as in Chaucer's narra-tives, with love and the fate of lovers; all of them represent ideas which inter-ested Chaucer and which he had sometimes treated in extenso. Here I shall mention first the 'powers' – Nature and Fortune – then the admirable human qualities of Pite and Gentilesse, and discuss this last idea in greater detail.

Chaucer's 'noble goddese Nature', 'the vicaire of the almyghty Lord', presides over the vivid scenes in the park in *The Parlement of Foules*. Her realm is one of plenitude and the infinite variety of species, characterized by life, harmony, concord, and temperance – although here on earth there are plenty of examples of disharmony and excess, both tragic – as in the stories of sorrowful lovers depicted in the temple of Venus – and comic – in the arguments and quarrels of some of the birds. Nature is concerned with generation, with the continuation of life; the influence of this great central idea is suffused through all of Chaucer's works, expressing itself in a concern with 'naturalism', in descriptions of ideal beauty or of ideal landscape, in a loving attention to the details of a natural description, or to the contrarieties of species.

There is nothing surviving in Scotland which can match *The Parlement of Foules* as a vivid 'philosophical' poem. There are examples, of course, of 'spring openings' and ideal landscapes, in which there are sometimes echoes of Chaucer, and there are hints of some interest in the more general idea of Nature. In *The Kingis Quair*, for instance, in that scene reminiscent of the *Knight's Tale* in which the imprisoned author (soon to be 'converted' to love) looks out at the 'gardyn fair', hears the nightingales singing 'the ympnis consecrat / Of lufis use', and sees a lady of surpassing beauty – 'In every poynt so guydit hir mesure ... That Nature myght no more hir childe avance' – we have an obviously 'Chaucerian' collocation. And later in the poem there is a fine formal landscape with a catalogue of 'bestis ... mony diverse kynd' which is developed from the *Parlement*, but put to a different use. The river of crystal water is

> full of lytill fischis by the brym
> Now here now there with bakkis blewe as lede
> Lap and playit, and in a rout can swym
> So prattily, and dressit tham to sprede
> Thair curall fynnis as the ruby rede,
> That in the sonne on thair scalis bryght
> As gesserant ay glitterit in my sight.   (1065–71)

This is an elegant and appreciative echo and expansion of Chaucer's *Parlement* (187–9), where 'colde welle-stremes, nothyng dede / ... swymmen ful of smale fishes lighte, / With fynnes rede and skales sylver bryght'. Henryson too has a 'parliament' of 'fourfuttit beistis' of considerable variety in his fable of 'The Trial of the Fox', and prefaces his 'The Preaching of the Swallow' with a pageant of the seasons as part of a demonstration of the wisdom and providence of God that may be perceived through his creatures. But although something very like Chaucer's view of Nature and her domain informs his view of the animal and human world of the *Fables*, he seems less interested in formal or 'philosophical' analysis than in the dramatic portrayal of the disorder – both comic and tragic – in that orderly domain, and of the curious effects of 'contrarieties'. Dunbar, although we tend to notice the clever way he will allude to or adapt an individual Chaucerian phrase in a formal nature description (transforming, for instance 'the silver droppes hangynge on the leves' of the *Knight's Tale* into the more 'enamelled' 'The perly droppis schake in silvir schouris' of *The Goldyn Targe*), shows in his *The Thrissil and the Rois* that he can use the *Parlement of Foules* for larger purposes: there, when 'Dame Nature' summons all birds, animals, flowers and herbs to appear before her, the suggestion of her joyous plenitude and the triumphal songs of all the birds are part of the celebration of the forthcoming royal marriage (the 'occasion' is clearer in this poem than in the *Parlement*; and in a rather typically Scottish way, Dunbar, like Henryson, uses the scene for 'advice to princes' on the right rule of their domains). Finally, an example from outside the obviously 'Chaucerian' tradition: in that very merry tale, *Colkelbie Sow*, there is a typically skittish adaptation. When the unfortunate sow is on the point of being killed, there is a thrilling rescue by her own kind, introduced by the remarks

> I keip nocht now to commoun
> All beistis, for to blausoun
> Of that divers naturis,
> Complexionis and cullouris ...
> Nor of the foulis of the are,
> How sum with clos feit thay fare
> And sum devidit the nails,
> Nor of the fische with thair scalis.
> All this I set asyd now ...[5]

and by a comically elaborate demonstration that swine are 'luvand beistis', and much more loving than dogs are.

In the case of Fortune there is no such elaborately 'philosophical' starting-point as the *Parlement*. The little Boethian poem called *Fortune* with its dramatic opposition of the 'pleintif' and of (an eloquently defensive) Fortune gives a formal miniature of a conflict that is expressed more memorably in Chaucer's narratives in the speeches of various sufferers. Medieval artists of course were extremely fond of the depiction of the goddess with her wheel, often with the favoured climbing high upon it while the unfortunate are cast down; the literary equivalent of this scene, the long formal description (as in King Arthur's dream towards the end of the alliterative *Morte Arthure*) is not found in Chaucer. Like his follower Spenser later, he seems to prefer to allude to what was obviously an extremely familiar iconographical image: thus he says of the war of the Trojans and Greeks, that 'Fortune on lofte / And under eft gan hem to whielen bothe / After hir course' (*TC*, I, 138–40). But not only is he fully conversant with the various (mostly derogatory) descriptive terms applied to Fortune, and fascinated as a narrative poet by the often apparently unpredictable flux of events, but he constantly attempts to explore the meaning and nature of fortune, fate, destiny and chance, the roles of gods, planets, and spiritual powers.

Echoes of and parallels to these ideas and discussions can be found in the later Scottish writers, especially those of the more obviously 'Chaucerian' cast. With deliberation, the poet of *The Kingis Quair* describes how in his prison he read the book of Boethius, and how the reading provoked meditation on the power of Fortune, how 'that on hir tolter quhele / Every wight cleverith in his stage, / And failyng foting oft (quhen hir lest rele), / Sum up, sum doun: is non estate nor age / Ensured – more the prince than [is] the page' (57–61). Appropriately, in his dream he is later sent by Minerva (who has alluded to the clerkly disputes on freedom and predestination) to beseech Fortune for aid; when his spirit has descended 'to ground ageyne', he finds himself in a wonderful landscape, where the harmony of the sound of running water, and the amazing variety of animals seem almost to be a setting for the goddess Nature, instead of Fortune, who is there with her wheel, and a sinister pit beneath it. The formal description of the traditional image is unlike Chaucer's practice; in setting it in a terrestial landscape, idyllic but subject to change, James was no doubt recalling either a literary passage like that in the alliterative *Morte Arthure*, or one of those visual depictions which set the scene in a landscape. For Henryson too, the theme is a central one: like Chaucer, he has a narrative artist's fascination with the flux of events; and his more general and 'philosophical' treatments range from the tragic – in *The Testament of Cresseid*, with its dark and questioning presentation of the 'drerie destenye' imposed by the cruel gods – to the comic – as in the marvellous moment in 'The Fox, the Wolf, and the Husbandman' when the fox remarks to the unfortunate wolf disappearing down to the bottom of a well in a bucket, 'Schir ... thus fairis it off fortoun: / As ane cummis up, scho quheillis ane uther doun.' There is an ingenious satiric adaptation of the traditional Fortune with her wheel in Dunbar's poem on Antichrist (53.6 ff.) where in answer to the poet's complaint against her contrariousness, the goddess appears to him in a dream 'with ane fremmit cheir', insists on her power, advises him 'nocht to stryfe aganis my quheill', and prophesies that his troubled spirit will not find rest nor will he receive a benefice until an abbot clad in eagles' feathers shall fly in the air from east to west like a falcon (this will be a sign of the coming of Antichrist and of the impending end of the world). Dunbar keeps this 'nyce' dream hidden from everyone, until he hears it said that an abbot (Damian, of Tungland) is indeed planning a flight: 'Within my hairt confort I tuke full sone; / Adew, quod I, My drery dayis ar done ...'

The group of emotions covered by the words 'pite' or 'routhe' are often associated with the concept of 'gentilesse'. Chaucer is fond of remarking that it 'renneth soone in gentil hert'. He extends it from its traditional courtly role as one of the qualities of the beloved lady to a much more powerful and intense emotion in love and in other human relationships. It is a desideratum in a 'gentil' ruler (the Parson quotes Seneca to the effect that a man in high estate should show 'debonairetee and pitee' to his subjects); it is sometimes almost indistinguishable from a religious concept of compassion or of charity; it is sometimes aroused by the sight of patient suffering (Patience is, of course, one of the traditional means of overcoming the slings and arrows of outrageous Fortune); it is a natural affection, associated especially with the tender hearts of women. It is not hard to find echoes of these ideas. In *The Kingis Quair*, for instance, the 'womanly pity' of the goddess Venus is such that because of the cruel 'unkindness' of men on earth she weeps down crystal tears from which spring fragrant flowers. In Henryson, the quality is shown by the 'gentill' Troilus, and is vehemently expressed by the narrator in the *Testament* when he laments the cruelty of the 'crabbit' gods; in the rough world of the *Fables*, it is rarely straightforward: a fox finds his father dead, and 'throw naturall pietie', picks up the corpse, carries it to the peat-hole full of water and tosses it in, 'and to the Deuill he gaif his banis to keip'. Dunbar makes a traditional appeal in a love poem to the lady's 'womanlie petie' (12:28); and, like Chaucer and Henryson, he will sometimes generate ironic undertones: the Widow in *The Tretis of the Tua Mariit Wemen and the Wedo* feigns sorrow and tears for her departed spouse so successfully that all are moved to wonder at the way she 'lelely . . . luffit hir husband': 'Yone is a pete to enprent in a princis hert, / That sic a perle of plesance suld yone pane dre!'

The frequent occurrence in Chaucer's writings of the word 'gentilesse' – and associated words for 'nobility' or various 'noble' qualities, like 'curteisie' or 'honour' or 'trouthe' – is an obvious indication of a long-standing interest in this complex of ideas.[6] Chaucer seems to share a general view that 'nobility' of behaviour should be expected of those of noble birth, although it is not necessarily dependent on noble birth. 'Gentil' can of course mean simply 'nobly-born' as well as 'noble in spirit'; a kind of 'courtly' or 'chivalric' gentilesse can perhaps be distinguished, which suffuses works like the *Knight's Tale* or *Troilus and Criseyde*. Here 'gentil' speech or deeds are recognized and admired by others, and honour – the desire to have 'a passant name' – is important, as well as generosity of spirit. But gentilesse is also a quality ascribed to the Virgin Mary; there is an ideal of saintly gentilesse which finds its truest exemplum in Christ. Chaucer also seems to have been especially interested in the idea of 'true nobility' or 'nobility of soul': the contention which argues strongly that nobility does *not* depend on birth or lineage. This ancient idea, influenced by Christian concepts of the equality of souls before God or the paradox of 'humility' fused with 'sublimity' in the incarnation of Christ, came to Chaucer from Seneca, Juvenal, Boethius, Jean de Meun, and, especially, Dante. It is a tradition which seems to have appealed particularly to 'intellectual' writers (significantly it is taken up and discussed by the later Italian humanists).

In Scotland, it is easy to find examples of 'chivalric' or 'courtly' gentilesse, the nobility of heart that is ideally found in noble knights and ladies. In Dunbar, for instance, a personified Gentrise is one of the companions of Suete Womanhede in *The Goldyn Targe* (10.165); it is one of the ideal qualities of a lady in the lyric 'Sweit rois of vertew and of gentilnes' (8.1) and is used in the eulogy of Margaret Tudor in *The Thrissill and the Rois* (50.175), where the nightingale sings, 'Haill Naturis suffragene / in bewty, nurtour and every nobilnes, / In riche array, renown and gentilnes'. In 'Into this Warld may none assure' (63.26) he laments its demise in this wicked world in those of high estate: 'All gentrice and nobilitie / Ar passit out of he degre'. 'Nobility' is a necessary quality in rulers: in a characteristically Scottish 'advice to princes' passage in *The Thrissill and the Rois*, Nature alludes to the idea when she adjures the 'awfull Thrissill' to be 'discreit' – 'Nor latt no wyld weid full of churlichenes / Compair hir till the lileis nobilnes.'

Outside the 'Chaucerian' makars, the tradition seems to have flourished from the time of Barbour's *Bruce*, where the king is presented both as a tenth 'Worthy' and as an ideal commander, uniting in the heroic manner valour and prudence. But although much in the *Bruce* sounds like echoes of earlier heroic poetry, Barbour can delight in the 'chivalric' surface of things – knights in their armour shining like angels – and the excitement of battle. The splendour of 'courtesy' is assumed and celebrated in the later Scottish romances, like *Lancelot of the Laik* or *Clariodus*; in *Golagros and Gawane* the 'gentrice' of Gawain, that legendary 'flower of courtesy', is expressed in a finely generous gesture towards his defeated opponent. These romances are similar to the chivalric literature of late medieval France and Burgundy.

Such interests also lie behind some non-fictional works. There seems, for instance, to have been – as in England and France – a taste for manuals of chivalry and war. There is a Scottish version of Caxton's *Order of Chivalry*. And there is a translation (by Andrew Cadiou) of Alain Chartier's *Le Breviaire des nobles*, *The Porteous of Noblenes*, which was printed by Chepman and Myllar in 1508.[7] Chartier's work consists of a series of ballades which define *noblesse* and its duties; *Noblesce* herself 'appears' first, and introduces the twelve cardinal virtues of a noble life: Foppy [Faith], Loyaulté [Lawté or Treuth], Honneur, Droiture [Ressoun], Proesce [Worthyness], Amour, Courtoisie, Diligence, Necteté [Clenlyness], Largesce, Sobresse [Soberness], and Perseverance. This statement of a code, a 'manuel où la chevalerie était invitée à prendre chaque jour sa leçon de morale nécessaire à son relèvement',[8] seems to have been immensely popular in France; no doubt in Scotland it appealed both to an interest in 'chivalry' and in the proper conduct of rulers. The *Porteous* is in fact more than a curiosity; it is an example of highly competent Scottish prose, with the retention of the recurring refrains of the verse original giving a curiously interesting rhythmical effect. We also have a reference to another favourite medieval didactic 'chivalric' kind, the biography of a real-life 'flower of chivalry' (like that of Bayard by the 'Loyal Serviteur'). Lord Bernard Stewart of Aubigny (*c.* 1447–1508), a famous Scottish general in the French service, called like Bayard 'un grand chevalier sans reproche', was certainly one of these.[9] His return to Scotland in 1508 was celebrated by Dunbar in a ballade, where he is described (35.81) as 'prynce of fredom and flour of gentilnes'. Here Dunbar promises to return to record at length his great deeds 'in France, in Bertan, in Naplis and Lumbardy'. But Stewart died in Scotland,

and all that Dunbar has left us is an elegy for this 'flour of chevalrie'. For a surviving Scottish 'chivalric biography' we have to wait until the mid-sixteenth-century *Historie of Squyer Meldrum* by David Lindsay,[10] a very lively verse account of the success of this soldier in war and in love. His deeds like 'the famous deidis / Of our nobil progenitouris' should be a mirror to us, inspiring us to follow 'Vertuous deidis ... And vicious leving to eschew' (unlike the great Lancelot, Meldrum was no adulterer). With this, and with other examples of 'chivalric' literature, we are often close to the splendid pageantry and martial excitement of the *Knight's Tale*.

Henryson seems to have been much less attracted to this 'chivalric' gentilesse than other Scottish writers. At the beginning of his *Orpheus and Eurydice* he uses the traditional idea that the recording of the great deeds of noble ancestors will incline the heart of a prince or lord 'the more to vertu and to worthynes, / Herand reherse his eldirs gentilnes', but his evocations of the glittering scenes of courtly life are brief and plangent. Thus Cresseid, among the lepers, in her lament sorrowfully recalls former scenes of happiness: 'Quhair is thy garding with thir greissis gay ... / Quhair thou was wont full merilye in May / To walk and talk the dew be it was day ... / With ladyis fair in carrolling to gane / And se the royall rinkis in thair ray ...?' When she has been admitted to the leper-house there is a moment of bitter satire, when the lepers presuming that she was 'of nobill kin' took her in 'with better will'. One element in her 'passion' is that she has to suffer in an extreme form the lot of common forked humanity. And yet the brief upward movement at the end of the poem, when she comes to a kind of self-knowledge, seems to be set off by the memory of the love of the 'gentil' and 'nobill' Troilus, who rides past 'royallie' with his knights.

The world of the animal fable is not one in which this kind of 'gentilesse' is likely to flourish; but in the *Fables* we can see Henryson using the words 'gentill' and 'gentrice' in a variety of ways, ironic and serious. In this world, the appearances of things are deceptive, and it is hard for creatures to see clearly. Thus the cock, confronted by a splendid jewel, praises it for its nobility – 'O gentill jasp, O riche and nobill thing ... Thow art ane jouell for ane lord or king' – and rejects it because 'it ganis not for me' – 'Rise, gentill jasp, of all stanis the flour ... Thow ganis not for me, nor I for the.' But the *moralitas* makes all this ironic. The cock has been deceived; the jasp is not 'gentill' because of its appearance and monetary value, but because of its hidden inner meaning – 'this gentill jasp ... betakinnis perfite prudence and cunning'. Elsewhere we are shown, in traditional Aesopic fashion, that it is perilous for creatures to move out of their 'estate' – as in the case of the wether pretending to be a dog (which shows, says the *moralitas*, 'that riches of array / Will cause pure men presumpteous for to be' (2595–6)), or the cock who succumbs to the flattery of the fox (a figure of 'nyse proud men, woid and vaneglorious / Of kin and blude, quhilk is presumpteous' (591–2)). Nobility of spirit is usually commented on because it is absent. The mean-spirited 'churl' in 'The Preaching of the Swallow', who sows the seed and sets nets to catch the birds is said to be 'of gentrice spoliate' (1895; and is a figure of the fiend). Those in positions of power regularly act in a way which is cruelly 'un-gentle'. In 'The Sheep and the Dog' for instance, the unjust persecution of the sheep by the wicked wolf-judge is moralized as the oppression of the 'pure commounis' by 'tirrane men',[11] and the sheep in its lament bitterly complains of the abuses of this cruel upside down world: 'The pure is peillit, the lord may do na mis / Now is he blyith with okker maist may wyn; / Gentrice is slane, and pitie is ago' (1309–12). (The opposition of the outgoing, altruistic generous impulses of 'gentrice' and 'pitie' and the mean, self-obsessed 'cursit syn of covetice' is a common one.) An idea of 'true nobility' clearly underlies the 'advice to princes' doctrine of 'The Lion and the Mouse' where the humble mouse's appeal to the 'gentrice' (1461) of the mighty lion produces an act of 'pitie' and mercy that is recommended to 'lordis of prudence'.

It is noteworthy that Henryson seems more interested than Chaucer in working out the implications of these ideas in contemporary social life, and much less in the intense, abstract discussion of 'true nobility' that we find in the *Wife of Bath's Tale*. It may well be that this is partly because he is less involved than Chaucer was with earlier treatments (notably that of Dante), and partly because contacts with Italian humanism seem to have been later in Scotland than in England (where we have, for instance, Tiptoft in the fifteenth century translating one of the many humanist treatises on 'true nobility'). But the idea is certainly there in Henryson, and it is probably true to say that he holds 'that "nobility" is a condition accessible to every individual, no matter what his social station'.[12] At the end of the period, there is another more general treatment of 'nobility' in Douglas's *Palice of Honour*. And that ideas of true 'gentilesse' were current in fifteenth-century Scotland may be shown by a couple of comic examples outside the 'Chaucerian' tradition.

In the second part of *Colkelbie Sow* there is an episode – half romance, half parody – in which Colkelbie meets an old man with 'a pretty maid' twelve years old – 'But suth to say scho was not lyk to be /A worldly wicht, so windir fair wes sche, / So weill nurtourit as scho had nurischeit bene / In closter or court, dochter to kyng or quene.' 'This amiable innocent Adria', who sounds like a romance version of Griselda or Virginia, is the daughter of a mysterious palmer; she marries Colkelbie's son Flannislie, and they rise to high estate in France. In the even more high-spirited *Taill of Rauf Coilyear* (an adaptation of the 'king-in disguise' motif), the emperor Charlemagne finds lodging with a tetchy collier, whose very first rough answer provokes the ironic remark 'Thow semis a nobill fallow, thy answer is sa fyne', and there follows a stream of allusions to 'courtesy': the king standing back to allow Rauf to go in first is called 'uncourtes' ('gif thow of courtasie couth, thow hes foryet it clene') and seized by the neck. A similar piece of 'forgetfulness' earns him a blow under the ear, and another reproof – 'thow suld be courtes of kynd and ane cunnand courteir'. And so it continues. In spite of his wife's warning, 'it is not my counsall bot yone man that ye knew / To do yow in his gentrise', Rauf fulfils his promise to visit his unknown guest at court. Another comic contest in 'courtesy' with the knight Roland, and a splendidly uneasy moment when he sees the emperor in all his magnificence ('To ken kingis courtasie, the devill come to me, / And sa I hope I may say or I chaip heir . . .'), the 'carll' is made a knight 'for his courtasie'. Not the least of the poem's comic excellences is the even-handed way it deals with obsessive single-mindedness in both 'gentils' and 'carls'.

With the possible exceptions of Henryson and Douglas, none of the later Scottish writers can lay claim to the title of 'un grand poète philosophique', but in a variety of ways one can see them grappling with the ideas that fascinated Chaucer, and producing different treatments and answers. It is clear that those cosmological and ethical questions which so engaged Chaucer continued to excite interest and argument.

NOTES

1 *The Kingis Quair*, ed. J. Norton-Smith (Oxford, 1971), ll. 1374–5 (but they were also 'superlative . . . /In moralitee'); Henryson, *Testament of Cresseid*, in *The Poems of Robert Henryson*, ed. Denton Fox (Oxford, 1981), l. 59; Dunbar, *The Goldyn Targe*, in *The Poems of William Dunbar*, ed. J. Kinsley (Oxford, 1979), l. 257; (all references to these poets are taken from these editions).

2 The phrase is that of Deschamps; the idea is one that has been stressed by Derek Brewer in his various studies of Chaucer.

3 *The Quare of Jelusy*, ed. J. Norton-Smith and I. Pravda (Heidelberg, 1976).

4 *The Asloan Manuscript*, ed. W. A. Craigie, *Scottish Text Society*, NS 14 (1923), I, pp. 271–98.

5 *Colkelbie Sow*, in *Colkelbie Sow and the Talis of the Fyve Bestes*, ed. Gregory Kratzmann (Garland Medieval Texts 6, New York and London, 1983), ll. 187–97.

6 Cf. D. Gray, 'Chaucer and Gentilesse', in *One Hundred Years of English Studies in Dutch Universities*, ed. G. H. V. Bunt, E. S. Kooper, J. L. Mackenzie, and D. R. M. Wilkinson (Groningen, 1987), pp. 1–27.

7 There is also a copy of the Asloan MS. (ed. Craigie, I, pp. 171–84); French text in *The Poetical Works of Alain Chartier*, ed. J. C. Laidlaw (Cambridge, 1974), pp. 393–409.

8 P. Champion, *Histoire poétique du quinzième siècle* (Paris, 1923), I, p. 92.

9 Cf. D. Gray, 'A Scottish "Flower of Chivalry" and his Book', *Words*, 4 (1974), pp. 22–34.

10 Ed. J. Kinsley (London and Edinburgh, 1959).

11 Similarly in 'The Wolf and the Lamb', the tyrannical wolf is a figure of three kinds of 'ravenous wolves': fraudulent lawyers, 'mychtie men', and 'men of heritage' who oppress their tenants.

12 See Robert L. Kindrick, 'Kings and Rustics: Henryson's Definition of Nobility in *The Morall Fabillis*' in *Proc. of the 3rd International Conference on Scottish Language and Literature (Medieval and Renaissance)*, ed. R. J. Lyall and F. Riddy (Stirling and Glasgow, 1981, pp. 271–81), p. 275.

7

The planetary gods in Chaucer and Henryson

JILL MANN[1]

Cresseid's vision of the planetary gods occupies a position of central importance in *The Testament of Cresseid*. It is by far the longest of the static rhetorical
set-pieces which punctuate the poem, and it constitutes the pivotal moment
in Cresseid's passage from prosperity to misery. The visual power of the
linked series of portraits lodges it securely within the sequence of mental
images – the aged poet huddled by the fire in his 'oratur', the deformed
Cresseid, the jewels showered into her lap – into which the poem resolves
itself in the memory. In giving the planetary gods a role in the narrative
dynamics of his poem, Henryson is following in the steps of 'worthie
Chaucer glorious' – the Chaucer of the *Knight's Tale* and the *Complaint of
Mars* as well as of *Troilus and Criseyde*. In what follows, I propose to examine
both the resemblances and the differences between the two poets in their use
of this cosmological dimension to the narrative action; they will not only
reveal the intelligence and creativity of Henryson's response to Chaucer, but
will also lead into an understanding of the structural principle underlying
the *Testament* and of Henryson's conception of his own relation to its
subject.[2]

Chaucer's introduction of the planetary gods into his poetic narratives has
as its single most important effect the creation of an enlarged perspective on
the course of events.[3] This opening-out of perspective is most vividly – and
disturbingly – felt in Book III of *Troilus and Criseyde*, where the cosy domestic
interior of Pandarus' supper-party suddenly gives way to a vision of the dark
forces of the wheeling cosmos outside.

> And after soper gonnen they to rise,
> At ese wel, with herte fresshe and glade;
> And wel was hym that koude best devyse
> To liken hire, or that hire laughen made:
> He song; she pleyde; he tolde tale of Wade.
> But at the laste, as every thyng hath ende,
> She took hire leve, and nedes wolde wende.

> But O Fortune, executrice of wierdes,
> O influences of thise hevenes hye!
> Soth is, that under God ye ben oure hierdes,
> Though to us bestes ben the causez wrie.
> This mene I now: for she gan homward hye,
> But execut was al bisyde hire leve
> The goddes wil, for which she moste bleve.
>
> The bente moone with hire hornes pale,
> Saturne and Jove, in Cancro joyned were,
> That swych a reyn from heven gan avale
> That every maner womman that was there
> Hadde of that smoky reyn a verray feere;
> At which Pandare tho lough, and seyde thenne,
> 'Now were it tyme a lady to gon henne!'   (610–30)

The shift in perspective here makes itself felt in the phrase 'us bestes'; the human scale is diminished, and men dwindle to beasts seen from the 'hevenes hye' crawling on the surface of the earth below. The shift in perspective is accompanied by a change of mood: a sinister note of foreboding strikes across the cheerful security of the supper-party, heralding and anticipating the doom-laden atmosphere of Books IV and V. But the change of mood is only one of the effects of this sudden change in perspective: even more important is its function as a dramatic representation of the limits of human knowledge and human control. Pandarus, securely measuring the world by the human scale, sees only the convenience of the rain, arriving as he had forecast, to provide a plausible excuse for Criseyde to stay overnight. The limits of this human-centred perspective are made apparent to the reader by the sense of contraction as we return to the domestic cheerfulness of the dinner-party in the last two lines: Pandarus' laughter, in its turn cutting across the mood of disquiet represented by the women's fear, with brilliant economy re-establishes the gaiety of the opening stanza, but it also makes us conscious of Pandarus' obliviousness to all but his own concerns. Despite his earlier care in consulting the astrological omens (II, 74–5), Pandarus fails to take into account the planetary conjunction which is the antecedent cause of the rain, a conjunction in which the benign effects of Jupiter are outweighed by the malevolent association of Saturn and the moon in Cancer.[4] Under this conjunction, the love-affair of Troilus and Criseyde is consummated, and its malevolent effects are realized in the unhappy end to their love.

We are not, of course, to blame the whole tragedy on Pandarus' failure to consult his astrological tables; it is rather that his inability to comprehend the full range of the forces at work in the situation he so confidently believes he is manipulating represents for us the inevitable limits of the human grasp on the causes and the control of events. The planetary gods here stand for everything that the human-scale view of events leaves out of account: the vast area of the unknowable, of future and contingent events. The planets in this conjunction are not chosen simply for their malevolent nature, but for what more precisely they represent: Saturn (by virtue of his Greek name Kronos) represents Time, and the moon, Change.[5] Time and Change bring the love between Troilus and Criseyde to fruition; Time and Change will destroy it. We can see already how perceptive a reader of Chaucer Henryson was, for he identifies the same two planetary gods – Saturn and the moon – as responsible for Cresseid's harsh fate.[6] In Chaucer, Time and Change bring about her treachery, in Henryson they bring about its punishment.

This same shift in perspective is the most important function of the debate between the planetary gods in Chaucer's *Knight's Tale*. From the human point of view, Arcite's death is 'an accident'; his horse suddenly shies and he is thrown, with fatal consequences. The hidden cause of this, made visible to the reader though not to the figures in the story, is the 'furie infernal' sent by Saturn. Saturn does not, however, in this tale act as a free agent; he acts as a planet. It is in his planetary role that he describes himself, itemizing the disastrous effects of his baleful influence.

> 'My cours, that hath so wyde for to turne,
> Hath moore power than woot any man.
> Myn is the drenchyng in the see so wan ...
> I do vengeance and pleyn correcioun,
> Whil I dwelle in the signe of the leoun ...
> My lookyng is the fader of pestilence ...'   (2454–69)

It is his planetary role that gives Saturn the power to determine Arcite's fate, since his 'wyde cours' subordinates all the planets beneath him to his influence. And the other 'gods' too act not with divine freedom, but in accordance with their planetary natures: Mars and Venus respond favourably to the prayers of Arcite and Palamon not out of personal choice, but because they are appealed to at the appropriate astrological moments, the hours when they are most susceptible to earthly influence.[7] Palamon and Arcite therefore in one sense determine their own fates, but in getting – literally – what they asked for, they also get *more* than they asked for. The limits of human comprehension and control are again dramatized. The forces they activate wear to them the personal aspect of gods, but their power resides in their impersonal role as planets – planets whose movements and influences are determined not by themselves, but by the First Mover, whose controlling presence behind the planetary debate is as invisible to us as the controlling presence of the planetary gods is to the spectators of the tournament, and of which we are reminded only in Theseus' long final speech.[8]

Identifying the planetary gods as 'hidden causes' of the catastrophe does not, that is, involve identifying them as its *ultimate* causes. The perspective of the First Mover, seeing all things and all causes in a single moment of eternity, is one that by definition lies beyond human comprehension; the illumination afforded by the sudden shift to the planetary perspective can only teach us to imagine that yet another perspective is possible, not afford us access to it. The enlargement of vision that comes with the shift to the cosmic scale yields not knowledge but a realization of ignorance; it reveals the play of unseen and incalculable forces which will always endow human actions with repercussions and consequences unimagined by the human actors. Attempting to fashion the world into the shape of their own designs, human beings are unwitting pawns in the hands of greater powers fashioning larger designs of their own.

Yet, as I have already suggested, these larger powers are likewise pawns involuntarily acting out larger designs.[9] Their very role as planets instructs us in this: their motions – and thus their effects – are involuntary, determined by the physical laws of the universe. Chaucer's *Complaint of Mars* derives its witty comedy from precisely this equivocation between a conception of the planetary gods as persons, endowed with freedom of choice and action, and a conception of them as astral bodies, inexorably moved on their courses by the laws of the cosmos. The 'love-affair' between Mars and Venus is created by a temporary conjunction between the planets, and it comes to an inevitable end as their planetary motions separate them once more and bring Venus into contiguity with Mercury instead.[10] If, in the *Knight's Tale* and *Troilus and Criseyde*, the planetary gods scatter human misery in their wake, provoking bitter human complaints against their callous injustice, in the *Complaint of Mars* we see one of these same planetary gods himself reduced to the same uncomprehending misery and helplessly questioning the purpose of God's design. With a blasphemy even more far-reaching than Cresseid's, he accuses God not merely of having destroyed his happiness, but of taking a sadistic pleasure in instilling in men the passionate desire for what will prove to be their ruin.

> Hit semeth he hath to lovers enmyte,
> And lyk a fissher, as men alday may se,
> Baiteth hys angle-hok with som plesaunce
> Til many a fissh ys wod til that he be
> Sesed therwith; and then at erst hath he
> Al his desir, and therwith al myschaunce;
> And thogh the lyne breke, he hath penaunce;
> For with the hok he wounded is so sore
> That he his wages hath for evermore. (236–44)

He compares his lady's beauty to the magical power of the legendary brooch of Thebes, which created in those who beheld it an obsessional desire to possess it, and in those who possessed it, an obsessional fear of losing it (245–56). Just as its victims might blame their unhappiness not on themselves, but on the craftsman who had given the brooch its dreadful power, so it is God who is to be blamed for creating the beauty which lures men to their destruction.

> So fareth hyt by lovers and by me;
> For thogh my lady have so gret beaute
> That I was mad til I had gete her grace,

> She was not cause of myn adversite,
> But he that wroghte her, also mot I the,
> That putte such a beaute in her face,
> That made me coveyten and purchace
> Myn oune deth – hym wite I that I dye,
> And myn unwit that ever I clamb so hye.   (263–71)

The poem offers no answer to this passionate accusation; we are left with the vision of a universe where the planets, like men, are the helpless victims of a divine will whose motivations and sympathies remain totally inscrutable.

These, then, are the poetic purposes for which Chaucer introduces the planetary gods into his narratives, despite his declaration in the more sober 'scientific' mood appropriate to the *Treatise on the Astrolabe*, that 'these ben observaunces of judicial matere and rytes of payens, in whiche my spirit hath no feith' (ii, iv). And Henryson uses them for the same poetic purposes in the *Testament of Cresseid*, to the extent that he too achieves a simultaneous vision of voluntary and involuntary action by representing the physical forces of the cosmos in the personalized form of gods.[11] 'In themselves', as MacQueen points out, 'they are neither friendly nor hostile; they are the indifferent laws of the universe' – laws which express themselves in the natural processes of 'time and change, growth and decay'.[12] It is these laws which 'punish' Cresseid's infidelities with leprosy; the parallel conception that she is punished for her 'blasphemy' against Venus and Cupid represents the 'intentionalist' view of the universe to which Cresseid, at this point in the poem, stubbornly clings.[13] It is, in other words, an allegorical fiction which functions properly only when it is penetrated – as it is when Cresseid renounces her view of supernatural malevolence to identify the sources of her misery in herself: 'Nane but my self as now I will accuse' (574). Like Troilus and Criseyde consummating their love under the auspices of Saturn and the moon, Cresseid has unwittingly entwined her own actions with the movements of forces greater than herself, which will absorb those actions into their own operations and lend them consequences beyond the reach of her will. Cresseid's final lament shows an acceptance of this larger cosmic life, of 'the way things are', in that she abandons her intentionalist view of the universe; she ceases to seek for causes outside herself and instead turns inwards to examine herself and her own contributory role in determining the way things are – the only area of the cosmos over which she has control and for which she is responsible.[14] But recognition of this contributory role necessarily carries with it the recognition that it is now too late for it to be retracted or for its effects to be reversed. It is, therefore, a kind of Stoic acceptance of her degradation that animates her final lament, rather than Christian remorse and penitence. A. C. Spearing acutely comments on the 'factual quality' which marks Henryson's presentation of suffering in this poem, and observes that this 'factuality' extends to embrace the retrospective contemplation of Cresseid's willed actions themselves. In this poem, 'the concept of misfortune

... include[s] the sins men *choose* to commit'.[15] It is a factuality that is both harsh, in its refusal to pretend that things can be otherwise, and compassionate, in its clear-sighted recognition of this very harshness.[16]

Henryson, then, like Chaucer, uses the planetary gods as a poetic means of representing man's need to recognize his place in a universe whose laws are enacted through him and yet irrespective of him. Yet there are differences between his presentation of the planetary gods and Chaucer's which are significant of the specific functions they have to serve in the *Testament*. The first of these differences is a simple – but crucial – change in the direction in which the cosmos is imaginatively traversed. Chaucer's creations of a cosmic perspective all take the form of a movement upwards and outwards. The imagination soars to the outermost limits of the universe and thence turns to gaze back on the 'litel spot of erthe' far below. In these aerial flights Chaucer is following a long and rich literary tradition. Troilus rising through the cosmos to 'the holughnesse of the eighthe spere' (v, 1809) imitates not only Boccaccio's Arcita, but also the flight of Boethius' Philosophy.[17] Chaucer himself, rising aloft in the clutches of the eagle, repeats Dante's upward flight to Purgatory in the talons of the same bird,[18] and compares his experience with the cosmic ascents described by Martianus Capella and Alan of Lille (985–90).[19] In the *Parliament of Fowls*, Chaucer recapitulates Cicero's *Somnium Scipionis* in recounting the vision of 'the lytel erthe' vouchsafed to Scipio from the 'sterry place' to which his ancestor Africanus had led him.[20] In all these cases, the aerial flight represents a liberation from earthly concerns; the elevation to a higher plane of being or understanding. And it is the same sort of elevation we are temporarily granted in the narrative passages from *Troilus* and the *Knight's Tale* examined earlier.

Henryson's *Testament* makes a striking contrast to this venerable tradition. For here the order in which the planets appear suggests a movement *downwards and inwards*, beginning with Saturn as outermost of the planets and working down in order as far as the moon. This downward motion is emphasized by the fact that the planetary gods themselves descend from their spheres to appear in assembly before Cresseid. This simple inversion of the normal upwards and outwards movement creates a sinister effect of claustrophobia; the cosmos seems to be bearing down on Cresseid. This same downwards and inwards movement is found in Henryson's *Orpheus and Eurydice*, where it has a moral significance, spelled out in the conclusion of the poem: the intellective part of the soul, represented by Orpheus, is forced to descend from heaven to the depths of the earth to which its appetitive part, represented by Eurydice, is by nature confined (428–34; 445–54).[21] But in the *Testament* the descent has emotional rather than moral significance: we feel the weight of circumstance that Cresseid has to bear. The universe is 'top-heavy'; man's smallest actions invoke a crushing burden of inevitable consequence. It is by this apparently simple stroke that Henryson achieves much of the grim atmosphere of his poem.

The second difference between Henryson's planetary gods and Chaucer's is less easy to isolate, but is nevertheless, I think, perceptible. It consists in the greater degree of formal stylization which characterizes Henryson's portraits, and which gives them the static pictorial quality of emblems. Chaucer provides something of a model for this pictorial method of presentation in his portraits of Venus, Mars and Diana in his descriptions of their respective temples in the *Knight's Tale*. Yet the parallel is not exact, for the reason that the static pictorial quality is here appropriate to the fact that Chaucer is describing not the gods themselves, but artistic representations of them; when we later see the gods in action in the planetary debate, they are not described at all.[22] Moreover, whereas Henryson's portraits resolve themselves smoothly into coherent visual terms (an artist could take them as a set of instructions), Chaucer's descriptions accumulate a set of visually unco-ordinated features, which sometimes seem to belong to a statue and sometimes to a painting. (The difficulty of translating these descriptions into visual terms is amply evident in both the preliminary sketches and the final versions of Burne-Jones's illustrations to these passages in the Kelmscott Chaucer.)[23] The link between Henryson's portraits and the self-consciously decorative use of descriptions of the pagan deities in a work such as the *Assembly of Gods* is much more evident.[24] There is nothing of this late-medieval 'encyclopedic' feeling in the informal spontaneity of Chaucer's handling of iconography.

The emblematic nature of Henryson's portrait-sequence is not however simply a manifestation of fifteenth-century taste: it draws attention to an equally formal pattern on which the sequence is founded – a pattern of opposition. The menacing picture of the aged Saturn, old, ugly, hung about with ice and hail, is followed by the mellow description of Jupiter, vigorous, handsome, garlanded with flowers, benevolently counteracting the disastrous effects of his father's influence. Mars and Phoebus form a similarly contrasting pair: the god of war appropriately fierce and glowering, the sun-god appropriately radiant and life-giving. The last of these contrasting pairs is formed by Mercury and Cynthia, with the traditional conception of each in this case delicately 'touched up' to accommodate it to the pattern. Thus Mercury is presented with positive emphasis on his skill in rhetoric, music and medicine, and as attractively clothed in scarlet and fur, while his traditional role as god of theft, cheating and lying, is blandly inverted in Henryson's assurance that he was 'Honest and gude, and not ane word culd lie' (252). Cynthia, on the other hand, has no trace of the virgin beauty of the huntress Diana. Her colour is leaden and muddied, her clothing 'gray and full of spottis blak', and decorated with the bent, thornladen figure of the Man in the Moon. The odd man out in the sequence of contrasting pairs is, it will be seen, the planet Venus, who nevertheless fits into the pattern by virtue of containing a whole set of oppositions within herself.

Venus was thair present, that goddes gay,
Hir sonnis querrel for to defend, and mak
Hir awin complaint, cled in ane nyce array,
The ane half grene, the vther half sabill blak,
With hair as gold kemmit and sched abak;
Bot in hir face semit gret variance,
Quhyles perfyte treuth and quhyles inconstance.

Vnder smyling scho was dissimulait,
Prouocatiue with blenkis amorous,
And suddanely changit and alterait,
Angrie as ony serpent vennemous,
Richt pungitiue with wordis odious;
Thus variant scho was, quha list tak keip:
With ane eye lauch, and with the vther weip,

In taikning that all fleschlie paramour,
Quhilk Venus hes in reull and gouernance,
Is sum tyme sweit, sum tyme bitter and sour,
Richt unstabill and full of variance,
Mingit with cairfull ioy and fals plesance,
Now hait, now cauld, now blyith, now full of wo,
Now grene as leif, now widderit and ago.   (218–38)

This picture of Venus, as critics have noted, has more in common with
Chaucer's pictures of Fortune than with the traditional iconography of
Venus, 'naked, fletynge in the large se', with her garland of roses and her
fluttering doves.[25] Henryson presents love as an experience which concen-
trates in a particularly acute form the alternation of ecstasy and pain, beauty
and ugliness, which constitutes the experience of man's life – or woman's life.
For Cresseid's history is in itself an illustration of Venus' 'gret variance'; the
goddess's shifts from 'perfyte treuth' to 'inconstaunce' are an iconographic
reflection of her own instability.[26]

This emblematic sequence of portraits thus formulates the cosmos in terms
of a binary principle of contrast, which juxtaposes youth and age, benevolence
and cruelty, beauty and ugliness, sweet and sour, without diminishing or
blurring the opposition between them.[27] And in this respect the portrait-
sequence formalizes and focusses a pattern of contrasts that runs through the
whole of the *Testament*. The importance of this pattern was eloquently
conveyed several decades ago by Kurt Wittig: 'From the opening contrast
between bleak cold and ardent love to the epitaph "lait lipper lyis deid"
written in letters of gold, sustained thematic contrast is the source from which
the immense tension of the *Testament* arises.'[28] More recently, Douglas Gray
has spoken of 'the great oppositions of the poem – cold and hot, "faded" and
"green" love, age and youth, ugliness and beauty', and commented 'in the
manner of a tragedy it holds contraries in tension'.[29] This binary perception of
experience determines Henryson's choice of the 'ubi sunt' form for the next
rhetorical set-piece of the poem. The 'ubi sunt' mould likewise juxtaposes

unmediated extremes: joy and misery, beauty and ugliness, luxury and penury, past and present (this last most important of all, as we shall see). The last of the visual images that the poem lodges in our mind is, significantly, an image of startling contrast: the hideously deformed leper with the shower of jewels in her lap. The epitaph that Troilus writes for Cresseid represents her history in terms of contrasting extremes without attempting a reconciliation between them: 'flour of womanheid' – 'lait lipper' (608–9). The 'factual' tone of the poem allows these contradictions to exist without attempting to explain or suppress them. Wittig comments on the 'tightlipped reticence' which is 'achieved by Henryson's use of contrast. When pathos seems to rise to the highest pitch, the poet looks away and sees the common reality of every day'. The devastating infliction of leprosy on Cresseid is followed by the ordinariness of the child's arrival to announce supper.[30]

Chaucer too, of course, conceives of the story of Troilus and Criseyde as illustrative of a principle of change and alternation, the inevitable passage from 'wo to wele' and back again. But Henryson gives us a far greater sense of strain in the baffling suddenness of the passage from one to the other. This is partly due to the different scale of his poem: Chaucer's far longer narrative can absorb the processes of change into the leisurely passage of time, while in Henryson the change is dramatic and abrupt. But it is also due to the greater prominence Henryson gives to *physical* suffering. Here again he differs from Chaucer, whose interest is almost entirely in mental and emotional suffering. His description of Arcite's death constitutes the only exception, and it is interesting that this occurs in a tale which had so much else to contribute to Henryson's *Testament*. In the medical details of Arcite's death we find indeed the same grim factuality as pervades the whole of Henryson's poem. Meta- physics gives way to the simple physiological facts: the 'whys' which Arcite's death calls forth are here answered by the simple logic of the laws of matter. Why did Arcite die? Because the 'clothered blood, for any lechecraft, / Corrupteth ...' – and so on, through the grim vision of a man as a collection of blood and lung-pipes and muscles, as a machine which simply ceases to function. But this is, in the whole of Chaucer's poetry, an isolated and unusual moment. When, in the *Complaint of Mars*, Mars responds to his loss of love by raising the eternal question 'why?', it is the suffering caused by beauty of which he complains. Henryson's conception of suffering makes this version of it seem a luxury: beauty may be terrible in its effects, but far more terrible is the loss of beauty, the hideous bodily deformation that annihilates person and identity.

In inventing this terrible form of punishment for Cresseid, Henryson appears to many critics much more cruel to her than Chaucer,[31] and he has in the past been blamed for the generally harsher attitude to her that prevailed among Renaissance writers.[32] I should like to argue, however, that Henry- son's compassion for Cresseid goes much farther than his echo of Chaucer in his proclaimed intention to 'excuse als far furth as I may / Thy womanheid, thy wisdom and fairnes' (87–8). This compassion appears, paradoxically enough, in the culminating moment of Cresseid's suffering, the moment when the burden of self-knowledge is added to the weight of physical affliction. Troilus' lavish gift stimulates in Cresseid the first true recognition of what she has done and what she has become. The binary oppositions characteristic of this poem culminate and climax in the refrain to her lament: 'O fals Cresseid and trew knycht Troilus!'[33] As elsewhere, there is no attempt to mediate between these extremes; they are held separate by virtue of the gulf between past and present, a gulf which Cresseid's leprosy makes it impossible to bridge, and which severs the two lovers to such an extent that each seems to be encountering only the ghost of the other. Cresseid's lamenting contrast between herself and Troilus registers with painful intensity the opposition between them, and by the same token, the opposition between her past and present selves. The poignant contrast between past and present recalls her earlier 'ubi sunt' lament, yet here it has a quite different significance: here she is not complaining that her past has been taken away from her, but is registering the fact that she has distanced herself from it by her own actions.

Chaucer's Criseyde has none of this self-recognition. We see her not only lying to Troilus (in her letter to him), but also lying to herself, trying to shuffle off the awareness of what she has done by parting assurances that she will 'never hate' Troilus and fully appreciates his worth, and by attempts to convince herself that *this* relationship will be for keeps (v, 1069–85). Chaucer's cruelty to Criseyde is precisely this final portrayal of her as imprisoned in dishonesty. It is, in the context of this poem, a necessary cruelty, because Chaucer is writing of Troilus' tragedy, in which this spiritual deformation of Criseyde plays a vital part. The loss of his love depends not on Criseyde's removal from Troy, nor even on her falling in love with another man, but on her ceasing thereby to exist as the Criseyde he had known. Henryson, in contrast, chooses to write the 'fatall destenie' (62) of Cresseid, not of Troilus, and his compassion resides in the simple fact that his poem gives back to Cresseid a *role*, the role of self-recognition that Chaucer had denied her.[34] Chaucer's Criseyde vainly tries to use the future to wipe out the past: 'To Diomede algate I wol be trewe.' Henryson's Cresseid, in contrast, allows the past to re-constitute itself with the force of a terrible destructive challenge to the present; so far from trying to wipe out the past, she allows the past, one might say, to wipe out her.

> 'O Diomeid, thou hes baith broche and belt
> Quhilk Troylus gaue me in takning
> Of his trew lufe', and with that word scho swelt.   (589–91)

It is Henryson's generosity to Cresseid that he allows her this passionate re-integration with her former self, an identification so intense that her present life is consumed by her dead past.

Henryson's consciousness of his own responsibility towards Cresseid is evident, I believe, in the vision of the planetary gods, to which I return for the

last time. For Saturn and Cynthia are not the only gods involved in passing
sentence on Cresseid: it is Mercury who is chosen spokesman for the gods, and
who advises that the planets with highest and lowest spheres (again we note
the juxtapositions of extremes) should devise her punishment. The significance of Mercury's role has not escaped the notice of former critics:
MacQueen suggests that he represents Poetry,[35] and even closer to the mark
is Jennifer Strauss, who suggests that he is a representative of Henryson
himself.[36] The odd little detail which gives the clue is the description of his red
hood as being 'heklit atouir his croun, / Lyke to ane poeit of the auld fassoun'
(244–5). The difficulty of tracing any precise links between poets (old-
fashioned or not) and a particular way of wearing the hood even tempts one to
suppose that Henryson might be amusing himself and his immediate audience by a description of his own preferred style of headgear.[37] However that
might be, the association between Mercury and the figure of the poet is not in
doubt.

Viewed in this light, Henryson's poker-faced assurance that Mercury is
'Honest and gude, and not ane word culd lie' becomes much more than an
attempt to suppress the unfavourable aspects of Mercury's character: with its
obvious irony acknowledged, it draws attention to the lying nature of poetry.
With adroit blandness, Henryson represents the poet – himself – not as the
inspired prophet of truth, but as a word-spinner, a teller of tall stories and an
inventor of fables.[38] The opening of his poem has already prepared us for this
in the qualifications with which he hedges about his description of the 'vther
quair' in which he pretends to have found his narrative:

> Quha wait gif all that Chauceir wrait was trew?
> Nor I wait nocht gif this narratioun
> Be authoreist, or fenʒeit of the new
> Be sum poeit, throw his inuentioun . . .   (64–7)

Henryson acknowledges his own role in 'newly feigning' the history of
Cresseid by giving to himself not only the passive role of the narrator, reading
the story in his 'vther quair', but also the active role of Mercury, the
poet-figure who determines the final destiny of his heroine.

Again, Chaucer had preceded him, not only in his constant equivocations
about the 'auctoritee' of his writings, but more specifically in acknowledging
his own responsibility as poet in fixing the destinies of Criseyde and of Dido.
He does this by attributing to them the laments in which they foresee their
own future imprisonment within the unsympathetic stereotypes of story and
song – an imprisonment which Chaucer reinforces to the extent that he
rehearses once again Criseyde's betrayal and Dido's shame.[39] Yet it is,
paradoxically, his very imagination of their laments which represents the
degree to which he has in fact liberated them from that imprisonment, inviting
the reader to participate in the imaginative retrieval of a living multi-
dimensional human experience behind the flat record of narrative events.
Henryson similarly takes responsibility for his own poem: in locating the

source of Cresseid's judgement and punishment in Mercury, he locates it in himself, eschewing the pretence that it emanates from any higher moral authority. He acknowledges his own cruelty to Cresseid; he does not attempt to hide his own role as creator of the fiction behind the mask of divine retribution.

Henryson is thus at his most Chaucerian in doubting Chaucer's authority: 'Quha wait gif all that Chaucer wrait was trew?' It is from Chaucer that he will have learned to doubt the implicit claims of the story-teller to omniscience and objectivity, and will have learned also that the 'inventiounes' of a poet can be 'authoreist' only by the poet's overt acknowledgement of his personal responsibility for them, an acknowledgement which must include the recognition that in creating his own miniature world he wins none of the privileges that belong to divine judgement. In making himself merely the humble reader of another poet's story, or including himself among the Canterbury pilgrims, Chaucer both evades responsibility and accepts it: he rejects the poet's quasi-divine claims to omniscience and moral judgement while at the same time identifying his own vision as the limited and partial source of the narrative. Henryson too includes himself in the fictive level of his poem as a way of demonstrating his own consciousness of the difference between poetic justice and divine justice. So far from arrogating to himself the harsh execution of a rigorous moral orthodoxy, Henryson shares with Chaucer a humility before his creation, a humility perceptible in the 'factuality' with which he endows it. Many poets after Chaucer happily imitated his practice of introducing themselves as narrator-actors in their own poems. Henryson's distinctiveness as a reader of Chaucer and as a creative poet in his own right is evident in the fact that he has a true understanding of what Chaucer's introduction of himself into his poems *means*.

NOTES

1 It is a pleasure to dedicate this essay to Derek Brewer, whose colleague I have been privileged to be for fifteen years, and whose friendship I have enjoyed for even longer, since the time when his generosity and interest in Chaucer led him to seek out and introduce into the circle of Cambridge medievalists a stray Oxford graduate student with what he thought 'an interesting research topic'. My personal gratitude is undimmed by the later knowledge that this instance of 'humane medievalism' in action is merely characteristic of him.

2 All quotations from Henryson are taken from *The Poems of Robert Henryson*, ed. Denton Fox (Oxford, 1981). Recent scholarship on Henryson is helpfully summarized by Louise O. Fradenburg, 'Henryson Scholarship: The Recent Decades', in *Fifteenth-Century Studies: Recent Essays*, ed. Robert F. Yeager (Hamden, Connecticut, 1984), pp. 65–92.

3 The following paragraphs recapitulate, for the sake of comparison with Henryson, some parts of my article on 'Chance and Destiny in *Troilus and Criseyde* and the *Knight's Tale*', in *The Cambridge Chaucer Companion*, eds. Piero Boitani and Jill Mann (Cambridge, 1986), pp. 75–92.

4 Jupiter's influence presumably brings about the immediate happiness which the lovers are about to experience.

5 Saturn's Greek name, Kronos, is conflated with the Greek *chronos*, meaning time. For Saturn as representing Time, see Jean Pépin, *Mythe et allégorie: les origines grecques et les contestations judéo-chrétiennes* (Paris, 1958), pp. 328–35, and Raymond Klibansky, Erwin Panofsky and Fritz Saxl, *Saturn and Melancholy* (London, 1964), pp. 133, 154, 162, 177–8, 185, 193. For the moon as an image of change, see *House of Fame*, 2114–16, and the *Complaint of Mars*, 235.

6 The significance of Henryson's choice of these two planets was perceived by Muriel Bradbrook, 'What Shakespeare Did to Chaucer's *Troilus and Criseyde*', *Shakespeare Quarterly*, 9 (1958) 311–19, at p. 313, and by John MacQueen, *Robert Henryson* (Oxford, 1967), p. 81, but neither critic notes that Henryson follows Chaucer in this.

7 John Livingston Lowes, *Geoffrey Chaucer* (London, 1934), pp. 10–13.

8 In claiming that Saturn is 'the supreme deity' in the *Knight's Tale*, and that Theseus 'is simply mistaken in referring Arcite's death to the "grace" of Jupiter', A. C. Spearing leaves out of account Theseus' reference to the First Mover, and thus the determinist view of planetary influence (*Criticism and Medieval Poetry*, 2nd edn (London, 1972), p. 176).

9 Cf. Chaucer's *Man of Law's Tale*, 295–308, which depicts the planets as 'hurled' and 'crowded' by the superior force of the 'cruel' Primum Mobile, their own baleful influence thus being due, paradoxically, to their impotence. For fuller discussion of this passage, see my article on 'Parents and Children in the *Canterbury Tales*', in *Literature in Fourteenth-Century England*, eds. Piero Boitani and Anna Torti (Tübingen/Cambridge, 1983), pp. 165–83, at pp. 169–71.

10 For an analysis of the poem in astronomical terms, see J. D. North, 'Kalenderes Enlumyned Ben They: Some Astronomical Themes in Chaucer', *Review of English Studies*, n.s. 20 (1969) 129–54, at pp. 137–42, and J. C. Eade, *The Forgotten Sky: A Guide to Astrology in English Literature* (Oxford, 1984), pp. 109–14.

11 Cf. Douglas Gray's comment on Henryson's creation of 'a kind of double motivation, in that we believe at the same time that men are helpless before the gods, and yet are moved by emotions and vices within themselves' (*Robert Henryson*, p. 175).

12 *Robert Henryson*, p. 70.

13 Ralph Hanna III rightly emphasizes that the planetary council does not (as it does in the *Knight's Tale*) have an independent existence guaranteed by the narrator, but is reported as a dream seen by the swooning Cresseid; in this dream, 'Cresseid sees mainly what she wants to, a kind of cosmic conspiracy which is devoted to reducing her to causeless ruin' ('Cresseid's dream and Henryson's *Testament*', in *Chaucer and Middle English Studies in Honour of Rossell Hope Robbins*, ed. Beryl Rowland (London, 1974), pp. 288–97, at p. 295). While agreeing with Hanna that Cresseid's vision invests the cosmic powers with a spurious intentionalism, I think he underestimates the degree to which Henryson conceives those powers as more than a figment of Cresseid's imagination.

14 Cf. E. Duncan Aswell, 'The Role of Fortune in *The Testament of Cresseid*', *Philological Quarterly*, 46 (1967), 471–87, esp. pp. 486–7.

15 *Criticism and Medieval Poetry*, pp. 184 and 190.

16 'The *Testament of Cresseid* is a compassionate poem as well as a harsh one ... Nevertheless, the compassion of the narrator does not blur the harshness of the universe as he sees it' (ibid., p. 190).

17 Boccaccio, *Teseida* XI, 1–3, and Boethius, *De consolatione Philosophiae* IV, m. 1. For references to other parallels, see the notes to this passage in the Riverside Chaucer.

18 *Purgatorio* IX, 19–30; cf. also Dante's backward vision of the 'little threshing-floor' of earth from the sphere of the fixed stars in *Paradiso* XXII.

19 The first Book of Martianus' *De nuptiis Philologiae et Mercurii* briefly describes the flight of Mercury and Apollo through the heavens to Jupiter (27–30); Book II is almost entirely devoted to the heavenly ascent of Mercury's bride Philology (117–99). Book IV of Alan of Lille's *Anticlaudianus* relates the heavenly ascent of Prudentia to request a soul for the 'new man'.

20 The *Somnium* concludes Cicero's *De re publica*; Chaucer probably knew it only second-hand, as the basis of Macrobius' *Commentarii in Somnium Scipionis*.

21 This section of Henryson's *Orpheus* seems to have been influenced by Macrobius (see Denton Fox's Introduction to his edition, pp. cviii–cix), who describes Platonist theories concerning the descent of the soul from its heavenly abode under 'the weight of earthly thoughts', accumulating the attributes of material existence as it sinks through the planetary spheres until at last it is imprisoned in a terrestrial body (*Comm. in Somnium Scipionis* I, xi, 10 – xii, 16). This idea of the soul's descent into the body also influences the account of Urania's descent through the spheres, at the request of Natura, in the *Cosmographia* of Bernard Silvestris (II, v). Descending order is also followed in Martianus' account of the 'rivers flowing down from heaven' shown to Virtue by Mercury, which represent the planetary spheres (I, xiv), as in his description of the 'colonization' of the spheres by the Muses (I, xxvii). Troilus' appeal to the planetary deities at *Troilus and Criseyde*, III, 715–32, also follows a downward movement, with the exception of an appropriate displacement of Venus to head of the series. These examples are, however, few in comparison to the instances of the 'upward and outward' pattern, and none of them provides a precedent for the unique effect of the downward movement in Henryson's *Testament*.

22 In the *Parliament of Fowls*, Chaucer similarly passes from the static descriptions of the figures in and around the Temple of Venus – which C. S. Lewis called 'mere pageant figures put in for decoration', introducing an 'alien Renaissance quality' derived from their Boccaccian source (*The Allegory of Love* (Oxford, 1936; corr. edn London, 1938), pp. 174–5) – to the lively debate centred on the figure of Nature, whom Chaucer pointedly does *not* describe, merely referring us to the lengthy portrait in Alan of Lille's *De planctu Naturae* instead of imitating it.

23 See Duncan Robinson, *A Companion Volume to the Kelmscott Chaucer* (London, 1975), esp. pp. 29–31, 40–3. The difficulty of envisaging a statue of Mars which stands in a (stone or wood?) cart, has two stars over its head, and a wolf eating a man at its feet, and is then said to be 'depeynted' with 'soutil pencel' is a good example of the problems. Cf. also Burne-Jones's comment on the difficulty of rendering the allegorical figures in the *Romaunt of the Rose*: 'I wish Chaucer would once for all make up his unrivalled and precious mind whether he is talking of a picture or a statue'; quoted by G[eorgiana] B[urne]-J[ones], *Memorials of Edward Burne-Jones*, 2 vols. (London, 1904), vol. II, p. 217.

24 *The Assembly of Gods* (formerly attributed to Lydgate) was edited by Oscar Lovell Triggs, *EETS*, e.s. 69 (London, 1896). The portraits of the gods seated at Apollo's banquet occupy lines 253–385. In suggesting Henryson's debt to this work, Marshall W. Stearns largely confined himself to similarities between the two accounts of a 'trial by the gods' (*Robert Henryson* (New York, 1949), pp. 70–2), and it is this more limited influence that is rejected by Denton Fox in the Introduction to his edition (p. lxxxvi, n. 1). My own point concerns its more generalized role as

representative of the classicizing current in late-medieval literature. Cf. R. J. Lyall's comment, in combating MacQueen's claim that the portraits derive from Boccaccio's *De genealogia deorum*, that what links Henryson and Boccaccio 'is not so much the particular detail as the iconographic approach itself' ('Henryson and Boccaccio: A Problem in the Study of Sources', *Anglia*, 99 (1981), 38–59, at p. 44).

25 See the *Book of the Duchess*, 626–49 (especially 633–4). The passage in the *Knight's Tale* (1530–9) which describes how 'geery [changeable] Venus' imbues lovers with her own changeability is the most likely stimulus for Henryson's linking of the two figures, though this has not previously been noted by Henryson critics. Other examples of the fusion of Fortune and Venus are noted by Howard R. Patch, *The Goddess Fortuna in Medieval Literature* (London, 1967), pp. 96–8, but they are not numerous. On the traditional iconography of Venus, see Meg Twycross, *The Medieval Anadyomene: A Study in Chaucer's Mythography*, Medium Aevum Monographs, n.s. 1 (Oxford, 1972).

26 On the affinity of Venus and Cresseid, see Jennifer Strauss, 'To Speak Once More of Cresseid: Henryson's *Testament* Re-Considered', *Scottish Literary Journal*, 4, ii (1977), 5–13, at pp. 10–11, and Gray, *Robert Henryson*, p. 186.

27 The alternating pattern of the portraits is noted by MacQueen (who classes Venus among the hostile powers), *Robert Henryson*, p. 71; Lee Patterson (who likewise classes Venus as hostile, and makes an unconvincing claim for Cynthia as 'odd man out'), 'Christian and Pagan in *The Testament of Cresseid*', *Philological Quarterly*, 52 (1973), 696–714, at p. 701; R. J. Lyall (who notes 'the careful alternation of favourable and unfavourable deities' as one of the features in the portrait sequence that are 'quite manifestly independent of any possible source'), 'Henryson and Boccaccio', p. 53. So far it has not been noted that it is the internal contradictions in the portrait of Venus that enable Henryson to preserve the pattern of contrasting pairs even with an odd number of planets.

28 *The Scottish Tradition in Literature* (Edinburgh/London, 1958), p. 47. Cf. also the earlier remarks of E. M. W. Tillyard, *Five Poems 1470–1870* (London, 1948), pp. 8–9; Wittig (p. 47) cites Tillyard's observation that it is 'a contrast between knowledge and ignorance that underlies the tragic irony of the sublime scene ... when the lovers meet for the last time'.

29 *Robert Henryson*, pp. 169, 192.

30 *The Scottish Tradition*, p. 46.

31 Louise Fradenburg provides a convenient summary of the polarized critical views on the question of whether Henryson is hawk or dove in his treatment of Cresseid ('Henryson Scholarship', pp. 79–80).

32 See Hyder E. Rollins, 'The Troilus–Cressida Story from Chaucer to Shakespeare', *PMLA*, 32 (1917), 383–429, esp. pp. 397, 400; a corrective to this view is to be found in Gretchen Mieszkowski, 'The Reputation of Criseyde 1155–1500', *Transactions of the Connecticut Academy of Arts and Sciences*, 43 (1971), 71–153.

33 Cf. Douglas Gray, *Robert Henryson*, p. 202.

34 Cf. Gregory Kratzmann, *Anglo-Scottish Relations 1430–1550* (Cambridge, 1980), pp. 72–3, 85–6.

35 *Robert Henryson*, p. 81.

36 'To Speak Once More of Cresseid', pp. 11–12.

37 Priscilla Bawcutt attempts to remove the difficulty by arguing that it is the 'croun' (of laurel) which marks the poet ('Henryson's "Poeit of the Auld Fassoun"', *Review of English Studies*, n.s. 32 (1981), 429–34); this still leaves the 'heklit' red hood unexplained.

38 Cf. Douglas Gray, *Robert Henryson*, p. 187: 'Perhaps we are also meant to recall that even poets of "the auld fassoun" were sometimes accused of being liars.'
39 See *House of Fame*, 345–61; *Troilus and Criseyde*, v, 1058–64.

8

Gavin Douglas: 'Off Eloquence the flowand balmy strand'

RUTH MORSE

To begin with the idea of Douglas as a Scottish Chaucerian is to pre-empt a complicated issue, not least by making Chaucer central to Douglas's projects. Gavin Douglas was the third son of the Earl of Angus, a Scottish aristocrat before he was a prelate of the universal church. His ambitions were Scottish; he sought his advancement there. His university training in Paris gave him a grounding in scholasticism while he shared with his university acquaintances the newer learning, historical and literary. He knew the latest editions of Virgil and the most recent research into Scotland's past. Scotland's status as a nation and Scotland's place in European vernacular culture (or equally vernacular literature's place in Scotland) occupied him throughout his life. He went to Chaucer for the literary idiom he needed, but he fought both Chaucer's interpretation of Virgil and his elevation of love as a premier subject. His humanist ambitions reveal themselves in numerous ways, none of which apparently contradicted the human ambitions he revealed as a Douglas.[1] His working life as a poet probably occupied a dozen or so years, from about 1501 (*The Palice of Honour*) to 1513 (the translation of the *Aeneid*). Instead of writing three works, one each in the low, the middle, and the high style, he displays an ambition to write something that would be both a translation, and a true translation, which meant *interpreted*, of Virgil's *Aeneid* while also creating a kind of meta-*Aeneid* which would go Virgil and Chaucer one better by enveloping the Roman epic in English pastoral, rolling the wheel of Virgil into one. It is Douglas's without being Douglas's, and increases Virgil's, English's, and his own fame all at once. Just as Chaucer enabled Douglas to respond to, to equal and overcome Virgil, so Virgil formed a shield against Chaucer's overwhelming influence upon any English-language poet. In Douglas's two long works we see him suspended between scholasticism and the new learning, between his Latin and his English predecessors as translators, commentators, and poets; seeking Fame or Honour; believing and disbelieving authorized accounts of the past; defending and suspecting the art of poetry; aspiring to and rejecting the *cursus honorum* of pastoral and epic.

Finally he was to reject the contemplative life of study and poetry altogether in favour of active involvement in the complex politics of his day. Throughout Douglas's poetry his anxieties are explicit, though it has to be recalled that displaying narratorial anxiety, indecision, or simple-mindedness was itself part of the homage he owed Chaucer. The path to honour, the claims of the poetic accounts of the past as models for politics and virtue, the desire to find and to found a *Scottish* English that would establish a rhetorically sophisticated vernacular, the anxious rivalry with his poetic forebears, the ambivalence to love as a high subject, the worry that the uncertainties of history included falsehoods among their truths, thus further complicating the responsibilities of the poet as interpreter – all these themes occupy him in both the long poems.

It would be foolish to divide Douglas's career into a humanist–literary phase followed by a political–intrigue phase. For one thing, he was not so much of a humanist as to eschew scholastic habits of interpretation, nor did his commitment to the disciplines of history overcome his loyalty to Scotland's claim to aristocratic ancestry. He worried about the stories of history, arguing and disagreeing with the foremost scholars of his day. Douglas studied in Paris, though little more than that he studied in Paris is known. It was probably there that he knew John Mair, the great Scottish scholar, as friend or pupil, or as a fellow member of one of the 'German' nations of foreign scholars. The interest in Mair, and in what Mair was interested in, seems to have continued to the end of Douglas's life. After he had composed his long dream poem, but before the eighteen-month period in which he says he translated Virgil,[2] he worked with fellow Scot David Cranston to compile the index to John Mair's 1509 *In Quartum*, lectures on the Lombard's *Sentences*, and his association with Mair is dramatized in the preface to Mair's next commentary volume published the following year, *Johannes Maior in primum Sententiarum* (Paris, 1510) where Cranston and Douglas are two voices in Dialogue. Cranston, or 'Cranston', voices the more traditional scholastic approach to the study of theology, while 'Douglas' (described as 'no less erudite than noble') cites Valla and invites Mair to come home to Scotland to 'cultivate the Lord's vineyard' and 'sow the seeds of the gospel by preaching'. The Dialogue is unattributed, and may be by Cranston rather than Mair himself; whoever wrote it, it is unlikely that it distorted Douglas's views.[3] The Dialogue, and chance asides in Mair's work, reveal what seems to have been a group concern with Scottish difference, a kind of linguistic and political proto-nationalism. In 1516, by which time the Virgil translation was complete and Douglas was heavily involved in court intrigue and the fortunes of his nephew, whose wife was Dowager Queen Regent, he shared the Dedication of Mair's Commentary to the Fourth Book of the Lombard's *Sentences* with Robert Cockburn, Bishop of Ross, and Mair carries what one hesitates to call a *joke* from the Dialogue into his dedicatory letter, associating himself with his social superiors as neighbours in Scotland:

These reasons have led me to dedicate this work to you, for not only is each of you like myself a Scottish Briton (*Scotus Britannus*), but also my nearest neighbour in my native land.[4]

This suggests some concern with, or at least some thought about, their place of origin and what that might have meant to them, which we also find later in their interest in the history of those origins. For as Douglas seems to have had reservations about Mair's theological studies, hoping that he could be persuaded to leave the university and return home to Scotland to a more active role, so also he seems to have had reservations about the austere results of Mair's historical researches, which threatened to deny Scotland's claim to have been 'founded' by a refugee from the fall of Troy – one of those common European ancestral myths. In London in 1522, at the same time as he was corresponding with Wolsey about Scottish (and his own) affairs, Douglas had time to discuss them with another historian and scholar, Polydore Vergil, who was then working on his own history of the British nations, and with whom Douglas shared his own preference for the traditional myths although Polydore Vergil seems himself to have inclined toward Mair's, and not Douglas's view.[5] Although at this distance the nexus of concerns can only faintly be discerned, there is nothing uncommon in the association of interests: history, origins, the relative demands of university or pastoral life, that is, the *vita contemplativa* or the *vita activa*, the sense of place and the political and linguistic nation. For Mair, and for Douglas, being a Scottish Briton is something to talk about. For Mair, the coincidence of language between England and Scotland was part of his preliminary geographical description, part of the literary conventions of a history. 'The third tongue of this island, and the chief, is the English, which is spoken by the English and by the civilised Scots.'[6] The Scots speak as their southern neighbours do. There is something of that tension which arises from being the same but different. For Douglas, writing in the vernacular, the requirement was more immediate.

Douglas needed a literary register for his *Eneados*, and it was Chaucer who provided it. Yet his is not the same, but slightly different, 'written in the language of Scottis natioun' (1 Prologue, 103), and he calls it Scottish to distinguish it from the English of Caxton. Even so, he allows southern forms, as scholars have long remarked; this is not Scots English as it was spoken, but an amalgam, indeed a series of amalgams.

The well-known lines from Douglas's *Palice of Honour* which contain the praise of Chaucer show him acknowledging while distancing his master.

> Sa greit ane preis of pepill drew vs neir,
> The hundredth part their names ar not heir.
> ȝit saw I their of Brutus' Albyon
> Geffray Chaucer, as A per se sans peir
> In *his* vulgare, and morall Iohne Goweir.
> Lydgait, the Monk, raid musing him allone.
> Of *this* Natioun I knew also anone

Greit Kennedie and Dunbar ʒit vndeid,
And Quintine with ane Huttok on his heid.   (916–24)[7]

By 1501 the association of poets had become traditional enough; what matters
here is that Douglas sets his trio of Scottish poets alongside the usual English
worthies, and that while they are all together at the court of the Muses, his
Muse of choice is Calliope, the epic muse, who is his saviour from the wrath of
Venus. Sometimes Douglas works by juxtaposition; sometimes by indicating
brief reservations or even explicit criticism. Here there is only the slightest
shift in pronoun to distance his vulgar, his nation, from Chaucer's. It may be
worth recalling that in *The Goldyn Targe* Douglas's older contemporary
Dunbar praises the English trio's achievements in 'oure tong', 'oure rude
language', 'oure speche' without this slight distancing.[8] Chaucer is for
Douglas not only the great English example of eloquence, but England's great
poet of love. Yet even in this vexed subject he was not perfect. Indeed, his
imperfections might have helped give Douglas the room he needed for his own
vulgar, so close to, but so different from, Chaucer's. Chaucer the model, the
mark to shoot at, influenced Douglas in many ways, which scholars have
explored in some detail. As a model for diction and register, as a source of
phrase and adapter of syntax, as an establisher of the Dream Poem, Chaucer's
importance is well known.[9] Above all, Chaucer's *House of Fame* stands as the
inspiration for Douglas's own first long poem, his *Palice of Honour*.[10]

The *House of Fame* presented Douglas with an important precedent which
resumed its own previous precedents by seeing the *poet* as the source, the
support, of Fame, and by linking the tradition of the poets' craft to history, in
the broad sense of the historical which obtained throughout the Middle Ages.
Especially in Douglas's third part, which links study and poetry, the stories
cited are those which made the history of the world, from Creation to the
coming of Antichrist (tactfully not described, though this omission means that
Douglas misses the chance to prophesy). The magical mirror which enables
Douglas to 'see' all these stories hangs from a tree in the court of Venus, but
Douglas-the-Dreamer is there under the protection of Calliope, the Epic
Muse, without whose intervention he would have been flayed in Part II. From
inside the Court of Venus Douglas can see outside to history (beyond the
Court of Venus Chaucer saw Fame).[11] History appears to counter love and to
offer an escape from it. Douglas-the-Dreamer first got himself into trouble
with the court by attacking love head on. This is more subtle. If this poem was
indeed written in 1501, that is, some dozen years before his translation of
Virgil (his own estimate accords suspiciously with the dozen years Virgil
worked on the *Aeneid*), it shows an early interest in history, and one that must
have antedated by perhaps as many as seven or eight years his association
with Mair. To say that Douglas is under Calliope's protection is to forget that
in fact Calliope delegates her client to an unnamed Nymph, who becomes
Douglas's guide, a kind of cross between Chaucer's Eagle and Dante's more

illustrious companions. The journey the Nymph leads the Dreamer through ends where it began, in a garden, which, when he wakes, leads him back to the garden outside the Dream Garden, in which he first fell asleep.[12]

The visions of the different courts along the way, the description of the great gate of the palace of honour, and the gods, or God, whom the increasingly dazed Dreamer sees (and by whom he is knocked unconscious), are not just a source of comedy, but also suggestions about different paths which may – or may not – lead to Virtue, which is in the end the sole road to salvation as well as to immortality of a more literary kind. The closer to the end of the poem, the more Douglas relies upon the Chaucerian route for his travelling Dreamer. What has not been remarked is that Douglas uses the old technique for dealing with convention: writing it backwards. In the three early Dream Poems Chaucer began with reading, and ended only with the beginning of writing (as in the *Book of the Duchess* and one of the *Legend* prologues). Douglas ends with a book. When his Venus, like Chaucer's Dream-Prologue Alceste, demands a penance from the poet, she does not merely set a subject; she hands it to him, literally, as a book. In three crucial stanzas Douglas makes his goddess, his dreamer, and his guide, set, promise, and misunderstand stories, biblical and Roman.

> 'Weill, weill,' said scho [Venus], 'thy will is sufficient.
> Of thy bowsum answer I stand content.'
> Than suddanelie in hand ane buik scho hint,
> The quhilk to me betaught scho or I went,
> Commanded me to be obedient
> And put in Ryme that proces than quite tint.
> I promisit hir, forsuith, or scho wald stint,
> The buik ressauand, thairon my cure to preif.
> Inclinand since, lawlie I tuik my leif.

> Tuitchand this bulk perauenture ʒe sall heir
> Sum time efter, quhen I haue mair laseir.
> My Nimphe in haist scho hint me be the hand,
> And as we samyn walkit furth in feir,
> 'I the declair,' quod scho, 'ʒone Mirrour cleir,
> The quhilk thow saw befoir Dame Venus stand,
> Signifyis na thing ellis to vnderstand,
> Bot the greit bewtie of thir Ladyis facis,
> Quhairin louers thinks thay behald all graces.'

> Scho me conuoyit, finallie to tell,
> With greit plesance straicht to the riche Castell,
> Quhair mony saw I preis to get Ingres.
> Thair saw I Sinon and Achitophell
> Pressand to clim the wallis, and how thay fell.
> Lucius Catiline saw I thair expres
> In at ane windo preis till haue entres,
> Bot suddanelie Tullius come with ane buik
> And strik him doun quhill all his chaftis quoik.   (1747–73)

True stories may defend the Palace of Honour, but they are no defence against subsequent commentators: beside these stanzas (in the version of the Edinburgh print of 1579) the London print of 1553 has side-notes, probably the work of its printer, Copland, whose misinterpretation rivals E.K. at his worst. By the second stanza we find 'By thys boke he meanis Virgil', which is perhaps a sensible retrospective judgement, especially if you fail to see the Chaucerian allusion. Troy might be said to belong to Venus if we think of Paris's choice of her to receive the apple dedicated 'to the fairest' as the ultimate cause of its destruction. The ambiguities, even contradictions, of Venus herself are explored throughout Douglas's work, as also in Chaucer's. Then we read, 'The Auctors conclution of Venus merour', which, since it is the Nymph's interpretation, and since she seems to be mistaken, does Copland little credit. Then beside the third stanza is the unobjectionable judgement that 'The Palice of honour is patent for honest vertuus men an not for vicius fals & craftye pepyll', except that if the Nymph really thinks that 'Semiramis, Thamar, Hippolita / Penthessilea, Medea, Zenobia' exemplify Virtue she is misinterpreting again. The *House of Fame* included notoriety ('diffame') and emphasized the arbitrariness of Fame's rewards and punishments; can Honour's Palace encompass Dis-Honour? We must think of it as a possibility raised only to be frustrated by the Dreamer's pitching into the water which awakens him. Perhaps the servants of the Epic Muse have a different view from us of what constitutes Virtue; certainly it is the Nymph's promise to show the Dreamer the punishments meted out to famous transgressors against Virtue which leads him to try to cross the river into which he stumbles, thus bringing the dream to an end. Douglas's ambivalence to love extends perhaps to rejection: he wakes up rather than describe any examples.

The dream has been a journey towards the Palace of Honour, and has taken the Dreamer through a sequence of courts along the way. Characters reappear, as if to suggest that little is left behind, and that reinterpretation itself is a recurrent feature of understanding. The Sinon and Achitophel whom we last see struggling to climb into the palace through a window first appeared to identify the court of Minerva to the Dreamer.[13] Perhaps the poet sees these courts as poetic subjects along the way, with Love, in the sense of devotion to Venus, taking its place among the rest. Douglas's ambivalence to Love amounts to contradiction, as his Dreamer both celebrates and blames the service of Cupid. This may, if only in part, be a response to the vagaries of Fame's rewards and punishments in Chaucer's poem. It makes the story of Aeneas, to which Douglas was to devote himself, part of Rome's story more than part of Love's story.[14] Douglas has more than one predecessor to rival and correct. One is Chaucer, whose first book so reorients the contents of Virgil.[15] The other is Caxton, whose translation of the French prose 'paraphrase', the *Eneydos* of about 1490, is perhaps better known for its prefatory remarks about the difficulties of translating a simple word like 'eggs' than for its content. Caxton never claimed to be translating Virgil. Given Chaucer's status as literary ancestor, perhaps some of the vituperation expressed about *Caxton* is displaced from a similar reaction to Chaucer's misdeeds. Douglas's ending, which uses the rhetorical tones of the end of Chaucer's *Troilus* to make the point about the transitoriness of worldly fame and prosperity, nevertheless manages to encompass the lessons of his *House of Fame*, which is that immortality of a kind is bestowed upon stories by the poets who tell them. There is no solution to the two central thematic anxieties: in historical writing, which is the highest poetry, truth and falsehood are compounded, and Love is both a source of wickedness and of good. Both Virgil and Chaucer are implicated in these dilemmas.

Douglas's Prologues to his thirteen-book *Eneados* form a series of *accessus* to Virgil's poem, addressing each in its own way the contents of the section to come, its themes and implications including the translation itself. Douglas exhorts Virgil and Chaucer, readers knowledgeable and ignorant, hostile and friendly, to read sympathetically. Caxton he simply blames for misrepresenting the contents of Virgil's poem. This is not quite a question of accuracy, or not a question of accuracy alone. Medieval translation came in numerous kinds; the most important division was between that meant to accompany the original and that meant to replace it. Caxton's book, written as it was in continuous prose without constant reference to the original, appeared to be a replacement text with pretensions to stand alone in English as a representation of the history of Troy and story of Dido. Although in fact Caxton makes it clear that his translation is of a French paraphrase, not of the original, Douglas will have none of it, and he sends his unfortunate rival up in his best 'flyting' manner.

His own translation is *both*. It can be used, and, indeed, Douglas recommends its use, by schoolmasters attempting to teach Virgil, as an accompaniment to the original.[16] It is, though, a replacement text of the highest order, translating, as it does, the whole text of the *Aeneid* as it was understood through the interpretations and commentaries of generations of scholars. Douglas calls it a comprehensive translation (1 Prologue, 309), and that it is, on a wholly unprecedented scale. Although Douglas seems to have abandoned the annotated commentary about halfway through the first book, his glossing within the text continues throughout, as commonly in medieval translations, like Chaucer's own of Boethius. The provision of a kind of dialogic commentary was more frequent in scholarly writing than in poetry, but of course Douglas was well-read in that, too. The prologues not only help the reader understand the text as Douglas thought Virgil intended and commentators elucidated, they drew its lessons for the Christian reader, as in the long sermon on love which precedes Book IV. This is already an extraordinarily ambitious project. The Prologues, however, do more. They create an equivalent to Virgil's earlier career as pastoral poet by making use at numerous points (pointed out by earlier critics demonstrating sources)[17] of both the *Georgics* and the *Bucolics*. They address the large concerns of poetic creation, and encompass the translation as it proceeds. In addition, as scholars have recently begun to notice, the prologues follow the cycle of a year in a calendar, if not a Shepherd's Calendar, then at least a poet's.[18]

As one might expect, thinking of Douglas's anxieties as displayed in his *Palice of Honour*, an ambition this large does not appear as a simple or a straightforward matter. In the course of the long Prologue to Book I no affirmation appears without its disclaimer, nor any disclaimer without a contradictory remonstrance. Caught between his rival translators, Chaucer and Caxton, caught between his models of unsurpassed eloquence, Virgil and Chaucer, caught by the combination of truth and falsehood elegantly set out in his original (which must needs house wisdom and not merely demonstrate beautiful expression), Douglas rebounds from topic to topic, using epanorthosis as his technique for correcting his claims immediately he has made them. Placing himself vis-à-vis Chaucer (1 Prologue, 349–449), Douglas commends his English master for his eloquence, then takes him to task for his claim to have translated word-for-word (which is, given the relative vocabularies of Latin and English, impossible). If Chaucer was eloquent, perhaps he was not eloquent enough. Then Douglas extends his criticism of Chaucer, who 'was evir (God wait) all womanis frend' (1 Prologue, 449) because he accused Aeneas of treachery to Dido. Perhaps Chaucer was too eloquent. When Douglas defers to Chaucer it is also to claim his place: he will be a better, a truer translator.

> Thought venerabill Chauser, principal poet but peir,
> Hevynly trumpat, orlege and reguler,
> In eloquens balmy cundyt and dyall,
> Mylky fontane, cleir strand and royss ryall
> Of fresh endyte throu Albion iland braid,
> In hys legend of notabill ladeis said
> That he couth follow word by word Virgill.
> Wisar than I may faill in lakar stile.
>
> (1 Prologue, 339–46; my punctuation)

If Douglas exaggerates Chaucer's claims to follow his author in order to enable himself to point out his failure, that is not an unusual way of dealing with rivals. What, of course, Chaucer said at the beginning of the 'Legend of Dido' was 'I shal, as I can, Folwe thy lanterne, as thow gost byforn' (*The Legend of Good Women*, 925–6) and nothing more specific. Douglas says nothing at all about the use he was to make of, for example, Chaucer's own Prologues, to which he reverts for his own last poem of introduction.

> The royss knoppys, tutand furth thar hed
> Gan chyp and kyth thar vermel lippys red,
> Crysp scarlet levis sum scheddand, baith atanys
> Kest fragrant smell amyd from goldyn granys
> Hevynly lylleis, with lokrand toppys quhyte,
> Oppynnyt and schew thar creistis redymyte;
> The balmy vapour from thar silkyn croppys

Distilland hailsum sugurat hunny droppys
And syluer schakaris gan fra levys hyng
With crystal sprayngis on the verdour 3yng
The plane pulderit with semly settis sovnd,
Bedyit full of dewy peirlys rovnd,
So that ilk burgioun, syon, herb and flour
Wolx all enbalmyt of the fresch liquour,
And bathit hait dyd in dulce humouris fleyt,
Quharof the beys wrocht thar hunny sweit,
By myghty Phebus operations
In sappy subtell exalations
Forgane the cummyn of this prynce potent.

(12 Prologue 123–41; my punctuation)

This is one of the preambles which elicits a title from the author, who calls it pearl of May. It is a match for the sad prologue to Book VII; that one was to have its letters illuminated in black in sign of the sad contents of war, this celebrates the promise of Rome and the completion of Virgil's text in letters of gold. The echoes of the opening of Chaucer's *General Prologue* include the close association, what one might call clustering, of Chaucerian vocabulary, including some small transformations (the 'flour/liquour' rhyme by itself would be mere coincidence, but in association with 'bathit' and the bees' transformation of the liquor into honey we can see Douglas rewriting Chaucer). Because Douglas like so many Chaucerians before him, works by amplification, it is difficult to quote a short passage; in the lines which follow these quoted, he expands 'smale foweles' to include swans and Phoebus' bigamous bird, one of whose wives he names as 'Partelot' (l. 159). The mixture of the *Nun's Priest's Tale* and the *Legend of Good Women* with the ostensibly higher register poems like *Troilus* is typical. Chaucerian imitation is also Virgilian imitation: here at the end Douglas lists his principal works as Virgil did, and quotes himself as Virgil quoted *himself* reminding his readers that he was the author of pastoral poetry.[19] 5 Prologue, too, had exploited the conventions of spring, but coming as it did at the end of the books concerned with 'the state of man' it was explicit about Virgil's craft and political intention. This second spring prologue looks forward to the results of the foundation of Rome, to the flawed promise of human society. Within the pastoral perfection of the natural scene lies Douglas's old ambivalence about love, for the May opening encompasses scenes of projected sexual conquest by two scheming men. While the birds praise Nature and Venus, the poet imagines himself roused from his bed to complete his translation. The *General Prologue*, the *Prologue* to the *Legend*, and the *House of Fame* have all contributed to make both subject and register for the new creation. In the first Prologue Douglas discusses the need for 'fouth' (plenty, copiousness), but as the prologues progress we see that not only has he plentiful vocabulary, he can manipulate registers in order to take us through a sequence of styles, styles which encompass the variety established by Virgil in his early poetry as well as by Chaucer and alliterative poets in theirs. The 'unmarked' register may be Chaucerian, but the marked registers include aureation as well as numerous complex rhyme schemes. The last four books move from 9 Prologue's discussion of the 'royal style' to the heavily, formally aureate praise of God in 10 Prologue (incidentally the only prologue to appear to exploit numerological appropriateness), which contrasts Virgil's court of the gods to the correct worship of the one true God. Then 11 Prologue celebrates the virtues of right kingship and the importance of magnanimity before 12 Prologue resumes the high Chaucerian 'royal' style to bring the series to a fitting climax. Like 6 Prologue, 12 Prologue is written in an eight-line stanza, and balances it. Douglas is keenly aware of style variation not only in Latin but in the Englishes of Brutus' Albion. The manipulation of Scottish English is part of Douglas's ambition; in expanding its resources Douglas makes it more like his model, Virgil. But in some ways he makes it more like his southern models, too. Not for him the views of some Renaissance translators, like Dolet, that the translation must not display calques of the original, that it must accommodate itself to the original without 'sacrificing' its own character. Douglas set himself to create a literary style, indeed a sequence of styles, for Scotland, as Chaucer had for England, and he set about to do it by representing, comprehending, the greatest and most serious of classical texts. That the styles are expressive Douglas tells us more than once; his satisfaction in 9 Prologue is the most striking. The Prologues do many things, and it must not be forgotten that they are, first and foremost, introductions to each book of his translation. As *accessus*, they introduce and tell us how to read; they are variations on the themes of the different books; they are counters to the temptations of the text. One of the functions of eloquence is to create an art of poetry for the 'Scottis natioun' while writing about subjects that teach history, moral and political example, the life of public man and the search for private virtue.[20] To take the Prologues in isolation from the rest of the translation and read them as the last gasp of Scottish Chaucerianism is at once to misunderstand Douglas's ambition and his understanding of Chaucer.

It is testimony to Douglas's success, if not to successive generations' understanding of the place of nature poetry in late-medieval/early-renaissance verse, that Douglas's nature-writing became not only a model for how to write about the seasons and the countryside, but an argument for the priority of romanticism in Scotland. The commentary tradition of interpretative translation lost its prestige at an early date, and Douglas's *Eneados* became a subject for misplaced debates about 'accuracy'. From Surrey to Pound, Douglas has been used, abused, and praised for qualities he would hardly have known he was displaying. His was a display of learning, clothed in his best rhetoric, which represented and explained the history and hidden wisdom of the great Latin poet–philosopher. This is consistent with his concern with Mair's explications of Peter the Lombard, or their shared passion for Scottish history – his active concern with Scottish dynasties led him to prison and to exile. Douglas may have thought he was writing a serious historical interpretative translation of Virgil's epic. He is not responsible for the ways his prologues have been extracted from their context.

David Lyndsay's Skeltonic/Chaucerian 'Testament of the Papyngo', so much concerned as it is with the practice of poetry, begins with a retrospect, familiar enough in some ways, disclaiming any skill or message, because all has been said and well said.

> Suppose I had Ingyne Angelicall,
> With sapience more than Salamonicall,
> I not quhat mater put in memorie;
> The Poetis auld, in style Heroycall,
> In breue subtell termes Rethorycall,
> Off euerilke mater, tragedie, and storie,
> So ornatlie, to thare heyche laude and glorie,
> Haith done Indyte, quhose supreme sapience
> Transcendith far the dull Intellygence
>
> Off Poetis now in tyll our vulgare toung;
> (For quy) the bell of Rethorick bene roung
> Be Chawceir, Goweir, and Lidgate laureate.
> Quho dar presume thir poetis tyll Impung,
> Quhose sweit sentence through Albione bene song?
> Or quho can now the workis cuntrafait
> Off Kennedie, with termes aureat?
> Or of Dunbar, quhilk language had at large,
> As maye be sene in tyll his golden targe?
>
> Quintyng, Mersar, Rowle, Henderson, hay & holland,
> Thought thay be ded that libells bene leuand,
> Quhi[l]kis to reheirs makeith redaris to reiose.
> Allace for one, quhilk lampe wes of this land,
> Off Eloquence the flowand balmy strand,
> And, in our Inglis rethorick, the rose,
> As of Rubeis the Charbunckle bene chose:
> And, as Phebus dois Synthia presell,
> So Gawane Dowglas, Byschope of Dunkell,
>
> Had, quhen he wes in to this land on lyue,
> Abufe vulgare Poetis prerogatyue,
> Boith in pratick and speculation.
> I saye no more: gude redaris may discryue
> His worthy workis, in nowmer mo than fyue,
> And, speciallye, the trew Translatioun
> Off Uirgill, quhilk bene consolatioun
> To cunnyng men, to knaw his gret Ingyne,
> Als weill in Naturall Science as Deuyne.[21]

In this discussion of the tradition inspired by Chaucer, which must include reactions against the image of that greatest of courtly makers, and attempts to find ways of making it new, it is worth remembering that the line leads down the centuries. For Scott himself made Douglas a very minor character within *Marmion* (David Lyndsay himself gets more attention from Scott). Perhaps there are few enough readers of *Marmion* now to make it worth recalling that Marmion has forged a paper which incriminates the young Wilton, with whose return, recapture of his reputation and beloved, and resistance to revenge upon the treacherous villain-protagonist, the tale ends. When Wilton has proof of his innocence it is to Gavin's father, Earl of Angus, that he presents the forgery, evidence of Marmion's guilt. Now the poet's view of the Bishop of Dunkeld is that of writer to writer, and he attributes to Gavin Douglas a natural pride in his accomplishment.

> Amid that dim and smoky light,
> Chequering the silvery moonshine bright,
>   A bishop by the altar stood,
>   A noble lord of Douglas blood,
> With mitre sheen, and rocquet white.
> Yet show'd his meek and thoughtful eye
> But little pride of prelacy;
> More pleased that, in a barbarous age,
> He gave rude Scotland Virgil's page,
> Than that beneath his rule he held
> The bishopric of fair Dunkeld.

By contrast the aged Douglas to whom his son is his 'boy-bishop', gives thanks that forgery remained out of the power of his warrior sons, in what we may think of as the man of action's reflection on the world of words:

> Thanks to Saint Bothan, son of mine,
> Save Gawain, ne'er could pen a line.[22]

NOTES

1 Douglas's political involvement seems to have increased, understandably enough, after Flodden. His nephew succeeded to the Angus title, and married Margaret Tudor, widow of James IV (who was killed, like so many, at Flodden). This alliance put the Douglases at the centre of Scotland's government, always vexed by competition among its ruling elite, until the Earl not only flaunted his mistress in public but also spent his wife's rents. Her attempts to divorce her unsatisfactory Douglas spouse redounded upon Gavin, whom she abandoned. His advancement in the Scottish church was always difficult, and his intrigues on behalf of his nephew with their southern neighbours opened him to accusations of treason by his Scottish enemies. Some of his correspondence survives, and is printed by John Small as a biographical preface to the first modern scholarly edition of Douglas, *Poetical Works: with Memoir, Notes and Glossary* (Edinburgh, 1874). When he died of plague in London, in 1522, he was probably in his late forties, and trying to come to some arrangement with Cardinal Wolsey that would allow him to return to Scotland and recover his own position.

2 After the epilogue with which the whole *Eneados* ends comes a second farewell which describes 'the tyme, space and dait of the translation' (vol. IV, p. 194) in

which Douglas claims to have completed his work on the feast of Mary Magdalene 1513 (22 July): 'It was compylit in auchteyn moneth space' (line 12), when Douglas would have been (if he was born in 1475) about 38. Douglas translated large quantities of commentary as well as the poem's 9896 hexameters (in modern editions), the so-called thirteenth book of Mapheus Vegius, plus thirteen prologues and the double epilogue. Readers may choose to doubt the literal truth of his claim. It seems probable that some of the work on Virgil was contemporaneous with Douglas's time in Paris working on scholastic texts and commentaries.

3 I am grateful to Professor J. H. Burns for elucidating the Dialogue for me. References to this period of Mair's life can be found reprinted in *A History of Greater Britain by John Major*, ed. and trans. Archibald Constable, Scottish History Society (Edinburgh, 1892), p. 414. Hereafter cited as *History*.

4 *History*, editor's introduction, p. xxxi.

5 Mair's *History* was published in 1521, the year before Douglas's death, and treated the story of Gathelus and Scota as fabulous and the traditional Scottish claim to Trojan descent as without foundation. Vergil says that he asked Douglas to provide him with some notes on the subject. There followed a conversation which Vergil represented, in the words of the English translator, as follows: 'As soon as I hadde redde these thinges, accordinge to the olde proverbe, I seemed to see the beare bringe foorthe her younglinges. Afterwarde, when for recreation wee mette together, as wee weare accustomed, this Gawine demaunded mie opinion. I aunswered, that as towchinge there originall I wowlde not greatlie contende, seing that for the moste parte all contries weare woonte to drawe the principles of there pedegree ether from the Goddes or from heroical nobles, to the ende that they which afterwarde being not easie of beeleefe minded to skanne and derive theim, when they showlde hardlie find enie thinge of more certaintee, they showld rather bee constreyned to beeleve it firmelie then enie farder to labour vainelie. But to bee short, this in noe wise kanne agree that the Scottes and Pictes, two mightie people, showlde soe longe reigne in the Ilond, showlde performe so manie battailes, showlde so often foyle the Britons and Romains, molest them, and vanquisshe them, and yet noe antique or grave writer once make rehersall of theim; especiallie seeing that Caesar, Tacitus, Ptolome, and Plinie (levinge to reherse the others) doe eche wheare in there histories make mention of the people named Trinobantes, Cenigmani, Segontiaci, Ancalites, Bibroci, Brigantes, Silures, Iceni, Ordulucae, Vicomagi, Elgouae, with the other contries of Brittaine; but of the Scottes and Pictes not a woorde, bie cause as yeat they weare not in this region, which forsothe is to bee thoughte the verie cause whie late writers have soe slacklie used the memoriall of theim. Wherefore I towlde him, even as frindlie as trewlie, that as concerning the Scottes and Pictes beefore there comminge into Britaine (which Bedas in his time hadd well assigned), it showlde not bee lawful for me to intermeddell, bie reason of the prescrit which is incident to an historien, which is that hee showld nether abhorre the discoveringe of falsehoode, nether to sybe suspition of favor not yeat of envy.

This Gawine, noe doubte a sincere manne, didd the lesse dissent from this sentence, in that it plainelie appeared to him that reason and trewthe herin well agreaed, so easilie is trewthe allwaise discolowred from feyned fansies.' (Quoted from Small, pp. clix–clx.) (Camden Soc. vol 1, p. 106.) By 1534, when Vergil's history appeared, Douglas had been dead twelve years, so that disagreement with his aristocratic friend no doubt had value without danger.

6 *History*, iv, p. 18.

7 Quotations from Douglas will be from *The Shorter Poems of Gavin Douglas*, ed. Priscilla Bawcutt (Edinburgh, 1967), which prints parallel texts of the two surviving '*Palices*' and *Virgil's* Aeneid *Translated into Scottish Verse by Gavin Douglas*, ed. D. F. C. Coldwell (Edinburgh, 1954–67) with line numbers in the text. While for reasons of orthography I have reproduced the Edinburgh *Palice* it is worth remarking that at this verse the London text shows one of its not-infrequent pointing hands. Emphases here and throughout are mine.

8 *The Poems of William Dunbar*, ed. W. Mackay Mackenzie (London, 1932), p. 119. It may nevertheless be worth remembering that in the course of Douglas's poetry he refers only to Chaucer, Gower, and Caxton and not to their theoretically equal Scottish poetic peers. This surely implies something not only about Douglas's real views about whose work counted, but also about his own ambition to take his place with his southern neighbours

9 Priscilla Bawcutt's analyses are the keystone of any study of Douglas's. My debts to her work will be obvious. Her *Gavin Douglas: A Critical Study* (Edinburgh, 1976) summarizes, but does not replace, her earlier articles, 'Gavin Douglas and Chaucer', *Review of English Studies*, n.s. 21 (1970), 401–21 and 'Douglas and Surrey: Translators of Virgil', *Essays and Studies*, 27 (1974), 52–67. Her recent 'William Dunbar and Gavin Douglas' in *The History of Scottish Literature: vol 1, Origins to 1660*, ed. R. D. S. Jack (Aberdeen, 1988), pp. 73–90, seems to resist some of the recent interpretations of Douglas's allegorical leanings.

10 The relations between Chaucer and Douglas were explored in a long article by John Norton-Smith, 'Ekphrasis as a Stylistic Element in Douglas's *Palis of Honoure*', *Medium Aevum*, 48 (1979), 240–53. Norton-Smith derived Douglas's structure from Chaucer's *House of Fame*, and showed how the invocations to Douglas's parts I and III were expanded from *HF*, Invocation to Book II, specifically ll. 520ff. But in counting the trees he denied that the wood could be allegorical. Mark E. Amsler is one of several scholars to point out the ways that Douglas's dream concerns him as a poet, poet for whom his craft is one of the ways of achieving honour and virtue. 'The Quest for the Present Tense: The Poet and the Dreamer in Douglas' *The Palice of Honour*', *Studies in Scottish Literature*, 17 (1982), pp. 186–208.

11 This interpretation differs from that of Gerald B. Kinneavy, who saw Calliope simply as poetry, rather than specifically as *epic* poetry, and for whom the vision in the mirror was a vision of everything that had happened rather than a commitment to history followed by brief allusions to fabulous, i.e. fictional characters of the likes of *Piers plewman* and *Robene Hude*. Nor has anyone remarked that the fictions which Douglas identifies are not love-stories. The effect would be quite different if instead of Piers Ploughman he saw Tristan, or for Rauf Coilyear he substituted Havelok. For Kinneavy, too, the section on music is mere 'digressio', not, as I hope to show, part of a scheme which encompasses the Virgilian, as well as the Chaucerian, examples. See his 'The Poet in *The Palice of Honour*', *Chaucer Review*, 3 (1969), 280–303.

12 Douglas adapted the 'Chinese Box' construction from Chaucer; though many of the details, the individual boxes, may have come from other dream poems, their combination is distinctly Chaucerian. Exaggerating the desert place found in the *House of Fame* into a wasteland typifies one of the characteristic Bloomian reactions to a great predecesor. Compare John Fyler's note on *HF*, 482–8 (p. 981). In Chaucer's poem Calliope, 'The myghty Muse', leads the singing around Fame. No doubt this stresses the status of Epic, a cue Douglas expanded.

13 It is through a window in the whirling house of wicker that Chaucer's eagle

introduces the dreamer into Rumour's domain (warning him that from here there is no exit); the last scene is thus a final destination, a search for Fame and a denial that the dreamer is searching for anything more than new stories. When Douglas uses Chaucerian details he makes them his own.

14 In interpreting this poem as in part a search for subject I am indebted to A. C. Spearing's discussion of the Dreamer's contradictions and confusions. See his *Medieval Dream-Poetry* (Cambridge, 1976), pp. 202–1.

15 See John Fyler's notes to *HF*, 240–382 and 314 (p. 980).

16 This is one of those apparently humble ambitions which yields rich fruit when analysed: not only is this to be a translation to teach teachers, it is to be taken as a model of eloquence by those teachers. Douglas's ambivalence throughout extends to chastising those he ostensibly asks to correct his work: unless they understand Virgil even better than the humble translator they are to hold their fire. By one of the ironies of history the translation was completed about eight weeks before Flodden. The opportunities for political manoeuvre which followed were certainly more than Douglas himself could, or would, resist.

17 As in Norton-Smith, 'Ekphrasis in *Palis of Honoure*'; Priscilla Bawcutt, 'Gavin Douglas and Chaucer', and 'The "Library" of Gavin Douglas', in *Bards and Makars: Scottish Language and Literature: Medieval and Renaissance*, ed. A. J. Aitken, M. P. McDiarmid and D. S. Thomson (Glasgow, 1977), pp. 107–26.

18 As, elegantly, Lois Ebin, 'The Role of the Narrator in the Prologues to Gavin Douglas's *Eneados*', Chaucer Review, 14 (1980), 353–65. Ebin takes Douglas to be enacting a journey to understanding.

19 First recognized in Priscilla Bawcutt's 'Library', p. 117. These examples may be taken to indicate the breadth of Douglas's ambition.

20 Edwin Morgan discusses length as an aspect of the translation as a mirror for princes in 'Gavin Douglas and William Drummond as Translators', in *Bards and Makars*, 194–200. This contrasts with the private (and partial) view of Penelope Schott Starkey, 'Gavin Douglas's *Eneados*: Dilemmas in the Nature Prologues', *Studies in Scottish Literature*, 11 (1973), 82–98.

21 *The Works of Sir David Lindsay*, ed. Douglas Hamer (Edinburgh, Scottish Text Society, 1931), vol. 1, pp. 56–7. Dated 1530, thus eight years after Douglas's death.

22 Sir Walter Scott, *Marmion*, VI, x and xv. I am grateful to Yvonne Burns for this lesson in Scottish descent lines. While the editors edited all the contributions to *Chaucer Traditions*, it fell (as it is my pleasure to say it always falls) to one of the contributors to read this essay: my thanks (as usual) to Helen Cooper.

9

Skelton's *Garlande of Laurell* and the Chaucerian tradition

JOHN SCATTERGOOD

Of all the English Chaucerians nobody wrote more about poetry, about the nature of the poetic tradition, and his own role in it than Skelton, and *The Garlande of Laurell* is in many ways his most considered statement. Usually his comments appear in the context of some other subject, but this poem is about poetry and nothing else. For all that, it is not a particularly unified or cohesive performance, partly due to the circumstances of its composition. From the astrological opening (XXI, 1–7)[1] it would seem that Skelton began the poem in 1495 on the occasion of a celebration at Sheriff Hutton Castle (Yorkshire) organized by Elizabeth Tylney Howard, Countess of Surrey, and her circle, to mark Skelton's laureations by three universities – Oxford in 1490, Louvain in 1492, and Cambridge in 1493. But the revised version published by Richard Fakes on 3 October 1523 included a defence of *Phyllyp Sparowe* (lines 1261–1366) which must post-date 1509 and a list of works including some which date from the early 1520s. In a sense, this is not unusual: Skelton's poems frequently grow by addition and augmentation. What is important in relation to *The Garlande of Laurell*, however, is that by 1523 its original celebratory purpose had waned somewhat, and it had become rather a retrospective review of a lengthy career spent on poetry, and an attempt at justifying that career.

In view of its subject matter, it is a less complacent poem than it might have been. Skelton's dream of fame is set in a forbiddingly unfavourable context. The traditional enemies of fame are chance, time and death, and Skelton contextualizes his examination of the subject as he meditates, at the beginning of his poem, on the mutability of things:

> In place alone then musynge in my thought
> How all thynge passyth as doth the somer flower,
> On every halfe my reasons forth I sought,
> How oftyn fortune varyth in an howre,
> Now clere wether, forthwith a stormy showre;
> All thynge compassyd, no perpetuyte,
> But now in welthe, now in adversyte.   (8–14)

In his despair he leans for rest on the stump of an oak tree in Galtres Forest, but it provides no comfort and merely reinforces those fears that are troubling his mind, for the once mighty and noble tree is now no more than an emblem of the ravages of time: its 'bewte blastyd was with the boystors wynde', its leaves were gone and the sap had left its bark (15–21). He aspires instead to the everlasting laurel, 'Enverdurid with leves contynually grene' (666), the symbol of poetic fame, and this is granted him, though with reservations. Pallas, goddess of wisdom and the deity controlling the academic curriculum ('Madame regent of the scyence sevyn' 53), vouches for Skelton's excellence and the Quene of Fame allows his name to be registered 'With laureate tryumphe in the courte of Fame' because he has spent his time 'studyously' (57–63), but this is only after a rigorous examination of his case and the raising of a number of serious objections. For Skelton, fame is not easily acquired. And even after he is acclaimed and accepted, once out of his dream the poem ends with another figure of transience – the double-faced Janus, Roman god of beginnings and endings, who is making calculations about time with his 'tirikkis' and his 'volvell' (1515–18). In order to come to terms with what constitutes everlasting fame for the poet Skelton meditates profoundly on the past and the future.

Everlasting fame, glory, and honour are frequent subjects in poetry and in *The Garlande of Laurell*, Skelton uses many traditional ideas. There is no agreement, however, about whether he used closely any specific source. It has been argued, by Edvige Schulte, that his inspiration came from Italian, from Dante's *Purgatorio* and from Petrarch's *Africa*, the *Triumph of Fame* Chapter III and from *Canzone* CCXXIII.[2] On the other hand, Gordon Kipling has seen the French *rhétoriquer* tradition, as developed in the courts of Flanders, as providing Skelton with models for this and other poems.[3] Again, Gregory Kratzmann proposes Gavin Douglas's *Palice of Honour* as a significant influence.[4] It may be that Skelton derived something from all these sources; it is clear that in *The Garlande of Laurell* he identifies himself with a tradition of poetry which he takes back to its mythic origins and which incorporates many languages and many periods both ancient and modern. But predominantly, this concern is with England and the English tradition. The poem is infused with a sort of literary nationalism: Skelton pays particular attention to the gate of the palace of Fame which is called 'Anglea' and which bears the English heraldic beast, 'a lybbard, crownyd with golde and stones' (588–95); and it is Gower, Chaucer, and Lydgate 'Theis Englysshe poetis thre' who escort him to the Quene of Fame (386–455). The most substantial earlier treatment of the subject of *The Garlande of Laurell* in English poetry was Chaucer's *House of Fame*, and this is the poem, as was long ago proposed, which seems to me most important to Skelton here.

It is perhaps unfortunate that A. S. Cook chose to make the case for the 'dependence' of *The Garlande of Laurell* on Chaucer by citing parallel passages.[5] His evidence shows that the same general ideas and literary strategies occur, but that there is no specific verbal correspondence. Though both poems are dream-visions in which the narrator confronts allegorical figures of authority, Skelton's poem is much simpler than the *House of Fame*: it is less inventive (there is no Dantean eagle to act as guide, and no aerial flight through the cosmos as there is in Chaucer's lines 496–1053); it is philosophically less enquiring (there is no disquisition on the way sound travels as in lines 765–852, or on the relation of rumour to fame in lines 1916–2120); and crucially it is much narrower in its conception of fame (there is no comparable equivalent to the various companies who put their cases to Chaucer's goddess in lines 1520–1867). Skelton is concerned, almost exclusively, with literary fame.

Yet something of Chaucer's poem is recalled by Skelton, though transmuted so as to be almost unrecognizable. In the *House of Fame* Eolus blows 'bad fame' or 'shame' out of his black trumpet to one company of petitioners:

> ... throughout every regioun
> Wente this foule trumpes soun,
> As swifte as pelet out of gonne
> When fyr is in the poudre ronne.
> And such a smoke gan out wende
> Out of his foule trumpes ende,
> Blak, bloo, grenyssh, swartish red,
> As doth where that men melte led,
> Loo, al on high fro the tuel.
> And therto oo thing saugh I well,
> That the ferther that hit ran,
> The gretter wexen hit began,
> As dooth the ryver from a welle,
> And hyt stank as the pit of helle.   (1641–54)

Chaucer is concerned to show how bad fame spreads, and uses, amongst other comparisons, some of the traditional images associated with vainglory – smoke and stench.[6] Though Eolus appears also in Skelton he is not an agent for the distribution of fame, being now no more than someone who performs ceremonial duties, calling for attention and such like. Yet Skelton remembers and responds to Chaucer's passage, though not by direct imitation. He takes Chaucer's simile, 'as pelet out of gonne', and literalizes it. He causes the presumptuously clamouring, unworthy figures who are besieging the palace of Fame to be scattered by gunfire from the walls:

> With a pellit of pevisshenes they had suche a stroke,
> That all the dayes of ther lyfe shall styck by ther rybbis.
> Foo, foisty bawdias, sum smellid of the smoke ...   (637–9)

– retaining the two traditional images. Similarly, in Chaucer 'good fame' from Eolus' golden trumpet is spread like a fragrance:

> And, certes, al the breth that wente
> Out of his trumpes mouth it smelde
> As men a pot of bawme helde
> Among a basket ful of roses.   (1684–7)

This reappears in Skelton as the fragrance from the olive-wood fire kindled by the phoenix in the top of the laurel tree in Fame's garden: 'It passid al bawmys that ever were namyd' (674). Though he steals odd lines here and there, Skelton rarely makes extensive use of literary sources: the relationship between these poems is not one of direct borrowing. Rather, Skelton engages with some of the ideas in the *House of Fame*, and in some of Chaucer's other poems, in order to define his own position.

Even a cursory examination of the two poems, however, is enough to indicate that Skelton makes claims for his own importance as a poet – claims about the status of the poet writing in English, about his relation to the literary tradition, about his role as a perpetuator of noble subjects, and about fame acquired through labour and the multiplication of readers – which are more substantial than Chaucer ever felt able to make. This, as I shall seek to argue, is not simply to be attributed to Skelton's vanity,[7] but is rather a reflection of a substantially different way of thinking about literature which had emerged in England in the hundred and fifty years separating the two poems, and of a new confidence which English poets were beginning to feel.

Chaucer sought to invest poetry with more dignity and significance than his predecessors in English. In a mode of high clowning, he frequently presents himself as a minstrel or a court entertainer and little more, but as A. C. Spearing rightly points out, the three invocations or apostrophes in Proem II of the *House of Fame*, imitated from Dante, are important in that Chaucer envisages, for the first time in English, the idea of poetry as a vocation, the idea of the poet as prophet, and the idea that sublime poetry was possible in the vernacular.[8] Chaucer is also the first poet in English to use the evocative image of the laurel, symbolic of the everlasting fame of poets: the Muse Polyhymnia sings 'with vois memorial in the shade / Under the laurer which that may not fade' (*Anelida and Arcite*, 18–19). And in Proem III to the *House of Fame* Chaucer asks Apollo, the god of poetry, for his help and promises, if he receives it:

> Thou shalt se me go as blyve
> Unto the nexte laure y see,
> And kysse yt, for hyt is thy tree.
> Now entre in my brest anoon!   (1106–9)

But he also knew about Petrarch's laureation in Rome in 1341, a ceremony which formed the model for similar Renaissance occasions, for he refers to 'Fraunceys Petrak, the lauriat poete' whose sweet rhetoric had spread the idea of poetry over all Italy (*CT*, IV, 31–3). But Chaucer never claims the laurel, and expresses no pretensions to fame through laureation.

This modesty clearly disappointed his fifteenth-century followers, for they repeatedly suggest that he ought to have been invested with the honour. Lydgate praises Chaucer for 'the golde dewe dropes of speche and eloquence' in English and says that he 'worthy was the laurer too have / of poetry',[9] and elsewhere suggests that he has an equal right to 'be registred in þe house of fame' with Petrarch.[10] Caxton, in the Prohemye to the second edition of the *Canterbury Tales* (1484), commends Chaucer 'the whiche for his ornate wrytyng in our tongue maye wel have the name of a laureate poete'.[11] And in the final stanza of *The Kingis Quair*, James I of Scotland extends the claim to include Gower as well as Chaucer, who were together 'Superlative as poetis laureate / In moralitee and eloquence ornate' (1373–9).[12]

When Skelton confronts Gower, Chaucer and Lydgate in *The Garlande of Laurell*, he honours them as the establishers and enrichers of the English language as a medium for poetry: one of them 'first garnisshed our Englysshe rude', and another 'nobly enterprysed/How that our Englysshe myght fresshely be ennewed' (386–91). He remarks, however, that 'Thei wantid nothynge but the laurell' (397) – an enigmatic line which has been read off as a not very subtle attempt on Skelton's part to enhance his own reputation, because he had been laureated, at the expense of theirs.[13] The implication of it, however, may be the same as when Lydgate, Caxton and James I had treated the subject earlier, that because of the nature and importance of their achievements in poetry these English poets ought to have been awarded the laurel, but had not been. In the *House of Fame*, Chaucer approaches Apollo's laurel but does not claim it, just as he approaches the palace of Fame, but not to get fame (1871–82). Skelton hesitates ('I made it straunge, and drew bak ones or twyse', 444) but not for long; fame and the laurel are his due, he feels, not necessarily because he is a better poet than his English predecessors, but because English poetry itself and its representatives, including Skelton, deserve more honour and in more formal terms than had been accorded to them previously. Skelton appreciated the importance for English poets of claiming fame through status: he insists on his titles of 'laureate' and, after 1512–13, of *orator regius*. He may be following the example of the *rhétoriquers* in this: Octavien de Saint-Gelays refers to himself as 'simple orateur du roi'.[14] But Skelton is the first English poet to feel able to do this.

In the second place, Skelton appears to have believed that fame consisted, in part, of belonging to a tradition of notable writers, of being able to set oneself in the context of illustrious predecessors. Norman Blake has pointed out the lack of a sense of tradition in much Middle English literature, and that 'texts often seem to appear quite fortuitously without past or future',[15] though they are sometimes used as sources or quarried for ideas. With Chaucer this altered. He habitually seeks to define his own position by referring to authors of the classical and medieval past, usually with a sense of uneasiness and anxious deference: at the end of *Troilus and Criseyde* he urges his 'litel bok' to 'kis the steppes' of 'Virgile, Ovide, Omer, Lucan and Stace' (v, 1786–92).

Chaucerian poets of the fifteenth century follow his example and, in addition, defer to him: he is referred to by Hoccleve as 'maister deere' or 'fadir reverent', and others echo this.[16]

Chaucer's method of definition by reference to other poets was taken over by Skelton's admirers (of whom in his lifetime there were many) and later by Skelton himself, who was doubtless encouraged by what he read about himself. The earliest praise of Skelton, by Caxton in 1490, sets him in a context of classical authors: 'he hath late translated the *Epystlys* of Tulle, and the *Boke of Dyodorus Syculus* and diverse other werkes out of Latyn into Englysshe ... as he that hath redde Vyrgyle, Ovyde, Tullye and all the other noble poetes and oratours ...'[17] In 1499 Erasmus goes further. Skelton has not only read classical authors, but is their equal: What Greece owes to Homer, and what Mantua owes to Virgil, by so much is Britain in debt to Skelton:

> ... Te principe Skelton
> Anglia nil metuat
> Vel cum Romanis versu certare poetis.[18]

[While you are its principal poet, O Skelton, England need fear nothing, for you are worthy to vie in versifying with Roman poets.]

This is elaborated by Roberet Whittinton in 1519 in his *In Clarissimi Scheltonis Louaniensis Poeti: Laudes Epigramma*. On Parnassus Apollo praises the 'monumenta suorum vatum' mentioning Homer, Orpheus, Musaeus, Aristophanes, Aeschylus and others among the Greeks, and Virgil, Ovid, Horace, Statius and others among the Romans. Then he turns to Britain, a land which nourishes poets, and at considerable length he praises Skelton for his rhetorical speech, his eloquence and his power to move. He is in no doubt about Skelton's claim to fame: 'Ecce virum de quo splendida fama volat', and he calls upon the Muses to make his glory eternal:

> Aeterno vireat quo vos celebravit honore
> Illius ac astris fama perennis eat.[19]

[Let him flourish in the eternal honour with which he celebrated you, and let his fame be perennial in the stars.]

Similarly, Skelton's contemporaries testify to his fame by setting him in a tradition of English poetry and among English poets. In 1510 the author of *The Great Chronicle of London*, perhaps Robert Fabyan, links him with William Cornish, Sir Thomas More, and Chaucer 'if he were now in lyffe'.[20] And a little later Henry Bradshaw twice defers to the authority of Skelton in association with Chaucer, Lydgate and Barclay.[21]

In *The Garlande of Laurell*, Skelton sets himself in a comprehensive tradition of poetry incorporating Greek and Latin authors, poets from the Middle Ages such as Petrarch and Boccaccio, Renaissance figures such as Poggio 'that famous Florentine' (372) and contemporaries such as Robert Gaguin; the list is closed by his three eminent English predecessors. In the fiction of his poem, the poets of this tradition approve his claim to fame: 'Triumpha, triumpha! they cryd all aboute' (1506). His vanity has provoked criticism from modern scholars, in part justifiably: 'For him, the poetic tradition which he evokes so fully seems to exist for his sake, rather than he for its ... the tradition of poetry exists in order that Skelton may be its latest and most glorious representative.'[22] But it has to be remembered that Skelton is here not claiming for himself anything more than his contemporaries thought he deserved.

When one turns, thirdly, to the subject of fame and poetry as perpetuation one finds on Skelton's part the same engagement with traditional ideas, with Chaucer and his followers, and the same desire to equal or outdo. The idea appears early that poets bestowed eternal fame on those whom they celebrated in their verses, and by doing so acquired fame for themselves.[23] Chaucer takes the idea up in the *House of Fame* where the notable poets of antiquity, whose durability is indicated by their positions on pillars of metal like caryatids, 'bar ... up the fame' (1461) of men, events and peoples of the past, like Aeneas, Caesar, Pompey, the Jews, the Greeks, the Trojans, or the fame of mythical personages, like the 'god of love' or Pluto and Proserpina. So far as is known, Chaucer never wrote for patrons, but his followers – Hoccleve, Lydgate, Ashby, and the like – appear to have sought readily the favour of the great and powerful, and in return provided the kind of verses which were asked for: apart from any material benefits which may have been forthcoming, to have a famous patron provided some assurance of acceptability and eminence for the poet. Frontispieces to presentation copies of poems which show the poet kneeling before the patron become common. So too do headings like the following to the copy of Lydgate's *Guy of Warwick* from BL MS Harley 7333 fol. 33r: 'Here now begynneþe an abstracte out of the Cronicles in Latyn made by Gyrarde Cornubyence the worþy Croniculer of Westsexse, and translated in to Englishe by Lydegate daun Iohan at þe requeste of Margarite Countas of Shrowesbury Lady Talbot fournyval and Lisle of the lyf of the most worþy knyght Guy of Warwike, of whos blood she is lyneally descended.'[24] The fame of one's ancestors and hence the fame of one's family and one's own fame may be procured and perpetuated in poetry.

Skelton's earliest datable poem is written firmly within this tradition. In *Upon the Dolorus Dethe ... of the ... Erle of Northumberlande* he seeks to 'make memoryall' for Henry Percy, the Fourth Earl, murdered by tax rebels at Topcliffe, near Thirsk, in 1489. He appeals to Clio, the muse of history, to help his 'elect uteraunce' by refreshing his 'homely rudnes' and adverts to the idea that poetry of this sort preserves fame:

> Of noble actes auncyently enrolde
> Of famous princis and lordes of astate,
> By thy report ar wonte to be extolde
> Regestringe trewly every formare date ...   (I, 15–18)

Whether Skelton was commissioned to write this poem is difficult to tell, but he offers his services to the son of the dead earl in a prefatory Latin verse: 'Ad libitum cuius ipse paratus ero'. And an elaborately written and rubricated copy of the poem is preserved in BL MS Royal 18. D. ii, a sumptuous Percy manuscript.[25] Thereafter, from time to time, but especially after 1512–13 in his capacity as *orator regius*, Skelton writes in praise of Henry VIII to memorialize his achievements and those of England. So when Skelton thinks of his own fame in *The Garlande of Laurell* it is partly in these terms: it depends on the mutual interest of those celebrated in poetry and the poet who celebrates them. The Countess of Surrey and her companions feel bound to 'rewarde' Skelton with an embroidered garland of laurel (779) to signal his pre-eminence as a poet because he has in the past celebrated the fame of ladies:

> ... of all ladyes he hath the library,
> Ther names recountyng in the court of Fame;
> Of all gentylwomen he hath the scruteny,
> In Fames court reportyng the same... (780–3)

In his turn he has to thank them, at the prompting of Occupacyon, with a series of lyrics 'In goodly wordes plesauntly comprysid' (813). The whole process is then perpetuated 'in pycture, by his industrious wit' (1096–9) by 'maister Newton', presumably a painter or illuminator. Skelton's frequent allusion to those who appear to be his patrons – the Percy family, Henry VIII, the Howards, and latterly Wolsey – was no doubt in part a recognition of kindnesses received or expected, but it may well also have had the function in his mind of establishing his fame by associating him with the famous.

However, the fourth aspect of the poet's claim to fame as treated in *The Garlande of Laurell* – the expenditure of labour over a long time to produce a body of work which will be read – is probably the most important to Skelton. The formula 'Idleness is to be shunned' is a favourite topic of the exordium among classical authors. Seneca's warning, 'Otium sine litteris mors est et hominis vivi sepulta' (Idleness without studies is death and a sepulture for a living man), was often quoted, and the practice of poetry came to be seen as a virtuous cure for sloth.[26] On one occasion Chaucer uses the idleness topic in a prefatory position: the Second Nun sees the telling of the life of St Cecilia as a way to avoid 'ydelnesse' by means of 'leveful bisyness' (*CT*, VIII, 1–28).[27] But the idea also occurs in the *House of Fame*: the seventh company ask for Fame but the goddess instructs Eolus to blow 'a sory grace' for them from his black trumpet because they are 'ydel wrechches' who will 'do noskynnes labour' (1771–810). Fame without labour is impossible, and for a poet labour consists of producing poems which will be read by posterity and recognized.

Chaucer worries about the stability of his texts at the end of *Troilus and Criseyde*: the 'gret diversite / In Englissh and in writyng of oure tonge' may cause the metre of his book to be ruined or its sense misunderstood (v,

1793–8). He curses his scribe Adam for his incorrect copying and complains that he has to 'rubbe and scrape' the parchment in correction of Adam's versions of his texts (6). These complaints may to some extent be traditional[28] and the second is deliberately amusing, but behind the comedy lies a deep concern for the lastingness of his works. And doubtless it was this same motive – the wish to establish his fame by ensuring his identification with certain works which he hoped would last – that caused Chaucer to include lists of his works in his writings. None of the lists is very formal or complete and all are contextualized by disparaging reservations about the poet's achievement. In the F Prologue to the *Legend of Good Women* it is said that 'he kan nat wel endite' though he has written a great deal about love (412–30). According to the Man of Law, 'thogh he kan but lewedly / On metres and on rymyng craftily' (*CT*, II, 47–8), Chaucer has told, in one place or another, all the seemly stories there are to tell – and he lists some of Chaucer's works about women. And in the Retractions to the *Canterbury Tales* Chaucer, in his own person, asks that God 'foryeve me the synne' of his secular writings which, nevertheless, he names along with those works which he feels are morally sound and need no apology (*CT*, X, 1081–9). In his habitual, self-deprecating way Chaucer talks himself down, but at the same time seeks to establish his fame, for the first time in English, by associating his name with a defined body of work.

Chaucer's followers pick up and develop these ideas, too. The idleness topic is frequently used – poignantly by George Ashby, who wrote while in the Fleet Prison, 'Thus occupying me' (I, 339).[29] Yet one of its most assiduous users was Caxton, than whom there can have been few more active men of letters. In his Prologue to the 1483 edition of the *Game of Chesse* he mentions that he undertook the translation 'in eschewyng of ydlenes',[30] and in the Prologue to *Charles the Great* (1485) he asks God for grace so that he may 'laboure and occupye myself vertuously that I may come oute of dette and dedely synne'.[31] Most interesting, however, in his Prologue to the *Golden Legend* (c. 1481) which begins with a quotation from Jerome, 'Do alweye somme good werke to th'ende that the devyl fynde the not ydle', and in a lengthy passage he adds quotations from a number of other authorities to the same effect.[32] Most of the Prologue is based on the introduction to the French version of the work which Caxton was using, but he adds a certain amount – notably an extensive but incomplete list of translations made before 1482 which justify the way he has spent his time. Though he worries, like Chaucer, about 'dyversite and chaunge in language'[33] and though he worries about his own literary capacities, he has faith in the virtues of hard work and productivity.

And so too does Skelton. The Quene of Fame makes the point to Dame Pallas that Skelton will have to be banished from her court 'As he that aquentyth him with ydilnes' (228) unless he can give a convincing account of his productivity. In response, Occupacyon reads off an enormous list of his works which, nevertheless, is said to be merely a selection 'in as moche as it were to longe a process to reherse all by name that he hath compylyd'. It is in many ways an odd list. Not all the descriptions of extant works are very accurate, and a great many of the works are evidently lost.[34] Perhaps some never existed at all, and it may be that the list is partly parodic. Chaucer's lists included items which, to a sixteenth-century reader such as Skelton as to a twentieth-century reader, must have appeared lost: 'Origenes upon the Maudeleyne' (F Prologue to *LGW*, 428), 'the book of the Leoun' (*CT*, x, 1087), and so on. It may be that Skelton invented his own 'lost' works in emulation of Chaucer. Yet he shows no uneasiness about the lastingness of his achievement: the stability of print was, no doubt, reassuring to him. Indeed, this very stability imposed its own pressures and responsibilities: 'Beware, for wrytyng remayneth of recorde' (89) warns Dame Pallas. On one occasion, in the person of Jane Scrope, Skelton complains that the English language is 'rude', 'cankered', and 'rusty', and that it is difficult to find the terms in which to write 'ornatly' (VII, 774–83). But this doubt about the capacity of the language for eloquence did not extend to fears about durability. At the end of *The Garlande of Laurell*, Skelton reassures his 'littill quaire' that though it is written in English and not Latin that does not mean that people will not read it:

> That so indede
> Your fame may sprede
> In length and brede. (1550–2)

His fame is assured through the multiplication of readers of his works – a point he makes in other places.[35]

It seems clear, therefore, that Skelton saw himself, in much the same way as his contemporaries saw him, as a poet whose lasting fame was secure: he had status because of his laureation, poetic identity because he belonged to a definable historical tradition which embraced classical authors and his illustrious English predecessors, a role as perpetuator and memorialist of the famous, and a body of work to his credit that was likely to be read down the ages. Yet, for all this, he is sufficiently self-aware and self-critical to realize that there were aspects of his poetry that might cause his fame to be questioned, and in *The Garlande of Laurell* he expresses these doubts.

They principally concern his satires and polemical verses. When questions are raised (64–77), Dame Pallas interprets the Quene of Fame's reservations about accepting Skelton into her court as having to do with the fact that he does not always write in the style of courtly compliment and that he is therefore 'sum what to dull' (79). In order to defend him she seeks to broaden the notion of what are acceptable forms of poetry, and to justify his use of more demotic styles. The lines:

> And if so hym fortune to wryte true and plaine,
> As sumtyme he must vyces remorde,
> Then sum wyll say he hath but lyttil brayne... (85–7)

express similar misgivings to lines in the opening of *Collyn Clout*:

> Or yf he speke playne
> Than he lacketh brayne. (XIX, 26–7)

What is being referred to here is the low style of direct invective used by Skelton in his later satires, which, he affirms in *Collyn Clout*, may be 'tattered and jagged', but, nevertheless, is of some substance: 'it hath in it some pyth' (xix, 58).[36] A few lines later Dame Pallas refers to the indirect Galfridian manner of political prophecy:

> A poete somtyme may for his pleasure taunt
> Spekyng in paroblis, how the fox, the grey,
> The gander, the gose, and the hudge oliphaunt,
> Went with the pecok ageyne the fesaunt ...   (100–3)

This is the mode of some lines of *Why Come Ye Nat to Courte?* (xx, 118–22), which he may have in mind here, and for most of *Speke Parott*, where Skelton defends himself by saying that metaphor and allegory shall be 'his protectyon, his pavys and his wall' (xviii, 202–3), presumably against charges that he has defamed and slandered those he writes about. The disadvantage of this style is its obscurity and difficulty. At the end of *Speke Parott*, Galathea asks in desperation for a change of style of the poem: 'Sette asyde all sophysms, and speke now trew and playne' (448), and this and other remarks indicate that Skelton had some sense that his readers found it hard to understand (292–8, 364–70). In *The Garlande of Laurell* Dame Pallas defends this manner by affirming that those who are 'industryous of reason' will find in 'suche an endarkid chapiter sum season', but even she admits it is 'harde' (xxi, 106–12).[37]

Skelton is also concerned about the fate of satirists: Dame Pallas recalls the banishment of Ovid by Augustus Caesar and the threats to Juvenal, perhaps by Domitian, because he 'rubbid sum on the gall' (92–8). She defends Juvenal by saying, 'Yet wrote he none ill', but she later admits that in this sort of writing it is difficult to satisfy everybody: '... harde is to make but sum fawt be founde' (112). These examples are adduced to help defend Skelton, 'to furnisshe better his excuse' (92). And, indeed, throughout his work he is conscious of his role as a controversialist, and aware that there are those who disagree with what he writes. The traditional prayer of the medieval poet:

> I aske no more but God, of his mercy,
> My book conserve from sklaundre and envy ...[38]

takes on an added force in Skelton's writings. Though it is not always possible to identify them, his enemies are not vague figures, for he often feels it necessary to answer specific charges. He writes a reply to the 'dyvers people' who thought his verses on the death of James IV at Flodden tasteless (xii 'Unto Dyvers People ...'). Similarly, he appends to *Why Come Ye Nat to Courte?* some lines 'Contra quendam doctorem/Suam calumpniatorem' – a doctor of canon law evidently, who has not been further identified. Some of his enemies are, however, known by name. In 1509 Barclay attacked *Phyllyp Sparowe* for its 'wantones'[39] and Skelton wrote a 115-line reply which is appended to the poem in the printed editions: he notes in the account of *Phyllyp Sparowe* in *The Garlande of Laurell* that some 'grudge' at his poem 'with frownyng countenaunce' (1257–8) and includes the reply, closing with the line 'Est tamen invidia mors tibi continua' (1261–375). And among the writers who are called upon to approve his laureation there is at least one former opponent who appears not to have entirely forgiven him:

> ... a frere of Fraunce men call Sir Gagwyne,
> That frowned on me full angerly and pale   (374–5)

– Robert Gaguin, with whom Skelton had earlier engaged in polemical exchange.[40] For a controversial writer fame does not imply universal approval, and it is Skelton's consciousness of this which, no doubt, caused him to ponder at length the case of Aeschines, defeated in controversy by Demosthenes in 330 BC. He is allowed a place in her court, according to the Quene of Fame, because he provoked Demosthenes to great works, because he was overcome by no one but Demosthenes, and because of his subsequent acknowledgement of Demosthenes' superior ability: 'though he were venquesshid, yet was he not shamyd' (161). There is generous inclusiveness in Skelton's conception of fame, particularly in relation to satirists and polemicists.

But Skelton's view of poetry was also an extremely inclusive one, and one which conferred a dignity and an importance on poetry and poets which was far greater than Chaucer or most of his followers ever felt able to give it. Poetry embraced everything and the poet's realm was everywhere. In the paradisal garden of the Quene of Fame performs no courtly entertainer and no love poet, but the Carthaginian bard Iopas who sang before Aeneas in Dido's palace, and, as in *Aeneid*, I, 740 ff., he sings of the whole cosmic order, 'Of Atlas astrology, and many noble thyngis ... Of men and bestis, and whereof they begone ...' (690–703), to which, as A. C. Spearing has acutely pointed out,[41] Skelton adds a line of his own which suggests that his subjects include the whole moral order also: 'How wronge was no ryght, and ryght was no wronge' (704). The poet is privileged to speak of all things.

It is a large claim but Skelton develops and goes beyond it in *A Replycacion*, his last extant poem. Here he undertakes to defend the Christian faith against heresy by means of satirical verse and in the course of his poem he also finds himself defending the right of poets to deal with theological matters,[42] for which he uses the impeccable authority of Jerome who, in his letter to Paulinus prefacing the Vulgate, had praised the poetry of the psalms of David:

> Than, if this noble kyng,
> Thus can harpe and syng
> With his harpe of prophecy
> And spyrituall poetry,
> And saynt Jerome saythe,
> To whom we must give faythe,
> Warblynge with his strynges

> Of suche theologicall thynges,
> Why have ye than disdayne
> At poetes, and complayne
> Howe poetes do but fayne?   (XXIV, 343–53)

What is more, says Skelton, those who disparage the 'fame matryculate/Of poetes laureate' (357–8) do wrong, because poetic inspiration comes from God, and it is this which causes poets to write:

> ... there is a spyrituall,
> And a mysteriall,
> And a mysticall
> Effecte energiall,
> As Grekes do it call,
> Of suche an industry
> And suche a pregnacy,
> Of hevenly inspyracion
> In laureate creacyon,
> Of poetes commendacion,
> That of divyne myseracion
> God maketh his habitacion
> In poetes whiche excelles,
> And sojourns with them and dwelles.
>
> By whose inflammacion
> Of spyrituall instygacion
> And divyne inspyracion
> We are kyndled in suche facyon
> With hete of the Holy Gost,
> Which is God of myghtes most,
> That he our penne dothe lede,
> And maketh in us suche spede
> That forthwith we must nede
> With penne and ynke procede...   (365–88)

Skelton fuses classical and Christian ideas about poetic inspiration in this comprehensive defence. It rests on a well-defined tradition but probably takes its immediate origin from Boccaccio's *De Genealogia Deorum Gentilium* XIV, 7: 'Thus poetry, which ignorant triflers cast aside, is a sort of fervid and exquisite expression, in speech or writing, of that which the mind has invented. It proceeds from the bosom of God, and few, I find, are the souls in whom this gift is born, indeed, so wonderful a gift it is that true poets have always been the rarest of men. This fervor of poetry is sublime in its effects: it impels the soul to a longing for utterance ...'[43] And this inspiration, given to the few, rare poets, operates whether they write for 'affection', 'sadde dyrection', or 'correction' – that is to say, it encompasses satire. It is hard to imagine how a Christian poet could make a more complete vindication of his practice: the poet partakes of the divine, and this validates all aspects of his art.

In *The Garlande of Laurell* Skelton tries to come to terms with his poetic lineage, particularly with Chaucer, and to establish a claim to fame by justifying a career spent in the service of poetry. Skelton is not unaware of possible criticisms of past writers: according to Jane Scrope, Gower's English is 'old / And of no value told' (VII, 784–5); Lydgate is difficult and 'some men fynde a faute / And say he wryteth to haute' (811–12). Skelton's references to Chaucer, however, are always admiring, though it is equally clear that he recognizes how different he is. In Seneca's terms Skelton resembles him 'as a child resembles his father, and not as a picture resembles its original'.[44] And that he should be more assertive than Chaucer is perhaps not surprising. In the *House of Fame*, if the Egle is to be believed, poetry is for Chaucer something to be indulged in 'when thy labour doon al ys', a bookish, essentially solitary, pastime which keeps him in ignorance of 'tydynges' from far and near in the world at large (641–60). And though this may not be the whole truth, it is at least part of it: Chaucer recognizes the marginal nature of poetry and the poet in his society, though he is uneasy about it and takes some, albeit hesitant, steps to change things. Skelton, in a way that was becoming common, confident of the all-embracing relevance of poetry and confident also of his capacities and status as a poet, seeks to put himself at the centre of things, whether the sphere is social, political or spiritual. Part of Skelton's self-respect, indeed, derived from his status as a poet. When he defends himself in verse against Sir Christopher Garneshe[45] he says on one occasion: 'I am laureat, I am no lorell' (XIII, iii, 14) and, no doubt pleased with the pun, elaborates on it later:

> A kynge too me myn habyte gave
> At Oxforth, the universyte,
> Avaunsid I was to that degre;
> By hole consent of theyr senate,
> I was made poete lawreate.
> To cal me lorell ye ar to lewde... (XIII, v, 80–5)

Skelton had acquired a way of thinking in which it was inconceivable for a 'laureate' to be a 'lorell' (= worthless person, wretch). The dignity of the poet's calling enhances and validates the dignity of the individual. The essentially modest claims for their status and art characteristic of most Chaucerian poets are insufficient to contain this.

NOTES

1 *John Skelton: The Complete English Poems*, ed. John Scattergood (New Haven and London, 1983). References and quotations are from this edition.

2 'Skelton, Petrarca e l'amore della gloria nel *The Garland of Laurel*', *Annali Istituto Universitario Orientale Napoli, Sexione Germanica* 5 (1962), 135–63, repr. in *La Poesia di John Skelton* (Napoli, 1963).

3 'John Skelton and Burgundian Letters', in *Ten Studies in Anglo-Dutch Relations*, ed. Jan van Dorsten (Leiden and London, 1974), pp. 1–29.

4 *Anglo-Scottish Literary Relations 1430–1550* (Cambridge, 1980), p. 165.

5 'Skelton's *Garland of Laurel* and Chaucer's *House of Fame*', *Modern Language Review*, 11 (1916), 9–14.

6 See Piero Boitani, *Chaucer and the Imaginary World of Fame* (Cambridge, 1984), pp. 161–3. Many of the ideas on fame and poetry which I use were suggested by this comprehensive survey.

7 See, for example, the remarks in *The Poetical Works of John Skelton*, ed. Rev. Alexander Dyce, 2 vols. (London, 1843), vol. I, p. xlix. See also H. L. R. Edwards, *Skelton: The Life and Times of an Early Tudor Poet* (London, 1949), pp. 22–3 for a similar judgement.

8 *Medieval to Renaissance in English Poetry* (Cambridge, 1985), pp. 22–30. I am much indebted to this fine account of the poem. See also the interesting article by Vincent Gillespie, 'Justification by Good Works: Skelton's *The Garland of Laurel*', *Reading Medieval Studies*, 7 (1981), 19–31.

9 See *The Lyfe of Our Lady*, ed. J. Lauritis, R. Klinefelter and V. Gallagher (Pittsburg, 1961), lines 1628–34. See also *Chaucer: The Critical Heritage*, ed. Derek Brewer, vol. I, 1385–1837 (London, 1978), p. 46.

10 See *Troy Book*, ed. H. Bergen, 4 vols., EETS, e.s. 97, 103, 106, 126 (London, 1906–20) III, 4534–59. See also *Chaucer: The Critical Heritage* vol. I, p. 48.

11 *Caxton's Own Prose*, ed. N. F. Blake (London, 1973), p. 61. See also *Chaucer: The Critical Heritage*, vol. I, p. 76.

12 ed. John Norton-Smith (Oxford, 1970).

13 A. C. Spearing, *Medieval Dream Poetry* (Cambridge, 1976), p. 214 says he deals 'patronisingly' with them. See also Stanley Eugene Fish, *John Skelton's Poetry* (New Haven and London, 1965), pp. 231–2. Compare the interesting account of Richard Firth Green, 'the lavish praise which fifteenth-century writers heaped on Chaucer, Gower, and, later, Lydgate was rarely completely disinterested; living poets were manifestly raising their own stock by venerating their predecessors' (*Poets and Princepleasers: Literature and the English Court in the Late Middle Ages* (Toronto, 1980) p. 208).

14 See H-J. Molinier, *Essai Biographique et Littéraire sur Octavien de Saint-Gelays: Évêque d'Angoulême 1468–1502* (Rodez, 1910), pp. 58–9. See also Pierre Jodogne, 'Les Rhétoriquers et l'Humanisme' in A. H. T. Levi (ed.), *Humanism in France at the End of the Middle Ages and in the Early Renaissance* (Manchester, 1970), pp. 160–1.

15 *The English Language in Medieval Literature* (London, 1977), p. 14. See also pp. 21–7 for other relevant comments on this problem.

16 *Hoccleve's Works*, ed. F. J. Furnivall, EETS, e.s. 61, 72 (London 1892–7), III, ll. 1961–2. See also *Chaucer: The Critical Heritage*, vol. I, p. 62.

17 *Caxton's Own Prose*, p. 80.

18 See *Skelton: The Critical Heritage*, ed. A. S. G. Edwards (London, 1981), pp. 44–5.

19 *Ibid*, pp. 49–53.

20 *Ibid*, pp. 46–7.

21 *Ibid*, pp. 47–8.

22 See A. C. Spearing, *Medieval to Renaissance in English Poetry*, p. 243.

23 For the background to the idea of poetry as perpetuation, see E. R. Curtius, *European Literature and the Latin Middle Ages*, trans. W. R. Trask (London, 1953), pp. 476–7.

24 See *The Minor Poems of John Lydgate*, ed. H. N. MacCracken, 2 vols. EETS, o.s. 107, 192 (London, 1911–34), vol. 2, p. 516.

25 On this poem see my essay 'Skelton and the Elegy', *Proceedings of the Royal Irish Academy*, 84 C10 (1984), 333–47; and for some interesting comments on the

manuscript see Mervyn James, *Society, Politics and Culture: Studies in Early Modern England* (Cambridge, 1986), pp. 83–90.

26 On this topic see Curtius, *European Literature*, pp. 88–9, whence I derive the example from Seneca.

27 On the background to this Prologue, see Richard Hazleton, 'Chaucer and Cato', *Speculum*, 35 (1960), 357–80.

28 See R. K. Root, 'Publication before Printing', *PMLA*, 28 (1913), 417–31. For a famous instance see Petrarch's complaint in *Epistolae de Rebus Senilium*, v, i, in Franciscus Petrarcha, *Opera* (Basel, 1581), pp. 790–2.

29 *George Ashby's Poems*, ed. Mary Bateson, *EETS*, e.s. 76 (London, 1899), p. 12.

30 *Caxton's Own Prose*, p. 88.

31 *Ibid*, p. 68.

32 *Ibid*, pp. 88–9.

33 *Ibid*, p. 80.

34 For a comprehensive survey, see R. S. Kinsman and Theodore Yonge, *John Skelton: Canon and Census*, Renaissance Society of America: Bibliographies and Indexes No. 4 (New York, 1967).

35 See, for example, the epigraphs to *Speke Parott*: 'Lectoribus auctor recepit opusculy huius auxesim. / Crescet in immensem me vivo pagina presens / Hinc mea dicetur Skeltonidis aurea fama.' [By his readers an author receives an amplification of his short poem. The present book will grow greatly while I am alive; thence will the golden reputation of Skelton be proclaimed]. See also *Why Come Ye Nat to Courte?* 29–30: 'Hec vates ille / De quo loquntur mille' [About these things the famous bard of whom a thousand speak]. This is repeated at the end of the poem.

36 For the deliberately rustic nature of *Collyn Clout* see R. S. Kinsman, 'Skelton's *Colyn Cloute*: The Mask of Vox Populi', in *Essays Critical and Historical dedicated to Lily B. Campbell* (Berkeley and Los Angeles, 1950), pp. 17–23. For the literary antecedents for this style see A. R. Heiserman, *Skelton and Satire* (Chicago, 1961), 208–43.

37 For the stylistic affinities of *Speke Parott* see Heiserman, *Skelton and Satire*, pp. 126–89.

38 *The Court of Sapience*, ed. E. Ruth Harvey (Toronto, 1984), lines 69–70.

39 This comes in 'A brefe addicion to the syngularyte of some new Folys' added to his *Shyp of Foles*; see *Skelton: The Critical Heritage* p. 46. In 1519 the grammarian William Lyly attacked Skelton as 'neither learned nor a poet' (see *ibid*. p. 48).

40 See also *Why Come Ye Nat to Courte?* 718–41. For Skelton's dispute with this man see H. L. R. Edwards, 'Robert Gaguin and the English Poets 1489–1490', *Modern Language Review*, 32 (1937), 430–4. Another enemy appears to have been Rogerus Stathum, referred to by means of a number code in *The Garlande of Laurel* 742–65; he is also called Envyous Rancour, but so far as is known was not a poet.

41 *Medieval to Renaissance in English Poetry*, p. 246.

42 For the background to this problem see Curtius, *European Literature*, pp. 214–27, and for the sixteenth-century development of some of these ideas John N. King, *English Reformation Literature: The Tudor Origins of the Protestant Tradition* (Princeton, 1982), pp. 14–19, 209–31.

43 Quoted in the translation of Charles G. Osgood, *Boccaccio on Poetry* (Princeton, 1930), pp. 39–42.

44 *Ad Lucilium Epistulae Morales* LXXXIV, 7–8 '... quomodo filium, non quomodo imaginem ...' from *Seneca* ed. and trans. by Richard R. Gummere, 10 vols. (Loeb Classical Library: Cambridge, Mass., 1970), vol. 5, pp. 280–1.

45 For the background to these poems see Helen Stearns Sale, 'John Skelton and Christopher Garnesche', *Modern Language Notes*, 43 (1928), 518–32.

10

Chaucerian metre and early Tudor songs

JOHN STEVENS

The *Fayrfax Manuscript* (*c.* 1505) is one of three major songbooks which contain virtually all that survives of English secular songs from the late fifteenth and early sixteenth centuries.[1] It has several claims on the attention of anyone interested in the period: the repertory it presents seems to reflect not only some secular and 'occasional' tastes of Henry VII's court narrowly considered but also a wider world of traditional fifteenth-century pieties. There is one claim, however, of particular interest to students of literature – the way its composers set English words:

> The novelty was to attend to the words of the poems they chose in such a way as to see them, and set them, as physical sound-objects of an individual kind ... [This manuscript] is the earliest source in which one finds the careful and observant copying [in music] of English speech-sounds.[2]

This new musical practice is, of course, of interest in itself, since it is one of the symptoms of a changing 'aesthetic'. But it could also throw some light on a problem that needs all the light it can get – the rhythm of late fifteenth-century 'Chaucerian' verse.[3]

In this essay I shall attempt to assess some of the evidence relating to verse-sound, and therefore possibly the *spoken* performance of verse, which the surviving musical settings seem to offer. The four main headings of the discussion are: (1) word-sound; (2) line-structure; (3) intonation, enjambement, stanza-form; (4) the rhythm of the line. But, first, two preliminary questions need to be aired.

It is sometimes assumed that only certain types of verse are apt for musical setting. If this were true of the period we are considering, then clearly all we could hope for would be some light on so-called 'musical' verse. Fortunately it is not. 'Any Tudor lyric could be set to music in a traditional style'; the evidence relates, then, to almost the whole spectrum of written verse available.[4]

However – and this brings us to the second preliminary question – what does this 'evidence' amount to? Are we entitled to assume that the composer was hearing the sounds of *verse* in his head when he wrote his setting? Or was he hearing simply words as he would have heard them in *everyday speech*? This distinction does not, of course, matter to those of us who believe that the basis of courtly metres in the fifteenth-century high style was courtly speech itself. But for others, who believe that under the lumber of courtly verse up to Wyatt there was an iambic line struggling to free itself, a metrical pattern diverse from and in tension with natural speech, then the most that could emerge from the proposed analysis would be knowledge of the speech-sounds, of 'voice', not of the metrical base. This could in fact be no negligible gain, since information about the way our ancestors talked is interesting in itself and must be relevant to *any* theory of their metres. However, I share the first view and shall briefly set out the reasons for it as I shall be arguing on that assumption.

There are, to put the issue in the crudest terms, two basic views that one may take of fifteenth-century courtly-clerical metre – the metre of long-line verse with a syllable-count of ten or so syllables per line. Either, it is attempting alternate weak and strong stresses, constituting what later is called an iambic line, with the allowable 'reversed feet' and 'substitutions';[5] or, it is made up of integral units of ordinary speech, *selected* certainly, for desired qualities of length and rhythm, but not dismembered and put together again differently. The first of these views is not generally held today (except in the special case, as it is regarded, of Chaucer), though it still has learned supporters. It tends to rest on the, to me, extraordinary belief that poets had simply forgotten how to do it, i.e. how to create alternate stresses,[6] or, no less strange, on the idea that the rapidly changing language stultified their efforts to control metre. We are left with the second option – metres based on speech-units. What 'long-line' models were present to late medieval authors? On the one hand, they had contemporary French and Italian verse with irregularly accented lines but much stricter syllabic system, and, on the other hand, Middle English alliterative verse with its widely variable number of syllables but stricter, balanced, arrangement of stresses. There was also the palpable presence of Chaucer, the acknowledged master ('ther is no makyng to his equipolent'), whom they may have seen as combining qualities of both – the syllabic (i.e. syllable-counting) and the 'balanced' (but now un-alliterating). One of the interests of the present investigation will, I hope, be that it provides hints towards a 'reading' of verse which, though late, is still in the Chaucerian tradition. It is important to understand the 'Chaucerians', if only because no theory of Chaucer's metre which merely attributes stupidity and incompetence to his self-styled imitators is going to be thoroughly convincing.

The courtly poems which survive, with or without music, do appear indeed to be a compromise (to what degree conscious?) between the two main traditions. There are many poems, and many lines in poems, where the poet seems to write under no other constraints than those of approximate line-length and the need to com-pose ('put together') harmonious lines. The latter, it should be added, is no mean requirement – as exponents of *vers libre* know. The *Fayrfax Manuscript* can show many examples of medieval *armonia*.[7] Turning to the musician's role, I cannot see evidence that he, any more than the poet, felt constraints of a metrical kind – that is, the constraints of an external, pre-ordained pattern *within the line* – except the mid-line pause. His constraints were the rhythm of speech itself within the line and the structure of the stanza outside it.

There is a further good reason, as I have argued elsewhere, for believing that late medieval verse is 'com-posed speech'.[8] It is the nature of the mid-sixteenth-century effort, practically a 'campaign', to replace it with something else: this, in the words of Tottel's preface to the *Songs and Sonets*, was to be verse one would recognize by 'the stateliness of the stile removed from the rude skill of common eares'. Tottel's definition of 'stateliness' rested on resolutely iambic metre. 'What happened, in brief, was the replacement of a system based on the norms of speech ("O wombe, o belly, o stinking cod!") by one based on an external pattern (ti-tum, ti-tum, ti-tum).'

(1) **Word-sound**

The information one would like to have concerns the pronunciation (or not) of final syllables; the pronunciation (or not) of medial syllables; instances of unusual hiatus or elision; the accentuation of words when it differs from modern expectations, and especially of romance words ending in *aunce* or *aunt*. We may also hope to find hints about the duration of syllables and perhaps about their intonation.

(i) Final syllables
The final *-e* causes no problems, as one might expect by this date; it is either silent or elided. The final *-es* (*-is*, *-ys*) is much more often sounded than not. So, in the following single stanza song, all the plural forms and the genitive in line 1 have two notes of music:[9]

> Lett serch your myndis ye of hie consideracion!
> Beholde the soveren sede of this rosis twayn,
> Renewde of God for owre consolacion
> By dropys of grace that on them down doth rayn
> Thorough whose swere showris now sprong there is ayen
> A rose most riall with levis fressh of hew,
> All myrthis to maynten, all sorous to subdewe.   (F8)

Of particular interest because they must indicate some indeterminacy, and therefore the possibility of flexible practice, are instances in the songs where a plural, e.g. *paines* (F31, mm 64–5), or a genitive, e.g. *sonnes* (F32, m 65), is treated differently in the various voices.[10] Other examples are *nedes* (F38, mm 99–101), *soules* (F32, mm 37–8), *thinges* (F47, mm 25–6).

Final *-ed, -id, -yd*, is normally sounded and takes a separate note. Thus in 'But why am I so abu*syd* ... And my service allway refu*syd*' (F17, mm 5–7; 28–9); or, in 'I love, lov*ed* and lov*ed* wolde I be' (F21, mm 3–6). Here again, a certain indeterminacy is evident, as in the interesting double setting of the fifteenth-century devotional poem, 'Woffully araid' (F33 William Cornish; F35 [William] Browne). The poem is full of past participles in *-ed*, often paired in sound-play. Cornish's treatment is the expected and consistent; he singles out the suffix with a separate note. (It is worth noting that the scribe can suggest his own intentions with his spelling: 'araid' and 'naid' in the burden, clearly indicating monosyllables. But only the music gives proof that he means what he spells.) Browne, however, allows himself licence in this line, 'They mowid, they grynned, they scornyd me' (st.2); each suffix is set in two ways.

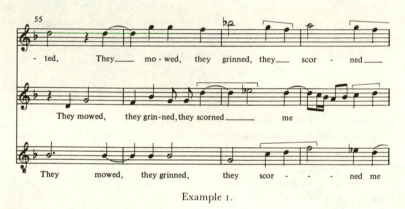

Example 1.

The third-person singular ending *-eth* in the present tense is almost invariably sounded and so set.[11]

(ii) Medial syllables

This is another issue on which the musical settings can be most helpful, since in 'syllabic' songs, such as those of F, either a note is provided for a syllable or it is not. (It is reasonable to refer to the songs as 'syllabic' because although they also feature melismas, sometimes of considerable length, established convention seems to demand that in this English style the text of any one phrase should generally be set entire before the melisma takes over.) The largest category of medial syllables refers to words with the suffix *-cion*. One of the court-songs towards the end of the manuscript, 'Jhoone is sike and ill at ease' (F40), with a stylistically inept and rather tasteless text, makes use of aureate rhyme in the second stanza – *lynyacion, recreation, formacion, conjuracion* – presumably for comic effect. Every occurrence of the suffix *-acion* is trisyllabic. The convention is consistently observed throughout the manuscript. Another class has the suffix *-ial: special, specially, celestial*; the *-i* is always sounded. Other less expected musical renderings (sometimes producing apparently hyper-metrical syllables) include *benedicite* with the second *e* sounded; *besherew*, like-wise; *every* – this common word is almost invariably set with care as a tri-syllable. Least expected of all, *goodly* (F26, line 2) is musically a trisyllable, '*go-od-ly*'.[12]

Example 2.

Conversely, *iyevyn* is disclosed as a disyllable, whilst *sovereyn*, normally trisyllabic, may lose its middle syllable.

(iii) Accentuation

For the student of metrics and verse-sound, however, accent and stress are primary considerations.[13] It is the absence of information about these, for instance, not about vowel-quality, which leaves even the rhythm of Chaucer's verse problematic for many of us. Music, carefully used, may sometimes produce some scraps at least of the desired direct evidence.

None of the categories of word-sound so far discussed have involved complicated musical judgements. Because of the precise underlay it is generally easy to see whether a syllable is to be sounded separately by the singer, or not. The question of accentuation raises subtler problems. There are three ways in which music may indicate stress; they correspond to the ways in which speech itself does the same thing. They are duration, pitch and intensity. Often, as we shall see, one syllable in a word will have both a longer and a higher note.[14] This double emphasis (duration, pitch) in a single voice-

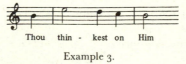

Example 3.

part leaves no room for doubt; but things are not always as straightforward as this, since the demands of harmony or counterpoint in a *part*-song (the songs range from two to four voices in the *Fayrfax Manuscript*) may result in conflicting evidence. The third component of stress, intensity, is by far the most baffling. In part-writing, even when as in the present song-book it is truly polyphonic, intensity may result in two separate ways – from an impulse of the musical metre (a rhythmic effect) or from a particular moment in a harmonic progression (e.g. a cadence point, or, paradoxically, a marked dissonance – though this is more applicable to slightly later music).

I shall consider the accentuation of polysyllables in two categories: first, the traditionally troublesome derivation ending in *-aunce* or *-aunt*. Their manuscript spellings vary between these and the modern spelling without the 'u'; I shall use the manuscript spelling in every case. There are about twenty words of some interest in this category. Those for which modern stressing seems to be confirmed are:

> aqúayntance (F19)   álliaunce (F44)   alégeaunce (F11)   ćontynaunce
> [countenance](F40)   góvernaunce (F15)   remémbraunce (F23)
> sémblaunce (F14)   sérvaunt (F63)

Even in these cases the positive evidence is not always consistent. An instance as unambiguous as this is rare.[15]

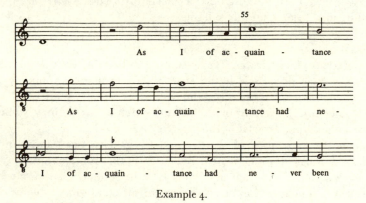

Example 4.

The treatment of 'variaunce' in F26 raises a question. How much weight should be given to the final syllable in view of the fact that the cadence is (in modern terminology) 'interrupted'? In this instance voices ii and iii are conclusive at least for the primary stress 'váriànce'.[16]

The words for which a French stressing of the final syllable is indicated are:

> ássurànce (F21)   dísplesaùnce (F23)   plesánt (F46)   répentaúnt (F34)

Less certain are

> constaunce (F23)   enerytaunce [inheritance](F44)   pleasaunce (see example 2)
> suraunce (F34).

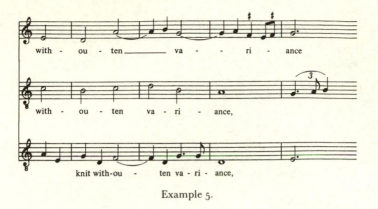

Example 5.

The kind of difficulty encountered can be illustrated from 'assurance'. In F21, the word occurs in rhyme-position and is clearly accented in un-modern fashion on first and last; in voices i and iii pitch and duration reinforce each other.[17] In F23, on the other hand, 'assurance', *again in rhyme*, has the opposite

Example 6.

stressing with equal clarity; here the pitch-shape is decisive, but it is confirmed by the musical metre – i.e. the stressed syllables occur 'on the beat'. (Note, however, the displacement of the beat, characteristic of close counterpoint, in voice i.)[18] (See example 7.) The moral of this example is the obvious one, that there were at this time, as there still are today, a number of words of variable stress and that those borrowed from other languages were naturally prone to ambiguity. But it is a matter for particular note that, contrary to what one might expect, the rhyme does not always have the effect of requiring a strong last syllable. The anonymous poem, 'That was my woo' (F23), is a sort of *locus classicus* for romance rhymes, and I give it later entire with the accents as suggested by the musical setting.

The second category of accentuations includes all other words. Space does

Example 7.

not admit of a full list, let alone the necessary scrutiny of individual cases; but it will be noted that even this selective list contains again a majority of romance-derived words, for some of which the music supplies alternative stressings.[19]

créatùre egáll énterlỳ fórthi fórtuned
ímmortál ínferàl matérnal, máternàl
náture, natúre pité térrestriàl, terréstriàl tóward
viságe

(2) Line-structure: mid-line break or pause

One aspect of post-Chaucerian courtly-clerical verse which often has been noted is the tendency of many lines to fall into two halves, the natural and unforced rendering of which seems to require, as in alliterative verse, some sort of pause or break in mid-line, usually marking the end of a phrase. The existence of such a break has generally been associated with the virgule, raised stop or other manuscript symbol. I should like now to examine the evidence which the *Fayrfax Manuscript* provides on this point.

The songs of the *Fayrfax Manuscript* are themselves metrically varied and they naturally show considerable variety in the way they treat the line. But it is in the long-line poems above all that the problem of the break is most important and baffling. The first song in the book, with words dating back to the early fifteenth century, is the most obvious example of a poem consisting of 'balanced' lines, as they have been called:

The farther I go the more behynde	1
The more behynde the nere my wayes ende	1/2
The more I sech, the wers can I fynde	0
The lyghter leefe the lother for to wende	2
The trewer I serve the ferther out of mynde	2

Thoo I go lose   yet am I teyd with a lyne   2
Is it fortune or infortune this I fynd?   0

The figures on the right-hand side indicate whether none, one, or both the voices in the two-part song have a musical rest in the middle of the line. In five of the seven lines the expected pause is marked in this way. Line 2 is the odd one, the explanation of the second pause being a melisma of purely musical *rejouissance* on the word 'nere'. The style of these early songs (as they appear to be) can be highly melismatic – the three- and four-part songs are less so – but, as previously remarked, the melismas are generally confined to the ends of phrases (i.e. of the half-lines). Melisma is, indeed, quite commonly used to mark or to reinforce the expected break (See, for example, the last two lines of 'Alas it is I that wote nott what to say' (F14)). When a rest is used as a marker, one retains a sense of the line as a whole as a single temporal unit consisting of two phrases, as in example 8.[20] When a melisma takes its place or supplements it, little sense of the line unit remains.[21] (See example 9.) It is not, however, essential to have either of these two markers – rest or melisma – since the shape of the musical 'sentence' may convey the effect in itself, by means of melodic or harmonic progression.[22]

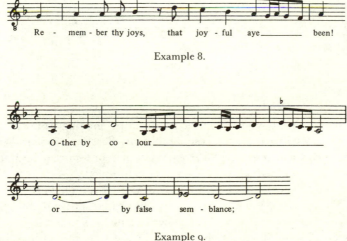

Re - mem - ber thy joys,   that   joy - ful   aye_____ been!

Example 8.

O -ther by   co - lour_____

or_____ by false   sem - blance;

Example 9.

In example 10 voices i and ii have shapes that naturally divide after the word 'loved', and this is reinforced harmonically by the return to the tonic in m 4 – also, one may add, by a change of texture from chordal (mm 1–4) to contrapuntal (m 5 onward).

The songs become progressively more complex, musically speaking,

Example 10.

throughout the first two-thirds of the manuscript, moving from two-part to three-part to four-part pieces (the ambitious Passion carols). With the extension of musical resources, further ways of representing the line-break occur and are combined with those already mentioned.

To sum up, the evidence of the *Fayrfax Manuscript* gives firm support to the idea that it was normal in long-line courtly poems for there to be a *felt* break, a short pause, a 'performance comma', however one likes to put it, in mid-line. It is not an absolutely consistent feature of the musical settings but it is strongly represented one way or another in a great number of them.

(3) Intonation; enjambement; stanza-form

By way of conclusion I shall, in a moment, analyse stanzas from one or two poems and examine the movement of the verse. But, by way of clarification, a few preliminary observations may be helpful.

First, I am aware of having neglected certain aspects of sound-structure which the reader might reasonably expect to see treated. *Intonation* is a feature of speech as pitch-relations are of music. Of all the insoluble problems of historical phonology intonation is perhaps the most intractable. Written music – until recently the only known way of recording the relation of pitches to words – might be expected to be of some use. But there are very few styles of word-setting that can be relied upon to convey the truth about everyday speech-melody formalized in verse. Is the style of the earliest Tudor court-songs one of them? This is doubtful. One characteristic pitch-movement of the setting of the long line is in the form of two small arches. This may indeed represent the intonation of speech, but it is also a very common melodic type in music. Moreover, there are many types of melodic progression patently uninfluenced by verbal intonations.

Concerning *enjambement* little needs to be said. As a verse procedure it is rare, since the basic structural unit of late medieval verse-rhythm is the line and not the paragraph. In long-line poems this feature is marked in the musical settings by the same devices as were described above as marking the mid-line break. To mark the end of the line, however, melismas, sometimes of considerable length, are much more prominent.

The musician, then, is conscious not only of the inner structure of the line but also of the line as a unit in itself. What conventions, if any, govern his *treatment of the stanza* or of the poem as a whole? The answer to this is that he follows quite strict conventions but they are not of a kind that throw any light on the main question – the spoken performance of late medieval verse. It does not come as a surprise to discover that the formal structures of the verse are regarded as given. There are two *formes fixes* – the carol and the rhyme-royal stanza.[23] In the carol the formal division into Burden and Verse (B VI, B VII, B VIII, ... B) is always observed, even when the form is modified, as it is in the more ambitious examples (F30–6), for example). In rhyme royal the stanza is almost invariably set in two sections with a major cadence after the fourth line, irrespective of the sense of the words. In many cases, as in the first stanza of 'That was my joy is now my woo and payne' (F23, quoted below p. 152), no unnatural effect is created: there the series of four antitheses is concluded in line 4 ('That was my wele is now my most grevaunce.') and the second half of the stanza opens with a question – 'What causyth this?' But in 'So fer I trow from remedy' (F4) the subjects of the sentence are separated from their main verb by a melisma of fourteen measures and by the mid-song cadence with a complete arrest of forward movement

> So mekyll dred, so lytyll trust [cadence]
> Cannot be well for to be wisht

Similar nonsensical breaks occur in F3 (main clause/consecutive clause), in F5 (subject/main verb), and in other songs. Common sense again suggests that this purely musical structure cannot represent the way the stanza was spoken.

Thus musing in my mind

Example 11.

(4) The rhythm of the line

We are now in a position, I hope, to draw together the threads of this analysis in the consideration of particular poems. The music helps us to a more certain reading of a poem such as the following (F19) with its irregular syllable count.

11 Thūs músyng in my mínd   grétly mérvelyng
14 Houghévyr súch dyvérsite   in ón persón may bé
15 So góödly   so cúrtesly   so géntill in behávyng
13 And so sódenly will cháunge   in évĕry degré
11 As sólen as státely   as stránge tóward mé
12 As Í of aquáyntance had néver býn afóre

13 Wherfóre I hópe to fýnd a spécïàll rémedy
12 To létt it óver páss   and thýnk therón no móre.

(I omit the detailed commentary which would support the markings which I have entered in the text.) What the setting does, as in practically all the songs of this manuscript, is to provide a rhetorical reading of the text, or enable us to reconstruct one, such as some early printed punctuations do. But the setting does more – it enables us to be much more sure which syllables were sounded, and which not; it establishes some essential stressings (the middle syllable of 'aquayntance' for instance is lengthened, heightened and rhythmically weighted in all three voices); and it interestingly suggests that two of the lines had no pause in the middle.

A poem of special interest is 'That was my joy is now my woo and payne' (F23) mentioned earlier because of its abundance of romance words; the regularity of the syllable count (ten syllables per line – none of the final -e's are sounded) is quite unusual. The decasyllabic pattern is established in the first four lines, all of which are in the syntactical pattern of the first. The pattern happens to be an iambic one but after that the decasyllables continue mostly in other rhythmic groupings except in the refrain line.

That wás my jóy   is nów my wóo and páyne;
That was my bliss is now my displesaunce
That was my trust is now my wanhope playne;
That wàs my wéle   is nów my móst greváunce.
5 What caúsȳth thìs   but ónly yowre plésâunce
Onrýghtfullỳ shewyng mé unkýndness,
That háth byn your fayre lády and mástreṡs.

Nor nóght cowde hàve   wolde I névyr so fáyne
My hárt is yoùrs   with so grét assúrance.
10 Wherfóre of rýght ye shúld my gréffe compláyne,
And with pítë háve me   in remémbraūnce
Múch the ráthir   síth my súryd constaùnce
Wolde in no wíse for jóy nor hévynèss
Have bút yoursélfe, fayre lády and mástrés.

As the markings show, there are many lines (e.g. 6, 8, 12) which cannot be read naturally with alternating stresses. With their natural speech contours, which the music seems to preserve, these are the kinds of line which Wyatt preferred and which Tottel eliminated. Such lines fall with perfect felicity, I should maintain, into the general rhythmic pattern of the poem. They sound well when read aloud; they are only 'irregular' if an anachronistic 'iambic' regularity is looked for. If we are content to look for 'harmonicall concent', the *armonia* of proportioned words and phrases, we can surely be well content with this poem.[24] It is an example of what in medieval terminology was required by *ritmica*:[25]

'rhythmical' theory is that which in the matter of verbal 'scansion' [i.e. a reading of the words as verse] seeks to know whether the words cohere well or badly [xiii cent.]

To sum up – in the absence of any other rational and convincing hypothesis about the rhythmic principles of the high-style post-Chaucerian verses, it seems reasonable to pay serious attention to the possibility that these unusually sensitive musical renderings of the text convey a contemporary 'reading' of the poems. This reading represents the poetic line as a stable, separable unit. Its rhythmic organization – and this is the most important point – is achieved through the combination into a whole of units of natural 'prose' speech – heightened perhaps but not dismembered. Only two constraints are observed in this long-line verse – an approximate length of line and, normally, a mid-line break. Iambic lines occur, in some poems quite frequently, but these represent *only one way* of creating a 'harmonicall concent'. They do not constitute, as in later verse, a norm so insistent that any deviation from it will be heard as creating a tension between 'voice' and metrical pattern – a tension which in English verse from *c.* 1550 to *c.* 1920 has to be realized in the way the verse is performed. In the fifteenth century there is no conflicting metrical pattern; the sound of the 'voice' is the sound of the verse, unmodified by a notional metre co-existing with it. Was the absence of this tension perhaps one of the features of verse technique which the early Tudor poets found and imitated in their 'maistir Chaucer'? If so, then the secret of Chaucer's rhythm may be an open secret after all.

NOTES

1 The *Fayrfax Manuscript*, BL Add.MS 5465, is printed in Appendix A of my *Music and Poetry in the Early Tudor Court*, 2nd edn (Cambridge, 1979). All references to texts of the early Tudor songbooks are to this edition; the capital letters R, F, and H refer to *Ritson's Manuscript* (BL Add.MS 5665), the *Fayrfax Manuscript* and to the so-called *Henry VIII's Manuscript* (BL Add.MS 31922) respectively. The music of the three songbooks is edited in three volumes of the Musica Britannica series: *Music at the Court of Henry VIII*, Musica Britannica, 18, 2nd edn (London, 1969) contains the songs of H; *Early Tudor Songs and Carols*, Musica Britannica, 36, (London, 1975), the songs of F and R; and *Medieval Carols*, Musica Britannica, 4, 2nd rev. edn (London, 1958), the carols of R.

2 *Early Tudor Songs and Carols (ETSC)*, introd., p. xvii. The issue is discussed more extensively in *Music and Poetry in the Early Tudor Court (M&P)*, ch.6.

3 There has been no previous study of the musical texts designed to contribute to our knowledge of the rhythmical problem.

4 *M&P*, p. 107.

5 The classical term, 'foot', for a unit of metre, is to my knowledge never used by Middle English writers except to refer to *quantitative* verse. See *MED* s.v. fot (8). Chaucer's ref. in *MkT*, VII, 3169 is typical: 'And they [tragedies] been versified comunly / Of sixe feet whiche men clepen exametron'. The vernacular term

'iambic' (with others of the class) is not medieval; it is first recorded in the 1570s (*OED*).

6 C. S. Lewis pointed out (*English Literature in the Sixteenth Century* (Oxford, 1954), p. 225) that Wyatt for instance was perfectly capable of 'ticking out' iambics 'with the ruthless accuracy of a metronome' when he wrote in poulter's measure.

7 I discuss the concept of *armonia*, harmoniousness, in ch.11 of *Words and Music in the Middle Ages* (Cambridge, 1986), espec. pp. 375–85.

8 *The Old Sound and the New* (Cambridge, 1982), pp. 7–8, q.v. for the quotations and references in this paragraph.

9 Music in *ETSC* no. 28 by Hamshere; one voice-part is missing from the MS.

10 Additional references to the musical setting of these words can be traced through *A Complete Concordance to the Songs of the Early Tudor Court*, by Michael J. Preston (Leeds, 1972).

11 See, however, the contradictions of F36 (*ETSC* no.56, m[easure] 25–6: voice ii, disyllabic; voice iii monosyllabic. (NB the underlay in voice i should be emended to give a further *di*syllabic rendering [MS sleith].) See also 'My love sche morneth [monosyll.] for me' (H25).

12 The underlay to the musical text of F26 (*ETSC* no. 46), mm 15–19 should be emended to show the trisyllable in all voices.

13 They are unfortunately not much treated in E. J. Dobson's *English Pronunciation, 1500–1700*, 2nd edn (Oxford, 1968), chiefly it seems because of the comparative paucity of the evidence. Dobson, however, points out that the most important difference in accentuation between *c.* 1500 and the present is that 'in the former there survived extensive secondary stress' alongside more modern 'single stressing' (p. 445).

14 F38; *ETSC* no. 58, mm 25–8.

15 F19; *ETSC* no. 39, mm 53–6.

16 F26; *ETSC* no. 46, mm 43–5.

17 F21; *ETSC* no. 41, mm 12–14.

18 F23; *ETSC* no. 43, mm 35–6.

19 For references, see *Concordance* (note 10 above).

20 F32; *ETSC* no. 52, mm 100–3.

21 F14; *ETSC* no. 34, mm 49–56.

22 F21; *ETSC* no. 41, mm 1–9.

23 The main repertory of late fifteenth-century carols is in MS R (see note 1 above); but their musical style and style of word-setting, although elaborated, belongs to an older tradition than that of the carols of F.

24 'Harmonicall concent': see Puttenham, *The Arte of English Poesie*, ed. G. D. Willcock and A. Walker (Cambridge, 1936) p. 64, 'Poesie is a skill to speake & write harmonically.'

25 From a treatise by Lambertus (before 1279); see *Words and Music*, p. 422 (note 7 above).

11

Aspects of the Chaucerian apocrypha: animadversions on William Thynne's edition of the *Plowman's Tale*

THOMAS J. HEFFERNAN

The single most important aspect of the formation of Chaucer's canon is the record of critical judgement which adjudicated between the apocryphal and the authorial works. Despite this important inter-textual relationship, the judgement of R. H. Robbins, and most recently Russell Peck, that 'the Chaucer apocrypha is at present the most neglected area of Chaucer and fifteenth-century studies' is substantially correct.[1]

For the last half century, all the major editions of Chaucer, namely those of Robinson, Baugh, Fisher and the Riverside, have accepted the cumulative judgements of Tyrwhitt, Bradshaw, Skeat and Hammond concerning the canon. There is no explicit analysis in Howard's biography or in the general preface to the Variorum Chaucer of the apocrypha's relationship to the canon as a problematic nor of the heuristic process out of which the canon evolved.

Baker, however, in addressing the rationale for a variorum in his preface to the facsimile of the Hengwrt Manuscript acknowledges that 'Chaucer's text has never had the stable tradition that Milton's has had, and as a result each century has had its own Chaucer.'[2] Baker's remarks, if restricted to the idea of text as strictly authorial composition, are undoubtedly correct. However, the canons of most medieval authors share this lack of stability. The fixed canon had to await the development of print and more sophisticated editorial methods. Indeed it seems to make little sense to impute to a medieval author a standard derived from a print culture It is closer to the spirit of the Middle Ages to view the transmission of the *oeuvre* of a medieval author in an organic fashion – that is as an evolutionary process which incorporates additional items into the tradition as the reception of the tradition changes.

This evolution indicates a self-conscious critical historiography, i.e. the ability to distinguish at the level of the particular between historical periods. That the Middle Ages had not achieved such a critical historiography can be demonstrated, for example, by the virtual absence of all questions concerning the identity and number of books in the New Testament: their historiography was still largely informed by a system based on belief and not by scepticism.

For the early printers of Chaucer, in particular William Thynne, we see the development of a post-medieval historiography, not because he makes the right judgements about what should be included in the canon but because in one or two of his judgements, especially that of the *Plowman's Tale* and the *Pilgrim's Tale*, singularly mistaken ones, he illustrates clearly this critical historiography.[3]

Chaucer's canon evolved alongside a substantial body of virtually contemporary apocryphal texts attributed to him. Hence the process of editorial adjudication, beginning with Shirley, has always had as one of its primary tasks identifying those genuine works amongst a corpus of spurious, albeit virtually contemporary, compositions, which vary in quality from works that were likely to have been Chaucer's, to those like Chaucer's, to poor imitations, and lastly to works which despite their claims could not have been by Chaucer.

Prior to the end of the last century, the judgement whether a text was genuine or not was often indebted to extra-textual biases: the complex political, social, moral and religious beliefs which informed the editor's historical imagination. This insinuation of the social climate in editorial judgement is not always evident nor necessarily recognized by the editor. Yet it is demonstrably present in a number of past editors of Chaucer, for example in Francis Thynne's account of his father's discussion with Henry VIII about the merits of the *Plowman's Tale* in his edition of the works, and illustrates extra-textual pressures upon the canon.

I

From Shirley to Skeat the apocrypha grew to a corpus slightly in excess of one hundred poems. Indeed, despite Tyrwhitt's excisions in his edition of 1775, Alexander Chalmer's edition of 1810 still included some 17,000 lines of poetry and reinstated texts like the *Plowman's Tale* which, although cut by Tyrwhitt, reappeared tentatively categorized as 'Certain Works of Geffrey Chaucer annexed to the Impressions printed in the years 1561 and 1602'. Twenty-five years after Chalmer's edition – a period which saw the Catholics seeking greater privileges in England – Cowden Clarke defended the authenticity of the *Plowman's Tale* and in so doing (whether wittingly or not) reaffirmed the gains made by the Church of England against that of Rome.[4]

The principal reasons for this lack of a stable textual tradition are well known to most Chaucerians: the absence of any holograph manuscripts; and unlike Gower, the lack of any substantial evidence of Chaucer's personal commitment to an accurate reproduction of his works (notwithstanding his plea for scribal care and his understanding of the vagaries of language change in *Troilus and Criseyde*, v, 1793–8); and his own ambiguous comments concerning the items which comprised his *oeuvre*.[5] Perhaps the most difficult factor which stands in the way of establishing an exact canon of Chaucer's works is the oblique nature of the poet's own remarks concerning his work. If we further consider the absence of a chronology of publication (with the single exception of the date 'The yeer of oure Lord 1391, the 12 day of March at midday' in the *Treatise on the Astrolabe* Pt II, 1, 7) it is clear that we cannot reconstruct an accurate order or canon from the poet's own testimony.

Whether in the Prologue to the *Legend of Good Women*, the Introduction to the *Man of Law's Tale* or the *Retraction* at the end of the *Canterbury Tales* (its own authenticity often questioned) Chaucer's concern for an exact catalogue of his works seems less than rigorous. His conclusion to the enumeration of his compositions in the *Legend of Good Women* may be intentionally oblique: 'He hath maad many a lay and many a thing' (*LGW*, F, 430), and 'many another book, if they were in my remembrance, and many a song and many a leccherous lay' (*Retr*). Such authorial commentary, if not a traditional topos, is hardly designed to establish these unnamed texts as an important part of his work. Indeed Chaucer's remarks are indicative of a psychology of the self with such a limited view of individual autonomy that modern notions of literary 'ownership' are singularly out of place.

Aside from such remarks concerning the existence of a considerable body of unnamed lyrics, Chaucer did cite a number of more substantial compositions by name – compositions which by virtue of their being named suggests his interest in unambiguously fixing them as his. In the Prologue to the *Legend of Good Women* he refers to two works of translation no longer extant, *Of the Wreched Engendrynge of Mankynde* (G, 414), and *Orygenes upon the Maudeleyne* (G, 418), as well as to 'many an ympne for your halydayes, / That highten balades, roundels, virelayes' (F, 422–3). Despite divided opinion on the matter, it seems most plausible to conclude that the first of these works which he cites, *Of the Wreched Engendrynge of Mankynde*, was a prose translation of the whole of Pope Innocent III's well-known *De Miseria Humane Conditionis* completed *c.* 1385–95. The text he called *Orygenes upon the Maudeleyne*, if genuine, would have been a translation of the pseudo-Origen's dramatized and rhetorically sophisticated homily *De Maria Magdalena* (of probable Cistercian provenance), based on Mary's response to Christ's empty sepulchre in John 20.11–18.[6] Although the extant manuscripts of the *De Miseria* are considerably greater in England during Chaucer's life than those of the *De Maria*, the *De Maria* was none the less popular in England in the fourteenth century. Indeed both the *De Miseria* and the *De Maria* appeared together in fourteenth-century devotional *florilegia* like Cambridge University, Peterhouse MS. 219 and Paris, Latin MSS. 2049 and 2568. The point worth underscoring here is, if Chaucer did translate both these texts, that such an endeavour indicates a considerable interest and commitment on Chaucer's part to what he refers to as 'and othere bookes of legendes of seintes, and omelies, and moralitee, and devocioun'.[7]

The additional works Chaucer mentions in the Prologue have been extremely difficult to identify. Formal love poems of this sort were commonplaces of the courtly sensibility of the late fourteenth and fifteenth centuries. Many of the apocryphal lyrics attributed to Chaucer by Pynson, Thynne, Stow and Speght for example, are virtually indistinguishable from the English lyrics of Charles d'Orléans or those of Sir Richard Roos of Leicestershire. Chaucer's equation of balades, roundels and virelays with hymns is quite curious. The extant medieval hymns/*ympne*[n] (songs used primarily for liturgical worship) for festal day/halydayes celebrations – the bulk of which would have been the feasts in the *sanctorale* – are for the most part, in theme and in structure, unlike the balade, the roundel or the virelay. Even if Brusendorff was right that the use of the names of such works in authorial lists is simply a convention, there is precious little evidence that his early editors accepted it as such.[8] Pynson, Thynne and Stow did their level best to credit him with anonymous verses which seemed to them Chaucerian, basing their judgements not only on stylistic and thematic grounds, but on the exigencies of present politics.

The hagiographies, homilies and pious readings mentioned by Chaucer are unidentified. However, if we assume that these non-extant works were genuine, it is reasonable to assume that in their composition Chaucer would have followed a method like the one he used in translating Jacobus de Voragine's *Passio Sancte Caeciliae* in his *Second Nun's Tale*:

> For bothe have I the wordes and sentence
> Of hym that at the seintes reverence
> The storie wroot, and folwen hire legende.   (VIII, 81–3)

If it is correct that in such works Chaucer exercised considerable care in translating both the word and the thought, then not only would the canon of his work be considerably larger but it would have increased in the direction of rather substantial 'pious' works. This expanding canon – the growing inclusion of materials which both reflected a changed sensibility among his readers and served to prejudice the response of future readers – created a rather different image of Chaucer for the generation following his own. The poet whom Thomas Usk described in the *Testament of Love* (a work accepted even by Tyrwhitt as genuine) as love's 'owne trewe servaunt' became by the end of the fifteenth century the poet of philosophical speculation and moral injunction. John of Ireland, a fifteenth-century member of the faculty of philosophy at the University of Paris, mentions approvingly a passage concerning God's providence and free will in the *Troilus* (IV, 953–1085) in his *Meroure of Wisdom* and evidently knew the *Parson's Tale*.[9]

II

Early Tudor literary output, certainly that prior to 1530, was almost exclusively concerned with orthodox religious and ecclesiastical themes – this is more typical of the North than of the South East or East Anglia. For example, the commonplace book of Thomas Ashby (an Augustinian canon of Bridlington) is entirely medieval in spirit; the most contemporary author Ashby cites is Jean Beleth. John Gysborn, a Praemonstratensian canon, serving as a parish priest at Allington in Lincolnshire 1520–30, also left a commonplace book very similar in sentiment to Ashby's, replete with late-medieval pious themes and traditional authors.[10] Such conservative religiosity was not restricted to the parish priest, typically limited by economics and a rudimentary education. The major clerical library of the early reign of Henry VIII was that of William Melton, chancellor of York (d. 1528). Melton's incomplete will of 1527 includes at least 100 titles from his library, and although it mentions some works of the leading humanists, they are mainly biblical and patristic. Thus despite the strength of early humanism, the traditional corpus of medieval catholicism remained the intellectual affective prop which supported Tudor piety and learning immediately prior to Henry's break with Rome. Janelle pointed out a half-century ago that English printers, up to the very moment of the Reformation, printed the most traditional and orthodox literature.[11] Thus, it made the best of historical sense for William Thynne, acting in concert with the Henrician reforms, to charge Chaucer with the authorship of such avowedly Lollard texts as the *Plowman's Tale* and *Pilgrim's Tale*.

Thynne's critical judgement was in part a product of the prevailing image of Chaucer. The most frequently anthologized of his works during the fifteenth century were the sententious moralizing compositions, like the *Clerk's Tale* (six times), the *Prioress's Tale* (five times) and the *Melibee* (five times).[12]

If we grant that the readership for his work became more religiously and socially conservative as the fifteenth century advanced, those of his works which celebrate obeisance, like that of the *De Miseria* and the *De Maria* would undoubtedly have contributed to his reputation. Thus it is puzzling both in light of this well-acknowledged drift in the change of his readership (from the court circles of the late fourteenth century to the landed gentry of the fifteenth) and the growing anthologizing of booklets of his work containing apocrypha from the middle of the fifteenth century (e.g., Bodleian Library 638 and MS. Tanner 346), that neither of these works of translation survives.[13]

None the less, Chaucer's growing reputation as a poet of real genius for the *contes moralisés* provided a substantial tradition of reception to those intent on seeing Chaucer as a proponent for a type of ecclesiastical reform, uniquely concerned with the abuse of ecclesiastical authority. For the Court of Henry VIII, especially during the tumultuous thirties, following the promulgation of the Act of the Submission of the Clergy (1531), the Statutes of Annates and Appeals, and most crucially the Act of Supremacy (1534), the need was for an edition of the most celebrated of the ancient English poets which, with whatever else it might provide its Tudor readers, should be able to evidence a healthy disrespect for church authority, especially that of the Bishop of Rome. Such works of literary apologia supporting Henrician reforms are evident as early as Richard Sampson's *Oratio* and Edward Fox's *Opus Eximium* (both published in 1534). In early 1534 Berthelet, already functioning as the King's printer, offered his services to Cromwell, thus strengthening his connection with official policy against Rome. Godfray, a friend of Berthelet and the printer of Thynne's 1532 folio edition of Chaucer's works, printed in 1534 Valla's 'On the Donation of Constantine', a work William Marshall heartily recommended to Cromwell on the grounds that 'surely I thinke there was never better boke made and sett for the defasing of the Pope of Rome than this'.[14]

Thus it was precisely when an icon of Chaucer as a paragon of clerical reform and a satirist of clerical abuse was most needed (second quarter of the sixteenth century) that we have Thynne making a substantial increase in the apocrypha (adding nineteen new items), and particularly, in the case of the *Plowman's Tale* (and in his abortive attempt to get the monarch to approve the *Pilgrim's Tale*) attributing to Chaucer a fifteenth-century text of unmitigated Lollard sentiment. Chaucer now appeared as an early advocate of the independence of the Church of England, a royalist before a Papist. Towards the end of the century Foxe could claim that Chaucer's Wycliffite sympathies were utterly transparent especially in such works as the *Plowman's Tale*.[15] We can imagine that Bale, Godfray, Thynne and other Henrician propagandists of the mid 1530s would have shared such a sentiment. Indeed Henry himself appears to have had a shrewd and timely interest in Lollardy and in Wyclif. He sent Edward Leighton with a letter (2 August 1530) from himself to the convocation of the University of Oxford requesting the University to send to him at Windsor the articles for which Wyclif was condemned and the judgements of the Council of Constance which upheld that condemnation.[16] In light of such royal interest it is perfectly consonant to note that the Archbishop of Canterbury in a letter of 20 July 1536 argued that Wyclif was wrongly condemned by the Council of Constance.[17] Henry was a man of strong passions whose sympathies were well known. It certainly seems to be the case that the leaders of the Pilgrimage of Grace thought that Henry's minions in the North were virulently anti-Papist. The reputation of a civil servant like Sir John Bulmer, was that of 'a lollard and a puller down of Abbeys'.[18] And one Crystofer Carlyll said in public (29 January 1537) 'that the King was never made supreme Head but by a sort of heretics and lollards'.[19]

In the midst of the most heated of these charges and counter charges, in the midst of this open rebellion from the north, we find William Thynne receiving money to succour those church authorities in sympathy with Henry's reforms (e.g., on 20 May 1532 Thynne was given one hundred marks for Nicholas Hancocke, late prior of Christ's Church in Aldgate, London), and to serve as a type of quartermaster for the King's army mustered at Ampthill (30 October 1536).[20] Surely such particular service in that court at that time indicates someone who, aside from the obligations of office, shared his King's passion.

In Thynne's audience before Henry VIII (?c. 1531), when he asked approval to print the combatively anti-clerical *Pilgrim's Tale*, he prudently sought Henry's protection from Wolsey's expected anger. Thynne had reason to fear Wolsey: his son Francis writes that his father 'was heaved at by Cardinal Wolseye his olde enymye'.[21] This enmity dated from the time that William Thynne allowed Skelton the use of his residence, Erith in Kent, in order to complete his satire *Colyn Cloute*.[22]

It is important to be reminded that with Speght's edition of 1602 virtually forty per cent of the canon was spurious, and hence Renaissance response to Chaucer was largely shaped by the editorial judgements of Pynson, Thynne, Stow and Speght. For example, Speght adds *Jack Upland* to his 1602 edition almost 70 years after John Gough printed it in 1536. Thus, some of the longest and most controversial items attributed to Chaucer between the middle 1530s and 1602 were works which gave succour to the foundation of the English church. Chaucer's reputation as proto-protestant reformer was to become an intellectual credo of English protestant propagandists for centuries to come.

Indeed Chaucer's Renaissance reputation for learning was directly linked to proto-protestant items from the apocrypha, most notably the *Plowman's Tale* and *Jack Upland*. On this basis William Vaughn in his *The Golden Fleece* (1626) refers to Chaucer as 'that arch heresiarch'. Milton, in his pamphlet *Of Reformation Touching Church-Discipline in England* (1641), lauds Chaucer's historical reformist insight in the *Plowman's Tale* writing: 'And this was a truth well knowne in *England* [the evil of Constantine's Donation] before this *poet* [Ariosto] was borne, as our *Chaucer's* Plowman shall tell you by and by upon another occasion.'[23]

Despite the efforts of Tyrwhitt to rid the canon of such literary 'rubbish', as late as the nineteenth century the later Romantics persisted in seeing Chaucer as both a political and religious reformer. Isaac D'Israeli believed Chaucer an ardent supporter of Lancaster, Wyclif, and the commons. While Leigh Hunt was convinced that Chaucer (echoing Vaughn), working in the cause of 'his friend' Wyclif, 'took pleasure in exposing the abuses of the church'.[24] The *Plowman's Tale* had become a leitmotif for a national Christianity striving to be born on English soil; it continued to serve the ends of anti-Catholic sentiment and English xenophobia until the middle of the nineteenth century.

III

Of all the narratives attributed to Chaucer by Thynne none has as interesting a publication history as the *Plowman's Tale*. Indeed Chaucer's Plowman is the only one of the Canterbury Pilgrims to have been favoured with the attribution of two apocryphal tales. We shall concern ourselves not with Hoccleve's poem which as Wawn says 'was subsequently rewarded with oblivion' but rather with the variant printed by Thynne which, despite Tyrwhitt's excision, continued to be taken as genuine as late as Cowden-Clark in 1835.[25]

The *Plowman's Tale*, 1380 lines long employing an eight-line stanza of alternating rhymed lines with five stresses to the line, is a form similar to that first developed and used by Chaucer in the *ABC* and in the *Monk's Tale* but with considerably more alliteration. The poem consists of a prologue and three major divisions; but these latter do not seem to support a necessary thematic or structural exigency.

The tale takes the form of a debate between a griffin and a pelican, with the griffin both embodying and defending the Roman church against the pelican's accusations of corruption. The pelican wishes to restore the church to its primitive Christian simplicity while the griffin rationalizes the need for structure as a way of maintaining a complex human organization. Such oppositions are a traditional topos of late medieval religious debate poetry. The bald dialectic was favoured by reform movements throughout the Middle Ages from the Waldensians to the later Lollards in the Court of Henry VIII, and is redolent of the complaint literature of the early fifteenth century, e.g., *Pierce the Ploughman's Creed* (see *Plowman's Tale* l. 1066). The point of such debate literature is not to present sophisticated arguments, nor to ape the scholastic *quaestiones*, nor even to present an even-sided debate, but to propagandize. In this respect the *Plowman's Tale* is typical: in the first 990 lines the griffin speaks but two lines (ll. 716 and 990), the first of which is a question! Clearly we have here the husk of the genuine debate.

Aside from the usual generalized diatribe against the clergy's corruption, wealth, ignorance, sexual promiscuity, disdain for the poor, simoniacal practices, and episcopal and papal abuse of power, the pelican singles out the office of the King as a model of the proper use of authority. The closing fifty lines of Part II are a bold contrast between the beneficent practices of the King and those of the Church: the King taxes only with the permission of Parliament while the Church taxes indiscriminately; while the King's law provides for a right of redress, the Church's is without appeal. The very roles of King and Church in England are now reversed: whereas in the past the King and his law were the paramount authority arising from the commons, now the Church is a tyrant and her law absolute. Such a sorry situation, the poem argues, is the inevitable result of the Church's failure to recognize the appropriate sphere of its ministry: the Church can no longer claim membership in the *civitas Dei* as it has given itself over wholly to *civitas hominis*.

Such polarizing sentiments were completely congruent with the needs of the Henrician reformers and the intention of Henry in promulgating the Act of Supremacy. Thynne's attribution of the *Plowman's Tale* to Chaucer, whose poetic reputation in early Tudor England was second to none, perforce invested these tired old saws not only with a legitimacy borne out of Chaucer's authority but also cloaked their nascent nationalist implications with the same unimpeachable imprimatur.

The argument presented so forcibly by the pelican was not limited to a plea for clerical reform but rather proposed that here truth and morality (i.e., native English qualities) were pitted in a titanic struggle with falsehood and corruption (i.e., things foreign, Roman). Henry became the *defensor fidei* against the Papal antichrist. The strategy was for Henry and the English Episcopacy to seize the high road, to take the position that they were the true church doing battle against a usurper – a standard reformist posture. Further, the *Plowman's Tale* was used quite deliberately to support a latent xenophobia which in turn made the Henrician reforms seem not only absolutely essential but imperative for the survival of the English nation. For this apodictic, albeit disingenuous, truth to prevail, the Chaucerian attribution had to be demonstrated beyond cavil. It is well to remember that the *Canterbury Tales* (among other books) was named in a Lincoln diocese proceeding of 1464 against the suspected Lollard John Baron of Amersham.[26] And by the 1540s the *Canterbury Tales* had acquired an 'heretical connection' precisely because of the insertion of the *Plowman's Tale*. It comes as no surprise to see Foxe attributing *Jack Upland* to Chaucer and Speght including it in his edition of 1602.[27] Sir Francis Thynne in his *Animadversions* (1598) reports that Sir John Thynne (his older cousin) told him that the Parliament was going to include Chaucer's works with 'Bookes to be forbidden ... had yt not byn that his woorkes had byn counted but fables'.[28] Between 1390 and 1540 Chaucer's reputation changed to embrace such polarities as the poet of *fin' amour*, of *contes moralisés*, and finally that of religious heresy.

IV

Wawn's study of the language of the *Plowman's Tale* confirms a composition date of the early fifteenth century, and thus supersedes Bradley's and earlier theories concerning Tudor interpolations in the tale itself.[29] Notwithstanding this early date for the original text and what Hudson has called the 'remarkable conservatism' by sixteenth-century editors in their treatment of medieval texts, it would be to read the historical circumstances naively not to suspect that Thynne or Godfray wanted to see in this anti-Papist polemic a genuine composition and thus strove to add it (and other apocrypha) to the genuine canon.[30]

The *Plowman's Tale* has had a most complex publication history. Although there is no manuscript copy extant, Speght in his preface for this tale in his 1598 edition remarked that '... I have seene it in writen hand in Iohn Stowes library in a booke of suche antiquity, as seemeth to haue beene written neare to Chaucers time'.[31] Although Speght's remarks have often been greeted with some scepticism because of recent work on the obvious archaisms of the language, it now seems entirely probable that Speght could have seen an early fifteenth-century text in Stow's library. Moreover, the anti-Papal sympathies of Henry's court would have served as a magnet

drawing from their secret recesses many a hitherto hidden manuscript with
Lollard sympathies.

A number of prominent Lollard missionaries were active in London during
the second decade of the fifteenth century. John Hacker of Coleman Street,
and his fellow Londoners, Maxwell and Stacey, regularly travelled into the
rural countryside (taking with them heterodox vernacular preaching texts)
seeking to make converts amongst the agrarian classes. Thomas Manx, who
was burned to death in Smithfield in 1518, claimed to have made 700
converts. John Colet, Dean of St Paul's, according to Erasmus's *Colloquies*,
read Wyclif's books and had Wycliffites present at his sermons. And we know
that John Tyball and Thomas Hilles, both well-known Lollards, came to
London in 1526 bringing 'certayne old bookes' for the widely-known
Lutheran sympathizer Dr J. Barnes. Is it not within the realm of probability –
remembering that Godfray printed the earliest single version of the *Plowman's
Tale* 1531–6 – that among those old books brought to or resident in London,
books which served a fairly substantial Lollard community, was perhaps a
copy of the *Plowman's Tale* written as Mr Speght put it 'neare to Chaucer's
time'?

The publication history of the tale still contains some thorny problems. The
evolutionary manner in which the tale intruded itself into the canon should
allow us a singular insight into Tudor editorial judgement. Indeed since the
tale appears in two different positions in Thynne's versions (the so-called
third folio is undated), both after the *Canterbury Tales* and before the *Parson's
Tale*, an accurate date for the tale in the undated edition can highlight not
only editorial judgement but perhaps the way the Henrician reforms intruded
themselves into that judgement.[32]

The earliest extant separate printing of the poem by Thomas Godfray is an
undated folio of 1532–6. The poem does not appear in Thynne's first black
letter folio edition of Chaucer (1532) which was printed by Godfray with a
preface by Sir Brian Tuke (d. 1536) secretary to Henry VIII. Thynne did,
however, use Godfray's text of the *Plowman's Tale* in his second edition of
Chaucer's works in 1542 of which there were two issues bearing the imprints
of W. Bonham (STC 5096) and John Reynes (STC 5070); with the exception of
their imprints both versions are identical.[33] In this 1542 edition (in the main
all the versions of the works printed after 1532 through Urry's edition of 1721
are emended reprints of the 1532 edition with the placement of the *Plowman's
Tale* inserted immediately before the *Parson's Tale*) the text of the *Plowman's
Tale* appears for the first time and concludes the *Canterbury Tales*. According to
Sir Francis Thynne, his father placed the *Plowman's Tale* after the *Canterbury
Tales* because his collation of manuscripts of the prologues of the *Parson's Tale*
made clear to his satisfaction that the *Manciple's Tale* preceded the *Parson's
Tale*, and thus the elder Thynne was not certain of 'where to place the
Plowman's Tale'. Even if we are to believe Sir Francis Thynne – he was only a
child when his father died and his *Animadversions* were written in December

1599, full fifty-seven years after the 1542 edition, with the express intention of correcting Speght's edition of 1598 – neither he nor his father seriously doubted but that the *Plowman's Tale* belonged in the *Canterbury Tales*. If his comment about his father's method of treating the *Plowman's Tale* is true then we cannot say categorically that it was William Thynne who decided to place the *Plowman's Tale* before the *Parson's Tale* in the undated or so-called third folio.

The third folio (Brewer calls it a 'bookseller's reprint of Thynne'), whatever its status, contains a number of difficult problems not the least of which is the result of its not having been dated.[34] Tyrwhitt dated the version from 1546; Skeat *c.* 1550; and the STC 1545. In addition, this version bears four different imprints: W. Bonham (STC 5071), R. Kele (STC 5072), T. Petit (STC 5073) and R. Toye (STC 5074). Whether we accept Hetherington's arguments for all four working collaterally as printers of this version or follow McKerrow's scepticism, what does seem clear from the number of printers involved is its popularity. The single difference between this version and that of 1542 is that the *Plowman's Tale* has been placed before the *Parson's Tale*. What can we infer from this repositioning? It seems reasonable to propose that the tentative attribution of the *Plowman's Tale* to Chaucer in the 1542 version met with some positive reception. Given that Chaucer's reputation from the late 1530s was seen to be increasingly in sympathy with the Henrician reforms, it is more likely to suppose that by this time, the printers (post 1542) were not seeking to create a climate for readers' approval – William Thynne had already accomplished that by his printing of the *Plowman's Tale* – but rather were responding to what was an established view of Chaucer as an early English herald of the Reformation. Thus the printers set the *Plowman's Tale* in its 'proper' place in the *Canterbury Tales*, before the *Parson's Tale*, where it was to remain, despite Tyrwhitt's efforts, as a balm for those who viewed Chaucer as a harbinger of English non-conformism for almost three centuries.

NOTES

1 D. Howard, *Chaucer: His Life, His Works, His World* (New York, 1987); F. W. Bonner, 'The Genesis of the Chaucer Apocrypha', *Studies in Philology*, 48 (1951), 461–81; N. F. Blake, 'The Relationship between the Hengwrt and Ellesmere Manuscripts of the *Canterbury Tales*', *Essays and Studies*, n.s. 32 (1979), 1–18; more recently John Bowers suggested at the New Chaucer Congress in Philadelphia (March, 1986) that the *Tale of Gamelyn* might be added to the canon ('The Evolution of *The Canterbury Tales* after 1400'); A. S. G. Edwards, *The Unity and Authenticity of 'Anelida and Arcite': The Evidence of the Manuscripts*, forthcoming; a session on the canon was held at the New Chaucer Congress, Vancouver (August, 1988); R. H. Robbins, 'The Chaucerian Apocrypha', in *A Manual of the Writings in Middle English: 1050–1500*, vol. 4 (New Haven, 1973), p. 1071; R. A. Peck, *Chaucer's 'Romaunt of the Rose' and 'Boece', 'Treatise on the Astrolabe', 'Equatorie of the Planetis', Lost Works, and Chaucerian Apocrypha* (Toronto, 1988), p. 243.
2 D. Baker, p. xviii in *The Canterbury Tales*, ed. P. G. Ruggiers (Norman, 1979).

3 A. N. Wawn, 'The Genesis of *The Plowman's Tale*', *The Yearbook of English Studies*, 2
   (1972), 21–40; and his 'Chaucer, *The Plowman's Tale*, and Reformation Propaganda: The Testimonies of Thomas Godfray and *I Playne Piers*', *Bulletin of the John
   Rylands Library*, 56 (1973–4), 174–92. Skeat's edition remains the most accessible,
   W. W. Skeat, *Chaucerian and other Pieces* (Oxford, 1897), VII, pp. 147–90.

4 This is even true to some extent of Tyrwhitt. Hench demonstrated that the actual
   form of Tyrwhitt's edition is based on the 1687 reprint of Speght, A. L. Hench,
   'Printer's Copy for Tyrwhitt's Chaucer', *Studies in Bibliography*, 3 (1950), 265–6;
   Windeatt has shown that Tyrwhitt followed Urry's practice of imposing a
   considerable number of metrical emendations on his text, B. A. Windeatt, 'Thomas
   Tyrwhitt', *Editing Chaucer: The Great Tradition*, ed. P. G. Ruggiers (Norman, 1984),
   pp. 123, 132–3, 274, n. 7; see also A. S. G. Edwards, 'Editorial Problems in Later
   Middle English Literature', in *Manuscripts and Texts*, ed. D. Pearsall (Woodbridge,
   1985), pp. 46–8; Robbins, *The Chaucerian Apocrypha*, p. 1071.

5 Francis Thynne's comments concerning the manuscript in his father's possession
   containing the phrase *Examinatur Chaucer* are tantalizing but of little value since no
   one has seen it.

6 R. E. Lewis, 'What Did Chaucer Mean by *Of the Wreched Engendrynge of Mankynde*?'
   Chaucer Review, 2 (1968), 139–58, and his *De Miseria Conditionis Humanae* (Athens,
   Ga., 1978), pp. 17–31. J. P. McCall, 'Chaucer and the Pseudo-Origen *De Maria
   Magdalena*: A Preliminary Study', *Speculum*, 46 (1971), 491–509, and R. Woolf,
   'English Imitations of the *Homelia Origenis de Maria Magdalena*', in *Chaucer and Middle
   English Studies in Honour of Rossell Hope Robbins*, ed. B. Rowland (London, 1974),
   pp. 389–90.

7 R. F. Green, *Poets and Princepleasers* (Toronto, 1980), pp. 161–6. In the *Retraction* he
   mentions a work called 'the book of the Leoun ... and othere bookes of legendes of
   seintes, and omelies, and moralitee, and devocioun' (*Retr*, x, 1087). The most likely
   source for this *dit amoreux* would be an adaptation of Machaut's *Dit du Lyon*, a
   courtly allegory in which the hero learns a lesson along with the promise of *fin'
   amour*.

8 Aage Brusendorff, *The Chaucer Tradition* (London, 1925), pp. 432–3.

9 J. A. W. Bennett, 'Those Scotch Copies of Chaucer', *Review of English Studies*, n.s. 32
   (1981), 294–6.

10 For Ashby, see Durham Univ. Lib. MS Cosin v, v, 19, and for Gysborn, BL MS
   Sloane 1584. See also A. G. Dickens, 'The Writers of Tudor Yorkshire', in
   Reformation Studies (London, 1982), pp. 219–20; and his *Lollards and Protestants in the
   Diocese of York* (London, 1982), p. 138; see also J. A. F. Thomson, *The Later Lollards*
   (Oxford, 1965), p. 192–201.

11 P. Janelle, *L'Angleterre catholique à la veille du schisme* (Paris, 1935).

12 C. A. Owen, Jr, 'The *Canterbury Tales*: Early Manuscripts and Relative Popularity',
   Journal of English and Germanic Philology, 54 (1955), 104–10; D. S. Silvia, 'Some
   Fifteenth-Century Manuscripts of the *Canterbury Tales*', in *Chaucer and Middle English
   Studies in Honour of Rossell Hope Robbins*, ed. B. Rowland (London, 1974), pp. 153–63.

13 The change in audience from men such as Clifford, Fastolf, Scogan, Sturry,
   Clanvowe, Gower, Usk and Hoccleve to the wealthy country households of the
   fifteenth century, like the Berkeleys of Wymondham in Leicestershire, the Grey-
   stokes or the Sherbrookes of Nottingham, while it reflects a growing appropriation
   by a landed class, further suggests that while these members of the gentry found
   their values being reinforced by aspects of his work their positive response in turn
   created a new image of the poet. See M. N. Hallmundsson, 'Chaucer's Circle:

Henry Scogan and His Friends', *Medievalia et Humanistica*, 10 (1981), 129–39; T. Turville-Petre, 'Some Medieval English Manuscripts in the North-East Midlands', in *Manuscripts and Readers in Fifteenth-Century England*, ed. D. Pearsall (Woodbridge, 1983), pp. 126, 139, and J. Boffey, *Manuscripts of English Courtly Love Lyrics in the Later Middle Ages* (Woodbridge, 1985), pp. 13, 130–5.

14 J. K. McConica, *English Humanists and Reformation Politics* (Oxford, 1965), p. 136.

15 G. Townsend (ed.), *The Acts and Monuments of John Foxe*, 5 vols. (London, 1837), IV, pp. 249–50, in a discussion of the Episcopal censure of vernacular books between 1518–21.

16 J. S. Brewer (ed.), *Letters and Papers Foreign and Domestic of the Reign of Henry VIII*, vol. IV, pt III 1529–30 (London, 1876), p. 2946, no. 6546. Hereafter cited as *Letters and Papers*.

17 J. Gairdner (ed.), *Letters and Papers*, vol. IX, p. 53, no. 124, item 9.

18 *Letters and Papers*, vol. XII, pt I, p. 454, no. 1011.

19 *Letters and Papers* vol. XII, pt I, p. 128, no. 275.

20 *Letters and Papers*, vol. V, p. 485, no. 1065, and *Letters and Papers*, vol. IX, p. 374, no. 937.

21 Francis Thynne, *Chaucer: Animadversions*, ed. G. H. Kingsley, *EETS*, o.s. 9 (London, 1865), p. 7.

22 W. Nelson, *John Skelton, Laureate* (New York, 1939; reprt. 1964), who notes a copy of *Colyn Cloute* printed by Godfray (but not recorded by the STC) which is in the Woburn Abbey Library. See also Greg Walker, *John Skelton and the Politics of the 1520s* (Cambridge, 1988), pp. 116–17.

23 A. N. Wawn, 'Chaucer, Wyclif and the Court of Apollo', *English Language Notes*, 10 (1972), 17; C. F. E. Spurgeon, *Five Hundred Years of Chaucer Criticism and Allusion 1357–1900*, 3 vols. (New York, 1960), I, p. 220.

24 F. W. Bonner, 'Chaucer's Reputation during the Romantic Period', *Furman Studies*, 34 (1951), 12–14.

25 Hoccleve's poem is extant in Christ Church, Oxford MS CLII, appearing after the *SqT*, and in Ashburnham MS 133; A. N. Wawn, 'Chaucer, *The Plowman's Tale*, and Reformation Propaganda ...' p. 174.

26 M. Aston, *Lollards and Reformers: Images and Literacy in Late Medieval Religion* (London, 1984), p. 208.

27 P. L. Heyworth (ed.), *Jack Upland* (Oxford, 1968), pp. 5–6.

28 G. H. Kingsley (ed.), 'Francis Thynne, *Chaucer: Animadversions*', *EETS*, o.s. 9 (London, 1865), p. 7.

29 Wawn, 'The Genesis of *The Plowman's Tale*', 39–40.

30 A. Hudson, *Lollards and Their Books* (London, 1985), p. 245.

31 *Geoffrey Chaucer: The Works 1532, with supplementary material from the Editions of 1542, 1561, 1598 and 1602*. A facsimile with introduction by D. S. Brewer (London, 1969); see Speght's 'Arguments to every Tale and Booke'. See also W. W. Skeat, *The Works of Geoffrey Chaucer* (London, 1905), a facsimile with introduction of Thynne's edition of 1532.

32 I believe the date of 1546–50 for this edition is too late. Indeed I suspect from remarks made by F. Thynne in his *Animadversions* that it is possible to date this folio earlier, perhaps even in his father's lifetime.

33 See the bibliography on these early editions (1532–1687) by J. R. Hetherington, *Chaucer 1532–1602* (Birmingham, 1964/7). Contains an appendix on the 1687 folio.

34 Brewer, section III.

12

The shape-shiftings of the Wife of Bath, 1395–1670

HELEN COOPER

The multitude of readers who have been captivated, since Chaucer's own time, by the Wife of Bath, is matched by the multitude of different interpretations of her. She is shrew, virago, *femme fatale*; she is the voice of feminism, or the projection of centuries of male misogynist fantasy. She represents Eve, or all of mankind that refuses to be born again in the Redemption; she stands for joy and vitality against a life-denying and cheerless orthodoxy. Her character is a mirror of Chaucer's own, a patchwork pastiche of other people's writings, open to deep Freudian psychoanalysis, or the greatest creation before Falstaff.[1] She is the antifeminists' nightmare come true, whom no man within the fiction of the *Tales* can resist when once she has marked him down.

There is some evidence for all of these contradictory readings in the text, and Chaucer adds yet more through the way he tells the Wife's *Prologue* and *Tale*. The one thing that everyone who has ever heard of the *Canterbury Tales* knows about it, that the Wife demands female sovereignty in marriage, is itself put into doubt by the end of both her *Prologue* and her *Tale*. The vicissitudes of her relationship with her fifth husband, the clerk Jankin, end not with their fight but with their reconciliation:

> I was to hym as kynde
> As any wyf from Danemark unto Ynde,
> And also trewe, and so was he to me. (III, 823–5)

She may be a biased reporter, but the ending of her *Tale* endorses her words here, as the hag-turned-beauty ensures the bliss of her marriage in the way one might least expect:

> She obeyed hym in every thing
> That myghte doon him pleasance or likyng.
> And thus they lyve unto hir lyves end
> In parfit joye. (III, 1255–8)

This is as much of a transformation on the moral side as the physical metamorphosis that has turned the bride from loathly to lovely.

168

Such shape-shiftings characterize every aspect of both the Wife and her *Tale*'s protagonist. The hag occupies an undefined border area between human and fairy. She is a fairy-tale character, yet she delivers a hundred-line speech on the nature of true virtue that is one of the most serious and impassioned pieces of poetry Chaucer ever wrote. Above all, she is a projection of the Wife herself, serving for her as a kind of wish-fulfilment, as a way of running time backwards –

> Age, allas, that al wole envenyme,
> Hath me biraft my beautee and my pith. (III, 474–5)

In the old woman, Alison of Bath can recover her youth, her beauty and her sexual attractiveness.

The Wife's *Prologue* and *Tale* do not exist independently either of each other or of the rest of the *Tales*. She herself gets into the end of the *Clerk's Tale* as a counter-example to patient Griselda, and its Envoy is sung for 'love' of her; in the *Merchant's Tale* she is cited by the dotard January's upright counsellor as an expert on marriage.[2] That she opens a debate on marriage that ranges across these and several other tales (the *Franklin's*, *Melibee*, the *Nun's Priest's*) has become one of the critical commonplaces of the work. These other tales do not necessarily present views contrary to the Wife's: given the multiplicity of opinions contained within her *Prologue* and *Tale*, that would scarcely be possible. In *Melibee*, Prudence, who is as much a personified virtue as a good wife, offers the theoretical justification for women's counsel (VII, 1055–1155), of which the loathly lady's discourse on the nature of *gentillesse* is the finest example. The definition the hag gives of true nobility, of virtue independent of high birth, is in turn embodied in the Wife's counter-type, Griselda. More surprising still is that the ending of the story of Griselda advocates a mutual respect and consideration as the basis for marital bliss very much in the manner of the end of the Wife's tale: if the newly beautiful bride does everything to her husband's pleasure, Walter does Griselda 'feithfully pleasaunce' (IV, 1111).

In addition to all this, the loathly lady is, it seems, a fairy queen, one of three such figures in the *Tales*. She herself is apparently to be identified with the 'elf-queene' described at the opening of the *Wife's Tale*, who

> with hir joly compaignye
> Daunced ful ofte in many a grene mede, (III, 860–1)

for it is just so that the knight finds the hag and the troupe of dancers later. Furthermore, there is no explanation given of her ability to change shape in terms of her being a woman cruelly enchanted, as happens in the analogues: it is not that the knight breaks a spell, but that she chooses to show herself as beautiful. The two other elf-queens of the *Tales* make their appearance later than the Wife's, so implicitly inviting comparison with her. The fairy who is the object of Sir Thopas's quest is notable most for her difference from the loathly lady, and she had to wait until the sixteenth century for Spenser to suggest a connection between them. More immediately significant in the context of the *Tales* is the Proserpina of the *Merchant's Tale*, whom Chaucer makes into the queen who dances in January's garden with 'al hire fayerye' (IV, 2038–41), and who enables the rebellious wife of the story to have her will and get away with it.

If the Wife can adopt such a multitude of shapes within the text – the loathly lady being only one projection, though one that in turn generates other forms – it is no wonder that readers and imitators of Chaucer over the two centuries following her creation should show her undergoing a further series of metamorphoses, as each shape hatched others. Almost all the modern readings of the Wife are foreshadowed in these early responses to her: the exceptions are exegetical–allegorical interpretations, supposedly medieval but unsupported by any contemporary evidence, and, more predictably, the psychoanalytical. Medieval and Renaissance readers ascribed to her neither suppressed inner meanings, nor a suppressed subconscious. She was, however, very much a vital character; to Thomas Nashe, in 1592, she was one of the prime examples of the immortality that poetry can give.[3] It was not until the generation of classicizing poets of the end of the seventeenth century that she was treated as an antiquarian phenomenon, to be polished up to a new standard of poetic elegance. Dryden may have given her *Tale* literary respectability, but it is more of a tribute to her continuing potential for subversion that in 1632 the printer of the broadside ballad of *The Wanton Wife of Bath* was imprisoned for outraging Reformation religious orthodoxy as the Wife had once outraged Catholicism.[4]

The Wife's refusal to stay within the bounds of her own text is apparent from the moment of her creation. By the time Chaucer wrote his *Envoy to Bukton*, where she is recommended as necessary reading on the subject of matrimony, she had clearly acquired a notoriety among Chaucer's real-life audience similar to that she bears among his fictional pilgrims. Some of the scribes of early manuscripts of the *Tales* reacted to her with more asperity, adding pointed comments in the margin or occasionally even furnishing extra lines. The scribe of the Ellesmere Manuscript displays a nice touch of indignation at the sufferings of her abused husbands:

> Bihoold how this goode wyf served hir iij first housbondes whiche were goode olde men.[5]

More enthusiastic misogyny comes over from the marginal comments on CUL MS Dd. 4.24, which endorse with a 'Verum est' or 'Nota' women's superior ability in swearing and lying, their inordinate desire of anything forbidden, their inability to keep a secret, their wickedness and contrariety, that flattery facilitates seduction, and the proverb against allowing wives to go on pilgrimages.[6]

Against such a background, it is all the more surprising that the one

appearance of the Wife in the various fifteenth-century additions and supplements to the *Canterbury Tales* shows a very different side of her. The anonymous author of the *Tale of Beryn* was a very attentive reader of the *Tales* indeed;
and he picks up, not the commonplaces of her husband-baiting or women's
unregenerateness, but her fondness for 'gossibs', for chatting with congenial
female company (see III, 529–38). The *Beryn* Prologue describes the pilgrims'
activities when they finally reach Canterbury, the Wife's among them:

> The wyff of bath was so wery, she had no will to walk;
> She toke the Priores by the hond: 'madam! wol ye stalk
> Pryuely in-to þe garden, to se the herbis growe?
> And after, with our hostis wyff, in hir parlour rowe,
> I woll gyve ȝewe the wyne, & yee shull me also.'[7]

The author may lose some chances for comedy, but his ability to make the
Wife do the slightly unexpected, but none the less right, thing, is closer to
Chaucer's treatment of her than the stereotype of the shrewish wife so widely
mothered on her elsewhere.

The Wife's spreading fame outside the immediate context of the *Tales*
during the fifteenth century certainly owed more to this stereotype: every
mention of her brings with it an implied *frisson* for the male of the species. The
'friend' who advises Hoccleve to write in praise of women mentions her as
authority for the fact that

> wommen han no ioie ne deyntee
> þat men sholde upon hem put any vice,[8]

and the allusion carries with it an unmistakable threat of retribution.
Elsewhere her name is used more openly as a rallying-call to the sect of what
the Clerk calls 'archewyves': a wife in one of Lydgate's disguisings, for
instance, cites her instructions on 'howe wyves make hir housbandes wynne
heven' on behalf of all married women who

> clayme maystrye by prescripcyoun,
> Be long tytle of successyoun
> Frome wyff to wyff.[9]

The Jane Scrope of Skelton's *Phyllyp Sparowe*, running through her life's
reading, gets through the rest of the *Canterbury Tales* in four lines before she
homes in with a kind of shocked admiration on

> the Wyfe of Bath
> That worketh moch scath
> Whan her tale is tolde
> Among huswyves bolde,
> How she controlde
> Her husbandes as she wolde,
> And them to despyse
> In the homylyest wyse,
> Brynge other wyves in thought
> Their husbandes to set at nought.[10]

Chaucer's Wife insists both on her domination of her husbands and on her sexuality, and the latter invited a further antifeminist interpretation as promiscuity. By the early seventeenth century, Richard Brathwait, in his commentary-paraphrase on the Wife's *Prologue*, could take it for granted that what Alison calls 'love' should be redefined as 'lust'.[11] He seems to be drawing on an alternative stereotype to the shrewish wife, of promiscuous womanhood, that had been associated with the Wife for over a century. It appears in works such as Dunbar's *Tua Mariit Wemen and the Wedo*,[12] where the three women divide up Alison's experience of unhappy marriage and cheerful widowhood between them, and add a measure of overt lechery that Chaucer holds back from. The 'tretis' is most strongly indebted to the whole antifemi-nist background it shares with the Wife's *Prologue*, but it seems to have been Chaucer who provided Dunbar with the seed of the poem, and with some of its details – such as women's fondness for showing themselves off at plays and 'preichingis' and on pilgrimages. A similar debt to misogyny in general and Chaucer in particular is owed by a ballad of about 1520 entitled *The boke of mayde Emlyn that had V Husbandes and all kockoldes*,[13] which caps Emlyn's wifely dominance by having her dispose of her third husband by pushing him down a well. The Wife of Bath does not get a specific mention, but the ancestry of the gaily-apparelled spinner suggests itself on a number of occasions:

> If her husbande said ought,
> Loke what she sonest cought,
>   At his heed she wolde it flynge
> She wolde saye, lozell thou
> I wyll teche the, I trowe,
>   Of thy language to blynne;
> It is pyte that a knaue
> A prety woman sholde haue,
>   That knoweth not golde from tynne.
> I trowe thou jalouse be
> Bytwene my cosyn and me . . .   (pp. 15–16)

Such techniques of husband-baiting are identical to the Wife's. Like her too, Emlyn is ready to accuse her husbands of impotence, to exchange an old and inadequate husband for 'a yonge lusty one', and to mourn briefly (with the aid of an onion in her handkerchief) between successive marriages. There is a certain admirable energy in all this, but the ballad ends as condemnatory in a manner very far from Chaucer. Emlyn represents a whole conglomerate of crimes as well as sins, and she finishes up being punished both by men (in the stocks) and by God, with the 'rodde of pouerte'.

An attempt from the end of the sixteenth century to model a work on the *Canterbury Tales* runs into similar problems of stereotyping: its Wife figure has something of both the loathly lady and Maid Emlyn about her. *The Cobler of Caunterburie*, first published in 1590, is a collection of prose tales supposedly told by six passengers on a barge travelling down the Thames from Billingsgate to Gravesend. They include an 'old wife', in part at least because such a figure seems to have been considered an essential element in imitating the *Tales*; as the final narrator puts it,

> We haue imitated ould Father Chaucer, hauing in our little Barge, as he had in his trauell sundry tales, and amongst the rest, the old wiues tale.[14]

All the narrators are described in doggerel verse immediately before their tales. The account of the old wife owes a little to the *General Prologue* portrait of the Wife of Bath, rather more to the topos of the hideous old woman that underlies both the hag of the *Wife's Tale* and other literary figures such as Skelton's Elinour Rummyng:

> Crooked was this beldam for age,
> Huffe shouldred, and of a wrinckled visage:
> And as hir backe and necke was croked,
> So was hir nose long and hooked . . .   (1902–5)

> Shee was mouthed like a sparrow,
> Gated like a wheelbarow,
> And of long time beforne
> Nat a tooth in hir head had she borne   (1910–13)

(the collocation of 'gated' with the lack of teeth may pick up the Wife's being 'gat-tothed', I, 468). She shares her prototype's fondness for 'gossibs', and her fellow-passengers' fondness for strong drink. Her clothes, in contrast to the Wife's, are distinctive more by age and eccentricity than flamboyance, but she does have an enormous red hat 'like a bushel' (compare the Wife's ten-pounder coverchiefs, buckler-sized hat and red stockings).

The tale she tells is much more predictable in type than the romance Chaucer eventually chose for Alison of Bath. It is a fabliau about an adulterous wife, based on two stories from the *Decameron*[15] – the sort of story Chaucer seems to have had in mind originally for his own Wife, if the present *Shipman's Tale* were indeed assigned to her. The wife of the old woman's tale twice persuades her husband of her innocence despite all evidence to the contrary, and the moral that the other passengers in the barge draw from it is close to that offered by the Proserpina element of the *Merchant's Tale*:

> Euery man began to commend the wit of a woman, who on the sudden is euer most quick, & percing, able so soone to yeeld a peremptory excuse, as the occasion is ministred.   (p. 74)

The Merchant's elf-queen Proserpina had given May and all women after her a ready answer: this wife is one of those to benefit.

The second half of the old woman's story is of particular interest for the history of the re-workings of the *Wife of Bath's Tale*, for it appears again as the sub-plot in a Jacobean dramatization of Chaucer's story of the knight and the loathly lady, John Fletcher's *Women Pleas'd*.[16] The two 'old wives' tales', of the road to Canterbury and the barge to Gravesend, are brought together to constitute a single play.

It must be admitted that the play adapts both its source plots very freely. One in particular of the changes Fletcher makes, however, paradoxically brings him back towards the Wife of Bath: the play finishes as a justification of the women at the expense of the men. The wife of the fabliau sub-plot turns out to have only virtuous intentions. The loathly lady of the main story undergoes, and passes, her own test of faithfulness, for she is in fact the knight's true lover, a princess who has followed him into exile disguised as a hag after the quest for the answer to the riddle had been imposed on him as a punishment for daring to court her.

The *Wife's Tale* ends with a series of logically related but ultimately contradictory turns of plot. The answer to the question of what women most desire is *sovereyntee*: the hag exerts her mastery over the knight first against his will, in demanding marriage, then with his co-operation, as he allows her to choose whether she will be old and faithful, or beautiful with all its attendant dangers. His free granting of *maistrie* to her results in her transformation to a young woman both beautiful and true; but their 'parfit joye' lies also in her obeying him in everything that pleases him. *Women Pleas'd* runs into a similar series of equivocations and contradictions, though by somewhat different ways. The forms of both the question and its answer are morally condemnatory, as Chaucer's are not:

> Tell me what is that onely thing,
>   For which all women long;
> Yet having what they most desire,
>   To have it do's them wrong.   (v, i, 127–30)

> ... In good or ill
> They desire, to have their will;
> Yet when they have it, they abuse it,
> For they know not how to use it.   (138–41)

The action of the play, however, runs counter to such moral rigidity, for it is only when the women are allowed to exercise their wills that a happy and peaceful ending becomes possible – a happy ending that is asserted to be in accordance with 'heavens hand' (v, iii, 79). Belvidere, the princess disguised as a hag, sheds her foul appearance to offer her beloved Silvio the same choice as Chaucer's loathly lady gives her husband: beautiful and wanton, or ugly and virtuous. Her acknowledgement that she is truly herself, both fair and virtuous, follows on Silvio's committing the choice to her 'soveraigne will'. With the removal of the supernatural aspects of the story, there is a strong implication that true identity and personal freedom are related: that she can show herself in her true shape, both physical and moral, only when she can make such a choice for herself. Nor is such freedom limited to the central pair of characters. Belvidere has a rival suitor who has been waging war to gain her

hand; he agrees to allow her widowed mother to choose an alternative bride
for him, and she deploys the same ideas to declare that she will herself marry
him:

> I thank ye Sir, I have got the mastry too,
> And here I give your Grace a husbands freedome.
> Give me your hand, my Husband.   (v, iii, 100–2)

'Mastry' enables freedom, just as the bride of the *Wife's Tale* exercises her
maistrie in obedience.

Any perceptive reading of the *Wife's Tale* requires some such conclusion; it
is more surprising to find that Fletcher gives a similar thematic treatment to
his sub-plot, despite its being based on the fabliau of the adulterous wife from
Boccaccio and the *Cobler of Caunterburie*. In the play, the young and beautiful
wife Isabella is driven to the brink of unfaithfulness by her husband's treating
her *as if* she were old, ugly and low-born, the three qualities the knight of the
Wife's Tale holds against his bride:

> Do you think to famish me,
> Or keep me like an Almes-woman in such rayment,
> Such poore unhandsome weeds? am I old, or ugly?
> I never was bred thus: and if your misery
> Will suffer wilful blindnesse to abuse me,
> My patience shall be no Bawd to mine owne ruine.   (i, ii, 46–51)

If 'the happinesse of youth and beauty' is only 'to live a slave', Isabella will
make her own freedom. She is converted back onto the path of virtue, in the
nick of time, by her husband's own conversion. When he is prepared to make
her 'Mistris of [her] fortune' (v, ii, 6), she will freely exercise her will in love
and faithfulness. The moral of both plot and sub-plot is expressed in the final
lines of the play, spoken by Belvidere's mother:

> How to preserve a wife, and keep her faire,
> Give 'em their soveraign wills, and pleas'd they are.   (v, iii, 112–13)

The widening of the import of the story to a general principle of morals
(conveniently indistinguishable, in this case, from self-interest) is made
possible largely because of the absence of the fairy element. Its removal
scarcely makes the plot more credible; as a story, indeed, it is rather more
successful with the human implications taken out. A broadside version of the
Wife's Tale made by Richard Johnson in 1612, *A New Sonet of a Knight and a
Faire Virgin*,[17] shows how attractive it can be at the simplest level of fairy-tale:

> I read how, in King Arthur's time,
> A knight, as he did ride,
> Did meet a virgin faire and bright
> About the greene-wood side.   (p. 68)

All the elements that make for complexity in the original (the Wife as
narrator, the *gentillesse* speech) or in Fletcher's re-working (the women's role

as moral centre) are abandoned here in favour of concentration on the story alone. No connection is made, for instance, between the terms of the answer to the riddle —

> It seems to me that soveraignetie
> Is that that women love best   (p. 70)

— and the loathly lady's transformation. She does not even promise faithfulness to offset her warning of youth and beauty:

> Sir, quoth she, were not you better have me
> Being both shrewd and old,
> Then to have youth that, for a truth,
> Should make you a cuckold?   (p. 71)

The style does not, however, invite ambiguous or ironic interpretations: it is a wish-fulfilment poem, not for an ageing woman, but for every man who wants a pliant and beautiful bride that he doesn't deserve.

The *New Sonet* is exceptional among later treatments of Wifely material in its avoidance of moral interpretation. When moral readings became the point at issue, writers had a much harder time with the matters raised by the *Tale*. Spenser is the most striking example. He quarried the *Canterbury Tales* frequently for ideas and motifs for the *Faerie Queene*, especially in Books II to VI; and female sovereignty is one of his recurrent themes. Where Chaucer explores a paradox, however, Spenser runs into a contradiction:

> Such is the crueltie of womenkynd,
> When they have shaken off the shamefast band,
> With which wise Nature did them strongly bynd
> T'obay the heasts of mans well ruling hand,
> That then all rule and reason they withstand,
> To purchase a licentious libertie.
> But vertuous women wisely vnderstand,
> They they were borne to base humilitie,
> Unlesse the heauens them lift to lawfull soueraintie.[18]   (v, v, 25)

The grudging exception made in the last line obviously stems in part from the historical and cultural circumstances of the work's composition, its nature as an encomium of the ruling Queen; but the detail of the narrative confirms that something more complex is at issue.

The Wife of Bath would certainly not fall within the category of 'vertuous women' as Spenser defines it here. Her desire for the supposedly male role of sovereignty is declared throughout her *Prologue* and *Tale*, and is implied by her portrait in the *General Prologue*. With her sharp spurs, her shield-sized hat and her readiness to indulge in physical battle with her fifth husband, she is something of a virago — a female warrior. Chaucer has no literal female warriors; but the *Faerie Queene* contains several characters who bear some resemblance to such a prototype, and their diversity is disconcerting.

Britomart is the most important. She is pursuing only a single husband, but she is unquestionably pursuing him. Womanly submission is not her most apparent quality: she enters the work when she turns her invincible lance on the hero of the previous book, and defeats him. As her first action, this is of particular importance for defining her allegorical nature; and so is her first speech, which borrows *verbatim* the lines of the *Franklin's Tale* that are customarily read in conjunction with the debate on sovereignty in marriage:

> Ne loue be compeld by maisterie;
> For soon as maisterie comes, sweet loue anone
> Taketh his nimble wings, and soone away is gone.[19]

If Britomart were solely a personified virtue, such matters might be reconcilable with the views Spenser expresses elsewhere on women's need to be ruled; but she is very much woman – a woman who embodies a virtue, certainly, but not a virtue given allegorical form by the linguistic accident of the gender of abstract nouns. Spenser emphasizes her quality as a pseudo-historical character within his debate on women's proper role in society, this time in terms distinctly at odds with most of his statements on the subject:

> But by record of antique times I find,
> That women wont in warres to bear most sway,
> And to all great exploits them selues inclind;
> Of which they still the girlond bore away,
> Till enuious Men fearing their rules decay,
> Gan coyne streight lawes to curb their liberty;
> Yet sith they warlike armes haue layd away,
> They haue exceld in artes and pollicy,
> That now we follish men that prayse gin eke t'envy.   (III, ii, 2)

The equality of the sexes in personal relationships that Britomart advocates is here extended to women's supremacy in every function in society.

By virtue of being equal with the best, Britomart can be the acceptable face of female superiority; by the nature of her name virtue, Chastity, she can represent the acceptable face of female sexuality. She is never taken as a threat to the established order, as the Wife of Bath is. It is rather her 'demonic opposites' who take to impermissible and unbridled lengths her rejection of celibacy and her ability to overthrow the males she meets. Some of these opposites, such as Malecasta (III, i), represent promiscuity of a kind rather different from the Wife's, though they fall within the tradition of Dunbar's lustful widows or 'mayde' Emlyn. Others, notably the giantess Argante and the amazon Radegund, are warrior figures who have more in common with the Wife, or with the literary relations of her *Tale*.

Radegund differs from both Britomart and Argante in that the men she overcomes surrender to her at least in part voluntarily. She appears in Book V, when she defeats Artegall, dresses him Hercules-style in women's clothes, and sets him to the women's occupation of spinning in the company of all the other men she has similarly overthrown. She thus represents unjust female dominance – dominance, that is, contrary to the justice that Artegall embodies. Even here, however, Spenser will not commit himself whole-heartedly to a reading of the episode based solely on gender, for Radegund is finally overcome, not by men, but by Britomart. She restores the proper rule of men, but only by the paradoxical means of taking over the government herself:

> She ther as Princess rained,
> And changing all that forme of common weale,
> The liberty of women did repeale,
> Which they had long usurpt; and them restoring
> To mens subiection, did true Iustice deale;
> That all they as a Goddesse her adoring,
> Her wisedom did admire, and harkened to her loring.   (v, vii, 42)

Patriarchy, it is implied, is the right and proper order of things, even when it has to be instigated and supported by a woman, and when the woman has to be metaphorically elevated to a 'goddesse' to justify her otherwise illicit sovereignty. The *Wife's Tale* and *Women Pleas'd* insist on the paradox of free-dom in obedience; Spenser seems to be asserting the patriarchal principle against the drift of his own text.

Argante, the giantess of unrestrained sexual appetite of III, vii, brings no such moral contradictions with her, and she would seem at first glance to have few connections with Chaucer. She is, however, the sister of Ollyphaunt, and it is through her brother that her genealogy becomes clear. Ollyphaunt takes his name from the giant who ranges the borders of Faerieland in *Sir Thopas*, and whose overthrow will, in the foreseeable course of Chaucer's plot, be a prerequisite of Thopas's winning his elf-queen. The giantess of promiscuity is the female twin to that Ollyphaunt whose literary ancestor bars the way to those who would venture on enchanted ground – and it is worth remembering that Arthur's dream of his own elf-queen, Gloriana, is itself based on *Sir Thopas*. Read allegorically, Argante is 'will' in its medieval and Elizabethan sense of sexual appetite: she is a type of sexual voraciousness whose female will is a perversion of true sovereignty, and especially the true sovereignty of the virgin Faerie Queen. She stands not only for the negation of social or political sovereignty, but also for a lack of self-mastery. She is an unconquer-able and demanding female – in many ways (though not in narrative image) like a promiscuous version of the Wife, one larger than life in the most literal sense – but Spenser has her represent the uncontrollable sexual appetite of the *male*: that is why the Squire of Dames is her principal victim, and why she is pursued by another virgin warrior, Palladine. Even so, the allegorical interpretation is no more than a gender-neutral gloss on a deeply antifeminist episode.[20] The Squire recounts his easy conquest of nine hundred women within a year, and his near-total inability to find any who resist him, to the accompaniment of hearty laughter from his male auditors. The one truly chaste woman he has met, interestingly enough, takes a form similar to the

Wife of Bath's principal counter-type, Griselda: a country girl of 'low degree' who yet embodies virtue, chastity and 'simple truth' (III, vii, 59).

As such, she is a figure unique in Spenser. The reasons for her uniqueness become clear from his one close allusion to the *Wife's Tale*: an allusion ascribed by antonomasia to Chaucer, but which actually ends up saying the precise opposite of its original.

> True is, as whilome that good Poet sayd,
> The gentle mind by gentle deeds is knowne.
> For a man by nothing is so well bewrayd,
> As by his manners, in which plaine is showne
> Of what degree and what race he is growne.   (VI, iii, 1)

The hag instructed her bridegroom that 'he is gentil that dooth gentil dedis' (III, 1170), that the 'moost vertuous' is the 'grettist gentil man' (1113, 1116), that 'Crist wol we clayme of hym oure gentillesse'; other narrators from the Clerk to the Parson endorse her words. For Spenser, 'gentle manners' are born of 'gentle blood' (VI, iii, 2). The debate occurs in the book of Courtesy, where Calidore repeatedly shows his superiority not only to the discourteous but also to the low-born. His sojourn among the shepherds is marked by his outdoing them in courtesy and bravery, and the true-love he finds there, Pastorella, is no Griselda figure. As with Perdita, or with Calidore himself, her superiority to the society that has nurtured her is innate: she is high born.

'Of Court it seemes, men Courtesie doe call',[21] but, as with the issue of female sovereignty, the tenor of the narrative in the *Faerie Queene* pulls away from Spenser's statements on the subject. Calidore's stay in the country of the shepherds may be a diversion from his quest, but it is also the allegorical core of the book, as the House of Holiness is of Book I: the Blatant Beast, the enemy to Courtesy that Calidore pursues, has never been known there. Courtesy is displayed in practice by the old shepherd Meliboe as much as by any of the high-born characters; and the vices associated with the court, such as ambition, discontent, and slander, have no place in the pastoral world. Spenser's distance from the loathly lady's speech on *gentillesse* is not in fact so great as might appear. The shepherd world exemplifies many of the ideas she puts forward. More striking still, the central scene of the episode – the still centre of this allegorical heart of the book, and in many ways the key passage of the whole work – borrows directly from the *Wife's Tale*, from the finding of the elf-queen and the dance of the disappearing ladies.

The knight of the *Tale* comes across his dancers on a green 'under a forest syde'. Their disappearance as he approaches confirms the suggestion that they are the fairies of the opening lines of the story, with the loathly lady who remains behind as their 'elf-queen'. Calidore comes on his ladies, dancing to the music of the shepherd Colin Clout, on Mount Acidale, on an 'open greene' surrounded by trees; he guesses that they may be fairies (VI, x, 17), though their true identity is more subtle. When he steps out from 'the couert of the wood', the dancers vanish, leaving only Colin. It is not the shepherd-poet, however, who is the focus of the episode: that honour goes to the woman in the centre of the dance, 'she to whom that shepheard pypt alone'. She disappears along with the rest of the vision, as Gloriana, to whom she is compared (VI, x, 28), disappears in the manner of Thopas's elf-queen when Arthur wakes from his dream. Unlike the loathly lady, she is not a shape-shifter from hideous to beautiful, nor does she offer a choice between virtue with ugliness or beauty with its risks. The options in the *Faerie Queene* are between her being lovely and present, or lovely and absent; and neither Calidore nor Colin has any choice in the matter. Before Calidore, she vanishes; and for Colin, she comes only at her own will. She represents neither female sovereignty nor female caprice, but that yet more capricious and more demanding quality, poetic inspiration.

This is perhaps the closest that the Wife, through her projection in the *Tale*, comes to apotheosis. Spenser works his way towards such a culmination by imaginative engagement with the narrative possibilities offered by the *Tale*, not with the thematic uses Chaucer makes of those possibilities. There is one work that shows a much greater commitment to exploring what Chaucer actually makes of the Wife, and which brings her, if not to literary apotheosis, at least to a fictional salvation.

This is the broadside ballad of the *Wanton Wife of Bath* – a poem, to judge from its publishing history, that was found deeply subversive. Its first seventy years of existence are on record only in terms of a series of attempts to suppress it. On 25 June 1600, the Stationers' Register records an order for all copies to be burned and its printers and publishers to be fined, 'and ther imprisonment is respited till another tyme'. Henry Goskin, summoned before the Court of High Commission in June 1632 for printing it, was shown no such leniency, and finished up in Bridewell. The earliest surviving copy – one of many different prints – dates only from 1670.[22]

The subversiveness of the broadside is due to its picking up the Wife's attacks, not on her husbands, but on the patriarchs and saints. She spends much of the first part of her *Prologue* in vigorous debate with St Paul, St Jerome and assorted other antifeminist or pro-celibacy writers, and religious orthodoxy does not emerge well from the battle. She has been accused by the exegetical school of (male) critics of misreading the Bible, or, more specifically, of failing to take orthodox interpretation into account; and the latter at least is true. She herself admits to preferring the text to the commentary: if Solomon and the rest of the patriarchs were polygamists, she sees no reason to gloss the fact out of existence. Once the boundaries of licit or authorized biblical interpretation are transgressed, pious orthodoxy – and especially celibate orthodoxy – is going to have a hard time.

The broadside, like the *Prologue*, is concerned with overstepping these bounds. The charges against Henry Goskin specified as much: in the ballad 'the histories of the Bible are scurrilously abused'. But if the surviving copies are true to the earlier versions, it is plain speaking rather than abuse that is at issue, just as it is in the Wife of Bath's own presentation of biblical history and

Church tradition. Both wives may select what suits their own arguments, but orthodoxy can scarcely claim that it does otherwise. Of all the various forms the Wife took down the centuries, the *Wanton Wife* represents the most attentive and responsive reading of Chaucer.

> In Bath a wanton wife did dwelle,
>   As Chaucer he doth write;
> Who did in pleasure spend her dayes,
>   And many a fonde delight.
>
> Upon a time sore sick she was,
>   And at the length did dye;
> And then her soul at heaven gate
>   Did knocke most mightilye.
>
> First Adam came unto the gate:
>   Who knocketh ther? quoth hee.
> I am the wife of Bath, she sayd,
>   And faine would come to thee.
>
> Thou art a sinner, Adam sayd,
>   And here no place shalt have.
> And so art thou, I trowe, quoth shee;
>   Now, gip, you doting knave.
>
> I will come in, in spight, she sayd,
>   Of all such cherles as thee;
> Thou wert the causer of our woe,
>   Our paine and misery;
>
> And first broke God's commandiments,
>   In pleasure of thy wife. —
> When Adam heard her tell this tale,
>   He ranne away for life.   (1–24)

A similar fate befalls a succession of patriarchs and saints, many of them referred to in the *Tales*, who attempt to deny her entry and are sent scuttling for their pains. Not all are male: both the prostitute Mary Magdalene, here identified with the woman taken in adultery, and the throat-cutter Judith, who is cited by the Merchant as a model woman (IV, 1366), receive similar treatment. The excesses of male lust provide her with an especially congenial line of attack, used against Lot, David, and Chaucer's Wife's favourite, Solomon:

> The woman's mad, quoth Solomon,
>   That thus doth taunt a king.
> Not half so mad as you, she sayd
>   I trowe, in manye a thing.
>
> Thou hadst seven hundred wives at once,
>   For whom thou didst provide;
> And yet, god wot, three hundred whores

Thou must maintain beside ...   (57–64)

Hadst thou not bin beside thye wits,
  Thou wouldst not thus have ventur'd;
And therefore I do marvel much
  How thou this place hast enter'd.   (69–72)

Another prime target of the *Prologue*, St Paul, would not appear to make such an easy victim, but the 'wanton wife's' description of his love of persecution as a 'lewd desire' is enough to establish that there are worse things than sexual promiscuity.

The verbal brawling at Heaven's gate eventually rouses Christ himself, and only to him does this latter-day Wife of Bath humble herself.

Sore have I sinned, Lord, she sayd,
  And spent my time in vaine;
But bring me like a wandring sheepe
  Into thy fold againe.

O Lord my God, I will amend
  My former wicked vice:
The thief for one poor silly word
  Past into paradise.

My lawes and my commandiments,
  Saith Christ, were knowne to thee;
But of the same in any wise,
  Not yet one word did yee.

I grant the same, O Lord, quoth she;
  Most lewdly did I live;
But yet the loving father did
  His prodigal son forgive.

So I forgive thy soul, he sayd,
  Through thy repenting crye;
Come enter then into my rest,
  I will not thee denye.   (121–40)

There is no attempt here to sanitize the Wife's sins, but neither are they condemned by any standard short of Christ's. Compared with the charges that the Bible enables her to bring against those on the safe side of the gates, her own 'wicked vice' appears mild indeed; and compared with their self-righteousness, her outspokenness has distinct virtues. The outraged establishment of the seventeenth century took the attitude not of Christ but of the patriarchs – the attitude satirized in the Wife's *Prologue*. The unsuppressibility of the broadside suggests an abundance of buyers who took a kinder view. The ballad-reading populace of England had their last sight of the Wife of Bath entering the gates of Heaven; and Chaucer, one suspects, would have approved.

NOTES

1 For an assortment of such views, see e.g. D. W. Robertson, Jr, *A Preface to Chaucer* (Princeton, 1962) pp. 317–31 (for theological readings); Alfred David, *The Strumpet Muse* (Bloomington and London, 1976) chapter IX (the Wife as self-revelation by Chaucer); Beryl Rowland, 'Chaucer's Working Wyf', in *Chaucer in the Eighties*, ed. Julian N. Wasserman and Robert J. Blanch (Syracuse, 1986) pp. 137–49 (the Wife as traumatized by her early sexual experiences); and two pieces by E. T. Donaldson, 'Designing a Camel: or Generalising the Middle Ages', *Tennessee Studies in Literature*, 22 (1977), 1–16 (the Wife *versus* men, from St Paul to the twentieth century), and *The Swan at the Well* (New Haven and London, 1985), pp. 129–39 (the wife and Falstaff).

2 IV, 1170 ff., 1685–7.

3 *Pierce Penilesse his Supplication to the Diuell*, in *The Works of Thomas Nashe*, ed. R. B. McKerrow (reprint ed. F. P. Wilson, Oxford, 1958), I, 194.

4 For the history of the ballad, see Caroline Spurgeon, *Five Hundred Years of Chaucer Criticism and Allusion* (Chaucer Society, 1914–25), I, 288, IV (Appendix A), p. 54; for the text, see n. 22 below.

5 See the transcription of Ellesmere given in *The Canterbury Tales: A Facsimile and Transcription of the Hengwrt Manuscript*, ed. Paul G. Ruggiers (Variorum I, Norman, Oklahoma, 1979) p. 234 (gloss at line 193).

6 See the transcript edited by Frederick J. Furnivall as *The Cambridge MS* (Chaucer Society, 1901–2): glosses to lines III (D) 227–8, 519, 980, 780, 509, 655–8. The lines numbered 44a–f in modern editions may be Chaucerian, or may represent scribal or editorial creativity: they appear only in this MS.

7 *The Tale of Beryn*, ed. F. J. Furnivall and W. G. Stone (*EETS*, e.s. 105, 1909), lines 281–5. *Beryn* is preserved in a single MS of the *Canterbury Tales*, Northumberland 455.

8 Thomas Hoccleve, *Dialogus cum Amico*, lines 694–6, of 1421–2 (ed. e.g. by M. C. Seymour, *Selections from Hoccleve* (Oxford, 1981) p. 91).

9 *A Mumming at Hertford*, lines 168–70, in *The Minor Poems of John Lydgate*, Part III, ed. H. N. MacCracken (*EETS*, o.s. 192, 1934), pp. 675–82; compare the Wife's *Prologue*, III, 489–90.

10 John Skelton, *The Complete English Poems*, ed. John Scattergood (Harmondsworth, 1983), p. 87 (lines 618–27), of *c.* 1504. For other allusions to the Wife, see Spurgeon, I, 44–5, on knowing 'the wifes lyfe of Bath' by heart (*The Chances of the Dyse*, *c.* 1440); and I, 82, on an allusion to her *Tale* (*The Pilgrim's Tale*, *c.* 1536).

11 See *Richard Brathwait's Comments in 1665 upon Chaucer's Tale of the Miller and the Wife of Bath*, ed. C. F. E. Spurgeon (Chaucer Society, II, 33, 1901) p. 62. Although the work was not printed until 1665, it was written before 1617: see pp. x–xi.

12 *The Poems of William Dunbar*, ed. James Kinsley (Oxford, 1979) no. 14; compare in particular lines 70–2, 473–4, with the Wife's *Prologue*, III, 555–8.

13 Printed by John Skot; it is edited by E. F. Rimbaut for the Percy Society, vol. VI (1842), pp. 13–29.

14 *The Cobler of Caunterburie and Tarltons Newes out of Purgatory*, ed. Geoffrey Creigh and Jane Belfield (Medieval and Renaissance Texts 3, Leiden, 1987), p. 74. The description of the old woman is on pp. 68–9, her tale on pp. 69–74. The work was popular enough to justify a reprint in 1598, and various references to it survive, including some in Gabriel Harvey's marginalia to his copy of the 1598 edition of Chaucer's Works. In 1630 a revamped version appeared entitled *The Tinker of Turvey*, but two new characters were introduced into this who displaced the old woman.

15 *Decameron* 7,1 and 7,8. In the latter, a husband discovers a string tied to his wife's toe as a signal to her lover; when she realizes she has been found out, she persuades her maid to take her place in the bed. The husband beats up the woman he presumes to be his wife, but when he returns in the morning with various members of her family, she shows herself to be unscathed and accuses him of whoring and drunkenness instead.

16 Ed. Hans Walter Gabler in *The Dramatic Works in the Beaumont and Fletcher Canon* (general ed. Fredson Bowers), vol. v (Cambridge, 1982), pp. 441–538. Its probable date is 1619–23, but either the play or an earlier form of it seems to have been in existence by 1603 (see pp. 443–4).

17 In *A Crowne-Garland of Goulden Roses*, Percy Society vi (1842), pp. 68–71.

18 All quotations from the *Faerie Queene* are from the edition by A. C. Hamilton (London, 1977).

19 *FQ*, iii, i, 25; cf. *CT*, v, 764–6.

20 It is based on the host's tale in Ariosto, *Orlando Furioso*, xxviii.

21 *FQ*, vi, i, 1.

22 A facsimile of one of the surviving copies of the ballad appears in *The Pepys Ballads*, intr. W. G. Day (Cambridge, 1987), ii, 39. As some of the lines are cropped from this, and there seem to be some corruptions in the text, I have used the closely similar version given in Thomas Percy's *Reliques of Ancient Poetry* (1765), vol. iii, ii, 12. Here too it proved offensive, and was removed from the third and fourth editions of the anthology. There are numerous variants in the surviving broadside prints: a list is given in *The Roxburghe Ballads*, ed. Joseph Woodfall Ebsworth, vol. vii (1890), pp. 215–16. The story of the sinner at heaven's gates has earlier analogues, but its association with the Wife of Bath has a particular appropriateness.

13

The genius to improve an invention: transformations of the *Knight's Tale*

PIERO BOITANI

In his long Preface to the *Fables*, Dryden not only compares the authors of the stories he translates for the collection, but also discusses their sources. What he says about the first of the tales is very interesting in this respect. After giving the 'Noble Poem' of Palamon and Arcite an epic status 'perhaps not much inferiour' to that of the *Iliad* and the *Aeneid*, Dryden maintains that he had thought this story to be 'of *English* Growth, and *Chaucer*'s own'. But, he adds,

> I was undeceiv'd by *Boccace*; for casually looking on the End of his seventh Giornata, I found *Dioneo* (under which name he shadows himself) and *Fiammetta* (who represents his Mistress, the natural Daughter of *Robert* King of *Naples*) of whom these Words are spoken. *Dioneo e Fiametta gran pezza cantarono insieme d'Arcita, e di Palamone*: by which it appears that this Story was written before the time of *Boccace*; but the Name of its Author being wholly lost, *Chaucer* is now become an Original; and I question not but the Poem has receiv'd many Beauties by passing through his Noble Hands.[1]

It is rather strange that, having made the connection between Boccaccio, the author of the *Decameron*, and Dioneo, one of the characters in the *Decameron*'s frame who is said to have 'sung' of Arcite and Palamon, Dryden should not suspect that the story had been first written by Boccaccio himself.[2] But the most important aspect of Dryden's source-hunting in the Preface is not philological accuracy – it is, rather, an attitude towards his poetic forebears which reveals a good deal about Dryden's own approach to the *Fables*. In these, he mostly translates or adopts stories written by Homer, Ovid, Boccaccio, and Chaucer. The general problem of 'borrowing' pre-existing material becomes, therefore, a personal one, and Dryden sublimates any 'anxiety of influence' from which he may suffer by inserting himself into the universal pattern of literary imitation. Neither Ovid nor Chaucer, he declares, were great inventors, the former having only 'copied the *Grecian* Fables', the latter having taken most of his stories 'from his Italian Contemporaries, or their Predecessors'. Yet Dryden significantly extends his considerations on the practice of 'translation' or 'adaptation' to the whole of English culture, thus implicitly shifting the focus to make room for himself: 'the Genius of our Countrymen in general' is, he writes, 'rather to improve an Invention, than to invent themselves; as is evident not only in our Poetry, but in many of our Manufactures'.

As a generalization, this statement hardly holds water. However, my intention in this essay is to see whether it applies to the particular chain of literary works which stem from Chaucer's *Knight's Tale*: *The Two Noble Kinsmen* of Shakespeare and Fletcher, and Dryden's own *Palamon and Arcite*.[3] The story of Palamon and Arcite has at least two features in common with that of Troilus and Cressida. The first is an aspect of the history of European literature, and hence of the European imagination: and this is their passing from the hands of Boccaccio to those of Chaucer, Shakespeare, and Dryden. The second may be one of the reasons for their extraordinary success, and this is that at the centre of both stand two men and a woman.[4] In the Troilus and Cressida plot we are presented with a version of the love triangle that ends up in betrayal on the part of the lady – a variation of the adultery pattern which is common in Western literature since its very beginning. In the Palamon and Arcite story we find a version of an archetypal moment of animal life: the fight of two males for the same female.

Violent animal imagery characterizes both the *Knight's Tale* and Dryden's *Palamon and Arcite*, and it also surfaces in *The Two Noble Kinsmen*. The martial Muse, whether in romance, epic, or drama, is of course fond of lions, tigers, bears, and boar, and in his attempt at recreating the classical epos in the *Teseida* Boccaccio uses similes that go back, through Statius' *Thebaid*, to Virgil's *Aeneid*, and ultimately to Homer's *Iliad*.[5] By concentrating such imagery into very dense clusters Chaucer reveals that he is not merely imitating the epic style, but in fact introducing into the story an elemental, instinctual fury absent in his source. The scene in which the two lovers meet for their duel in the grove is a characteristic instance of this. They are first compared to hunters waiting for the lion or the bear (1637–48); then, when the fight begins, the hunters become animals, and three similes are piled upon each other in quick succession:

> Thou myghtest wene that this Palamon
> In his fightyng were a wood leon,
> And as a crueel tigre was Arcite;
> As wilde bores gonne they to smyte,
> That frothen whit as foom for ire wood.   (1655–9)

Fletcher, who handles the corresponding scene of *The Two Noble Kinsmen*,[6] drops this kind of imagery, not essential on a stage where two actors can shout at each other and effectively mimic their 'ire' by brandishing swords. But a bear simile is used by Shakespeare during Arcite's and Palamon's first encounter (III, i, 68), and Theseus likens them to 'a pair of lions, smeared with prey' when, in Shakespeare's first act, he recalls their fighting in the battle over Thebes (I, iv, 18).

Shakespeare and Fletcher, however, are, as we shall later see, interested in different animal correlatives. Dryden, on the other hand, keeps Chaucer's images and indeed 'fortifies' them according to his conception of what an epic poem should be like,[7] but he also 'improves' Boccaccio's and Chaucer's 'invention' by catching precisely the archetypal meaning of the scene. His two boars do not merely, like Chaucer's, foam at the mouth 'for ire wood'; they show us their bristles and their tusks and make us hear their grunts and groans. In short, his Palamon and Arcite are really animal-like, and Dryden in fact adds an apparently superfluous detail which however reveals to us that he has fully understood the issue: two males are fighting for a female, the cause is 'love':

> Fell *Arcite* like an angry Tyger far'd,
> And like a Lion *Palamon* appear'd:
> Or as two Boars whom Love to Battel draws,
> With rising Bristles, and with froathy Jaws,
> Their adverse Breasts with Tusks oblique they wound;
> With Grunts and Groans the Forest rings around.   (II, 202–7)

Later in *Palamon and Arcite* Dryden shows himself much more aware of this element than Chaucer. In describing the paintings in the temple of Venus he mentions, following the *Knight's Tale* (1944), 'Medea's Charms' and 'Circean Feasts' (II, 505). Again, he adds a line which at first sight looks like a mere decorative filler or a pompous classical allusion, but which on a second reading points to deeper and wider implications:

> ... *Circean* Feasts,
> With Bowls that turn'd inamour'd Youth to Beasts.   (II, 505–6)

Thus, one of Dryden's 'improvements' consists in his making explicit a central theme of Chaucer's Tale – the contrast and complementarity of animal and human that the contest between Palamon and Arcite implies.[8]

In Chaucer, *eros* inflames the two lovers transforming them, as Dryden makes clear, into brutes. But in reading the *Knight's Tale* we also become aware that it is *eros* which turns both heroes into thinking human beings. Before falling in love, Chaucer's Palamon and Arcite dwell in the tower 'in angwissh and in wo'; after seeing Emily, they start arguing with logic (if not with actual sophistry, 1130–86). Soon after, they become philosophers expounding at length their views of the human condition (1251–67; 1303–24). Dryden keeps this feature of Chaucer's story. Shakespeare eliminates all philosophical considerations, but, as we shall presently see, highlights the contrast by underlining with greater emphasis than either his predecessor or his successor an opposition that lies at the heart of the story, that between *philia* and *eros*.

From the very beginning in Boccaccio's *Teseida* an essential feature of the

Palamon and Arcite plot is not only their contending for the same lady, but also their being both 'noble', 'of royal blood', and 'parenti', relatives. With Chaucer, this feature is made more prominent through repetition of words like 'cosyn', but Shakespeare and Fletcher place it at the very centre of their play, which is significantly entitled 'The Two *Noble Kinsmen*'. Thus, an opposition between 'nobility' and the basic human drive of possession in love – between courtliness and instinct, ultimately between culture and nature – is added to that between *philia* and *eros*. In turn, *philia* means both 'friendship' and 'kinship'. Our authors seem to be aware of the potentialities which this wide spectrum of contrasts opens up. The teller of the *Knight's Tale*, for instance, interprets the *philia–eros* dichotomy as one between Cupid and 'charity', between 'love' and 'felaweshipe'. In this, he is followed by Dryden:[9]

> O Cupide, out of alle charitee!
> O regne, that wolt no felawe have with thee!
> Ful sooth is seyd that love ne lordshipe
> Wol noght, his thankes, have no felaweshipe.
>
> (*Knight's Tale*, 1623–6)

> Oh Love! Thou sternly dost thy Pow'r maintain,
> And wilt not bear a Rival in thy Reign,
> Tyrants and thou all Fellowship disdain.
>
> (*Palamon and Arcite*, II, 166–8)

But Dryden emphasizes the 'friendship' element much more than Chaucer. Thus, when Arcite answers Palamon's argument on the 'Eldership of Right' with his 'no Law is made for Love', Dryden fills out the original, 'improving' it:

> If then the Laws of Friendship I transgress,
> I keep the Greater, while I break the Less   (I, 337–8)

At the end of the same scene he adds several lines that have no precedent in the Tale. Here, he underlines the turning of friendship into hate, with vivid visual touches and the inevitable insertion of the animal correlative:

> Great was their Strife, which hourly was renew'd,
> Till each with mortal Hate his Rival view'd:
> Now Friends no more, nor walking Hand in Hand;
> But when they met, they made a surly Stand;
> And glar'd like angry Lions as they pass'd,
> And wish'd that ev'ry Look might be their last.   (I, 352–7)

Shakespeare and Fletcher, however, are much more radical in their exploitation of such contrasts. They expand the *philia–eros* opposition at both ends and give a completely new turn to the instinctual–courtly dichotomy by introducing the subplot of the Gaoler's daughter's love for Palamon.

That Theseus and Perotheus love each other 'tendrely' we know already from the *Knight's Tale* (1196–1201) and indeed from classical tradition. But Shakespeare's Hippolyta describes this 'friendship' to Emilia in terms that go far beyond any Chaucer could conceive, as far in fact as to maintain that Theseus would be unable to choose between love for his wife and love for his friend:

> Their knot of love,
> Tied, weaved, entangled, with so true, so long,
> And with a finger of so deep a cunning,
> May be outworn, never undone. I think
> Theseus cannot be umpire to himself,
> Cleaving his conscience into twain and doing
> Each side like justice, which he loves best.   (I, iii, 41–7)

Shakespeare makes the theme much more relevant by adding a wholly new 'invention'.[10] Immediately after Hippolyta's statement, Emilia recalls her one-time playfellow Flavina. Pirithous' and Theseus' love, she says, 'has more ground, is more maturely seasoned,/More buckled with strong judgement, and their needs / The one of th'other may be said to water/Their intertangled roots of love' (I, iii, 56–9). She and Flavina, then both eleven years old, loved each other in total innocence, simply because they did, with no ulterior motive. The relationship between the two girls represents *philia* in all its complexity, in its primal child- and adolescent-like, purely homosexual quality. Indeed, it is opposed, and considered as superior to, love between different sexes: 'the true love 'tween maid and maid may be / More than in sex dividual' (I, iii, 81–2).

Not content with this, Shakespeare transforms the Arcite–Palamon relationship into one in which *philia* appears much more prominent and complex than in Chaucer. When we first see the two characters, Theseus' attack on Thebes is being launched. Arcite invites Palamon, 'dearer in love than blood', to leave the city and the vices of Creon's court (I, ii, 1 ff.). The *philia* between them is tinged with a Stoical, almost Brutus-like disdain for corruption and tyranny, and with a patriotic, almost nineteenth-century-like response to the call of king and country (I, ii, 98–103). The next time we see them, in the Athenian jail, all that is left to them is precisely their friendship. Thebes, friends, kindreds, 'games of honour' are gone (II, i, 60–79). They are prisoners, they think, forever, and in prison their youth 'must wither / Like a too timely spring'. Furthermore, they can entertain no hope of ever acquiring 'a loving wife', of knowing 'issue', of ever seeing 'figures of [themselves] to glad [their] age'. As Arcite puts it,

> This is all our world;
> We shall know nothing here but one another,
> Hear nothing but the clock that tells our woes.   (II, i, 94–6)

Philia becomes an existential necessity as well as a philosophical choice and a kind of proto-homosexual love:

From all that fortune can inflict upon us,
I see two comforts rising, two mere blessings,
If the gods please; to hold here a brave patience,
And the enjoying of our griefs together.

And here being thus together,
We are an endless mine to one another;
We are one another's wife, ever begetting
New births of love; we are father, friends, acquaintance;
We are, in one another, families.   (II, i, 111–14, 132–6)

From this we pass, within the same scene, to the harsh quarrel between Arcite and Palamon after they see Emilia. The tragic irony of their *philia* is fully exposed by the raging of *eros*.[11]

Lest we forget that this is the central theme of the play, Shakespeare now indirectly extends it to Emilia, who, in gathering flowers in the garden, picks a narcissus and exclaims, 'That was a *fair boy*, certain, but a *fool* / To love himself; were there not maids enough?', only to conclude: 'Men are mad things' (I, i, 174–5, 180). Two acts later, she has changed her mind. Fletcher seizes on Shakespeare's image with the gusto one would expect of the author of most of the Gaoler's Daughter's subplot. Emily is comparing her two lovers: she extols Arcite and despises Palamon, 'a mere dull shadow' to his cousin. She singles out all the defects of Palamon's appearance and character, but, suddenly, she sees them in a new light:

Yet these that we count errors may become him;
Narcissus was a *sad boy*, but a *heavenly*.
O, who can find the bent of woman's fancy?
I am a *fool*; my reason is lost in me,
I have no choice, and I have lied so lewdly
That women ought to beat me.   (IV, ii, 31–6)

Eros has conquered her, too; she is uncertain between Palamon and Arcite, but her 'fancy' now *cries* for both lovers (IV, ii, 52–4).

Emilia – the difference from Chaucer is quite remarkable – proclaims herself a fool. But the Gaoler's Daughter becomes, in the words of one of the peasants, 'as mad as a March hare' (III, v, 74). The animal image stands at the very centre of the play. The epic context, however, has been completely eliminated and replaced by popular, proverbial wisdom pointing to starkly naked *eros* if not to actual lechery.[12]

The subplot of the Gaoler's Daughter occupies nine scenes from the second to the fifth act of *The Two Noble Kinsmen*. There is no room here to illustrate in detail its furious, spectacular crescendo, but it is important to point out its most significant stages in order to understand how Shakespeare and Fletcher have altered Chaucer's romance. Already in the first scene of Act II the Gaoler's Daughter shows herself to be the opposite of Emilia. Emilia will never really manage to choose between Arcite and Palamon; the Gaoler's

Daughter immediately distinguishes between them and interestingly enough points to Palamon (II, i, 49–54). Two scenes later, the girl is already lost. Aware of the social difference between herself and Palamon, that 'to marry him is hopeless; / To be his whore is witless', she however deludes herself into thinking that, once she frees him from prison, he shall love her. She reconstructs with obsessive precision the stages of her falling in love with him: first came sight, then appreciation, then pity, finally love – an 'extreme' and 'infinite' love (II, iii, 14–15) which she herself shortly afterwards considers as 'beyond love, and beyond reason, / Or wit, or safety' (II, v, 11–12). In the fifth scene of Act II, although she is conscious of the fact that Palamon has paid her no attention, the girl fosters her illusion and mentally abandons herself to him:

> Let him do
> What he will with me, so he use me kindly;
> For use me so he shall, or I'll proclaim him,
> And to his face, no man ...   (II, v, 28–31)

The monologue from which these lines are taken closes Act II. Act III opens with the famous monologue in which Arcite sings his great hymn of love for Emilia, 'jewel o' th'wood, o' th'world', who has 'blessed a place' with her 'sole presence'. The two scenes are thus deliberately set in ironical contrast to each other: 'pure', exalted, courtly, male love against direct, improper, violent female *eros*. In the third Act, the latter's progress towards madness is inexorable. The girl is at first suspended between on the one hand the construction of a fictional reality[13] to fence off the realization that Palamon does not care for her, and on the other the recognition that this is a 'lie', that 'the best way is the next way to a grave, / Each errant step beside is torment' (III, ii, 33). Finally, she plunges into the storm. The sea images recall those of Shakespeare's later plays (*Pericles*, *The Tempest*, *The Winter's Tale*), but in fact Fletcher goes back to the 'tempest' in the mind of Lear (III, iv, 1–16).

After seeing her join the Schoolmaster and the peasants for the morris dance in III, v,[14] we find the Gaoler's Daughter again at the beginning of Act IV. Her Wooer describes her here as a sort of Pyramus looking for his Thisbe–Palamon ('gone to th'wood to gather mulberries'), but also as an Ophelia,

> her careless tresses
> A wreath of bulrush rounded; about her stuck
> Thousand fresh water flowers of several colours,
> That methought she appeared like the fair nymph
> That feeds the lake with waters ...   (IV, i, 83–7)

The topic of all her speeches when she appears again on the stage is, quite openly, her desire ('I must lose my maidenhead by cocklight', IV, i, 112), which she cries out roaringly, drowning all sounds of martial combat, precisely when, with another proverbial animal image, she announces her silence: 'yet I keep close for all this, / Close as a cockle' (IV, i, 129–30).

The culminating point of the subplot is, however, that which apparently brings it to its denouement – the moment when the fiction invented by the Doctor and played out by the Wooer 'cure' the girl. For the Gaoler's Daughter on the one hand really seems to believe that the man who stands before her and courts her is Palamon (v, ii, 80–2), but on the other a few minutes later seems to think that Palamon is far away (93–7), so that we have no way of determining whether she has accepted the fiction unconsciously or willingly. Thus, we perceive the last lines of the scene as a moment of supreme pathos: when, whatever his identity may be, she takes the Wooer as a *man* who will finally satisfy her desire without hurting her:

DAUGHTER   And then we'll sleep together.
DOCTOR   Take her offer.
WOOER   Yes, marry, will we.
DAUGHTER   But you shall not hurt me.
WOOER   I will not, sweet.
DAUGHTER   If you do, love, I'll cry.   (v, ii, 107–10)[15]

Shakespeare and Fletcher have then transformed the very coordinates of their story. While, following Chaucer, they show us two men in love with a woman, they add a woman in love with a man. The passion of the Gaoler's Daughter, the only functional motivation for which in the play is that of being instrumental to Palamon's liberation, constitutes a central ploy of *The Two Noble Kinsmen*. This is a passion that belongs to the lower classes and its explicitly sexual bent and violence highlight with dramatic irony what lies behind the apparently courtly contest of Palamon and Arcite. Thus, the contrast between the courtly and the instinctual, the cultural and the natural, is transposed onto a social plane (aristocracy vs. lower classes), but also, by its being extended to yet another realm of society, increased in intensity.

The role of the Gaoler's Daughter's plot is, however, more complex. The story of Palamon and Arcite traditionally presents us with a powerful image of male desire. The Gaoler's Daughter forcefully asserts the existence of woman's desire. If the former leads to a relentless struggle the final outcome of which is the death of one of the two suitors (*eros* gives way to *thanatos*), the latter leads to total madness. The two kinds of violence are presented as parallel and equally extreme, but there is a fundamental difference between them. Palamon's and Arcite's love for Emilia becomes a cosmic conflict, one between transhuman powers such as Venus and Mars, and its solution lies, as Theseus proclaims at the end of the play, with fortune and the gods. The Gaoler's Daughter's love is never reciprocated and arouses an exclusively inner conflict. In *The Two Noble Kinsmen* the wholly external violence of the contest between the two lovers becomes unbearable because it finds a counterpart in something that comes to divide the mind itself of a human being. The Gaoler's Daughter pays for her love with her own soul.

Finally, the solution is, in her case, wholly human. Neither fate nor the gods have anything to do with it. Like Arcite's in the *Knight's Tale*, here is a

'maladye/Of Hereos' and a 'manye,/Engendred of humour malencolik',[16] and
as such it is dealt with by a physician who shows himself to be both sensible
and radical, a genius of diagnosis as well as in stage directing: if necessary,
passion is treated by fiction, 'a falsehood ... with falsehoods ... combated'; in
any case it will be cured by sex. And while Arcite must die so that Palamon,
who was first in seeing Emily, can enjoy his 'right', the Gaoler's Daughter's
Wooer must pretend to be Palamon and promise to make love to her in order
to cure her. In other words, this time the male must die to himself, give up his
identity and at the same time satisfy his desire in order to help and love the
woman.

Shakespeare and Fletcher have, then, not just 'improved an Invention'.
They have radically re-invented a story, and perhaps their 'Fear' towards
Chaucer should not be seen as a purely rhetorical stance:

> Chaucer, of all admired, the story gives;
> There constant to eternity it lives.
> If we let fall the nobleness of this,
> And the first sound this child hear be a hiss,
> How will it shake the bones of that good man,
> And make him cry from under ground 'O, fan
> From me the witless chaff of such a writer
> That blasts my bays and my famed works makes lighter
> Than Robin Hood!' This is the fear we bring;
> For, to say truth, it were an endless thing,
> And too ambitious, to aspire to him.   (Prologue, 13–23)

Shakespeare and Fletcher have in fact changed the conception itself of love as
a force that presides over, or determines the fate of their characters. Thus, for
instance, the prayer of Chaucer's Palamon to Venus (v, i, 77–136) is a speech
full of contrasts between light and dark, positive and negative. In it, the might
of the goddess is exalted, but 'the emphasis is, throughout, on old age, and the
result is that what impresses us ... is not the power of love, but a series of
images of decay'.[17]

Dryden who, as we have seen, does not hesitate to stress the violence
implicit in Palamon's and Arcite's contest for Emily, considers love as such in
a wholly favourable way, celebrating Venus as creator in an enthusiastically
Lucretian, Chaucerian, and Spenserian hymn.[18] Before this Venus even the
lion 'loaths the Taste of Blood', and the male's hunt for the female becomes a
perfectly natural, even playful occupation (the opposite of what is happening
in the story at this point and of what earlier animal imagery had suggested):

> Creator *Venus*, Genial Pow'r of Love,
> The Bliss of Men below, and Gods above,
> Beneath the sliding Sun thou runn'st thy Race,
> Dost fairest shine, and best become thy Place.
> For thee the Winds their Eastern Blasts forbear,
> Thy Month reveals the Spring, and opens all the Year.
> Thee, Goddess, thee the storms of Winter fly,

Earth smiles with Flow'rs renewing; laughs the Sky,
And Birds to Lays of Love their tuneful Notes apply.
For thee the Lion loaths the Taste of Blood,
And roaring hunts his Female through the Wood:
For thee the Bulls rebellow through the Groves,
And tempt the Stream, and snuff their absent Loves.
'Tis thine, whate'er is pleasant, good, or fair:
All Nature is thy Province, Life thy Care;
Thou mad'st the World, and dost the World repair.   (III, 129–44)

The contrast between Mars and Venus is an integral part of the story ever
since Boccaccio's *Teseida*. When Venus herself turns into an ambiguous entity,
the conflict between the two divinities becomes less explicit. Individual
godheads occupy a far less prominent place in *The Two Noble Kinsmen* than in
the *Knight's Tale*: their temples, their quarrel, the intervention of Jupiter and
Saturn disappear. In Chaucer, Arcite's fatal accident is due to Saturn's direct
action – the god asks Pluto to send an infernal Fury to startle the hero's horse.
Shakespeare attributes the event to natural causes, endowing them with
saturnine qualities but refraining from decisive commitment:

              ... what envious flint,
        Cold as old Saturn and like him possessed
        With fire malevolent, darted a spark,
        Or what fierce sulphur else, to this end made,
        I comment not ...   (v, iv, 61–5)

What on the other hand becomes ever more oppressive in *The Two Noble
Kinsmen*, and particularly towards the end of the play, is the dark presence of
indeterminate divine entities, indicated simply as the 'heavenly powers' (v,
iii, 139) or the 'gods' (v, iv, 87, 100, 115, 120). Theseus alone returns – and
briefly at that – to the logic of his Chaucerian predecessor when, after Arcite's
death, he offers Palamon an explanation that points to Venus and Mars as to
the single gods that have dictated what he calls 'due justice' (v, iv, 105–9).
When Palamon replies with a statement about the inherently tragic condition
of man, who always loses what he most seeks (v, iv, 109–12), Theseus
responds with a speech where Fortune's paradoxical action and the gods'
profound justice are opposed to each other and at the same time seen as
complementary:

                     Never fortune
        Did play a subtler game: the conquered triumphs,
        The victor has the loss; *yet* in the passage
        The gods have been most equal ...

                     ... The gods my justice
        Take from my hand, and they themselves become
        The executioners.   (v, iv, 112–22)

Yet the conclusion of Theseus' speech – and of the play which ends with it – is
much more problematic. For meditating now on his own response to the

singular fate of Arcite and Palamon, the Duke of Athens seems to question divine justice. With an image that recalls *King Lear*,[19] he proclaims that human beings are 'children' and the gods 'charmers'. While the human condition is 'baffling', the gods are mere enchanters, magicians, illusion makers, tricksters. Thus, acceptance of 'that which is' means simply that the 'dispute' between men and gods is only suspended, that the deeply, essentially human 'question' is and will always be asked, is and will always be unanswered by the gods:

> ... O you heavenly charmers,
> What things you make of us! For what we lack
> We laugh; for what we have are sorry; still
> Are children in some kind. Let us be thankful
> For that which is, and with you leave dispute
> That are above our question. Let's go off,
> And bear us like the time.   (v, iv, 131–7)

Nothing is more unlike this than the conclusion of Theseus' speech in the *Knight's Tale*:

> What may I conclude of this longe serye,
> But after wo I rede us to be merye
> And thanken Juppiter of al his grace?   (3067–9)

Shakespeare and Fletcher have 'perverted' their Chaucer. On the other hand Dryden not only accepts fully the logic of Chaucer's Theseus, but even 'improves' on it by adding to his speech a whole new section on the formation, development, and death of man that makes the argument more cogent (III, 1066–81). Above all, he subtly modifies some details in the latter part of the tale so as to prepare the ground for a less traumatic ending. For example, Dryden's dying Arcite is as sad and pessimistic as Chaucer's in seeing men 'Now warm in Love, now with'ring in the Grave' (III, 795), but when he bequeaths the 'service of his ghost' to Emily, he adds an apparently gratuitous touch of pathos:

> But to your Service I bequeath my Ghost;
> Which from this mortal Body when unty'd,
> Unseen, unheard, shall hover at your Side;
> Nor fright you waking, nor your Sleep offend,
> But wait officious, and your Steps attend ...   (III, 781–5)

In fact, this anticipates the position Dryden takes on the fate of Arcite's soul after death. At first sight, he seems here to agree with Chaucer's Knight:

> But whither went his Soul, let such relate
> Who search the Secrets of the future State ...   (III, 845–6)

Then, he changes the approach. What becomes central is the insistence on the 'strong proofs', the belief that if there were no mystery faith would no longer count:

> Strong Proofs they have, but not demonstrative:
> For, were all plain, then all Sides must agree,
> And Faith it self be lost in Certainty.   (III, 847–9)

Dryden then appends a moral which has no antecedent in Chaucer, and finally spells out the theologically (and culturally) correct destination of Arcite's soul – precisely the opposite of what the Knight would wish to do:

> To live uprightly then is sure the best,
> To save our selves, and not to damn the rest.
> The Soul of *Arcite* went, where Heathens go,
> Who better live than we, though less they know.   (III, 850–3)

In other words, in Dryden an urge for consolation precedes the final re-composition of harmony such as we find in Chaucer. In the *Knight's Tale* consolation is the job of Egeus, who knows 'this worldes transmutacioun' and can therefore make the passage from Arcite's death to Theseus' later philosophical (and political) solution gradual. Dryden seizes on Egeus' speech, but adds two lines that have no counterpart in the original:

> With equal Mind, what happens, let us bear,
> Nor joy, nor grieve too much for Things beyond our Care.   (III, 885–6)

Here Shakespeare's Theseus would stop.[20] But in *Palamon and Arcite* these words represent only a first stage in the direction of final bliss. Thus prepared, the conclusion of Dryden's 'fable'[21] becomes a true neo-classical triumph such as Boccaccio may have dreamt of. In Palamon's prayer to Venus, Earth had smiled and the Sky had laughed to celebrate the goddess. Now, Venus herself smiles over Palamon. But, even more significantly, Eros and Anteros inflame bride and bridegroom during their 'sweet laborious Night'.[22] Eros and Anteros are sons of Venus by *Mars*. In Dryden's 'improvement' of Chaucer's *Knight's Tale* the harmony now and forever reigning between Palamon and Emily corresponds to total peace in heaven.

NOTES

1 *The Poems of John Dryden*, ed. J. Kinsley, vol. IV (Oxford, 1958). All quotations are from this text.

2 See Preface, 230–5, where Dryden shows that he does not know Boccaccio as author of the *Filostrato*, either, though he suspects that Chaucer's '*Troilus* and *Cressida* was also written by a *Lombard* Author'. In the Preface to his own *Troilus and Cressida, or Truth Found Too Late*, Dryden attributes the original story to 'one Lollius a Lombard, in Latin verse' (*The Works of John Dryden*, XIII, Berkeley, Los Angeles, London, 1984, p. 225).

3 The following are classic studies of the relationship between the *Knight's Tale* and *The Two Noble Kinsmen*, and between the *Knight's Tale* and *Palamon and Arcite*: A. Thompson, *Shakespeare's Chaucer: A Study in Literary Origins* (Liverpool, 1978), pp. 166–215; E. T. Donaldson, *The Swan at the Well: Shakespeare Reading Chaucer* (New Haven–London, 1980), pp. 30–73; W. H. Williams, '"Palamon and Arcite"

and the "Knight's Tale"', *Modern Language Review*, 9 (1914), 161–72, 309–23; W. Junemann, *Drydens Fabeln und ihre Quellen*. Britannica 5 (Hamburg, 1932); Earl Miner, 'Chaucer in Dryden's *Fables*', in H. Anderson and J. S. Shea, (eds.), *Studies in Criticism and Aesthetics 1660–1800* (Minneapolis, 1967), pp. 58–72; A. Middleton, 'The Modern Art of Fortifying: *Palamon and Arcite* as Epicurean Epic', *Chaucer Review*, 3 (1968), 124–43; T. J. Hatton, 'Medieval Anticipations of Dryden's Stylistic Revolution: *The Knight's Tale*', *Language and Style*, 7 (1974), 261–70. An overall view is presented by G. Galigani, *Il Boccaccio nella Cultura Inglese e Americana* (Florence, 1974).

4 An important study of this pattern in Chaucer is H. Cooper, 'The Girl with Two Lovers: Four Canterbury Tales', in P. L. Heyworth (ed.), *Medieval Studies for J. A. W. Bennett* (Oxford, 1981), pp. 65–79.

5 For example, see the transformations of the boar, lion, and lion/bear similes in *Teseida*, I, 38; VII, 106; VII, 119; *Thebaid*, IV, 494 ff.; *Aeneid* x, 707–13; *Iliad* XI, 414–19; XIII, 471–5; XVII, 61–9. And cp. *Knight's Tale*, 1638–42 and Dante's *Inferno*, XIII, 112–14.

6 With most modern critics, I assume that Shakespeare's share in the play includes the following: the entire Act I; II, i; III, i; III, ii (?), the whole of Act v except for scene ii. See the Introduction to N. W. Bawcutt's edition of the play in the New Penguin Shakespeare series (Harmondsworth, 1977). This is the text I use in the present essay.

7 See Middleton, 'The Modern Art of Fortifying'. On Dryden's *Fables* in general, see Earl Miner, *Dryden's Poetry* (Bloomington–London, 1967), pp. 287–323; J. Sloman, 'An Interpretation of Dryden's Fables', *Eighteenth-Century Studies*, 4 (1971), 199–211.

8 And see *Knight's Tale*, 1177–80: the hounds and kite image is reduced by Dryden in *Palamon and Arcite*, I, 342–3, but Aesop is (wrongly) mentioned as its author.

9 The image goes back to *Teseida*, v, 13, and ultimately to Seneca, *Agamemnon*, v, 259.

10 See P. Edwards, 'On the Design of "The Two Noble Kinsmen"', now in the Signet edition of the play by C. Leech (New York–Toronto–London, 1966), pp. 243–61; and G. Melchiori in his introduction to the play in *Teatro Completo di William Shakespeare VI, I Drammi Romanzeschi* (Milan, 1981), pp. 969–89. In what follows I am deeply indebted to both these studies.

11 Similarly, later on in the play (III, vi) the knightly brotherhood of Palamon and Arcite arming each other is opposed to the fury with which they fight the duel immediately afterwards. Here Fletcher expands an element already present in the *Knight's Tale* (1649–54), bringing it to extreme consequences.

12 See *Knight's Tale*, 1810, and, above all *Summoner's Tale*, 1327. The hare was seen as symbolic of lechery.

13 In which she paradoxically but significantly imagines herself as Pyramus and Palamon as Thisbe devoured by beasts (III, ii, 11–19; and see IV, i, 66–9).

14 The central scene of the play according to Melchiori, p. 984.

15 The end of the plot comes in v, iv where Palamon is about to be executed and the Gaoler tells him his Daughter is now 'well restored,/And to be married shortly' (27–8).

16 *Knight's Tale*, 1373–5; cp. the Doctor's words about the Daughter in *The Two Noble Kinsmen*, IV, iii, 47–9, and *Palamon and Arcite*, I, 522–42.

17 T. Spencer, 'The Two Noble Kinsmen', now in the Signet edition of the play, pp. 217–41 (237–8).

18 Chaucer, *Troilus and Criseyde*, III, 1–49; Spenser, *Faerie Queene*, IV, X, 44–6; Lucretius, *De rerum natura* I, 1–25.

19 Gloucester's lines in IV, i, 36–7; the change is as significant as the similarity.

20 The resemblance between these two lines and *The Two Noble Kinsmen*, V, iv, 134–6 is striking.

21 For the meaning of this term see J. Sloman, *Dryden: The Poetics of Translation* (Toronto, 1985), pp. 163–73. The book, prepared for publication by A. McWhir, is essential to an understanding of the Fables.

22 The only similar mythological apparatus is to be found at the end of Boccaccio's *Teseida*, XII, 68, 72, 77.

14

From the *Clerk's Tale* to *The Winter's Tale*

ANNA BALDWIN

That the *Clerk's Tale* was one of Chaucer's most popular tales in the fifteenth century there can be little doubt because it was excerpted more than any other tale apart from the *Prioress's Tale*.[1] That its popularity extended into the sixteenth century it will be my first aim to show, by looking at the evidence for Chaucerian influence on the two surviving 'Patient Grissel' plays (already investigated briefly by Thompson) and at the prose Chapbook and the Ballad on the same subject probably composed in the 1590s.[2] Chaucer's *Works* were published six times in the sixteenth century (by Pynson in 1526, by Thynne in 1532 – the edition from which I will quote[3] – 1542 and 1550, and in new editions in 1561 and 1598), and so would have been readily available to the authors of these four texts. Can his influence be seen in them, and if so what parts have they chosen to include or ignore, and why?

My second aim will be to see whether Greene was influenced by the Grissel story when he wrote *Pandosto* in 1588, and whether Shakespeare was influenced directly by either Chaucer's or any sixteenth-century retelling of the Grissel story when he adapted *Pandosto* into *The Winter's Tale* in (or shortly before) 1611.[4] E. T. Donaldson has forged a path for such a study by opening up the possibility that Shakespeare's Chaucer sources extend beyond the now well-established *Knight's Tale* and *Troilus and Criseyde*.[5] If Donaldson is right that Shakespeare was influenced by the *Merchant's Tale*, *Sir Thopas* and the Wife of Bath as well, then the likelihood is increased that he had read the *Canterbury Tales* as a whole, and found there the paradoxical patience, at once suffering and triumphant, which he celebrates in *The Winter's Tale*.

I will look first at the sixteenth-century Patient Grissel texts. Here the situation is complicated by the continued availability of Chaucer's foreign sources, to which the *Clerk's Tale* is often very close. These are: Petrarch's letter of 1373 'de Insigni Obedientia et Fide Uxoris' (derived but rather different from Boccaccio's *Decameron* x, 10 which remained untranslated until 1620), and one of its two fourteenth-century French prose translations, the *Livre Griseldis*. Both this and the other translation, that by Philippe de

Mézières, were in print in France by the sixteenth century, as was an early dramatization of Philippe's version, *L'Estoire de Griseldis*.[6] It has not previously been realized that two of the Renaissance English versions derive directly from French versions; indeed Walter is generally given his French name, Gautier. In order to discover whether Chaucer also influenced these and my other texts, I have had to concentrate on the distinctly original features of the *Clerk's Tale*, most of which are carefully detailed by Severs.[7] Briefly, Chaucer heightens the pathos of Griseldis' trial (partly by darkening the characterization of Walter and his sergeant), and gives a new realism to the relationship of husband and wife by allowing Griseldis to criticize Walter's changeability. I will attempt to keep only to distinctively Chaucerian features while searching for his influence in the following five texts. (I have not included among them *The History of Grisild the Second*, a political poem written in 1558 by the Catholic priest W. Forrest. Although this shows clear Chaucerian influence in the use of his protagonists' names (Grisild and Walter) and his rhyme–royal verse form, it is the history not of patient Grissel but of Katherine of Aragon, and takes little part in the tradition I wish to trace.[8])

(1) Chaucer's influence on the sixteenth-century 'Patient Grissel' texts

(i) Radcliffe's *De Patientia Griseldis* (1546–56?)[9]
Although the text is now lost, this play is very likely to be based upon Chaucer, as the author also wrote a lost *De Meliboeo Chauceriano*. It is conceivable that some of the Chaucer parallels noted below may be mediated through a knowledge of this Latin play, but very unlikely, since it was written only for performance by the boys at the grammar school at Hitchin and never printed.

(ii) Phillip's *Commodye of pacient and meeke Grissill* (1565–6)[10]
Although this morality play presents a wholly original approach to plot and characterization, it was probably inspired by *L'Estoire de Griseldis*, which had been printed in Paris in 1550. Both plays provide their Marquis, Gautier, with three principal courtiers and a sister, and his wife with a nurse, and verbal parallels may be found in the scene in which Grissill/Griseldis returns to her father, whose complaint to Fortune is unique to these two versions.[11] There are however also parallels between Phillip's play and 'Chaucerian' details of the *Clerk's Tale*. Ann Thompson has drawn attention to three of these:

a)   The author, in the preface of the play, is said to have written 'so simplye as hee coulde', eschewing 'Rethoricque' (10,13). This may derive from the Host's request to the clerk to 'speketh so pleyne' without 'termes' and 'fygures' (20,16).
b)   Gautier does not weep when he sends Grissill home, as he does in Petrarch's version (and *L'Estoire*).

c)   When Grissill is reunited with her children she appears to faint (stage direction,
       'fall downe' at 1956). Chaucer makes much more of this reunion than do his
       sources, and his Griseldis also 'swapte downe to the grounde' (1099). (This
       detail is in fact in the printed edition of de Mézières's translation, though it is
       simpler to assume Chaucer was the source.)

I would add:

d)   Both authors depict the servant who takes away Grissill's children with far
       greater ferocity than their sources; he is positively obsequious in *L'Estoire*.[12]
e)   Phillip's Grissill expresses her feelings more than any previous Griseldis apart
       from Chaucer's. In particular, both of these touchingly bid their daughter
       farewell, a detail not found in the sources nor in *L'Estoire*, which all highlight her
       refusal to give way to feeling at this point.[13]

More broadly, Phillip seems to show an understanding of the contradictory
feelings aroused by the two protagonists of Chaucer's *Tale*. In each case he has
expressed our negative feelings towards them by inventing a new character.
Grissill's nurse voices the outrage which we feel at the removal of the children,
in unflattering contrast to her unresisting mistress. Walter's role is split into a
loving but rather weak Gautier, and a malicious Vice, Sir Politicke Perswas-
ion, who personifies the obsession which drives Chaucer's Marquis, and who
initiates all the tests on his wife. This allows Gautier to express a quasi-Divine
pity for Grissill, just as God expresses his love for Job by allowing Satan to test
him. The resulting emotional and religious complexity in Phillip's play is
much more suggestive of Chaucer than of any of the French versions which lie
behind it.

(iii) The anonymous Chapbook *History of Patient Grisel* (possibly late
sixteenth-century, although the earliest edition is dated 1619)[14]
This novella claims to be a translation from the French, and a comparison
with the 1510 (?) Paris edition of *A Patience Griseldis: Marquise de Saluces*
reveals that it is based on one of the early printed editions of Philippe de
Mézières's version of the story. Verbal parallels are particularly frequent at
the beginning, and in spite of the laboured verbosity of the English translator,
and his indulgence in long and unattractive comments, it follows this
unChaucerian version of events pretty closely.[15] There is however one
possible parallel with one of Chaucer's most telling additions to the story:[16]
When the Marquis tells Grisel to sacrifice her son she replies, 'Take him then,
a Gods name, and if hee be marked for death, it is but the common brand of
all creatures; nay, if the mother may be a sacrifice of propitiation to appease
your disquiet, never was lamb so meek, nor holocaust so willing to be offered'
(ch. VI). This corresponds to Chaucer's own interpolated comment (at a
slightly earlier stage in the story);

> And as a lambe she sytteth meke and styll
> And let this cruel sergeaunt do his wyll   (538–9)

and indicates that the author has thoroughly recognized the religious implications of Chaucer's comment.

More tentatively I would suggest the influence of two mistranslations of Chaucer:

a) Grisel asks the Marquis not to torment his second wife because 'she is yong and peradventure of another straine, and so may want of that patience and government, which I, poore I, have endured' (ch. IX). This rather awkward sentence may be a mistranslation of Chaucer's lines:

She coulde not aduersyte endure.
As coulde a poore fostred creature.   (1042–3)

b) When the Chapbook author lodges Janicole in the cottage's single bed, while 'the sweet daughter made shift with the ground' (ch.1), he may be mistranslating Chaucer's more general statement that she 'made her bedde ful harde *and* nothi*n*g softe' (228). Petrarch does not specify who has the 'durum ... cubiculum' (II, 12: presumably both), and the French source says nothing about sleeping arrangements.

The Chapbook author may also have followed Phillip in insisting even more than his French source on the love and pity which Gualter feels for his wife, but conversely he has failed to provide a Vice figure to explain why he torments her. Grisel's behaviour is similarly inexplicable, for the author has omitted most of the religious reference which makes both Phillip's and Chaucer's stories intelligible *exempla*. Instead she emerges as a fairy-tale victim, whose trials of suffering are less like Job's than those of a rags-to-riches heroine.[17] The story is told for sentimental effect, sidestepping both Phillip's didacticism and Chaucer's disturbing realism.

(iv) The Ballad 'Of patient Grissel and a Noble Marquesse' (1593?)[18]
There are two early examples of this, one in a manuscript (dated 1600?), and one in Deloney's *Garland of Good Will*, first registered in 1593, though I will quote from the earliest extant edition, dated 1631. If Deloney did write this short ballad (as seems likely since he wrote most of *The Garland*), he may have been influenced both by Chaucer and by a memory of the *Lay le Freine*, a Middle English translation of Marie de France's *lai*.[19] Freine (Ash-tree), having been abandoned at birth, does not discover her parentage until she is decking her lover's bed, with Griseldis-like patience, for his marriage to her nobly brought-up twin sister. Grissel in the Ballad herself has twins, and her final return to the palace is also only to prepare the new bride's bedchamber. Another striking feature of this version is that the people and not the Marquis are the ultimate initiators of the test, for they demand he should 'put ... quite away' his 'beggars brat' (41,51), a phrase possibly taken from Phillip's play (911). This prompts the Marquis to make her suffer in order to win their sympathy (unsuccessfully, for they are still sneering at the second wedding, 166). Grissel is sent home *before* the gap in time during which her twins grow

up, and she goes wearing not the traditional smock, but a 'russet gowne' (133)
which the Marquis seems to have specially preserved.

This version of the story may seem to have little to do with Chaucer, but one
verse touchingly alludes to two of the passages in which Chaucer departs from
his sources. His Griseldis bids her daughter farewell directly, and regrets that
she dies (like Christ) for her sake.[20]

> Farewel my childe I shal the neuer se ...
> For this nyght shalte thou dyen for my sake.   (555, 560)

Although Phillip's Grissill does briefly bid her daughter farewell (1201), the
Ballad's wording and regret seems to be taken directly from Chaucer:

> Farwel, farwel (quoth she) my children deere,
>   neuer shal I see you againe:
> 'Tis long of me your sad & wofull mother here,
>   for whose sake ye must be slaine:
> Had I beene borne of Royall race,
> You might have liu'd in happy case:
>   but you must die for my vnworthinesse.   (89–95).

Deloney must have been attracted to this passage by its pathos and its
demonstration of Grissel's humility (as Thurber said, 'a woman's place is in
the wrong'). He does not develop Chaucer's religious implication that the
child is making a Christ-like sacrifice, as the Chapbook author had done when
he borrowed Chaucer's equivalent comparison between Griseldis and the
lamb. Instead, his radical changes go even further than the Chapbook does in
presenting Griselde as a fairy-tale victim rather than a religious *exemplum*. Like
all the other sixteenth-century texts, the Ballad also exonerates the Marquis,
insisting that he loves Grissel 'most dearley, tenderly, and entirely' (59). How
this is supposed to be compatible with his desertion of her for 'full fifteen
winters' (143) is not explained; such realism as Chaucer put into the
relationship is entirely ignored in order to exaggerate Grissel's trials and
increase the undoubted emotional effect of the poem.

(v) Dekker, Chettle and Haughton's *Pleasant Commodye of Patient Grissill*
(written in 1599 according to Henslowe's diary, produced in the 1600s, and
printed in 1603)[21]
T. Dekker, who is believed to be responsible for the splendidly realistic and
touching scenes of Grissill with her family, wrote two lost plays which may be
presumed to owe something to Chaucer: *Troilus and Cressida* and *Fair Constance
of Rome*.[22] However, it is difficult to find anything specifically Chaucerian in
these parts of the play, or, in the story of Grissill and Gualther, usually said to
be written largely by Chettle (the two must have collaborated on some if not
all scenes). The third collaborator, Haughton, who is credited by Hoy with
the Welsh dialect scenes, does seem to be influenced by Chaucer. These scenes
concern a Welsh virago, reminiscent of the Wife of Bath, who demonstrates

that husbands can be as easily tormented and trained as wives. This places
Grissill's story within a cynical context similar to that provided for the *Clerk's
Tale* by the 'Lenvoy de Chaucer', suggesting what Thompson calls 'a
dramatic equivalent for "the marriage group" of *The Canterbury Tales*' (p. 21).

The main plot of the play is not the Petrarchan version of the story, but
derives from the Ballad. Grissill gives birth to twins, is sent back with them to
her father's cottage dressed in russet, has to give them up, and lives with her
rustic family until sent for to attend Gualther's second marriage. The play
also shows the influence of Phillip's softening of the Marquis, particularly in
his wooing of Grissill and his continued muttered protestations of affection for
her.[23] Indeed at the end, as in Phillip's play, all admire Gualther's wisdom;
we are even invited, by the visual aid of plaited green osiers, to accept this as
the correct method for handling young wives.[24] Like Phillip too, Dekker
provides both a family group sympathetic to Grissill, and a court faction
which is hostile to her.

The play does however also have several Petrarchan features, and whereas
some of these (such as Grissill's request to Gualther not to torment his second
wife) can be derived from Phillip's play,[25] others can not. Thompson uses
several of these as evidence of Chaucerian influence,[26] but to accept her
arguments we must assume that none of the playwrights knew *L'Estoire*, the
French printed edition of de Mézières's translation, or the Chapbook (which
may indeed have appeared after the play). Two further parallels between this
play and Chaucer, neither noted by Thompson, must rest on the same rather
doubtful assumption:

a)   Dekker gives Gualther no motive for testing Grissill. Both Phillip and Deloney
      offer clear reasons which separate the testing side of Gualther from his loving
      side. Neither Chaucer nor the French versions do this.
b)   Gualther repents of his cruelty (v, 2, 205–6) as he does in Chaucer (1049–50),
      the Chapbook, and the French prose edition, but not elsewhere.

If the Petrarchan material in the play is taken from Chaucer, then it is not
passages which increase the story's pathos or religious message (as with the
Chaucerian material in the Ballad, Chapbook, or Phillip's play) which have
attracted Dekker and his collaborators. These are passages which highlight
the political dimension of the story, which expose how a high-born man can
wilfully tyrannize a low-born woman. The development of both the hostile
court faction, and the attractive rural family, considerably enhance this
theme. Both Balbulo, Grissill's loyal servant, and Laureo, her disaffected
student brother, bitterly criticize the Marquis's treatment of the helpless
Grissill, and even she is provoked by the loss of her children to exclaim:

> Farewell, farewell, deare soules, adue, adue,
> Your father sendes and I must part from you,
> I must oh God I must, must is for Kings,
> And loe obedience, for loe vnderlings.   (IV,2,140–3)

Even the nurse in Phillip's play never questions Gautier's rights in this way. There is potential for this interpretation of the story in Chaucer's Petrarchan version, particularly in the irony with which Walter's sense of himself as a servant is presented.[27] For example, he sends Griseldis home with the sententious remark:

> I may not done as euery ploughman may.   (779)

But the Petrarchan identification of Valterius' role with that of God necessarily implies that Griseldis, like Job or indeed like any mortal, can be rightfully tested by an apparently arbitrary divine power. Dekker's play is much more subversive, for in spite of the overt message for shrewish wives, Grissill's endurance not only shames her oppressor but questions his rights.

(2) The Influence of Patient Grissel on *Pandosto* and *The Winter's Tale*

It seems probable, then, that all the sixteenth-century Grissel texts owe something directly to Chaucer, whether it be to his actual words and images, or to his religious, political or emotional insights. I want now to turn to *Pandosto*, which may itself be loosely modelled on the story of Patient Grissel, and to *The Winter's Tale*, which though based on *Pandosto*, is sometimes closer to Phillip's or Dekker's Grissel plays, or even to the *Clerk's Tale* itself. Did Shakespeare recognize the shadow of the Grissel story behind *Pandosto*, and seek to restore the original theme of the testing of patience?

The first (defective) edition of Robert Greene's *Pandosto: the Triumph of Time*[28] is dated 1588, and so predates all the English Grissel texts except Chaucer's and Phillip's, but neither of the two printed French versions. Greene is known to have read some Chaucer,[29] but he had also spent some time in Italy, and could also have come across Boccaccio's original and untranslated story there. As McNeal noted in 1932,[30] the two parts of *Pandosto* could both owe something to the Patient Grissel story. In the first part we see a royal wife's patience being sorely tried by her husband, who believes her to be unfaithful, imprisons her, and sends two guards to take away and expose her infant daughter. In a passage which recalls Chaucer's own addition to his sources and has no equivalent in any preceding version besides a bare farewell in Phillip, she regrets that the child must die for her fault:

> ... thy untimely death must pay thy mothers debtes, and her guiltless crime must be thy gastly curse ... with a sorrowfull kisse I bid thee farewell, and I pray the Gods thou mayst fare well.   (pp. 166–7)

Bellaria also loses her son Garinter, who dies of grief during his mother's trial; the double grief kills her. In the second part of *Pandosto*, after a gap in time corresponding to that in Grissel's story, we see Bellaria's daughter Fawnia grown into a beautiful and hardworking shepherdess very like the young

Grissel. Dorastus, the son of Bellaria's supposed royal lover, has also grown into a huntsman-prince very like Walter, particularly when his father urges him to marry by pointing to the passing of time (p. 177). He chooses the unsuitably 'low-born' Fawnia, and elopes with her – fortuitously – to Pandosto's kingdom. Her unknown father sees in her, if not a second bride, at least a concubine, and after her identity has been revealed is sufficiently embarrassed by this to commit suicide. If Greene had used Chaucer's *Tale* then the only fundamental changes he has made are to invent a more realistic motive (jealousy) for the husband's trial of his wife; to develop the story of the second generation; and, by giving Fortune an intrusive role at every point, to substitute the theme of the 'Triumph of Time' for Chaucer's more moralistic theme of the 'Triumph of Patience'.

If this is so, then it is interesting to observe how nearly all of Shakespeare's (frequently discussed)[31] changes help to restore the original theme of the Grissel story. The most important change is the preservation of Hermione (Greene's Bellaria) to the end of the play, to enjoy a double reconciliation with husband and daughter and so to show the triumph of her patience. Leontes' own triumph of patience underscores Hermione's, for he has done penance under Paulina's direction for sixteen long years, while Hermione is patiently waiting for the oracle to be fulfilled. Even Camillo participates in this theme, for he patiently postpones his return home until it seems likely to be successful; in *Pandosto* Fortune engineers Fawnia's and Dorastus' return.

Shakespeare in fact takes pains to indicate that it is patience, and not time and fortune, which has triumphed.[32] Hermione's words and actions are often characteristic of Christian patience as it was celebrated by Elizabethan homilists. Coverdale clarifies the distinction between Christian and 'heathenish' patience.

> As Socrates ... thought that it was but a chance that he was afflicted; but David knew and confessed that his visitation and affliction came from God. (II Sam. 24; 1 Chron. 21)[33]

Bullinger, following the central patience text, Hebrews 12.5–11, explains that God 'doth, as a merciful father, chasten [men] to the amendment of their lives and safeguard of their souls'.[34] So Hermione accepts her prison-sentence willingly.

> This action I now go on
> Is for my better grace.   (II, 1, 121–2)

Moreover her words 'The king's will be performed' (115) evoke not only the patient man's submission of his will, but Christ's acceptance of his Father's will at Gethsemane (Matt. 26.39). Her analogy with the supreme *exemplum* of righteous patience[35] is also suggested when she tells her women not to weep, like Christ on the way to Calvary (II, 1, 118–19; Luke 23.28). Although she does not call suffering her cross, as Phillip's Grissill does –

> Blame not Fortune for my ouerthroe,
> It was the will of God, that it should be so: ...
> This crosse is to trye us, as hee doth his elect   (1767–70)

– Shakespeare's language suggests that suffering is a kind of Passion. Bellaria, on the other hand, sees patience as 'a shield against Fortune' (p. 165) even when the gods are invoked:

> If the divine powers be privy to humane actions (as no doubt they are) I hope
> my patience shall make fortune blushe ...   (p. 170)

Hermione uses this very speech, but Shakespeare alters it to show patience triumphant over tyranny, not Fortune, and to foretell a final Christ-like triumph of innocence over death:

> But thus, if powers divine
> Behold our human actions (as they do),
> I doubt not then but innocence shall make
> False accusation blush, and tyranny
> Tremble at patience.   (iii, 2, 28–32)

In this play we do observe 'tyranny/Tremble at patience' as we have in the *Clerk's Tale*.

   The triumph of patience may be felt however to be a theme too dear to Shakespeare and to the sixteenth century as a whole, to indicate any specific connections between *The Winter's Tale* and the Grissel stories. (Danby has shown its importance in *King Lear* for example.)[36] However, other changes which Shakespeare made to *Pandosto* make this comparison more plausible. In the first place Shakespeare, unlike Greene, suggests that both the queen's children are restored, for he repeatedly associated Florizel with the dead Mamillius (Greene's Garinter) at v, 1, 116–18, 132–3, and 175–7 where Leontes says

> What might I have been,
> Might I a son and daughter now have look'd on,
> Such goodly things as you!

Secondly, Leontes has far less cause for jealousy than had Pandosto, whose wife kept going in and out of Egistus' (Polyxenes) bedchamber, and walking with him in the garden (p. 158). This makes Leontes seem far more like the irrational Marquis, and so makes Hermione's inexplicable trial closer to Grissel's.[37] Thirdly, in both the Grissel story and Shakespeare the cruel father is offset by a kind father or foster-father; Grissel has Janicola; Perdita has the Shepherd. In *Pandosto* this opposition is confused because Fawnia has a foster-mother as well. More broadly, changes in social status and in relationship are embodied in changes of clothing in both the Grissel story and *The Winter's Tale*. In particular Perdita, unlike Fawnia, is seen first decked as a queen, then 'disguised' as a shepherdess, and finally restored to her courtly dress.[38]

Even if it is granted that Shakespeare was consciously using the Grissel story as a secondary source for *The Winter's Tale*,[39] can it be proved that he was using Chaucer's version of it? In many verbal details in fact the sixteenth-century versions are closer. The seasonal imagery which is so important in *The Winter's Tale* may have been suggested by Chaucer's association of the returning children with freshness and newness: the maiden is 'freshe, ful of gemmes clere' and her brother is 'Arayed ... fresshley in his manere' (779, 780). But the Ballad speaks of Grissel's exile for 'full fifteen winters' and Dekker, closer than either to Shakespeare, makes Grissill associate herself and her (unrecognized) daughter with winter and spring:[40]

> Onely I prostrately beseech your grace,
> That you consider of her tender yeares,
> Which as a flower in spring may soone be nipt
> With the least frost of colde aduersity.   (v, 2, 147–50)

Then again, there is no character in Chaucer's narrative to express the feelings of outrage and grief which the audience feel but the patient wife must suppress. The narrator fulfils this role in his asides, but Phillip supplies a nurse who seems a very model for Paulina and her husband Antigonus. Grissill's nurse attacks Gautier for unnatural cruelty, and offers to save his daughter from death:

> For I from hence will take my flight and hence be cleane exilde,
> This will I do oh worthie Lord, for safegarde of thy Childe.   (1177–8)

Paulina accuses Leontes of fancifulness, tyranny and injustice, and Antigonus offers to 'pawn the little blood which I have left/To save the innocent' and agrees to take the child 'quite out/Of our dominions' (II, 3,165,175).

The parallels between Shakespeare's play and Dekker's are particularly striking, and in any case it would seem improbable that Shakespeare did not know this excellent play. Dekker gives Grissill a father, a brother and a jocular servant, who resemble Perdita's entourage of shepherd, clown and Autolycus in more ways than one. In both plays the rustics are brought to court, which provides opportunity both for comedy and for contrasting the court's snobbish values and tyranny with rural simplicity and generosity. The contrast between false and true values is often expressed in surprisingly similar terms in the two plays; for example both Leontes and Gualther find disgrace in the similarity of their children's features to their own.[41] There are also verbal parallels,[42] of which perhaps the closest occurs at the climax of each play, when the mother is reunited with her children. Is Grissill's blessing

> Blessing distill on you like morning deaw,
> My soule knit to your soules, knowes you are mine   (v,2,196–7)

perhaps the inspiration of Hermione's?

> You gods, look down,
> And from your sacred vials pour your graces
> Upon my daughter's head!   (v,3,121–3)[43]

There is however one important aspect of *The Winter's Tale* which Shakespeare could not have found in any of the Grissel stories apart from Chaucer's. Phillip's and Dekker's Grissills follow tradition in remaining dry-eyed and inwardly calm.[44] Phillip's Grissill, after one emotional farewell to her daughter, offers Gautier 'pastimes sport' (1217) to show how little she is affected by it, and Dekker's Grissill triumphs over Gualther by her detachment from the suffering he has tried to inflict:

> It neuer toucht my heart.   (v,2,154)

Hermione is also 'not prone to weeping', but she does feel

> That honourable grief lodg'd here, which burns
> Worse than tears drown.   (II,1,108–12)

Moreover, although, like Bellaria, she does accuse her husband of tyranny III,2,114), she sees her greatest trial as the loss of this tyrant's love

> The crown and comfort of my life, your favour,
> I do give lost, for I do feel it gone,
> But know not how it went.   (III,2,94–6)

The sixteenth-century Grissels never express such a bitter sense of betrayal. They are either (like Phillip's and Dekker's) triumphant over feeling, or (like those in the Chapbook and Ballad) the suffering victims of a power they never question. Chaucer's Griseldis however is both triumphant and suffering. In an important addition Chaucer shows that she is aware of her own value and suffers for Walter's rejection of it

> Oh good god: howe gentill and howe kynde
> Ye seemed by your speche and your vysage
> The day that maked was our maryage; . . .
> Love is not olde as whan it is newe.   (852–7)

Griselde insists that *she* will never change (858–61), and in another addition Chaucer celebrates this special merit of feminine patience:

> There can no man in humblesse hem aquyte
> As women can: ne be halfe so trewe
> As women ben, but it befall of newe.   (936–8)

It is this faithfulness, this continuing love for a man she recognizes, by his cruelty and fickleness, to be unworthy of her love, which makes Griseldis' trials as harrowing as Hermione's.

The *Clerk's Tale* and *The Winter's Tale* are both 'symbolic stories' in Derek

Brewer's sense, and much of what he says about the first would apply equally interestingly to the second.[45] I hope that I have now shown that there may be a direct link between the two. Shakespeare may have imbibed some Chaucerian influence through the numerous sixteenth-century versions of the story, or he may conceivably have read Petrarch's original letter and there found the name of the heroine 'que divisim *perdita* videbantur' (VI,52). But I prefer to believe that it was in Chaucer's Griselde that he found a model for the suffering and yet triumphant love he wished to portray.

NOTES

1 Both appear six times; see D. Pearsall, *The Canterbury Tales* (London, 1985), p. 301, D. S. Silvia, 'Some Fifteenth-Century Manuscripts of the *Canterbury Tales*', in *Chaucer and Middle English Studies in Honour of R. H. Robbins*, ed. B. Rowland (London, 1974), pp. 153–63.

2 A. Thompson, *Shakespeare's Chaucer* (Liverpool, 1978), pp. 16–27; the Chapbook and Ballad are briefly discussed in C. Hoy, *The Dramatic Works of Thomas Dekker: Introduction, Notes and Commentaries to the Edition of F. Bowers*, vol. 1 (Cambridge, 1980), 129–47.

3 *The Works of Geoffrey Chaucer and Others, being a Reproduction in Facsimile of the First Collected Edition of 1532 from the Copy in the British Museum*, ed. W. W. Skeat (Oxford, 1905).

4 1611 is the date given by Simon Fordham of a performance of the play; his notes are reprinted in pp. xxi–xxii of the Arden edition ed. J. H. P. Pafford (London, 1963). This is the edition used here. For *Pandosto*, see n.28 below.

5 E. Talbot Donaldson, *The Swan at the Well* (New Haven, 1985); for Chaucer's influence on Shakespeare, see also: N. Coghill, 'Shakespeare's Reading of Chaucer', *Elizabethan and Jacobean Studies Presented to F. P. Wilson*, ed. H. Davis and H. Gardner (Oxford, 1959), pp. 86–99; K. Muir, *The Sources of Shakespeare's Plays* (London, 1977); Thompson, *Shakespeare's Chaucer*, H. E. Rollins, 'The Troilus–Cressida Story from Chaucer to Shakespeare', *PMLA*, 32 (1917), 383–429; C. Pettet, *Shakespeare and the Romance Tradition* (London, 1949); M. Bradbrook, 'What Shakespeare did to Chaucer's *Troilus and Criseyde*', *Shakespeare Quarterly*, 9 (1958), 311–19; A. S. Miskimin, *The Renaissance Chaucer* (New Haven, 1975); *Narrative and Dramatic Sources of Shakespeare*, ed. G. Bullough, VI (London, 1966).

6 E. Golenistcheff-Koutouzoff, *L'Histoire de Griseldis en France du XIVe au XVe siècle* (Paris, 1933, repr. Geneva, 1975), pp. 115–50 (he gives texts of both versions); *L'Estoire de Griseldis*, ed. M. Roques (Paris, 1957), p. xi.

7 J. Burke Severs, *The Literary Relationships of Chaucer's 'Clerk's Tale'* (New Haven, 1942, repr. Archon, 1972), particularly ch. 1 and IV and appendices, giving texts; H. G. Wright, *Boccaccio in England from Chaucer to Tennyson* (London, 1957), pp. 116–22.

8 W. Forrest, *The History of Grisild the Second*, ed. W. D. Macray (Roxburghe Club, London, 1875).

9 Described J. Bale, *Scriptorum Illustrium Maioris Brytanniae* (Basle, 1557–9) I, 700; see Hoy, *Dramatic Works*, pp. 131–2.

10 J. Phillip, *The Play of Patient Grissill*, ed. R. B. McKerrow (Malone Soc., London, 1909); see Wright, *Boccaccio*, pp. 173–8; Thompson, *Shakespeare's Chaucer*, pp. 20–4; Hoy, *Dramatic Works*, pp. 134–41.

11 See n.6 above and compare Phillip, *Grissill*, 1723–5, 1746–61 with *L'Estoire*, 2205, 2229–67. Other details indicating a French source include the betrothal scene and Grissill's welcome to the new bride (Phillip, *Grissill*, 551, 615–16, 1913; *L'Estoire*, 894–5, 2405–6); see Severs, *Chaucer's 'Clerk's Tale'*, pp. 235, 240.

12 See Severs, *Chaucer's Clerk's Tale*, pp. 140, 229–31; Phillip, *Grissill*, 1113, 1149–50, 1401–47; *Clerk's Tale*, 533–46, 673–86; *L'Estoire*, 1395–1412, 1703–15.

13 *Clerk's Tale*, 555, Phillip, *Grissill*, 1201ff.; cf. *L'Estoire*, 1413ff.

14 There is a copy (c.34.f.28) in Brit. Lib., with a frontispiece of Queen Elizabeth (suggesting an earlier date than 1619); it has been edited by H. B. Wheatley (Chapbook Soc., London, 1885), and by J. P. Collier in *Early English Ballads*, ed. T. Wright, et al. (Percy Soc., London, 1882), III; see Hoy, *Dramatic Works*, pp. 133–4.

15 No date or printer given for this copy (Brit. Lib. 12470, b.20). Examples of similarities include the Marquis's hearing of Grisel's virtue from others, her filling of *two* water-pots, her claim that her dowry was 'virginite, foy, reuerence et pouerte', and the Marquis's final sense of 'piteuse compassion'.

16 See Severs, *Chaucer's Clerk's Tale*, p. 233.

17 The full title of the Chapbook is 'The Ancient True and Admirable/History of Patient Grisel, A Poore Man's Daughter in France: Shewing/How Maides, By Her Example, In Their Good Behaviour/May Marriè Rich Husbands;/ And Likewise Wives by Their Patience and Obedience/May Gain Muche Gloriè' (see Hoy, *Dramatic Works*, p. 133).

18 *The Works of Thomas Deloney*, ed. F. O. Mann (Oxford, 1912), pp. 346–50; *A Transcript of the Register of the Company of Stationers in London: 1554–1640*, ed. E. Arber (London, 1875–94), II, 267, mentioned Wright, *Boccaccio*, p. 171, Hoy, *Dramatic Works*, p. 133. It is available elsewhere, e.g. *The Roxburghe Ballads*, ed. W. Campbell (London, 1874), II, 269–74. For authorship, see M. E. Lawlis, *Apology for the Middle Class*, (Bloomington, 1960), p. 158, n.10.

19 *Middle English Verse Romances*, ed. D. B. Sands (New York, 1966), p. 233–45.

20 See Severs, *Chaucer's 'Clerk's Tale'*, pp. 233–4; J. Mann, 'Parents and Children in the *Canterbury Tales*', *Literature in Fourteenth Century England*, ed. P. Boitani and A. Torti (Tübingen, 1982), pp. 165–83.

21 *The Dramatic Works of Thomas Dekker*, ed. F. Bowers (Cambridge, 1953), I, 207–98, see Wright, *Boccaccio*, pp. 207–11; Thompson, *Shakespeare's Chaucer*, pp. 24–7; Hoy, *Dramatic Works*, pp. 129–31.

22 See Hoy, *Dramatic Works*, pp. 144–6; Thompson, *Shakespeare's Chaucer*, pp. 30–3.

23 E.g. Phillip, *Grissill*, 638–750, 1337–41; Dekker, I, 2, IV, 1.

24 Phillip, *Grissill*, 2033; Dekker, V,2,214–18, 236–46.

25 Phillip, *Grissill*, 1934–6; Dekker, V,2,147–50.

26 Thompson, *Shakespeare's Chaucer*, pp. 24–7.

27 Mann, 'Parents and Children', p. 178; this is in Latin (I, 53–4, V, 5) and French (I,39–40, V, 11).

28 R. Greene, 'Pandosto, the Triumph of Time', ed. from 1588 edn in *Narrative and Dramatic Sources of Shakespeare*, ed. G. Bullough (London, 1975), VII, 156–99.

29 C. Camden, 'Chaucer and Greene', *Review of English Studies*, 6 (1930) 73–4; see C. F. Spurgeon, *Five Hundred Years of Chaucer Criticism and Allusion: 1337–1900* (Cambridge, 1925, I, 130, 131, 137 (five allusions).

30 T. H. McNeal, '*The Clerk's Tale* as a Possible Source for *Pandosto*', *PMLA*, 47 (1932), 453–60.

31 J. Lawlor, '*Pandosto* and the Nature of Dramatic Romance', *Philological Quarterly*, 41 (1962), 96–113; Arden edn pp. xxvii–xxxiii; S. R. Maveety, 'What Shakespeare

did with *Pandosto*: an Interpretation of *The Winter's Tale*', *Pacific Coast Studies in Shakespeare*, ed. T. H. McNeil and T. N. Greenfield (Oregon, 1966), pp. 263–79; Bullough, *Sources of Shakespeare*, pp. 123–4, 132; Muir, *Shakespeare's Plays*, pp. 240–6; C. Frey, *Shakespeare's Vast Romance* (Missouri, 1980), pp. 55–67.

32 *pace* I–S. Ewbank, 'The Triumph of Time in *The Winter's Tale*', *Review of English Literature*, 52 (1964), 83–100.

33 M. Coverdale, 'A Spiritual and Most Precious Pearl', pp. 84–194 in *Writings and Translations*, ed. G. Pearson, (Parker Soc., Cambridge, 1844), p. 178, see also Maveety, 'What Shakespeare did with *Pandosto*', (n.31) on Christian and pagan elements in the play.

34 *Bullough's Decades*, transl. H. L., ed. T. Harding, (Parker Soc., Cambridge, 1850), III, 93; see also Coverdale, 'Spiritual and Most Precious Pearl', pp. 108–15, *The Works of Roger Hutchinson*, ed. J. Bruck, (Parker Soc., Cambridge, 1842), p. 311.

35 For Christ as type of patience, see *Parson's Tale*, 662–8; Bruck, *Hutchinson*, pp. 316–20; Harding, *Bullough's Decades*, III, p. 86; etc.

36 J. F. Danby, 'King Lear and Christian Patience', *Elizabethan and Jacobean Poets* (London 1952, 1964), pp. 108–27. Danby maintains that the Christian patient does suffer pain.

37 *pace* P. Siegel in 'Leontes a Jealous Tyrant', *Reviews of English Studies*, n.s. 1 (1950), 302–7.

38 S. L. Bethell, *The Winter's Tale, a study* (London, 1947) discusses these changes of clothing, pp. 66, 93–6.

39 The two plots are briefly compared by J. H. P. Pafford, in the Arden edn of *The Winter's Tale*, p. lxiii and n.4.

40 For Shakespeare's possible use of Proserpina myth, and of F. Sabie's *Flora's Fortune* (written 'to expel the accustomed tediousness of cold winters nightes'), see E. A. J. Honigmann, 'Secondary Sources for *The Winter's Tale*', *Philological Quarterly*, 34 (1955), 27–38.

41 *Patient Grissil*, IV,1,16–17, 61–6; *Winter's Tale*, II, 3,97–9.

42 Cp. *Patient Grissil*, 1,2,276–7 with *Winter's Tale*, IV, 4,442–4.

43 This should be contrasted with Paulina's prophecy that vengeance is 'not dropp'd down yet' (III,2,202); it is characteristic of patience not to seek vengeance.

44 Tearlessness is part of the folk-story; see Severs, *Chaucer's 'Clerk's Tale'*, p. 5; inner calm is intrinsic to Augustine's and Gregory's formative definitions of patience ('aequo animo mala tolerare': Aug: *De Patientia*, ch.2); see R. Hanna III, 'Some Commonplaces of Late Medieval Patience Discussions: An Introduction', in *The Triumph of Patience*, ed. G. J. Schiffhorst (Florida, 1978), pp. 65–87, esp. p. 68.

45 See D. Brewer, *Symbolic Stories* (Cambridge, 1980), pp. 96–8.

15

The Virtuoso's *Troilus*

RICHARD BEADLE

Loquendi forma, scio, quòd mutata
Sit intra seculum; & verba mirè
Tunc temporis in precio, & laudata.
Nunc vel in desuetudinem abire:
Amabant etiam tunc (oportet scire)
Diuersis item saecis conciliare
Amorem: Artes variae sunt & rare.

Given a moment's thought, one recognizes that what is being said has a familiar ring, and perhaps recalls the source in English. The unusual but careful imitation of the rhyme scheme, and the ear for the rhythm of the original are strong clues. However when Chaucer wrote that 'in forme of speche is chaunge / Withinne a thousand yeer', and towards the end of his most ambitious work foresaw how the text of the *Troilus* might deteriorate, or become liable to misunderstanding over the years, he could scarcely have envisaged that before very long an able and well-meaning scholar-courtier would seek to provide the world with a parallel translation of the poem into Latin (together with a copious and erudite commentary) largely with the intention of protecting it from the ravages wrought by time through linguistic change.

Chaucer's critical heritage and the editorial history of his writings have been amply treated in recent years, but it is rare to find the name of Sir Francis Kinaston (1587–?1642) given more than a cursory mention in such contexts.[1] Apart from his posthumously published English works, the lyrical collection *Cynthiades* and the heroic romance *Leoline and Sydanis* (1642),[2] Kinaston's main published literary endeavour, from which the foregoing quotation is taken, was issued in 1635 under the title *Amorum Troili et Creseidæ libri duo priores Anglico-Latini* (Oxford, J. Lichfield). Though commonly described simply as a translation into Latin verse of the first two books of Chaucer's *Troilus*, it is as well to be precise about how the work is presented to the reader. There are good reasons for describing it as a parallel-text edition – the title suggests as much. A reprint of Speght's 1598 text of Books I and II of the *Troilus* is accompanied page-for-page and stanza-for-stanza by Kinaston's Latin rendering, and it is clear that the two were designed to be used side by side. Some trouble was taken to see that this novel literary event was appropriately heralded in the prefatory matter, which included an ample body of commendatory poems, ten in Latin, five in English, and one in a rather heavy-handed attempt at Chaucerian pastiche, printed in black letter.[3] Kinaston himself contributed an interesting preface 'Candido Lectori' outlining the principles on which he had proceeded, and he dedicated Book I to Patrick Young, keeper of the Royal Library, and Book II to John Rous, Bodley's Librarian. In the preface Kinaston promised that if the *Amorum Troili* were well received he would go on to publish a complete *en face* translation of Chaucer's poem accompanied by a body of explanatory notes – a proposal whose novelty (and in some respects whose modernity) has been largely overlooked by both Chaucerians and by historians of English literary scholarship in general.[4] The execution of this project occupied Kinaston during the later 1630s, and the work was completed in manuscript in 1639, and licensed for the press on 2 June 1640. Kinaston however died before his annotated version of the *Troilus* could be put into print, but the manuscript was preserved. It was later superficially consulted for Urry's edition of Chaucer (in places without acknowledgement), and speculatively printed in small part by Francis Waldron in 1796, before finally being acquired by the Bodleian in 1886.[5] In modern times 'the Kinaston Manuscript' has been better known to students of Henryson's *Testament of Cresseid* than to Chaucerians, partly because Kinaston, whilst including a translation and notes on the *Testament*, was the first English scholar to distinguish it as the work of a different author ('Mr Robert Henderson'), rather than lumping it together with Chaucer's work, in the tradition of the sixteenth-century black-letter editions.[6]

Kinaston's reputation as a Chaucerian was not assisted by his editor Saintsbury, who, in a phrase which has been repeated, stigmatized the poet's 'ultra-eccentric enterprise of translating *Troilus* into Latin rhyme-royal', though admitting his mastery of Chaucer's rhythm, and reserving some faint praise for the translation's charm.[7] Saintsbury however based his opinions on the published *Amorum Troili* of 1635, and was not aware of the existence of the completed translation, with its elaborate apparatus of Latin and English explanatory annotation, though the manuscript had been extracted by Waldron in 1796, and was noticed in the *Summary Catalogue* of the Bodleian western manuscripts in 1905.[8] Taken in the context of his life, work, and times, Kinaston's prolonged attention to the *Troilus* deserves better than this. The eccentricity of his undertaking emerges as more apparent than real, for it embodies a considered response to the problems of comprehension which had come to confront even the cultivated post-medieval reader of Chaucer, as well as intimating a significant enlargement of editorial attitude towards a major vernacular author of the past.

Francis Kinaston was descended from a well-established county family whose seat was at Oteley in Shropshire. Relatively little is known of Kinaston's early life and education.[9] He matriculated at Oxford (Oriel) in

1601, where his tutor was said to have been John Rous. After graduating as a BA in 1604, Kinaston proceeded immediately to Lincoln's Inn,[10] and was called to the Bar in 1611. More can be said of his career at court, which, in 1638,[11] he said had lasted for twenty-one years. Kinaston was knighted on 1 January 1618/19, and though Anthony à Wood generously attributed his elevation to the court's opinion that he was 'a man of parts', Colin Williamson has indicated evidence that he is more likely to have paid for the honour, a common path to royal preferment under James.[12] As well as becoming MP for Shropshire in 1620, Kinaston discharged a number of responsible offices at court. In 1621 he played a prominent part in the reception of the Russian ambassador Isaac Simanovitz,[13] and was for some time James's cupbearer. Samuel Hartlib's memoirs (*Ephemerides*), which contain a variety of valuable information about Kinaston and his activities set down in 1635–6, note that Kinaston's tenure of this office was not wholly successful: 'Was Cupbearer to K. James but trembled always so that he was faigne to resign that office. For hee is of a modest civil and somewhat timorous disposition'.[14] Kinaston's unsteadiness of hand did not however prevent him from progressing in 1624 to the more responsible post of Esquire of the Body,[15] which he continued to hold under Charles until his death, though his service was interrupted by family and financial difficulties.[16] The last decade of Kinaston's life, which was overshadowed by a prolonged and acrimonious legal wrangle with his father, was occupied as much by literary, intellectual and educational projects as by his work as a courtier, though he is known to have accompanied the king on his progress to Scotland in 1633.[17] The precise date of his death is not known, and the authorities follow Anthony à Wood in placing it in 1642, 'or thereabouts'.[18]

Kinaston's life as a courtier intersected with his artistic and scholarly leanings in a variety of ways which provide a first context for his work as a Chaucerian. In 1633 he marked Charles's coronation progress to Scotland by contributing English translations of eight Latin pieces by the well-known Scottish neo-Latin poet Arthur Johnston, *Musae querulae de regis in Scotiam profectione*. This progress may have been the occasion when Kinaston encountered the 'diuers aged schollers of the Scottish nation' from whom he said he had derived the correct attribution of the *Testament of Cresseid* and the personalia concerning Henryson with which he prefaced his Latin translation and annotations to the poem in the Bodleian manuscript. The results of further collaboration with Johnston were published under the title *Musae aulicae. Interprete F. K.* (1635), another bilingual work which includes addresses to the king attributed to various arts, sciences, and gentlemanly accomplishments: music, writing, languages, astronomy, geometry, medicine, arithmetic, chemistry, fencing and dancing. The publication of this work coincided with the educational initiative for which Kinaston is chiefly remembered, the Musaeum Minervae, a gentlemen's academy established under royal patronage at his house in Covent Garden in 1635. Though no direct link is made in

Musae aulicae, the group of arts, sciences, and accomplishments therein invoked has an unmistakable correspondence to the programme of studies announced by Kinaston in *The Constitutions of the Musaeum Minervae* (1636). The Musaeum, of which more will be said in a moment, was visited by the five-year-old Prince Charles and the two younger royal children on 27 February 1635, and for the occasion Kinaston wrote a suitably adapted masque, *Corona Minervae*, in which amidst the songs and dances the studies of Minerva are set forth, and the young prince presented with her crown. Though of no particular artistic pretension or merit, works such as these serve to establish Kinaston as a recognizable English Renaissance type, the gentleman scholar-courtier, whose facets had been variously described and prescribed in texts such as Elyot's *The Boke Named The Governour* (1531), Hoby's translation of Castiglione, *The Book of the Courtier* (1561), and Peacham's *The Compleat Gentleman* (1622). But a closer investigation of his intellectual interests – in no small part as they are evinced in his annotations to the *Troilus* and the *Testament* – suggests that Kinaston belongs more precisely to the group who have been described as the English virtuosi of the seventeenth century.[19]

The term virtuoso first appeared in an English context in the enlarged edition of Peacham's *Compleat Gentleman* that was issued in 1634, though the kind of person Peacham had in mind (he mentions Sir Kenelm Digby, Thomas, Earl of Arundel, and Nathaniel Bacon) had emerged as a cultural and intellectual phenomenon during the first two decades of the seventeenth century.[20] These virtuosi *avant la lettre* had significantly enlarged the scope of the scholar-courtier's concerns, partly under the influence of Francis Bacon's innovative approach to the issue of how human knowledge should be accumulated and organized, and Colin Williamson has summarized the type: 'A virtuoso was one who, in addition to the standard academic education, had a high degree of interest in a wide knowledge of the curious phenomena of the physical world, the marvels of science, relics of former civilizations, the products of the human mind in the plastic arts and mechanical contrivances, and the technicalities of traditional and new processes of manufacture.'[21] Francis Kinaston was as early an exemplar of the movement as any. In the *Athenae Oxoniensis* Anthony à Wood was to note that at Oxford in 1604 Kinaston 'took one degree in arts, and then left the university for a time without compleating that degree by determination, being then more addicted to the superficial parts of learning, poetry and oratory (wherein he excell'd) than logic and philosophy'.[22] One of the directions taken by his interests emerges a year later, when Kinaston is said to have stimulated a contemporary at Lincoln's Inn to compose 'Eight bookes of Poeticall Astrologie', as the author, John Glanvill, later attested in his dedication to the work.[23] Throughout his life Kinaston's literary concerns were matched by the virtuoso's characteristic curiosity about natural phenomena, and amongst his last compositions was a commendatory poem to the treatise *Mercury: or the secret messenger* (1641), by Bishop John Wilkins, one of the foremost exponents of the new science, and later effectively the founder of the Royal Society. But the most vivid impression of the breadth of Kinaston's abilities and concerns was recorded by Samuel Hartlib in his *Ephemerides* of 1635, beginning here with mention of the recently published *Amorum Troili*:

> Hase translated excellently old Chaucer. When his father dyes he wil bee worth a thous. lb. per annum.... Hee has a great booke in fol. of the most rare and excellent Master-pieces in Musicke with another of 40 voices. Hee hase a multiplying-glasse. An excellent Perspective which Mr. Ant. de Dnis said it was the best that ever hee had seene. A Namen-buch. Lapidem Aetiteni. A rare Ms. of Physical Experiments et Chirurgery. A Ms. of Ray[mond] Lullius never yet printed. Tabulam Germani Microcosmi in fol. which might serve exceedingly for a did[actica] Encycl[opaedia] Sing[ularum] d[e] Homine.... Many things are mathematically true which are not mechanically et con[tra] an observation of Sir Fr. Keniston. Also that Models faile often, as Drebbeli perpetuum mobile would moove or bee true in smal models but not in great. Hee presented to the K. a curious magnetical globe for a New Years gift at which the K. tooke great delight, and which hase many great Rarities in it.... A great lover of Music.[24]

The virtuoso's work on Chaucer jostles for attention amongst an impressive array of artistic, intellectual, and scientific interests, which must be treated selectively here. 'Mr. Ant. de Dnis' was Marco Antonio de Dominis, Archbishop of Spalatro, the scientifically able but notorious double-apostate who had been temporarily exiled in England from 1616 to 1622. In a note on *Troilus*, II, 445, 'Til I myn owne herte blood may see', Kinaston mentions that he had discussed with the Archbishop experiments he had carried out with the intention of observing the physical actions of the heart. The excellent optical instrument admired by the Archbishop was used by Kinaston to observe a comet in 1617, a fact which he mentions in a note on *Troilus*, I, 99–105. Further on in Hartlib's comments, 'Drebbeli perpetuum mobile' was the most celebrated of the numerous devices with which the inventor Cornelius Drebbel fascinated James and his courtiers, and this too makes an appearance in one of Kinaston's notes on the *Troilus*.[25]

Kinaston's empirical curiosity about natural phenomena seems to have been conspicuous even by the standards of the early seventeeth century.[26] However his habits of mind also illustrate the virtuoso's distinctively subjective or disinterested approach to the acquisition and use of knowledge, and the characteristic reluctance to proceed towards the framing of general or abstract principles on the basis of observation.[27] In its relentless, near-morbid curiosity Kinaston's is a sensibility comparable to that which Robert Burton brought to bear with a more exclusively bookish emphasis in the compilation of *The Anatomy of Melancholy*, which went through five editions in Kinaston's prime, between 1621 and 1638. Indeed, very soon after the latter date Kinaston was to quote the *Anatomy* and describe Burton as 'my most learned & deare freind' in one of his *Troilus* notes. The annotations which Kinaston provided to Chaucer's text contain an abundance of empirical and curious observation the significance of which remains to be assessed, but an aside in one of them may stand almost as an epigraph to this aspect of the virtuoso's sensibility as the annotator has there chosen to display it: 'Theis as any other thing*es* that shall seeme strange to the reader in theis Coment*es* I desire may be beleiued as set downe by one, who hath written nothing vppon trust, but what himselfe hath been an eie witnes of, & is found to be true & experimented.'[28]

The appearance of the pilot version of the *Amorum Troili* in 1635 coincided with Kinaston's foundation of the Musaeum Minervae, the academy where, as Houghton puts it, 'the studies of the virtuosi were embodied for the first time in a formal curriculum'.[29] Kinaston's original proposal for an academy was presented to the king at some time during 1632–3, and the royal licence was received in 1635, by which date a number of professors had been provisionally appointed. The licence formally conferred upon the academy the name of the Musaeum Minervae, together with a number of rights and privileges not unlike those enjoyed by university colleges in Oxford and Cambridge: a common seal, the status of a body corporate, and the right to possess land in mortmain. Kinaston was designated regent, and professors of philosophy and medicine, music, astronomy, geometry, languages, and fencing were nominated.[30] As has been mentioned above, the establishment of the Musaeum Minervae was marked by royal patronage of Kinaston's masque *Corona Minervae* in 1635, and in 1636 he published *The Constitutions of the Musaeum Minervae*, which served effectively both as the statutes of the institution and as a kind of prospectus. Though intelligently conceived, and constituted with care and the best of intentions, Kinaston's academy ultimately fared little better than those projected in preceding decades by Henry, Prince of Wales and Edmond Bolton.[31] No more is heard of it after 1638, owing, it appears, to a lack of financial support from distinguished patrons and a scarcity of suitable clientèle during plague years in the later 1630s.[32] Nevertheless, Kinaston's stated ideals in founding his academy lead back towards his interest in the *Troilus*. As well as providing scores of cues for the display of virtuoso knowledge in annotation, he plainly regarded Chaucer's poem as a great work of heroic idealism, a text which might be held up as an example to youth. In this regard, Kinaston's conception of his own role as regent of the Musaeum Minervae is worth quoting:

> the regent is to remember as he shall see opportunitie from time to time both publickly and privately, to excite the Noblemen and Gentlemen to vertuous and heroic mindes, by the example of the most renowned, but especially to set before their eyes the *Images* of the *Worthies* of our own *Nation*, and of their own Ancestours, in their severall families: so that having taken impression in the *Musaeum* from the best *Ide'as*, the whole kingdome of inferiour people, in those severall Counties, where they shall be distributed to live, and shine, may finde example, help, reason and happinesse in and being under them.[33]

Suitably-framed poetry occupied an important place in contemporary thinking about the cultivation of virtuous and heroic minds in well-born young
men. Peacham gave over a chapter of *The Compleat Gentleman* to poetry, urging
(with numerous examples) that 'if Mechanicall Arts hold their estimation by
their effects in base subiects, how much more deserueth this to be esteemed,
that holdeth so soueraigne a power ouer the minde, can turne brutishnesse
into Ciuilitie, make the lewd honest (which is *Scaligers* opinion of *Virgils*
Poeme) turne hatred to loue, cowardise into valour, and in briefe, like a
Queene command ouer all affections?'[34] Though it is not possible to demonstrate any direct connection between Kinaston's attention to the *Troilus* and
his educational enterprises, notes in the Bodleian manuscript indicate clearly
the light in which he viewed some of the principal characters:

> Chaucer ... hath made a most admirable & inimitable Epicke poeme
> describing in the person of Troilus a most compleat knt. in Armes & Court
> shippe, & a faithfull constant louer, & in Creseid a beautifull & most coie
> lady, which being once ouercome yeilds to the frailty of her sex.

> In the person of Hector our Poet describes twoe excellent vertues of a
> compleat kt., Valour, & curtesie in the proteccion of laydes.

(Bodl. MS, pp. 6, 13)

We have no means of defining for certain Kinaston's ultimate interest in
working so extensively on the *Troilus*, but the opportunity it presented to
display a virtuoso's knowledge in the annotations, combined with the heroic
idealism he perceived in the substance, suggests that his edition would surely
have been a model text for those engaged in study at the Museum Minervae.

Kinaston's first ostensible motives for presenting a parallel Latin translation of Chaucer's masterpiece were set out variously in the dedication and
preface to the *Amorum Troili* in 1635. It was his intention to preserve this 'gem
of a poem' from oblivion, and his work had the added virtue of making
Chaucer's genius accessible to those who understood no English:

> In aggredienda hac versione, duo praecipuè fuerunt in votis, Primò conservatio
> huius poematum gemmae an interitu & oblivione, quae ferè amissa erat, & a
> nostratibus vix intellecta, (saltem nemini in deliciis) ob verborum in eâ
> obsoletorum ignorantiam, quae in desuetudine abiêre. Diende illius Romano
> artificio munitae & ornatae tibi dedicatio, quam ob eruditissimi genij tui
> honorem, & nominis celebritatem, exteris gratiorem & acceptiorem non
> immeritò autumem.[35]

Comments on the obsolescence and 'rudeness' of Chaucer's language had
become commonplace in the sixteenth century. Though Speght, in his
editions of 1598 and 1602, had for the first time provided a basic glossary of
'The old and obscure words of Chaucer, explaned', it is clear that as well as
the presence of hard words, more gradual changes in pronunciation, morphology, syntax and so forth had rendered the reading of Chaucer a difficult
and resistant task to many by the early seventeenth century. Several of the

commendatory poems which accompany Kinaston's preface to the *Amorum Troili* remark specifically upon this issue, and (as is to be expected) are enthusiastic about the translator's ingenuity in meeting the problem.[36] Kinaston's further point, that his work would make Chaucer's poetry accessible to foreigners, is novel, and one of several indications that he perceived the possibility of the *Troilus* as what might later be termed a vernacular classic. Another is his explicit respect for the integrity of the original Chaucerian text as it had come down to him. The preface in fact airs two possible solutions to the problem of the obsolescence of Chaucer's language, either some form of modernization, or the preferred course of a parallel Latin translation. As to modernization, Kinaston is emphatic in rejecting a procedure which might in any way alter or obscure the sense of the original: 'Sed peccatum inexpiabile in MANES *Chauceri* admississe me existimarem, si vel minimum Iota in eius scriptis immutassem, quae sacra & intacta in aeternum manere digna sunt.'[37] In reaching a conclusion with such a marked respect for what he viewed as the authentic Chaucerian text Kinaston was possibly influenced by the nascent trend towards the modernization of ancient vernacular works represented by *The Life and Death of Hector* (1614), a free rendering of Lydgate's *Siege of Thebes*, sometimes attributed to Thomas Heywood, or the up-dated version of Hoccleve's *Tale of Jonathas* included by William Browne in the *Shepheards Pipe* (1614). He is unlikely to have been aware of an even more relevant work which remained unpublished: 'TROILUS and CRESIDA. Translated into our Moderne English. For the satisfaction of those who either cannot, or will not, take ye paines to vnderstand. By J:[onathan] S:[idnam]'.[38] Kinaston's instinct seems to have been to resist such developments, and he went on to argue in his preface that a supporting Latin version of the *Troilus* would have the virtue of rendering Chaucer's text forever stable and fixed ('eumque ... per omnia secula ... stabilem & immotem reddere'). This determination not to tamper with what was understood to be Chaucer's original text, but to seek to elucidate it by other means, was in contemporary terms an advanced editorial trait,[39] and as we shall see in a moment Kinaston was also on occasion concerned to establish (in the modern sense of the term) the text he was going to translate.

Kinaston's success in rendering accurately the Middle English (and Middle Scots) texts before him has been generally applauded, and the ingenuity shown in imitating the rhyme royal stanza in an alien linguistic medium has attracted particularly favourable comment. The Latin versions of the *Troilus* and the *Testament* undoubtedly read smoothly and easily, the substance is seldom other than lucidly expressed, and Chaucer's rhythm (as Saintsbury rightly observed) is most strikingly captured.[40] Less, however, has been said on the significant issue of how Kinaston set about establishing the sense of the texts he translated. Comments on the novelty or apparent eccentricity of Kinaston's work have tended to obscure the point that to translate a Middle English or Scots text can involve carrying out basic processes of textual criticism. The *Troilus* and the *Testament* had been subject to the same kinds of textual deterioration as the bulk of the writings attributed to Chaucer, editorial and compositorial errors accumulating as each sixteenth-century black-letter text was derived from its immediate predecessor, from Thynne down to Speght.[41] Speght's editions of 1598 and 1602 show no signs of having been improved by collation with early manuscript sources, but nevertheless, with its accumulated imperfections Speght's work naturally formed the raw material for Kinaston's Chaucerian studies. In doing so, however, it became the object of a closer textual scrutiny than was customarily given to a medieval English text, or indeed any vernacular work, in the early seventeenth century. As Denton Fox has recently observed of Kinaston's work on the less tractable text of Henryson's *Testament of Cresseid*, 'Kinaston was a man of considerable learning and poetic ability who was forced to produce an English text which made sense before he could translate it into Latin'.[42] In the case of the *Testament*, Kinaston took Speght's edition of 1598 as a copy-text, and Fox has noted a number of the emendations he introduced in the process of settling on a text to translate. Though Fox appears to take the emendations as original conjectures, there may be evidence that Kinaston also used Speght's edition of 1602 where he doubted a reading. In line 20, the manuscript gives a verse clearly derived from Speght 1598, 'Fro pole Artike come whisking loud & shill', but 'shill' has been deleted, and 'shrill', a reading also found in Speght 1602, has been substituted (Bodl. MS, p. 477). On the other hand, the manuscript's version of line 48 (a notable crux), definitely includes an original conjecture, and moreover one which in modern times has been independently proposed (by Skeat) and accepted in the standard text (Fox): 'While Esperus reioysed him againe', following Speght 1598, was first written, but 'Esperus' was subsequently altered to 'Esperance', and a marginal note added, 'esperance þat is hope' (Bodl. MS, p. 478). Kinaston was particularly accurate and effective in restoring lines 194–5, which in Speght 1598 are manifestly defective:

> Right tulsure like, but temperaunce in tene
> An horne blew...

Kinaston arrived at readings which also form part of the *textus receptus* nowadays:

> Right tulliure like but temperance in teene
> A horne he blew...   (Bodl. MS, p. 487)

adding in a note, 'Propter ignorantiam verae significationis Scotici vocabuli Tullieur erratum est fere in omnibus impressionibus in quibus perpaeram describitur Tulsur'.[43] These examples show that, where it was necessary for his purposes, Kinaston took steps to establish a satisfactory text by comparing differing authorities, or by means of conjectural emendation. His procedure in the *Troilus* itself (which would bear further investigation) appears to have been similar. At 1, 588 he evidently found what was derived from Speght metrically unsatisfactory, and interlined his own emendation: 'Wost thou not well that I am <thy> Pandare' (Bodl. MS. p. 49). In I, 145, 'But the Troyan iestes ... ' in Speght, he altered 'iestes' to 'gestes', doubtless to remove a wayward spelling which might be misunderstood (Bodl. MS, p. 15). On the other hand, at I, 445 he was misled by the erroneous division of the first word in his copy-text, 'For thy', and substituted 'he' for what he took to be a pronoun, 'For he full oft, his hot fire to cease' (Bodl. MS, p. 39). He was also less successful at the beginning of Book II, 1–2, introducing in the first line an additional reading from Speght 1602, and in the second a conjecture of his own:

> Out of theis blacke waues <let us> for to saile
> O wind, the weder <the heauen> ginneth clere.
>
> (Bodl. MS, p. 86)

Though Kinaston did not set out to be a systematic editor of Chaucerian writings, it is worthy of note that one here sees him applying to the texts techniques which were generally of much later development where the editing of early vernacular literature was concerned. Recourse to the comparison of varying authorities (if Speght's texts can for the moment be thus styled), and in particular the exercise of conjectural emendation are procedures which entered slowly and haphazardly into Middle English textual scholarship.[44] It might well be that the process would have taken a different course, had Kinaston's work ever been published.

No less advanced was Kinaston's urge to annotate, expound, and comment in an erudite way upon the *Troilus* and the *Testament*. The apparatus he supplied forms a large part of the Bodleian manuscript, but is unevenly distributed, and the intended disposition in the printed version is not clear. At the end of each book of the *Troilus* and at the end of the *Testament* is a substantial body of explanatory annotation in Latin. Interspersed amongst the stanzas of the texts themselves are further explanatory notes of variable length in English, together with interstanzaic and marginal glosses on individual words and phrases. The latter, which are particularly frequent in the earlier part of the manuscript, usually deal accurately with obsolete words and forms. In as much as they are concerned with grammar and morphology, these briefer notes, where the significations given are determined by the context, constitute an extension of the kind of apparatus provided in Speght's glossary of hard words. There is little to distinguish Kinaston's on-the-page glosses from what one finds in a modern student edition, e.g. (on *Troilus*, I, 93–6) 'Vnwist, vnknowing or ignorant, Penaunce, in trouble or destresse, What to rede, what course to take, Nist, that is she knew not'; (on *Troilus*, I, 273) 'stent þat is stayed'; (on *Troilus*, II, 248) 'ffremede þat is strange or coy'; (on *Troilus*, II, 413) 'defend þat is forbid me'; (on *Testament*, 155) 'frownced þat is wrinkeled' (Bodl. MS, pp. 10, 25, 103, 114, 485).

As to the longer explanatory notes, it is not clear why some are in English and some in Latin, or why the former are interspersed in the text and the latter gathered at the ends of the books. No distinction of substance seems evident in the points they comment upon, and it is possible that they were simply compiled at different times in the course of the work. Indeed, in several cases the material they contain and the references given are duplicated. The explanatory notes also vary considerably in their capacity to illuminate Chaucer's text, some taking the merest pretexts for leisurely displays of arcane knowledge. On the other hand, they provide practically an epitome of the range, depth, and quality of a seventeenth-century virtuoso's interests, and constitute a significant but neglected episode in the development of Chaucerian studies.

The points brought up in the notes cover a multitude of miscellaneous matters. Classical allusions are picked out, proper names traced to their supposed etymological origins, and scattered observations are unsystematically provided on a great variety of words, phrases, metaphors and ideas. A discussion of the invocation to Venus at the beginning of Book III of the *Troilus* (Bodl. MS, p. 210) is effectively a piece of critical commentary. Plants, gems, arms, music, antiquities, statues, pictures, books, authors, physical and celestial phenomena, magic, and a host of other topics either mentioned in or arising from the texts attract the annotator's attention. Kinaston's marked interest in natural science, noted above, is evident in numerous places. The comparisons made in *Troilus*, I, 524–5, '... as frost in wynter moone, / ... as snow in fire is soone', prompt a note on the experiments of 'the Chymists' concerning the physical nature of snow and ice (Bodl. MS, p. 44). References to magic and superstition are also frequent. *Troilus*, II, 1580, 'this charme I wol yow leere', elicits an ambivalent note on the 'horrible impiety' of trusting in charms such as 'Abra Cadabra written on a parchment & hung about ones neck' (against agues), but goes on to observe that 'the most worthy & religious frier Bacon in one of his Manuscripts which I haue seene in the Archiuis of the famous Vniversity of Oxford Library doth graunt þat God hath giuen power to words & sentences to do straunge thinges' (Bodl. MS, p. 192). Like a modern editor or commentator, Kinaston sought out up-to-date authorities on recondite points where the reader might feel the need for extraneous information. For example, he notes appropriately that *Troilus*, v, 319–20,

> The owle ek, which that hette Escaphilo,
> Hath after me shright al thise nyghtes two

refers to the fable (i.e. Ovid's) of the metamorphosis of Ascalaphus by Proserpina, but devotes most of his remarks to a digression on ominous birds in general, based on 'the most learned Gafarelle in his late published booke of vnheard of curiosities' (Jaques Gafarel, *Curiositez inouyes sur la sculpture talismanique des Persans* (1637); Bodl. MS, p. 403). Similarly, when Calkas is introduced at *Troilus*, I, 66, 'A gret devyn, that clepid was Calkas', the reader is referred to Jean Jaques Boissard's discussion of augurers in his *De*

Divinatione et Magicis praestigiis, de geniis etc. (1611) (Bodl. MS, p. 82). Boissard is again invoked in a note on the *Testament*, 127 (Bodl. MS, p. 513), as an authority on oracles, though Troilus' consultation with Apollo at *Troilus*, III, 540ff., '... to sen the holy laurer quake, / Er that Apollo spak out of the tree', elicits a darkly expressed direction for any reader interested in the physical manifestations accompanying the appearances of spirits: 'let him read the works of that Necromancer, whome Rablais calls his reuerend father in the diuell Picatrix, or Cornelius Agrippa, and he will be aboundantly satisfied' (Bodl. MS, p. 241).

Kinaston also has notes on many of the references made by both Chaucer and Henryson to astronomy and astrology, some of them drawing on contemporary understanding of the heavens as it was embodied in the publications of Kepler and Galileo (Bodl. MS, pp. 514, 515). Familiar lines such as *Troilus*, I, 837ff. ('Fortune is my fo', 'hire cruel whiel') and III, 618 ('influences of thise heuenes hye') give occasion for general discussions of judicial astrology,[45] whilst more specific references such as III, 624–5

> The bente moone with hire hornes pale,
> Saturne, and Jove, in Cancro joyned were,

and III, 715–17

> And if ich hadde, O Venus ful of myrthe,
> Aspectes badde of Mars or of Saturne,
> Or thow combust or let were in my birthe,

prompt useful notes respectively on the unusually portentous nature of the conjunction, and the technical terms 'Aspectes badde' and 'combust or lette', very much as one finds in modern editions (Bodl. MS, pp. 329, 202). Kinaston also noted and discussed the unnatural astronomy of lines 11–14 of the *Testament* long before it was recognized by modern students of the poem.[46]

The virtuoso's characteristic preoccupation with all manner of curiosities, antiquities, and 'rarities' finds ample scope for display in the annotations, sometimes yielding delightfully divagatory observations which can be as informative, if not more so, than what one finds in modern editions. For instance the 'relik, heet Palladion', which forms part of the setting for the first encounter of the lovers (*Troilus*, I, 153), is explained by Kinaston as follows: 'a siluer statue of Pallas or Minerua, which the Troians were foolishly persuaded came downe from Jupiter, & that as long as they kept that Statue, their Citty Troy should neuer be ouercome ...' He goes on to observe that it was eventually dishonestly acquired by Ulysses and Diomedes (as regards the latter's role in the poem, not a negligible point), and remarks in commonsensical fashion upon its likely size – presumably not large, 'like the Aegiptian Idolls of which I haue seene many, which haue bin lately digged vp out of ruines, some little smale puppet like thing & soe easily portable' (Bodl. MS, p. 16). Interest in ancient statuary and epigraphy was particularly strong in the 1620s and 1630s, and centred on the collection of marbles accumulated by another virtuoso, Thomas, Earl of Arundel. Kinaston clearly admired John Selden's learned dissertation upon them, *Marmora Arundelliana* (1628), for he draws on it at least twice in the *Troilus* annotations.[47] The procession of pagan deities in Henryson's continuation gave scope for copious remarks concerning their appearance and attributes. For example, the eloquent Mercury (*Testament*, 239–45), book in hand, with pen and ink, and wearing the poet's hood, furnished ideal material for a varied commentary. Kinaston was characteristically exercised by the anachronism of Mercury writing with pen and ink, and provided an informed discussion of ancient writing implements, 'in vsu apud priscos ante membranae aut papyri inuentionem', which he had seen in the Bodleian. The poet's hood prompted another lengthy note on the pictorial representations of poets, alluding to an ancient coin owned by Patrick Young showing Virgil, the delineation of Petrarch, and the sculpture on Chaucer's tomb in Westminster Abbey (Bodl. MS, p. 523).

Kinaston's annotations were strongly marked by the use of literary allusions and quotations intended to throw light on the text. Classical, medieval and contemporary sources are all employed. As has become customary, quotations from elsewhere in Chaucer's work are brought into notes on the *Troilus*. The 'cok, comune astrologer' of *Troilus*, III, 1415 is further illustrated by the now-familiar allusion to the *Nun's Priest's Tale*, VII, 2855–8; Troilus' consultation of Apollo's oracle at *Troilus*, III, 540–6 is paralleled by quotations from the *Knight's Tale*, where Emelye invokes Diana, and Arcite Mars (I, 2359–60, 2421–4; Bodl. MS, pp. 294, 240–1). Classical allusions and quotations are also frequent. *Troilus*, II, 104–5

> How the bisshop, as the book kan telle,
> Amphiorax, fil thorugh the ground to helle

is helpfully glossed by a quotation (with English translation) of the appropriate passage from Statius' *Thebais* (VII, 815ff.), the actual source of Pandarus' allusion to a book about 'th'assege of Thebes' having been identified a few lines beforehand (Bodl. MS, pp. 94–5). Again, going where modern editors have followed, Kinaston identifies the ultimate source of Chaucer's

> The swifte Fame, which that false thynges
> Egal reporteth lik the thynges trewe   (IV, 659–60)

as Virgilian, probably basing his discussion on *Aeneid*, IV, 188 (Bodl. MS, p. 347). Henryson's descriptions of Saturn and Jupiter (*Testament*, 155–82) are expounded with the assistance of appropriate material from Juvenal's *Satires* and Martial's *Epigrams*.[48] Contemporary authors are mentioned from time to time. The *First Anniversary* of 'the most excellently learned Doctor Dunne' is quoted in relation to *Troilus*, I, 910 ('Seynt Idiot') and IV, 659–60 ('The swifte Fame …'), whilst Marlowe's *Hero and Leander* is brought into an arch discussion of the propriety of a hawking metaphor in an erotic context, *Troilus*,

III, 1191–2, the lark and the sparrow hawk.[49] The fabled but obscure Wade, who is mentioned at *Troilus*, III, 614 ('He song; she pleyde; he tolde tale of Wade') is dealt with by Kinaston in a note which, though it is scarcely less exasperating than Speght's famous 'because the matter is longe and fabulous, I passe it ouer', at least suggests an avenue for further research:

> Tale of Wade &c. Chaucer meanes a ridiculous romance as if he had told a story of Robin Hood, for in his time there was a foolish fabulous Legend of one Wade & his boate Guingelot wherein he did many strange thinges & had many wonderfull aduentures, not much unlike that man & his boate in our time, who layed a wager, that he neuer going out of his boate, & without any other helpe but himselfe he would in a certaine number of dayes go by land & by water from Abington to London, & in his passage would go ouer the top of a square steepel by the way, which thing he performed, and wonne his wager.[50]

The foregoing examples must suffice to illustrate the remarkable novelty and the considerable learning displayed in this aspect of Kinaston's attitude to the presentation of medieval vernacular texts. Other notes deserve to be more widely known for the light they shed on the development of Chaucerian studies in his time, because the number of places where he takes precedence over eighteenth-, nineteenth-, and twentieth-century scholars is surprising. The following note discusses *Troilus*, I, 393–9, the stanza in which Chaucer makes mention of how 'myn auctour called Lollius' recorded all the details of Troilus' song, which he is about to set down:

> That Chaucer here makes mention of one Lolius his Author, whereas in truth there was neuer any such man, was it seemes to make þe world beleiue, that he himselfe was not the Author, but translator of this Poem: But it appeares in a most antient Manuscript, which was lent me by my most learned & most valued frend Mr John Selden, that he was the Author of it, for at the end thereof there is a soleme recantation penned by Chaucer expressing his sorrow & repentaunce, that euer he had bin soe vaine, as to write this poem & his Canterbury Tales, in which Manuscript (thought to be Chaucers owne hand writing) there is the Cooks Tale compleat, which is defectiue in the printed booke, & the truth is that Chaucer wittily intimates a pretty theft of his owne by excepting the tongues difference, for the three next following Stanzes are translated word for word out of Francis Petrarch his 103 Cansonet in the first parte of his Laura, by which it may be coniectured, that Chaucer writ this Poem after his being in Italy where he met Petrarch at the Marriage of Violante þe Duke of Millaines daughter, where it is probable he first sawe theis verses, & transcribed them, & translating them made them his owne.   (Bodl. MS, p. 36)

Apart from the spurious detail at the end concerning Chaucer's supposed meeting with Petrarch (which is taken from Speght's introduction), this note is of considerable interest. Though the Retractation found in many manuscripts of the *Canterbury Tales* had been printed by Caxton, it had not appeared in any edition of Chaucer's works published in the sixteenth or seventeenth centuries, and was therefore effectively lost. Credit for its rediscovery has hitherto been given to Thomas Hearne, who mentioned it in an appendix to his edition of Robert of Gloucester's chronicle published in 1724, but rightly it belongs to Selden and Kinaston.[51] For the identification of the Canticus Troili as a translation from Petrarch, Kinaston may well have relied upon his own knowledge and observation, though Thomas Watson, in his *Hekatompathia* (1582) had mentioned in passing that Chaucer had made a translation of the sonnet in question, but without stating where it was to be found.[52] The recognition that Lollius was intended as a fiction was of course a much later development in Chaucerian scholarship, and Kinaston's notion that Chaucer 'wittily intimates a pretty theft of his owne' after introducing the name at this juncture forms a neat critical point.

Kinaston plainly had an advanced interest in the primary materials for the study of Chaucer's life and works, and was acquainted with the contents of what we would now call unpublished life-records of the poet in the public collections. Details in the formalities described when Criseyde retires for the night at Pandarus' house (*Troilus*, III, 664ff.) suggested to him that Chaucer had first-hand knowledge of the duties of a squire of the body in ordinary to the king, the post Kinaston himself held as a courtier:

> some coniecture out of antient Recordes of Richard 2 time that Chaucer was a squire of the body & others affirme they haue seene a Record in a great case touching the bearing of a cote armour in contencion betweene Scroope & Grosuenor wherein Owen Glendore & Jeffery Chaucer were examined as witnesses & Chaucer stiled by the name of Sr. Jeffery Chaucer knt: but certaine it is he was stiled but squire in a Record of the last yeare of Richard 2 which was the yeare before he died, & he liuing till he was 72 years old is not likely he was knighted then. (Bodl. MS, pp. 249–50)

This is a much earlier allusion to the important discovery of Chaucer's role in the Scrope–Grosvenor controversy than its first appearance in print, which was in John Dart's contribution to the preface to Urry's edition of Chaucer (1721).[53] The circles in which Kinaston moved also gave him access to other source materials of primary importance. It is not known whether he was ever directly associated with the greatest antiquary and collector of the day, Sir Robert Cotton, but he certainly knew his son Thomas, and was able to make use of a Chaucer manuscript in the Cottonian library, since destroyed. The following is Kinaston's note on *Troilus*, I, 16, and Chaucer's reference to his 'unliklynesse' as a lover:

> For Chaucers personage it appeares by an excellent peice of him limn'd by the life by Thomas Occleue his scholler & coetanean, and now remaining as a high priz'd iewell in the handes of my honor'd frend Sr. Thomas Cotton knt: & Baronett, that Chaucer was a man of an euen stature neither to high, nor too lowe, his complexion sanguine, his face fleshie, but pale, his forehead, something broad, but comely smooth & euen, his eies rather little then greate cast most parte downward with a graue aspect, his lipps plumpe & ruddy & both of them of an equall thicknes, the haire in his upper lippe being thin & shorte of a wheat cullor, on his chin two thin forked tuffs, his cheeks of like cullor with the rest of his face, being either shaued or wanting haire, all which considered together

with his witt & education in the Court & his fauoure among the greate ladyes
one of whose women he married, it was his modesty rather then his fittnes to be a
louer made him speake of his vnlikelines.   (Bodl. MS, p. 3)

This description is of value because it refers, in all likelihood, to the portrait of
Chaucer which once formed part of what is now London, British Library, MS
Cotton Otho A. XVIII. Since the fire which ravaged the Cottonian library in
1731, only charred fragments of the manuscript remain. The picture did not
survive, but it is possible to tell from Kinaston's description that it was
another early example ('limn'd', in colour) of the 'Ellesmere–Hoccleve' style
of Chaucer portraiture which developed in the decade after the poet's death.[54]

When in 1914 G. Gregory Smith printed for the first time Kinaston's
annotated translation of Henryson's *Testament*, he remarked that in terms of
the history of English literary scholarship, the Bodleian manuscript represented a particularly early example of editorial attention to a vernacular
text.[55] The point is a substantial one. Setting aside special cases such as
E. K.'s glosses to the *Shepherd's Calendar* of Spenser, and Thomas Watson's
prose observations on his own translations in *Hekatompathia*, there is little to
compare with Kinaston's commentaries on the *Troilus* and the *Testament* until
the sixth edition of *Paradise Lost* (1695), which was issued together with
annotations by Patrick Hume. Kinaston's work was certainly advanced for its
time, and dealt with various issues which have since preoccupied editors of
Chaucer and Chaucerian writings. He was the first to correct the attribution
of the *Testament* in the standard edition, and the earliest post-medieval student
of Chaucer to note the existence in manuscript of the Retractation. He was
also concerned with the perennial question of the relationship between the
life-records of the poet and the works (noting for the first time the existence of
the Scrope–Grosvenor roll), and he left a valuable description of an early
manuscript portrait of Chaucer, since destroyed. The process of translating
the *Troilus* and the *Testament* involved Kinaston in activities which have much
in common with textual criticism, in the comparison of differing authorities
and the exercise of conjectural emendation. The extensive explanatory
annotation he provided was without precedent for a medieval English author,
and contained elements which were to become standard material in Chaucerian commentary. But though licensed for the press, the work was never
printed. Had it been published, and received as well as was the *Amorum Troili*
in 1635, the development of Chaucerian studies (particularly in the realm of
editorial presentation of the text) might have been rather different.

Taken on its own terms, Kinaston's work on the *Troilus* as finally assembled
in the Bodleian manuscript furnishes a striking insight into the peculiar
mentality of a distinctive type of seventeenth-century Englishman. The
atmosphere of a period much given to curious learning and learned curiosity
breathes in the pages, and to leaf through the manuscript is to find Chaucer
refracted through the diverse and subjective sensibility of the virtuoso.
Erudite associates – Selden, Cotton, Jonson, Young, Burton – wait with

information, advice, and material assistance at the commentator's elbow, and the nascent methods of natural science are brought to bear on the interpretation of Troilus' world. Kinaston's is a Renaissance Chaucer whose full acquaintance we have yet to make, and the unpublished book, at present something of an unvisited monument of English literary scholarship, anticipates many things that have taken generations to achieve.

NOTES

1 Basic information on Kinaston as a Chaucerian was collected by C. F. E. Spurgeon, *Five Hundred Years of Chaucer Criticism and Allusion 1357–1900* (Cambridge,1925), vol. I, p. 207, vol. III, pp. 66–9, and E. P. Hammond, *Chaucer: A Bibliographical Manual* (New York, 1908), pp. 396–8. He is the subject of only passing remarks in Alice S. Miskimin, *The Renaissance Chaucer* (New Haven and London, 1975), p. 189, n. 42, p. 230, n. 5, Derek Brewer in *Chaucer: The Critical Heritage* (London, 1978), vol. I, pp. 13, 20, 152, Paul G. Ruggiers (ed.), *Editing Chaucer: The Great Tradition* (Norman, 1984), and William Alderson, 'John Urry (1666–1715)', p. 108. The use made of Kinaston's manuscript notes on the *Troilus* (and on Henryson's *Testament*) in Urry's edition of Chaucer is not fully dealt with in the latter survey. Kinaston's qualities as a translator and a Latin metrist have however recently been given careful attention by L. V. Ryan in two articles: 'A Neo-Latin Version of Robert Henryson's *Testament of Cresseid*', in I. D. McFarlane (ed.), *Acta Conventus Neo-Latini Sanctandreani*, Proceedings of the 5th International Conference of Neo-Latin Studies, Medieval and Renaissance Texts and Studies, vol. 38 (Binghamton, NY, 1986), pp. 481–91, and 'Chaucer's Criseyde in Neo-Latin Dress', *English Literary Renaissance*, 17 (1987), pp. 288–302.
2 G. Saintsbury (ed.), *Minor Poets of the Caroline Period*, vol. II (Oxford, 1906), pp. 61–173.
3 The commendatory poems are reprinted in Spurgeon, *Chaucer Criticism and Allusion*, vol. I, pp. 207–15. The pseudo-Chaucerian verses (perhaps the earliest imitation of this kind) were by Francis James, who contributed another commendatory piece in the same manner (making incidental mention of Kinaston's *Amorum Troili*) to Achilles Tatius, *The Loves of Clitophon and Leucippe* englished by A[ntony] H[odges] (1638), sig. A6b.
4 Kinaston's preface is reprinted in Spurgeon, *Chaucer Criticism and Allusion*, vol. III, pp. 67–8. No history of Middle English literary scholarship at present exists, but see the useful preliminary survey by A. S. G. Edwards, 'Observations on the History of Middle English Editing', in Derek Pearsall (ed.), *Manuscripts and Texts: Editorial Problems in Later Middle English Literature* (Cambridge, 1987), pp. 34–48. Kinaston does not form part of Edwards' account.
5 The later history of the manuscript is traced in G. Gregory Smith (ed.), *The Poems of Robert Henryson*, vol. I (Edinburgh and London, 1914), pp. xcvii–xcix. In the posthumously-added 'Preface' to John Urry's edition, *The Works of Geoffrey Chaucer* (London, 1721), eleventh unnumbered page, sig. m, 'A Student of Christ Church' [Timothy Thomas] observes that the Kinaston MS had been in the possession of Henry Aldrich (1647–1710), Dean of Christ Church, during which time 'Mr. *Urry* procured some of the Notes to be transcribed, which have been made use of in the *Glossary*'. Francis Waldron (1774–1818) bought the MS at the sale of the library of the Rev. John Haddon Hindley in 1793, and printed *Troilus*, I, 1–84, together with

Kinaston's English notes and other annotations in his own, as *The Loves of Troilus and Creseid, written by Chaucer: with A Commentary By Sir Francis Kinaston: Never Before Published* (London, printed for and sold by F. G. Waldron ... 1796). Publication of more of the MS, promised by Waldron in the advertisement to this work, apparently never materialized.

6 Gregory Smith, *Poems of Robert Henryson*, vol. I, pp. cvi–clx, printed both the *Testament* and the parallel Latin rendering, together with many of Kinaston's explanatory notes. He also (pp. ciii–civ) gave an accurate transcription of Kinaston's long biographical note on Henryson. This note had already been copied without acknowledgement in Urry's edition, and Waldron (p. xxix) pointed out that Tyrwhitt had therefore been led into error in attributing it to Urry himself. See also D. Fox (ed.), *The Poems of Robert Henryson* (Oxford, 1981), pp. xiv–xv, xxvi, xcvii–ix, ciii.

7 Saintsbury, *Minor Poets of the Caroline Period*, vol. II, p. 64.

8 *A Summary Catalogue of Western Manuscripts in the Bodleian Library at Oxford*, vol. v (Oxford, 1905), no. 29640, Bodley Additional c.287, hereafter cited as 'Bodl. MS'.

9 By far the most accurate and comprehensive account of Kinaston, to which I am particularly indebted for details of his life, remains unpublished: Colin F. Williamson, *The Life and Works of Sir Francis Kinaston*, Oxford B.Litt. thesis, 1957. I am most grateful to Mrs Karina Williamson (McIntosh) for allowing me the use of a copy annotated by the author, and for permission to quote from it here.

10 The *DNB*, following Anthony à Wood (see n. 22 below), states that Kinaston migrated from Oxford to Cambridge, but this is due to a confusion with another man of the same name. The error was corrected by H. G. Seccombe, 'Notes on Sir Francis Kynaston', *Review of English Studies*, 8 (1932), pp. 311–12, but reappears in Ryan (1986) p. 482, (1987), p. 289, and Brewer, *Chaucer: The Critical Heritage*, vol. I, p. 152.

11 Williamson, *Francis Kinaston*, p. 12, quoting PRO, State Papers, Domestic Series 16, 439, no. 15.

12 Williamson, *Francis Kinaston*, p. 14, quoting the *Calendar of State Papers*, Domestic Series, 1619–23, p. 1, a letter of the Lord Chamberlain mentioning that on the occasion in question the king had 'made seventeen new Knights, men of no note'.

13 Kinaston alludes to the embassy in his MS notes on the *Troilus*, Bodl. MS, pp. 206–7.

14 G. H. Turnbull, 'Samuel Hartlib's Connection with Sir Francis Kynaston's "Musaeum Minervae" ', *Notes and Queries*, 197 (1952), p. 34.

15 Arguing from a reference in *Troilus*, IV, 1245 that Chaucer had himself once held the same office, Kinaston wrote a long note detailing the duties of an Esquire of the Body (Bodl. MS, p. 364). It was inaccurately transcribed into the glossary in Urry's Chaucer, s.v. *Morter*, the source being signalled by *Kyn*, at the end.

16 Williamson, *Francis Kinaston*, pp. 27–30.

17 Williamson, *Francis Kinaston*, p. 33.

18 Williamson, *Francis Kinaston*, p. 83, notes a list of Esquires of the Body made in 1641, in which Kinaston's name has subsequently been deleted and 'dead' added in the margin (PRO, Lord Chamberlain's papers, LC 3, 1).

19 Walter E. Houghton, Jr, 'The English Virtuoso in the Seventeenth Century', *Journal of the History of Ideas*, 3 (1942), pp. 51–73, 190–219.

20 Houghton, 'The English Virtuoso', pp. 58–62.

21 Williamson, *Francis Kinaston*, p. 84.

22 Anthony à Wood, *Athenae Oxonienses*, ed. P. Bliss (London, 1817), vol. II, col. 38.

23 Oxford, Bodleian Library, MS Ashmole 45 (IV). See W. H. Black, *Catalogue of the Manuscripts bequeathed unto the University of Oxford by Elias Ashmole* (Oxford, 1845), cols 70–1.

24 Turnbull, 'Samuel Hartlib's Connection with Sir Francis Kynaston's "Musaeum Minervae" ', p. 34.

25 Bodl. MS, pp. 117, 12. For de Dominis and Drebbel, see the entries in the *DNB*.

26 Cf. the anecdote quoted by B. A[gar] in *King James His Apopthegmes: or Table-Talke* (London, 1643), pp. 7–8: 'Sir *Francis Kinnaston* by experience falsified the Alchymists report, that a Hen being fed for certaine dayes with gold, beginning when *Sol* was in *Leo*, should be converted into gold, and should lay golden egges; which being tryed was no such thing; but became indeed very fat'.

27 Houghton, 'The English Virtuoso', pp. 56–8.

28 Bodl. MS, p. 152. For the reference to *The Anatomy of Melancholy* and Robert Burton see pp. 301–2, a note on Troilus' insomnia mentioned at *Troilus*, III, 1535ff. Burton owned a copy of Kinaston's *Amorum Troili*: N. K. Kiessling, *The Library of Robert Burton*, Oxford Bibliographical Society, NS XXII (1988), pp. 66–7.

29 Houghton, 'The English Virtuoso', p. 67.

30 T. Rymer, *Foedera*, vol. XIX (London, 1732), pp. 638–41, De Licentia speciali Francisco Kinaston Militi pro erectione Domus sive Collegii pro institutione Juvenum Nobilium in Artibus liberalibus. According to the licence, Kinaston at his house in Covent Garden 'plurima paravit Instrumenta mathematica & musica, Libros, Codices, Manuscripta, Picturas, Imagines cum aliis rebus antiquis, raris & exoticis plurimum estimandis, & haud modiocris valoris, ad pleniorem prefati Hospitii seu Societas usum & ornatum spectantibus'. The Musaeum was also to have professors of painting and engraving, dancing, and riding.

31 For the academies of Henry, Prince of Wales and of Edmond Bolton see respectively R. Strong, *Henry, Prince of Wales and England's Lost Renaissance* (London, 1986), pp. 8, 215, and E. M. Portal, 'The Academ Roial of King James I', *Proceedings of the British Academy*, 1915–16, pp. 189–208.

32 Williamson, *Francis Kinaston*, pp. 70–7.

33 *The Constitutions of the Musaeum Minervae*, p. 14.

34 Henry Peacham, *The Compleat Gentleman* (London, 1622), p. 80.

35 *Amorum Troili et Creseidae*, f. A3ᵛ.

36 Many notes on the first few pages of the Bodleian manuscript make it plain that Kinaston had gone out of his way to acquaint himself with various obsolete aspects of Middle English. On p. 1, in particular, he discusses at length Chaucer's inflections and rhymes, mentioning the assistance he derived from 'a most antient Grammar written in the Saxon tong & character, which I once saw in the handes of my most learned and celebrated frend Mr Ben: Johnson, & by which (out of doubt) Lilly our Grammarian made his Accedence'.

37 *Amorum Troili et Creseidae* f.†ʳ⁻ᵛ. Kinaston's commitment to this principle was in practice confined to matters of textual detail. In the Bodleian manuscript Books IV and V of the *Troilus* are somewhat condensed by omission, with Latin summaries of omitted material. L. V. Ryan, 'Chaucer's Criseyde in Neo-Latin Dress' (see n. 1 above), has recently argued that Kinaston's omissions were motivated by an adverse attitude to Criseyde.

38 On the modernized versions of Middle English texts mentioned see: F. Albert, *Über Thomas Heywoods The Life and Death of Hector, eine Neubearbeitung von Lydgates Troy Book* (Leipzig, 1909); W. C. Hazlitt (ed.), *The Whole Works of William Browne* (London, 1868–9), vol. II, pp. 178–98; H. G. Wright, *A Seventeenth-Century Modernisation of the*

First Three Books of Chaucer's 'Troilus and Criseyde' (Bern, 1960) on London, British Library, MS Additional 29494, *c.* 1630.

39 A. S. G. Edwards, 'Observations on the History of Middle English Editing' (see n. 4 above), pp. 36–8, notices a variety of attitudes in those who sought to present Middle English texts to contemporary readers, none of them resembling Kinaston's. In the Bodleian manuscript the English text is copied in secretary script and the Latin version in italic, possibly suggesting that in print the complete version would have followed the typography of the *Amorum Troili*, with Chaucer in black letter on the right-hand page of an opening, and Kinaston's parallel version *en face* in roman type.

40 For evaluations see the anonymous article in the *Retrospective Review*, 12 (1825), pp. 106–23, *Notes and Queries*, 1st Ser., 3 (1851), p. 297, quoting Robert Southey's view that Kinaston's work was 'the best serious piece of Latin in modern metre', and the detailed prosodic analyses in the two articles by Ryan cited above in n. 1.

41 The exact relationships between the various editions of Chaucer's works between those of Thynne and Speght remain to be worked out in detail, but see the preliminary account privately published by J. R. Hetherington, *Chaucer: 1532–1602: Notes and Facsimile Texts* (Birmingham, 1964; corrected repr. with additional matter to 1687, 1967).

42 Fox, *Poems of Robert Henryson*, pp. xcviii–ix.

43 Bodl. MS, p. 519.

44 Edwards, 'Observations on the History of Middle English Editing', *passim*, esp. pp. 41–2.

45 Bodl. MS, pp. 65–6, 245–6. The latter note also includes discussion of the hidden forces and astronomical affiliations of the lodestone, and mentions the researches of 'the most learned doctor Gilbert ... in his posthumus manuscript of his noua philosophia (of which there is but two copies extant)'. This was William Gilbert (1544–1603) author of the revolutionary treatise *De Magnete* (1600). His *De Mundo nostro Sublunari Philosophia Nova* remained unpublished until 1651. Kinaston must have seen either the original manuscript presented to Prince Henry (now British Library, MS Royal 12. F. XI), or the copy made for the use of Francis Bacon.

46 A. S. Cook, 'Henryson, *Testament of Cresseid* 8–14', *Modern Language Notes*, 22 (1907), p. 62. Fox, *Poems of Robert Henryson*, pp. 338–83, notices a number of points where Kinaston anticipated the observations of later commentators on the *Testament*.

47 Bodl. MS, pp. 82, 204–5.

48 Bodl. MS, pp. 516, 517; cf. Fox, *Poems of Robert Henryson*, p. 352.

49 Bodl. MS, p. 70 (*First Anniversary*, 109–10), p. 347 (*First Anniversary*, 3–4), p. 303 (*Hero and Leander*, II, 287–8).

50 Bodl. MS, p. 245. Williamson, *Francis Kinaston*, p. 8, suggests that Kinaston may be referring to the exploits described by A. N., *A True Relation of the Trauels of M. Bush* (1608), STC 18325.

51 Spurgeon, *Five Hundred Years of Chaucer Criticism and Allusion*, vol. I, pp. 306–7. It should be noted that the manuscript borrowed by Kinaston from Selden cannot have been what is now Oxford, Bodleian Library, MS Arch. Selden B. 14. a copy of the *Canterbury Tales* containing the Retractation, but not 'the Cooks Tale compleat' (i.e. *Gamelyn*). In his *De Synedris et Praefecturis Juridicis Veterum Ebraeorum* (Amsterdam, 1679), II, pp. 360–1, Selden digressed to discuss a *Canterbury Tales* manuscript containing *Gamelyn* which was in his possession. The details of Selden's discussion suggest that the copy in question had textual peculiarities not identifiable in any manuscript of the *Tales* at present known to be extant, but the matter

requires further investigation. This allusion was overlooked by Spurgeon, *Five Hundred Years of Chaucer Criticism and Allusion*, and by J. M. Manly and E. Rickert in their list of references to manuscripts of the *Canterbury Tales* in *The Text of the Canterbury Tales* (Chicago, 1940), I, pp. 606–45.

52 Thomas Watson, *The Hekatompathia or Passionate Centurie of Love (1582)*, facsimile edition with introduction by S. K. Heninger, Jr (Gainesville, 1964), p. 19.

53 Spurgeon, *Chaucer Criticism and Allusion*, vol. I, p. cix.

54 See M. Seymour, 'Manuscript Portraits of Chaucer and Hoccleve', *The Burlington Magazine*, 134 (1982), pp. 618–23, at p. 622. Professor A. S. G. Edwards draws my attention to another description of the portrait once in Cotton Otho A. XVIII, made by George Vertue at some time between 1721 and 1731: see *Walpole Society*, 20 (1931–2), Vertue Note Books, vol. II, pp. 47–8.

55 Gregory Smith, *Poems of Robert Henryson*, vol. I, p. ci.

16

Rewriting romance: Chaucer's and Dryden's *Wife of Bath's Tale*

A. C. SPEARING

This essay begins from two observations about Chaucer made by Derek Brewer: first that his 'inherited style' has its roots in the Middle English metrical romances; and second that he so unfailingly 'derides Arthurian romance' that it is at least partially true that 'Chaucer in his poetical character is decidedly anti-romantic'.[1] As a genre, romance hovers uneasily between the vagueness with which the terms *roman, romaunt, romaunce* were used in the Middle Ages and the backward glare of post-medieval attempts at more exact definition; but I think it unquestionably true that Chaucer regarded what *he* understood of what *we* mean by romance with derision; and that in his understanding what chiefly characterized romance was what his contemporary Thomas Usk praised him for avoiding in *Troilus and Criseyde*: 'nyceté of storiers imaginacion', foolishness of storytellers' fantasy – in a word, the unrealistic, the marvellous.[2] This did not prevent Chaucer from writing romances, but led him to experiment with the genre in highly original ways. To put it briefly, in three of his major poems Chaucer rewrites romance to make it more serious, more historical and more philosophical: he borrows from Boccaccio a setting in pagan antiquity, aims with the help of Boethius at a historical reconstruction of pagan thought, and reduces the marvellous to science and pagan religion. The three works I have in mind are *Troilus and Criseyde*, the *Knight's Tale*, and the *Franklin's Tale*. Two other *Canterbury Tales* may be regarded as critical rewritings of different aspects of romance as it already existed: the *Squire's Tale* is a generous and affectionate burlesque of all that is most complicated, sentimental and unrealistic in courtly romance, while *Sir Thopas* is a masterpiece of destructive comedy in its parody of the poetic and social ineptitude of the English tail-rhyme romances.[3] One other work of Chaucer's may also be considered a romance: the *Wife of Bath's Tale*. This is certainly not one of the Boccaccian–Boethian narratives of pagan antiquity, indeed it is Chaucer's only poem with an Arthurian setting; yet it does not appear to be a burlesque of Arthurian romance. The opening account of 'th'olde dayes of the Kyng Arthour' (857) rapidly turns into a satire on friars as the modern substitute for fairies, and the two moments of magic – the disappearance of the 'ladyes foure and twenty, and yet mo' (992) and the transformation of the Loathly Lady into a beautiful young lady – are neither exaggerated nor inept, but are simply passed over with the least possible emphasis.

The *Wife of Bath's Tale* can helpfully be seen, I suggest, as a diagnosis of romance;[4] and here it is useful to remember who tells it. A tradition of Chaucer interpretation that goes back to Kittredge and beyond sees the various *Canterbury Tales* as 'merely long speeches expressing, directly or indirectly, the characters of the several persons' who tell them;[5] and the *Wife of Bath's Tale*, preceded as it is by the longest and most purportedly autobiographical of all the pilgrims' prologues, appears to lend itself readily to such an approach. This tradition of interpretation remains so strong as still to seem merely natural to many readers; Derek Brewer has rightly resisted it, reminding us that many elements in the tales 'move between life and literature, defying any purely naturalistic interpretation, and not calling for any elaborate over-all reconciliation'.[6] There is a manifest inconsistency, in terms of naturalistic verisimilitude, between the unlearned Wife and the abundant learning displayed in her Prologue and tale; yet a characteristically 'Gothic' shift of perspective also enables her to enter her tale in a more partisan fashion than most of the pilgrims, as a self-appointed spokesperson for women and an expert on the crucial question of what it is they most desire. Since the Prologue represents the Wife as especially given to self-revelation, I find it easy to enter into the view which finds further and perhaps unconscious self-revelation in her tale. It is not only that the tale's conclusion, with the knight's submission to the Loathly Lady and their resultant happiness, reflects the ending of the Wife's 'autobiographical' Prologue, with the submission of her fifth husband and *their* happiness – so much can be understood as what the Wife intends. It is also that the Loathly Lady's magical transformation into a beautiful young woman and acquisition of a young and obliging husband can readily be seen as a presumably unintended revelation of the Wife's wishes for herself.[7] The only two occurrences in the Prologue of the exclamation 'allas' – so uncharacteristic in its helplessness of the Wife's indomitably energetic public personality – point to a parallel between her two hopeless longings to escape from consequences of the Fall. The directly-expressed wish of 'Allas, allas! That evere love was synne!' (614) is matched by a wish concerning 'age, allas, that al wole envenyme' (474) – and this finds full expression only in the wish-fulfilling dream of her tale.

More interesting, in my view, than what this tells us about the teller is what it tells us about the tale. What we call wish-fulfilment was evidently a familiar phenomenon to Chaucer, who knew well enough that dreams may provide the very satisfactions that waking life denies:

> The syke met he drynketh of the tonne;
> The lovere met he hath his lady wonne.[8]

He appears to recognize that romance, like this kind of dream, is above all a wish-fulfilling fiction; but he goes further, and asks whose wishes it fulfils. A typical pattern, perhaps the typical pattern, for Middle English romances is that a young knight undergoes one or more adventures, sometimes caused by magic, with the outcome that a truer conception of knighthood emerges and the knight gains a wife and land. Derek Brewer has pointed out that this often-repeated story offers symbolic reassurance about the possibility of growing up:

> The emerging adult successfully casts off childhood, frees himself or herself from parents, proves his capacity to stand on his own feet, finds his wife, or she her husband, and is then reconciled with the parents; in other words, is fully integrated into adult society. Fairy tales and most medieval romances are essentially stories of the successful *rite de passage*.[9]

Romances, however, unlike fairy tales, virtually always have a male protagonist; and this amounts to a structural bias of exactly the kind the Wife exposes in her Prologue when she asks 'Who peyntede the leon, tel me who?' (692). Just as the writings that constitute the apparently unquestionable authority of Christian doctrine are written from the interested viewpoint of 'clerkes ... withinne hire oratories' (694) – that is, celibate males[10] – so romances, equally unquestionable in their apparent naturalness and unanimity, also serve the interests of a specific group, that of the young male aristocracy. The *Wife of Bath's Tale* can be seen as a rewriting of romance that substitutes for this bias one closer to the Wife's heart; and the Loathly Lady's lecture is directed precisely against the values taken for granted by romances – nobility of blood, wealth, youth, and beauty.

It is easy to imagine a way of telling the story of the *Wife of Bath's Tale* which would make it a typical romance. A young knight, set an apparently impossible task, meets a fairy lady, transformed by magic into an ugly hag, who falls passionately in love with him. Against all expectation, she enables him to perform the task; showing courtesy and fidelity to a promise, he marries her, the spell is thus broken, and they live happily ever after. This is more like some other versions of the widely-known tale,[11] and it is seen from the usual romance point of view, that of the male protagonist; the position offered to the reader being one of identification with him and his wish for a happy ending, and the fairy lady being merely instrumental to this end. In the Wife of Bath's version, the story is magically transformed, so that its central figure becomes not a young unmarried aristocratic male but the character corresponding to herself as an old widowed non-aristocratic female – the Loathly Lady. The young knight is first degraded by the opening act of rape (a starting point found in none of the analogues), and is then displaced from the centre of the narrative. Once the Loathly Lady enters the story, the Wife almost completely disappears from it as the narratorial spokesperson for her sex, and her role is taken over by the Loathly Lady, who is henceforward the protagonist. Having trapped the knight into a rash promise, she forces him to marry her, enjoys his repugnance at being obliged to consummate the marriage, lectures him in bed at overwhelming length on the unromantic themes of the irrelevance of birth to *gentillesse*, the advantages of poverty, and the desirability of having an old and ugly wife; and only when he has submitted totally to her *maistrie* does she make herself young and beautiful. She also grants him her obedience, at least in sexual matters –

> And she obeyed hym in every thyng
> That myghte doon hym plesance or likyng.
> And thus they lyve unto hir lyves ende
> In parfit joye ...   (1255–8)

– but even this happy-ever-after ending is interrupted in mid-line[12] by a reminder that the *us* whom the tale is intended to please consists not of men but of women whose desire is first to dominate and then to outlive their husbands. The effect is as different from that of normal romance as would be a version of *Sir Gawain and the Green Knight* with Morgan la Fay as its central character.

The underplaying of the 'nyceté of storiers imaginacion' found in the *Wife of Bath's Tale* (just the opposite of the exaggeration of exoticism, idealization and marvel in the *Squire's Tale*) is an important part of its effect. Various consequences might be drawn from it, but one way of reading it is this. 'Th'olde dayes of the Kyng Arthour' (857) were no stranger than the friar-haunted present, and 'we' (that is, women) do not have to be transported to the realm of escapist fiction to be able to exercise power over men. 'Cast up the curtyn, looke how that it is' (1249), and you will see that magic is only a matter of wishes, and women's wish for *maistrie* can be achieved by the exercise of power in the real world: the Prologue gives hints enough.

When Dryden in his closing years prepared his *Fables Ancient and Modern*, he was already struck by the appropriateness of Chaucer's tales to their tellers. In the *Preface to the Fables*, that casually brilliant anticipation of so much subsequent Chaucer criticism, he offers a neoclassical version of the Kittredgian view:

> All his Pilgrims are severally distinguish'd from each other; and not only in their Inclinations, but in their very Phisiognomies and Persons ... The Matter and Manner of their Tales, and of their Telling, are so suited to their different Educations, Humours and Callings, that each of them would be improper in any other Mouth. Even the grave and serious Characters are distinguish'd by their several sorts of Gravity: Their Discourses are such as belong to their Age, their Calling, and their Breeding; such as are becoming of them, and of them only.[13]

Though for Dryden 'character' still had more of its original sense of 'type' than of the later sense of 'unique individual', it is evident that he, like many more recent readers, was incited to complete imaginatively the suiting of tale to teller that Chaucer carried out only in part. (Can we really say that the tales of the Monk and of the Man of Law are 'becoming of them, *and of them only*'? Twentieth-century scholars have attempted to argue such cases, but always unconvincingly.) Dryden relished 'the broad-speaking gap-tooth'd Wife of *Bathe*', yet, having determined to confine himself 'to such Tales of *Chaucer*, as savour nothing of Immodesty',[14] he did not translate her Prologue. This separation of the tale from its teller has interesting consequences.

Chaucer's version of the *Wife of Bath's Tale* contains many narratorial interventions. In some the 'I' is not necessarily attached to any particular narrator; thus the following chatty lines, while perfectly 'becoming of' the Wife, given that we know her to be the narrator, could equally well have been spoken by many of the pilgrims, or indeed by Chaucer himself:

> Now wolden som men seye, paraventure,
> That for my necligence I do no cure
> To tellen yow the joye and al th'array
> That at the feeste was that ilke day.
> To which thyng shortly answeren I shal:
> I seye ther nas no joye ne feeste at al ...   (1073-8)

Other interventions, however, can belong to the Wife only, because they use not singular but plural first-person forms to identify the speaker either with women in general – 'Pardee, we wommen konne no thyng hele' (950) – or more specifically with secular women; and Alisoun of Bath is the only such woman among the pilgrims. Lines 929–80 form the main section of this kind; indeed they include a passage in which Alisoun so fully makes the story her own that the various answers the knight gets to his question shift from third-person past – 'Somme seyden wommen loven best ...' (925) – to first-person present: 'And somme seyen that we loven best ...' (935). Interestingly, once the Loathly Lady is established as Alisoun's surrogate, she raises the argument to a higher plane, using 'we' to mean humanity in general –

> Crist wole we clayme of hym oure gentillesse,
> Nat of oure eldres for hire old richesse,   (1117-18)

– and it is not until the closing lines that the Wife snatches it back to mean wives.

There is doubtless more than one way to respond to Chaucer's Wife's claim to speak for secular women. The 'we' she adopts turns out to correspond to the definition of women by medieval men – garrulous, indiscreet, susceptible to flattery and to praise that they know to be undeserved, desirous of power over men – and the space she offers to share with female readers may thus be felt as confining or merely illusory. On the other hand, the intelligence and energy of her focus on sexual politics, combined with the merging of her 'we' into the Loathly Lady's to express an ethic genuinely superior to that of chivalry, surely makes her something more than a deceptive misogynistic caricature. In Dryden's retelling, that something more disappears. To be sure, the Wife is not completely expunged from his *Wife of Bath Her Tale*. Traces of her 'we' remain in the passage corresponding to Chaucer's lines 929–80 (D131–202); some instances, however, can be attributed to the knight's informants, for Dryden, unlike Chaucer, has him aiming specifically 'To learn *from Women* what they lov'd the best' (122: my italics). Thus in

> Truth is, says one, he seldom fails to win
> Who Flatters well, for that's our darling Sin,   (131–2)

'our' plainly belongs not to the Wife but to the 'one', and in other cases it is hard to tell whether first-person plurals belong to her or to female informants. Still, some of the first-person plurals in this passage clearly are retained from Chaucer's Wife, and so is the 'our' of the tale's final paragraph: 'And so may all our Lives like their's be led ...' (541). But such vestiges are anomalous in Dryden's version, for he greatly intensifies the separation of the sexes and commits himself far more explicitly than Chaucer to a male readership and a definition of woman as a deviation from the male norm.[15]

Here I must pause to note that Dryden's definition of woman is only a special case of his general Augustan habit of assigning individuals firmly to larger and more abstract categories, or indeed of substituting categories for individuals. An example will make this clear. Arthur, though he loves the story's 'hero', condemns him for his act of rape:

> Mov'd by the Damsels Tears and common Cry,
> He doom'd the brutal Ravisher to die.
> But fair *Geneura* rose in his Defence,
> And pray'd so hard for Mercy from the Prince;
> That to his Queen the King th'Offender gave,
> And left it in her Pow'r to Kill or Save:
> This gracious Act the Ladies all approve,
> Who thought it much a Man should die for Love.   (71–8)

The knight is here dissolved into the categories of 'th'Offender' and 'the brutal Ravisher'; Arthur becomes 'the Prince' and 'the King'; Geneura (Guinevere) 'his Queen'; and women 'the Ladies'. Most such categories are pinned down by definite articles, which leave no room for uncertainty; the neatness and concision of a line such as 'That to his Queen the King th'Offender gave' are possible only on the assumption of general agreement about the function and limits of each of the three categories it mentions. Similarly, when the knight returns with his answer, he is not just 'the Knight' (272) but 'the Criminal' (271), 'the *Culprit*' (273), 'Th'Offender' (276), and later 'the Suppliant' (311).

The story itself, turning in both versions on the qustion 'What thyng is it that wommen moost desiren' (c905), assumes the possibility of generalizing about women, though not necessarily about men: 'così fan tutte'. (The question may also arouse expectations of an improper physiological answer, in accordance either with the time-honoured male view that what women want must be what only men can give them, or with the Freudian sublimation of this view, according to which what women want is the one thing that men cannot give them. In both versions of the tale, any such expectation is disappointed: the commonest symbols of *maistrie* may be phallic, but no such symbols are introduced at the conclusion, and the story insists that what women want is not the symbol but the reality of power. Dryden, however, through jokes such as his favourite pun on death, as in line 78 quoted above, gives the expectation of a physiological answer so much encouragement that in his version the impropriety's conspicuous absence becomes a ghostly presence.) Dryden's way of phrasing the question – 'what the Sex of Women most desire' (97) – already strengthens the essentializing of 'women' as 'the Sex of Women'; and throughout his version it is women who are the chief objects of categorization. They are comparatively rarely just 'Women' (122, 240, 275, 290); more often, almost always with that knowing definite article, 'the Ladies' (77), 'the Sex of Women' (97), 'the Fair' (110), 'the Kind' (118, 134), 'the Female Kind' (124), 'the Sex' (129, 135, 285), 'Womankind' (146), 'the Mob of Women' (269), 'the Women' (307). Once, in the knight's answer to 'The Female Senate' (268), the categorization is attributed to a man: 'What all your Sex desire is *Soveraignty*' (279). More often, it is accepted by women: 'our offended Race' (89), 'our Kind' (90), 'our Sex' (153, 234), 'us Women' (298). 'Sex' is the word most frequently used to categorize women (but never men), and that favourite Restoration kenning 'the Sex' is particularly telling, with its implication that difference and indeed sexuality itself characterize only one of the sexes. 'The Kind' has a similar effect, and may further involve a sneering pun on women's 'Kindness' – that susceptibility to a virile rogue that they cover 'with dissembled Hate' (80) in debating the rapist's fate. 'Kind' and 'Race' are important terms in this story, since they are also used, in the knight's objection to marrying the Loathly Lady and in her answering lecture, to refer to the virtue supposedly deriving from noble birth. The knight first says that he would rather be beheaded than that 'any of my Race so foul a Crone shall wed' (333), then that even if she were less ugly,

> Thou art descended from so mean a Race,
> That never Knight was match'd with such Disgrace.   (368–9)

In her response, the Loathly Lady uses both terms with some frequency: 'Race' (378, 401, 455) and 'Kind' (385, 397, 426), indifferently with 'Descent' and 'Blood'. Dryden appears unconscious of the irony by which 'race' and 'kind' are deprived of their determining power when applied to rank, which descends in the male line, but not when applied to the female sex. Especially revealing is one of his additions to the Loathly Lady's lecture, a passage borrowed from Lucretius which attributes the blame for the contamination of noble descent to women rather than men:

> No Father can infuse, or Wit, or Grace,
> A Mother comes across, and marrs the Race.   (400–1)

One other aspect of Dryden's strengthening of the category of femaleness is worth mentioning. Again I must begin by noting that this too is only part of a more general tendency in his work. Chaucer follows the general practice of courtly French romance (though not of English romances such as *Havelok* or the alliterative *Morte Arthure*) in showing little concern with the political significance of kingship: with a flicker of his usual awareness of historical difference, he is content to speculate about Arthur's imposition of the death-penalty for rape simply that 'Paraventure swich was the statut tho' (893).[16] Dryden's thought, however, is deeply political, and he ingeniously applies to Arthur's court the satirical comparison of past and present introduced in the opening treatment of fairies and their modern successors:

> Then Courts of Kings were held in high Renown,
> E'er made the common Brothels of the Town:
> There, Virgins honourable Vows receiv'd,
> But chast as Maids in Monasteries liv'd:
> The King himself to Nuptial Ties a Slave,
> No bad Example to his Poets gave:
> And they not bad, but in a vicious Age,
> Had not to please the Prince debauch'd the Stage.   (61–8)

In this context, Arthur's granting of power over the condemned knight to Guinevere and her ladies (which for Chaucer is merely a narrative datum) is also seen in political terms, and female power is defined as an amusing parody of the normal situation in which power belongs to men. The ladies are first seen as forming a 'Female Parliament' –

> At last agreed they call'd him by consent
> Before the Queen and Female Parliament.
> And the fair Speaker rising from her Chair,
> Did thus the Judgment of the House declare ...   (80–3)

– and then, when the knight returns with his answer, they are represented as a 'Female Senate' (that is, as a female version of the House of Lords exercising its judicial function):

> The Female Senate was assembled soon,
> With all the Mob of Women in the Town:
> The Queen sate Lord Chief Justice of the Hall,
> And bad the Cryer cite the Criminal.
> The Knight appear'd; and Silence they proclaim,
> Then first the *Culprit* answer'd to his Name:
> And after Forms of Laws, was last requir'd
> To name the Thing that Women most desir'd.   (268–75)

Here for the real sexual politics of Chaucer's Alisoun is substituted a playful metaphor of sexualized politics which defuses the notion of female sovereignty precisely by being metaphorical.

In this respect, then, Dryden has undone Chaucer's rewriting of romance:

the male viewpoint is restored to its central position, though by Augustan rather than medieval means. Indeed, even the initial rape is now seen through the rapist's eyes. The 'male gaze', over which Chaucer passes in a single word – 'He saugh a mayde walkynge hym biforn' (886) – is treated more lingeringly and, not without complicity, as that of a human being appraising an animal (the knight dismounts from one only to mount another):

> It happen'd as he rode, a Damsel gay
> In Russet-Robes to Market took her way;
> Soon on the Girl he cast an amorous Eye,
> So strait she walk'd, and on her Pasterns high:
> If seeing her behind he lik'd her Pace,
> Now turning short he better lik'd her Face:
> He lights in hast, and full of Youthful Fire,
> By Force accomplish'd his obscene Desire.   (49–56)

Here 'obscene Desire' comes too late to neutralize the effect of 'Damsel gay', 'amorous Eye' and 'Youthful Fire': boys will be boys. Moreover, Dryden, here and elsewhere, undermines the tale's explicit social doctrine: in Chaucer the victim is just 'a mayde', while in Dryden her garb and destination, marking her as of lower social rank, evidently add to her attractiveness and suitability as prey. Similarly, later, the unChaucerian distinction between the 'Female Senate' and 'the Mob of Women in the Town' (269–70)[17] jars oddly with the Loathly Lady's teaching that 'Nobility of Blood/ Is but a glitt'ring, and fallacious Good' (382–3), finely though Dryden amplifies her lecture. (In the lecture itself, Dryden may be judged to have improved on Chaucer in an area in which Chaucer was a pioneer: sustained argument, at once rational and rhetorical, in English verse. But Dryden's ability to argue in verse persuasively, and even movingly, was rarely dependent on personal conviction. As Johnson put it, 'Give him matter for his verse, and he finds without difficulty verse for his matter.'[18]) The covert re-establishment of the social as of the sexual hierarchy can be connected with the virtual disappearance of the Wife of Bath as narrator, for her viewpoint was defined by her social rank and economic status as well as by her sex.

In another way too Dryden's rewriting of romance opposes Chaucer's. It might be supposed that an Augustan would sympathize even less than Chaucer with the elements in medieval romance that could be categorized as 'nyceté of storiers imaginacion'; but in fact we can already recognize in *The Wife of Bath Her Tale* that nostalgia for the imaginary that has coloured so much subsequent reading of medieval culture.[19] Dryden follows Chaucer in using the Arthurian opening as a peg for satire on the Church, and in part he updates Chaucer's topicality, writing jovially that

> ... in the Walks where wicked Elves have been,
> The Learning of the Parish now is seen,
> The Midnight Parson posting o'er the Green,
> With Gown tuck'd up to Wakes; for *Sunday* next,

> With humming Ale encouraging his Text;
> Nor wants the holy Leer to Country-Girl betwixt.   (34–9)

But Dryden, a papist convert writing under William III, is also attracted by what has become archaic in this satire directed against a Catholic England of priests and friars; and he further expresses a longing for the pre-rational past not uncommon in the Age of Reason but entirely foreign to Chaucer. The growth of an English literary tradition (not available to Chaucer because Chaucer was its originator) has reshaped Dryden's view of that past. With an allusiveness quite foreign to Chaucer,

> The elf-queene, with hir joly compaignye,
> Daunced ful ofte in many a grene mede   (c860–1)

is prettily elaborated and miniaturized, with the assistance of *Romeo and Juliet*, *A Midsummer Night's Dream*, *The Tempest*, and perhaps early Milton, to become:

> The King of Elfs and little Fairy Queen
> Gamboll'd on Heaths, and danc'd on ev'ry Green.
> And where the jolly Troop had led the round
> The Grass unbidden rose, and mark'd the Ground:
> Nor darkling did they dance, the Silver Light
> Of *Phoebe* serv'd to guide their Steps aright,
> And, with their Tripping pleas'd, prolong'd the Night.
> Her Beams they follow'd, where at full she plaid,
> Nor longer than she shed her Horns they staid,
> From thence with airy Flight to Foreign Lands convey'd.   (D3–12)

Dryden continues to elaborate the scene, expressing a feeling for what was lost as the necessary price of reformation and rationalism that can already be paralleled in earlier seventeenth-century poets.[20] Chaucer's prosaically dismissive couplet,

> I speke of manye hundred yeres ago.
> But now kan no man se none elves mo ...   (c863–4)

is drawn out as follows:

> I speak of ancient Times, for now the Swain
> Returning late may pass the Woods in vain,
> And never hope to see the nightly Train:
> In vain the Dairy now with Mints is dress'd,
> The Dairy-Maid expects no Fairy Guest,
> To skim the Bowls and after pay the Feast.
> She sighs and shakes her empty Shoes in vain,
> No Silver Penny to reward her Pain ...   (D16–23)

This world of fine fabling may be attributed to the superstition of swains and dairy maids, but there is no mistaking the regret in 'hope', 'sighs', and the repeated 'in vain'.

As the story proceeds, Dryden systematically expands those very exotic and supernatural features that Chaucer passed over as mere machinery. The knight's entry is touched with Spenser's archaizing of medieval chivalry – 'A lusty Knight was pricking o'er the Plain' (47)[21] – his emotional perturbation is treated far more sympathetically than by Chaucer, and when he encounters the fairies, Shakespeare and moonlight are once more called on to evoke a Gothick or Salvator-Rosan mood:

> In this despairing State he hap'd to ride
> As Fortune led him, by a Forest-side:
> Lonely the Vale, and full of Horror stood
> Brown with the shade of a religious Wood:
> When full before him at the Noon of night,
> (The Moon was up and shot a gleamy Light)
> He saw a Quire of Ladies in a round,
> That featly footing seem'd to skim the Ground:
> Thus dancing Hand in Hand, so light they were,
> He knew not where they trod, on Earth or Air.   (209–18)

The mysteriousness of their vanishing is intensified, as is the picturesque ugliness of the one who remains. She claims an uncanny knowledge of his thoughts, which he later attributes to diabolic influence:

> The Fiend thy Sire has sent thee from below,
> Else how cou'dst thou my secret Sorrows know?   (329–30)

Chaucer simply omits the journey of the knight and the Loathly Lady to court, but Dryden describes it at length as magically swift (256–63). More magic is hinted at after the knight has given his answer and we are told that the Loathly Lady 'was there unseen' (291): 'unseen' might mean 'unnoticed' but also suggests 'invisible'. And the final supernatural element, the Loathly Lady's transformation, is also written up in a more literary way, first as imaginary – 'could *Medea*'s Magick mend thy Face' (367) – and then as seen:

> He look'd, and saw a Creature heav'nly Fair,
> In bloom of Youth, and of a charming Air.
> With Joy he turn'd, and seiz'd her Iv'ry Arm;
> And like *Pygmalion* found the Statue warm.   (531–4)

If this example of neoclassicism at its most neoclassical seems to lack conviction, it may be because Dryden failed to draw here on the English tradition (Chaucer–Spenser–Shakespeare–Milton) that he knew and understood so well and that served him so well earlier in his version.

In this short essay, there are important aspects of Dryden's rewriting of the *Wife of Bath's Tale* with which I cannot deal. Among them are: the colouring of Chaucer's comparatively bare narrative with 'dramatic pictorialism';[22] the stylistic changes connected with the shift from a listening to a reading public (for example the substitution of elegant variation for the verbal repetition that is so prominent in the lecture of Chaucer's Loathly Lady); and the pervasive movement from concrete to abstract and from exemplary to analytic that may be epitomized by setting Dryden's 'Beware; for on thy Wit depends thy Life' (D99) alongside Chaucer's 'Be war, and keep thy nekke-boon from iren' (C906). But an overall aim of the rewriting seems to be the achievement of a narrative that, judged by neoclassical canons, would be more coherent and better-formed. Thus the themes of the narrative are made to emerge more explicitly. The politicization noted above is one example of this. Throughout, Dryden intensifies and systematizes Chaucer's occasional references to kingship and queenship. There is the satire on the immorality of the Restoration court; the reminder that 'Soveraign Monarchs are the Source of Right' (70); and a strong emphasis on kingship in the Midas exemplum. In Chaucer this concerns husbands and wives, and it is not even mentioned that Midas was a king; Dryden, by contrast, introduces him as '*Midas* the King' (157), then inserts a five-line digression on the need to conceal 'Monarch's Vices' from a populace sceptical of Divine Right (160–4), and proceeds to write of 'the royal Malady' (175), 'a Husband and a Prince' (182), 'the Secret of the King' (188), 'the King my Husband' (197), and 'A goodly Royal pair of Asses Ears' (198); his wife's knees become 'majestick mary-bones' (192) and she addresses the water 'as thy Queen' (196). Later in the story Dryden has the Loathly Lady vowing that 'Not all the Wealth of Eastern Kings' (321) would part her from her new husband, asking him whether his standoffishness is 'the Custom of King *Arthur*'s Court' (351), referring to Christ as 'The King of Heav'n' (386), and turning Chaucer's 'Bitwix this and the mount of Kaukasous' (C1140) of 'Betwixt King *Arthur*'s Court and *Caucasus*' (409). The formalizations of Guinevere's role as 'Speaker' and 'Lord Chief Justice' are part of the same pattern; royal status and royal power, belonging to men and amusingly reflected in their women (Midas' wife is 'his Ears of State' (166)), sometimes treated satirically but always with a sense of their unquestionable importance, are elevated systematically to thematic significance in Dryden's poem.

A similarly explicit theme is the secret lustfulness attributed to women. It is this that accounts for the mercy shown to the rapist by Guinevere and her ladies; the Loathly Lady is described as 'The liquorish Hag' (319), her determination to bed the knight thus being attributed to a purely selfish motive; and the thematic significance is clinched in the lines Dryden gives her when her husband flinches from her:

> When you my ravish'd Predecessor saw,
> You were not then become this Man of Straw;
> Had you been such, you might have scap'd the Law. (348–50)

This jolly triplet is worth pausing over. The elegantly categorizing 'my ravish'd Predecessor' connects the Loathly Lady with the victim of rape, and with its neat pointedness the triplet cleverly links the beginning of the story with its end – a link that Chaucer had neglected to provide. One can imagine Dryden congratulating himself on the improvement. Yet, just as the thematization of kingship undermines the message about the grounding of nobility in virtue, so, combined with this, the emphasis on female admiration for male potency undermines the message about the power relations between men and women. In the first case, Dryden has introduced a contradiction where none existed in Chaucer; in the second it is more a matter of his sharpening into contradiction divergent elements that lie side by side in Chaucer's text. Dryden puts as follows the knight's answer to the question what women most desire:

> What all your Sex desire is *Soveraignty*.
> The Wife affects her Husband to command,
> All must be hers, both Mony, House, and Land.
> The Maids are Mistresses ev'n in their Name;
> And of their Servants full Dominion claim.
> Thus, at the Peril of my Head, I say
> A blunt plain Truth, the Sex aspires to sway,
> You to rule all; while we, like Slaves, obey. (279–86)

The sharpening of this answer through antithesis and verbal play (wife/husband, maids/mistresses, rule/obey), while seeming to strengthen it, actually weakens its force, as does Dryden's similar antithetical sharpening of the Loathly Lady's triumph:

> Then thus in Peace, quoth she, concludes the Strife,
> Since I am turn'd the Husband, you the Wife ... (519–20)

The sharper, the less credible, and the more convinced we become that, after all, women do not mean it when they say they want sovereignty; women's rule is no more than a joke, and the real answer to the question what they desire is one known to any red-blooded man.

If finally I turn back to Chaucer's *Wife of Bath's Tale*, what in my view emerges from the comparison with Dryden is the positive value of the medieval poet's willingness not to be pointed, to allow the story to contain divergent meanings, alternative possibilities, loose ends, without necessarily tidying them up or even making them explicit.[23] The Loathly Lady's lecture makes the *Wife of Bath's Tale* one of Chaucer's most rhetorically directed poems; this must have been part of its attraction for Dryden, and in this as in so many respects Chaucer is the great innovator in whose work the seeds of later possibilities for English literature are already present. But they are present as seeds; and the temptation to find in Chaucer the full-grown blossoms that spring from them later needs to be resisted; this is as true of the 'fictional narrator' as it is of the fully thematized narrative. Chaucer's *Wife of Bath's Tale*, for all its teller's strength of will, is not entirely bent to her purpose and remains hospitable to a variety of readings. The almost inevitable tendency of academic interpretation is to find patterns and systems and to filter out what will not be reduced to pattern and system. One of the great merits of Derek Brewer's work has been to keep us aware of the medieval respect for stories as living sources of energy and storehouses of a human wisdom that goes beyond system; it is with that in mind that I offer this essay in affectionate tribute to him.

NOTES

1 'The Relationship of Chaucer to the English and European Traditions', in *Chaucer and Chaucerians*, ed. D. S. Brewer (London, 1966), 1–38, pp. 2, 4; 'Chaucer and Chrétien and Arthurian Romance', in *Tradition and Innovation in Chaucer* (London, 1982), 137–41, pp. 140, 139.

2 *The Testament of Love*, III, iv, in *Chaucerian and Other Pieces*, ed. W. W. Skeat (Oxford, 1897), p. 123. Cf. Brewer's useful distinction between the marvellous and the 'impossibly ingenious', and his statement that, whereas Chaucer 'accepts the marvellous in religious tales', 'In secular tales, specifically romance, [he] tends to exclude the marvellous, as far as he can, and even appears to despise it' ('Towards a Chaucerian Poetic', *Proceedings of the British Academy*, 60 [1974], 219–52, p. 226).

3 For argument in favour of this way of regarding the works mentioned, see my *Medieval to Renaissance in English Poetry* (Cambridge, 1985), pp. 34ff.

4 H. Marshall Leicester, 'Of a Fire in the Dark: Public and Private Feminism in the *Wife of Bath's Tale*', *Women's Studies*, 11 (1984), 157–78, sees the tale as a 'womanhandling' of a story 'which, as a chivalric romance, is in its original form an instrument of the dominant ideology and its values, such as loyalty and courtesy, that demonstrate male superiority' (p. 160); and Louise O. Fradenburg, 'The Wife of Bath's Passing Fancy', *Studies in the Age of Chaucer*, 8 (1986), 31–58, finds in it, along with its prologue, 'a demystification of romance' and 'a strong historical reading of the romance genre' (pp. 51, 56). I have been helped by both articles; it seems to me, however, that the former takes the Wife's consciousness for a solider fiction than it really is, while the latter, though splendidly intelligent and challenging, projects back into Chaucer a late twentieth-century reading of romance, thus writing another romance, in which 'capitalism' is the monster symbolizing all forms of constraint upon human freedom.

5 G. L. Kittredge, *Chaucer and His Poetry* (Cambridge, MA, 1915), p. 155.

6 'Towards a Chaucerian Poetic', p. 251. See also 'Gothic Chaucer', in *Tradition and Innovation*, 110–36, pp. 112–13; and the more recent critique of the Kittredge tradition by Derek Pearsall, *The Canterbury Tales* (London, 1985).

7 This appears to have been first suggested by Charles Owen, 'The Crucial Passages in Five of the *Canterbury Tales*: A Study in Irony and Symbol', *Journal of English and Germanic Philology*, 52 (1953), 294–311.

8 *The Parliament of Fowls*, 104–5.

9 *Symbolic Stories* (Cambridge, 1980), p. 11.

10 Cf. David Aers, *Chaucer, Langland and the Creative Imagination* (London, 1980), p. 84.

11 Gower's tale of Florent (*Confessio Amantis*, I, 1407–1861) writes the story somewhat differently, but still in terms of chivalric romance, with the knight as protagonist and central consciousness releasing the Loathly Lady from a magic spell.

12 Leicester, 'Of a Fire in the Dark', p. 173.

13 I quote Dryden from *The Poems of John Dryden*, ed. James Kinsley (Oxford, 1958), vol. IV; this is p. 1455, ll.426–35. (Where necessary for clarity line-numbers are accompanied by 'C' or 'D' to indicate Chaucer or Dryden.) Kittredge (*Chaucer*, pp. 153–4) recognized that Dryden was his predecessor in the 'human comedy' theory of the *Canterbury Tales*.

14 p. 1455, ll.453–4.

15 Dryden's assumption of a male reading public is revealed when he writes,
> Perhaps the Reader thinks I do him wrong
> To pass the Marriage-Feast, and Nuptial Song.   (338–9)

Here 'him' surely refers to the reader rather than to the knight.

16 D. W. Robertson, 'The Wife of Bath and Midas', *Studies in the Age of Chaucer*, 6 (1984), 1–20, p. 3, n. 8, notes that rape was a felony punishable by death in Chaucer's time.

17 Cf. Dryden's insertion of both anti-democratic and anti-tyrannical sentiments into his version of the *Knight's Tale* (III, 665ff. and 739), implying that inherited rank is the right basis for political order. On the political topicality of Dryden's translations, see William Frost, *Dryden and the Art of Translation* (New Haven, 1955), pp. 76–7.

18 Quotation from Johnson's *Lives of the Poets*. An especially fine addition of Dryden's is the triplet,
> Nobility of Blood is but Renown
> Of thy great Fathers by their Virtue known,
> And a long trail of Light, to thee descending down,   (439–41)

with its beautifully mimetic alexandrine.

19 Cf. Earl Miner, 'Chaucer in Dryden's *Fables*', in *Studies in Criticism and Aesthetics, 1600–1800*, ed. Howard Anderson and John S. Shea (Minneapolis, 1967), 58–72, p. 62: 'It cannot fail to strike a reader with both the medieval and Dryden's texts before him that in such alterations Dryden has "medievalized" the stories in a manner more often associated with the Romantics.'

20 E.g. Corbett's 'Proper New Ballad' and Herrick's fairy poems.

21 In view of what the knight does next, and of Dryden's predilection for indecent puns, his change of Spenser's 'gentle' to 'lusty' is probably meant to elicit an unSpenserian sense from 'pricking'.

22 See Anne Middleton, 'The Modern Art of Fortifying: *Palamon and Arcite* as Epicurean Epic', *Chaucer Review*, 3 (1968–9), 124–43, p. 126, drawing on Jean Hagstrum, *The Sister Arts* (Chicago, 1958), 178–210.

23 Anne Middleton, 'The *Physician's Tale* and Love's Martyrs: "Ensamples Mo Than Ten" as a Method in the *Canterbury Tales*', *Chaucer Review*, 8 (1973–4), 9–32, writes well of how 'The tales as Chaucer adapts them become consistently less neat, less economical, and far less palatable as ethical examples than their sources are' (p. 15).

17

Chaucer's religion and the Chaucer religion

CHARLES MUSCATINE

One of the most useful truisms in the study of literary reception – of the ways in which texts are read in times and places other than their own – is that reception has two aspects: it reveals something about the text itself and something about its new readers or critics. The most secure and satisfying reception-study finds these two aspects mutually explanatory. The assumption, at any rate, is that different ages or cultures do not so much misread a great text as make from it special abstractions, acutely suited to their particular concerns. The text that survives from age to age, receiving variant and sometimes antithetical interpretations, is typically not so much a compendium of perdurable truths that are sometimes misunderstood and sometimes distorted, but a structure so richly and complexly organized that different cultures, different audiences, can re-orient it (rotate it three-dimensionally as one might rotate an image in a computer) and then interpret it in ways that, however special, do answer to the work. The interpretation may often represent a very limited reception, depending on the limits of the receiving apparatus; but it receives something that is, after all, there. It responds to, and reveals, both aspects of the situation at once.

This, at least, has for a long time been the finding of leading students of the Chaucer tradition. Caroline Spurgeon's great collection of Chaucer criticism and allusion (1925) and Derek Brewer's *Chaucer: The Critical Heritage* (1978) are immensely satisfying works in that they provide just such mutual illumination between Chaucer and six centuries of English-speaking culture. Thus Chaucer's rhetoric both answers to and illustrates the fifteenth century's passion for a new ornament and eloquence in English. Chaucer's creditable learning is praised as early Humanism in the sixteenth century, and the attribution to him of such works as the spurious *Plowman's Tale* explains his enlistment in this period as a Lollard by anti-papal reformers. The growing interest in 'correctness' and polish, along with the progressive decay of the received text and the progressively antiquated appearance of Middle English explain, if they do not forgive, Chaucer's relative fall in popularity during the late seventeenth century and his frequently being modernized in the eighteenth. Brewer observes that during the eighteenth century, with the rise of the novel, Chaucer's poems 'begin to be read as novels' and that Thomas Gray, in 1760, finds in Chaucer undeniable but rarely noticed traces of Gothic Horror.[1] Chaucer's tenderness and sympathy are richly evoked by nineteenth-century critics, who also begin that preoccupation with Chaucer's realism, fed by an age of realism in fiction, that is still going strong today.

Indeed, the twentieth-century reception of Chaucer is in most respects a remarkably sensitive and accurate reflection both of his text and of twentieth-century sensibility. The vogue of Chaucer the realist was overlaid at mid-century by a decisive interest in Chaucer's ambiguity and irony, qualities, as Brewer says, 'that were not remarked on till the nineteenth century, and rarely then',[2] but that must henceforth be counted among his most characteristic traits as artist and as personality. And who will claim, reading the emergent poststructuralist interpretation of Chaucer, that this perennially cheerful and confident poet never expressed a twinge of the anxiety of influence, never wrestled with the slipperiness and intractability of language, never wrote a poem whose real theme was the agony of writing a poem?

There is, however, one additional aspect of the twentieth-century Chaucer that is most surprising and puzzling: the religious, almost puritanical Chaucer who emerges powerfully and suddenly at mid-century and is with us still. This Chaucer is an essentially new element in the Chaucer tradition; but it is peculiarly difficult to connect to late twentieth-century sensibility.

The new religious Chaucer can easily be distinguished from the figure who emerges from prior discussion of Chaucer's religion; it is a matter of distinguishing between Chaucer's doctrinal position and the quality of his piety, that is, the nature, range, depth, and intensity of his religious feeling itself. It is the latter, his enveloping religiosity, that seems to me to be a late twentieth-century discovery or preoccupation. The issue of his doctrinal position – whether he was orthodox or a reformer, whether a Lollard or not – was at its height in the Renaissance, and lost much of its energy with the purging of the spurious works from Tyrwhitt's edition on. It is for now fairly settled, with general agreement that Chaucer was a safely orthodox Catholic in doctrine. But this issue touched only tangentially, at best, on the deeper question, 'How *deeply* a Christian was Chaucer; or rather, how deeply does religion inform his work?' How deeply does his work express religious feeling? Where the doctrinal debate does touch on religiosity, it more often than not, and especially in the early twentieth century, lays Chaucer's religiosity open to serious question. Thus almost a century ago Thomas Lounsbury plausibly makes the case that Chaucer's temperament was not essentially religious at all. Chaucer's mind, Lounsbury thinks, was essentially sceptical. 'There are those', says Lounsbury, 'to whom faith is not so much a result of education or of conviction as it is a necessity of their being. It is natures of this kind that keep alive the religious flame in every age of doubt or unbelief ... It is hardly necessary to say that to this class Chaucer does not belong.'[3] To be sure, Chaucer has the capacity to feel 'the beauty of the life of sacrifice and devotion which inspires the purer and loftier natures that enter into the service of the church' (vol. II, p. 518); but Lounsbury actually traces a progressive dwindling in Chaucer's religiosity: the apostrophe to the Trinity at the end of the *Troilus* marks the height of his early, relatively religious phase. Thereafter, sceptical passages in the *Legend of Good Women* and the *Knight's Tale* point toward the full scepticism of the *Canterbury Tales* (vol. II, pp. 509–30).

Opinion through the middle of this century by and large supported Lounsbury's judgement; Chaucer the sceptic, Chaucer the detached, is of course hardly surprising in an age of science and of secularism. But it hardly prepares us for the new religious Chaucer, which has by now become so heavily settled in as to need no demonstration here.

It would, however, be a mistake to identify this view simply with the school of scholarship and criticism that one would perhaps think of first: the exegetical school associated for the past forty years with medieval studies at Princeton. The movement is broader than that, and has been carried on by a more central group of Chaucerians, who by now may have in varying degrees been influenced by the somewhat embattled and controversial exegetes, but who have remained independent of them, and have by themselves decisively coloured our view of the entire canon. Since there is scarcely room here to embrace so vast a subject, and since they have been especially revisionist as regards the *Canterbury Tales*, the point of this essay will perhaps be adequately made by reference to their criticism of that work alone.

The ur-text is the remarkable Johns Hopkins dissertation, *The Unity of the Canterbury Tales*, published in 150 copies in 1955 by Ralph Baldwin. Baldwin is among the first to have attributed sovereign importance of the idea of religious pilgrimage to Chaucer's *plan*, and to have followed out the idea in its grandest and fullest implications. If Kittredge had already dared say that the tales exist to illustrate the characters of the pilgrims,[4] Baldwin even more daringly finds that the pilgrims, along with their tales, exist for the pilgrimage. It, the pilgrimage, is the essential story that Chaucer tells:

> The drunken Miller, the rascally ecclesiastics, the Alisouns, the dutiful Parson and his brother – are all 'framed' in that common piety, a pilgrimage. Despite frivolities and arguments, rancor and raciness, they have been conjured into existence as wayfarers and they activate a drama that does not cease for each of them with his tale. The via of Pilgrimage and the viae of the Pilgrims merge and measure off a story whose milestones are visible only in terms of Him 'that hem hath holpen whan that they were seeke' [I(A) 18]. Some physical or spiritual sickness has put them *en route* to Canterbury, and one of the Enveloping Actions of the *CT* is the intercessory one of St Thomas à Becket, who is with them intentionally from the moment they convene at the Tabard. The 'ways that lead to Christ' are as various as the Specific Actions of these convergent pilgrims. And our approach to the text seems to indicate that, using the Host's

insistence on merriment as a foil, Chaucer has set his pilgrims on the road to
glory.   (pp. 78–9)

The secular tales are thus gathered and subsumed within the folds of a deeply
religious conception: life as a pilgrimage to the New Jerusalem. It is a
metaphor that Chaucer uses touchingly in his lyric *Truth*, and gives to the
Parson to introduce his telling of the last of the tales:

> To shewe yow the wey, in this viage,
> Of thilke parfit glorious pilgrymage,
> That highte Jerusalem celestial.   (x, 49–51)

Seen this way, the *Canterbury Tales* becomes an essentially religious work, the
Parson's Tale becomes an unprecedently important part of it, and Chaucer, in
his ripe maturity, becomes transcendently a religious poet.

The idea was apparently one whose time had come. By 1979, in a brief
survey of the state of Chaucer studies, Florence Ridley could confidently
say that 'all the individual Canterbury Tales must be seen in the context of
the last, *The Parson's Tale*. And in that light, even those tales which during
the process of their telling do, indeed, "sownen into synne," become
exemplars of the heedlessness and folly which each man must overcome if
he is to reach the ultimate shrine of heaven.'[5] In the same survey Ridley
reviews Donald Howard's *The Idea of the Canterbury Tales*[6] – three times the
length of Baldwin's book – devoted to the same general thesis, giving the
same importance to the structural and metaphorical power of the pilgrimage, and thus the same crucial importance to the *Parsons's Tale*. The idea
is a commonplace in the pages of the present decade's Chaucer criticism,
and comes to a peak of elaboration in V. A. Kolve's *Chaucer and the Imagery
of Narrative*, an intensely close reading of the first five of the *Canterbury Tales*.
Kolve not only seizes upon the idea of the religious Chaucer's religious
pilgrimage as the overarching structural idea of the poem; he also finds a
series of substructures of the same shape within the poem. Thus the pious
and hitherto rather unprepossessing *Man of Law's Tale*, in his reading,
becomes the climactic corrective, a 'provisional palinode', to what Kolve
takes as the first day's daring but unchristian excursions into pagan philosophizing and bawdiness.[7]

It is evident enough, then, that the religious Chaucer is a powerful new
reading which should, like the other great readings of the past, lead us to
deepened awareness of what is there in the text awaiting new appreciation.
But the reading remains, in my opinion, both surprising and troubling. Before
stating my misgivings, I should make clear what it is that I am not contesting.
In the first place, there is little doubt that for all or most of his life Chaucer was
a loyal Catholic, and – since his retractation seems both genuine and sincere –
that at the very end he was in a mood of deep, Christian contrition. It is also
clear that most of the mainstream critics, in contemplating the religious
Chaucer, have not done so crudely. They have been aware of, and have
confronted both aesthetically and historically, such apparent paradoxes as a

fundamentally Christian poem's containing a majority of secular, bawdy fabliaux; or of its having to be retracted by its author at all.

In general they have offered highly sophisticated explanations. Thus Alfred David sees the whole of the *Canterbury Tales* as a sort of *agon* between the secular artist and the Christian moralist who is the final victor.[8] Donald Howard comes to see the poems as a single confrontation: there are 'two books' within the *Canterbury Tales*; one book is the sequence of tales up to but not including the last, that represents the errant world, a world that is lost unless it be confronted, as it is, by the second, the Parson's tract on Sin and Penitence, which 'puts a qualification on art itself'.[9] Lee Patterson, rejecting the idea of pilgrimage or of anything else as the controlling pattern of the *Canterbury Tales*, sees the *Parson's Tale* (with the *Manciple's Tale* preceding) as the alternative offered to the meaninglessness and failure 'of the whole poetic enterprise': 'For his sober and prosaic treatise is a rejection of all personal speaking that does not confront, in the sacramental language of penance, the sinfulness of the human condition. It is not merely the qualifying complexities of language that are to be abandoned, but any language that does not deal with sin in the terms defined by the Parson.'[10]

The very sophistication of this sort of criticism is a source of concern; the case being made here is too neat, and, in a way, too full of thought. Going back to the question of religious sensibility, and for touchstones thinking of half a dozen of the best religious poets – of Dante, Langland, the Pearl poet, Donne, Milton, Hopkins – what does Chaucer teach us to feel? What, on balance, is his legacy as a religious poet? Most of what is being said about the new religious Chaucer is telling us relatively little that is new about the religious *quality* of his poetry, however much about the ideas of pilgrimage, of penance, of sin and contrition, of pride and charity, of art versus morality, and about the difference between the sensibility of the Age of Faith and that of our own. For lack of a new and finer delineation of his *religiosity*, his religion remains a rather mixed and not altogether impressive thing.

There are, of course, great and religiously moving moments in Chaucer; perhaps the greatest is in the ending of the *Troilus* (v, 1835ff.):

> O yonge, fresshe folkes, he or she,
> In which that love up groweth with youre age,
> Repeyreth hom fro worldly vanyte,
> And of youre herte up casteth the visage
> To thilke God that after his ymage
> Yow made, and thynketh al nys but a faire
> This world, that passeth soone as floures faire.

> And loveth hym, the which that right for love
> Upon a crois, oure soules for to beye,
> First starf, and roos, and sit in hevene above;
> For he nyl falsen no wight, dar I seye,
> That wol his herte al holly on hym leye.
> And syn he best to love is, and most meke,
> What nedeth feynede loves for to seke?

The pity is that moments like this are just isolated moments, and they rarely appear in Chaucer's avowedly religious works at all. As has been observed before, his career as a religious writer seems to have had a number of phases. The first possibly includes the *ABC* and the *Second Nun's Tale*. A lyric on the Blessed Virgin and a saint's life, they are usually classified as standard medieval fare, and suggest a youthful and rather passive, conformist religiosity. But they have a kind of integrity about them. Both are translations, and both are unembellished, presented much as they were received; they seem to say that if Chaucer's feelings were passive and conformist, he at least was perfectly honest about it, and pretended no more.

Practised readers of Chaucer notice at once that these presumably early works have almost no trace of pathos in them; and that marks them off from what might be construed as a later stage of his religiosity, which is engaged much with the Blessed Virgin and with images of suffering women and children. This pathetic religiosity, one that conveys powerful feelings of tenderness and pity, is to my mind at the highest level that Chaucer's *sustained* achievement as a religious poet ever reaches. Its masterpiece is the *Prioress's Tale*. There are some unforgettable passages in the pious tale of the Man of Law; this one (II, 841ff.) reminds us that Chaucer *could* write a great prayer:

> 'Mooder', quod she, 'and mayde bright, Marie,
> Sooth is that thurgh wommanes eggement
> Mankynde was lorn, and damned ay to dye,
> For which thy child was on a croys yrent.
> Thy blisful eyen sawe al his torment;
> Thanne is ther no comparison bitwene
> Thy wo and any wo man may sustene.
>
> 'Thow sawe thy child yslayn bifore thyne yen,
> And yet now lyveth my litel child, parfay!
> Now, lady bright, to whom alle woful cryen,
> Thow glorie of wommanhede, thow faire may,
> Thow haven of refut, brighte sterre of day,
> Rewe on my child, that of thy gentillesse,
> Rewest on every reweful in distresse.'

Moving as this note in Chaucer can be, it must be recognized as a very special note, that explores, however beautifully, only a narrow sector of religious feeling. It is not even an exclusively religious note, but can be found in secular dress in a number of other poems: the Hugelino episode of the *Monk's Tale*, the *Physician's Tale*, and the *Clerk's Tale*, and is closely related in Chaucer's sensibility to an even wider range of pathos (we might call it Ovidian pathos) to be found plentifully in the *Legend of Good Women* and the Dido episode of the *House of Fame*. Chaucer's pathetic religiosity, then, might more accurately be called his pathos in a religious vein, which does not lessen its value, but underlines perhaps his limitations as a religious poet. We come up against these limitations, almost embarrassingly, in the *Man of Law's Tale*, an overtly religious legend in which Chaucer repeatedly challenges himself to rise to the expression of deep religious feeling, and, except for the passages of pathos, fails. Chaucer – along with Langland and Dante – was at times capable of generating religious sublimity with the plain style, but here he reaches for it with high style, with rhetoric. The Christian noblewoman Constance somehow escapes being slaughtered with her fellow-Christians at a feast arranged by her pagan mother-in-law in Syria. She then is set adrift by wicked pagans in a rudderless boat, whence she drifts, in the course of years, to the coast of Northumberland. How, asks the poet, did she survive? His answer (II, 470–504) is poetically one of the lowest points in his entire *oeuvre*. We need contemplate only a couple of stanzas:

> Men myghten asken why she was nat slayn
> Eek at the feeste? Who myghte hir body save?
> And I answere to that demande agayn,
> Who saved Danyel in the horrible cave
> Ther every wight save he, maister and knave,
> Was with the leon frete er he asterte?
> No wight but God, that he bar in his herte.
>
> God liste to shewe his wonderful myracle
> In hire, for we sholde seen his mighty werkis;
> Crist, which that is to every harm triacle,
> By certeine meenes ofte, as knowen clerkis,
> Dooth thyng for certein ende that ful derk is
> To mannes wit, that for oure ignorance
> Ne konne noght knowe his prudent purveiance.   (470–83)

Passages like this, with their fillers, awkward rhymes, uneasy management of rhythm, and slackness of diction, remind us of a fact of Chaucer's life suggested in the *Prologue* to the *Legend of Good Women*, but too seldom reflected upon, that the poet was from time to time bidden by important people to write things 'and durste yt nat withseye' (F, 367). How else to account for work so ambitiously conceived and so cumbersomely executed?

Would that similar speculation could as readily account for the next problem that arises with Chaucer's new reputation as a religious author; and that is the unprecedented value it confers on the *Parson's Tale*. For there was never, perhaps, a less likely candidate for literary importance in the work of any great poet. The *Tale* is not poetry, of course, but a prose compilation from a sermon on penitence and a tract on the seven deadly sins, both originating in Latin. It is itself a tract, hardly intended that we should imagine it to have been recited aloud. (That would have taken about four hours and a quarter.) Until recently almost no one but specialists read it, and that under a species of compulsion. As literature, it rivals the work of Lydgate as a traditional object of derision. 'Nothing much more wearisome can well be imagined', says Lounsbury, 'than the worthy priest's disquisition on the various venial and deadly sins to which man's nature is exposed, and the various remedies against them. For the ordinary reader it is one long level of tediousness, save in two or three places where the preacher steps aside to denounce some particular manifestation of evil.'[11]

The new view of the religious significance of the *Canterbury Tales* has made its way with astonishing blitheness through a thicket of uncertainties about the status of the *Parson's Tale*. The problem is complex, and its more intricate considerations have no place here; but to indicate a few of its major aspects will suffice to illustrate the force and confidence of the new view itself.

The very authenticity of the *Parson's Tale* has long been challenged. The challenge has just as long been beaten off, mostly by the sensible observation that we cannot banish works from the canon just because we don't like them. It is possible still to argue that Chaucer could have owned and studied it without having translated it. But I see no reason, given Chaucer's apparent taste for such a dull piece of edifying prose as the *Melibee*, not to imagine the *Parson's Tale* also as Chaucer's, as produced at the behest of someone who could not be refused, or in a mood of contrition, or, most likely, as a laborious act of penance. The real problem – it is no less than an embarrassment – arises not so much from the presumption of Chaucer's authorship, as from its inclusion in the *Canterbury Tales* and its newly crucial significance as the last of them. Here we run up against the entirely uncertain history of the putting-together of the *Canterbury Tales*. We don't know who put them together. There is almost full agreement that the earliest and best manuscripts were assembled by persons other than Chaucer in the second decade after his death. The evidence of the manuscripts suggests that he left his desk or his files in a mess; that some of the tales in the final collection were written before he had an idea of a collection, and that only some were securely attached by him to the collection. Some bear no particular relation to the teller assigned, and it appears that from time to time Chaucer or someone else may have switched tellers. We know that the editors or scribes of the fifteenth century had a field day inventing orders of the tales, writing links to make them fit, and making ascriptions of pilgrims to them. Chaucer, in fact, left on his desk no book of the *Canterbury Tales*, but rather ten groups or fragments. Except for fragment I(A), which opens the work; for a scattering of (often irreconcilable) references to places and times of the day; and for the *Parson's Prologue*, which sounds genuine and which will introduce the last of the tales, Chaucer had not worked out, or at least had not written down, a plan for the order of the fragments. The inclusion in the *Canterbury Tales* of any work that happened by chance to be lying among his papers is a distinct possibility, whether done posthumously by his executors or editors, or by his family, or even, at the last moment, by himself. The fact that there is appended to the *Parson's Tale* in all the best manuscripts the pious retractation by Chaucer of all his sinful works – a retractation listing the *Canterbury Tales* among other works but indicating no more specific connection to it – makes it more than possible that the *Parson's Tale* found its way into the *Canterbury Tales* under unusual circumstances, perhaps in anticipation of death, and unrelated to the literary and artistic making of the rest of the work. All arguments about the plan or structure or sequence or even the canon of the tales have to be made with the circumspection imposed by these conditions.

Let us turn to the context of the *Parson's Tale* in the action of the poem. The *Parson's Prologue* seems genuine, and there can be little doubt that Chaucer's sense of decorum led him to feel that the Parson should tell the last tale. Boccaccio had had a similar feeling about ending the *Decameron*; secular as the work might be, the accomplishment, the completion of so great a work was in itself a sobering event, an occasion for humble thanksgiving, as would also be the accomplishment of a pilgrimage. There is every reason to feel the rightness of the Parson's awareness of the grand analogy between a pilgrimage to Canterbury and 'thilke parfit glorious pilgrymage / That highte Jerusalem celestial'. It is an important moment. There is likely a special poetic resonance in Chaucer's locating of the action vaguely and yet precisely: 'we were entryng at a thropes ende' (x, 12) he says, and it was four o'clock in the afternoon of the last day. The Host calls on the Parson 'to knytte up well a greet mateere', (x, 28) but characteristically he calls for a 'fable' (x, 29). The Parson will have nothing of fables, nothing even of verse. He will tell, he announces, 'a myrie tale in prose / To knytte up al this feeste, and make an ende' (x, 46–7). There is no problem with the word 'myrie' – we know enough about the terms for happiness and joy in religious contexts to accept 'myrie' as a religious term. But in the brief discussion that ensues, the Parson's imminent contribution is once again called a 'tale', once a piece dealing in 'vertuous sentence' (x, 63), and twice a 'meditacioun' (x, 55, 79). The Host, practical as ever, remarks that the sun is about to set – as it would be at four on an April afternoon in southern England – and asks the Parson to be economical – to recite 'in litel space'. Then comes, in the manuscripts, what we know as the *Parson's Tale*. The gross lack of dramatic verisimilitude here is one problem, though Chaucer did not always worry about verisimilitude if other and higher goals – as, for instance, philosophizing – were at hand. But it seems to me that the forecast of the *genre* of the *Parson's Tale* here must give us pause. A 'tale'? A 'meditacioun'? Well, a 'tale' might be almost any recitation; but how well does the *Parson's Tale* answer to 'a meditacioun'?

To my knowledge the question has not yet been given a satisfactory treatment; but for lack of a study of the meditation as genre in Middle English, we can at least consult the *Middle English Dictionary* under 'Meditation'. The overwhelming number – dozens – of examples of the word, dating from the early thirteenth century, illustrate its first meaning, which is 'meditation; contemplation; devout preoccupation; devotions; prayer'. A small second group of meanings simply show the first meaning in compound with certain verbs: to have or take or make or say one's meditation. Finally there is a third meaning, based on four examples which are reported to use 'meditation' to mean 'a moral discourse'. However, since two of the four are from the very passage we are examining, we must suspend judgement on them. The only two remaining examples of the meaning listed, from 1400, are from a translation of the well-known thirteenth-century life of Christ of the pseudo-Bonaventura. One is a translation of an *incipit*: 'Here byggynneth medytaciouns of the soper of oure lorde Ihesu And also of his passyun.' The other reads: 'Y wil the lere a medytacyun Compyled of crystys passyun and of hys modyr . . . what peynes they suffred thou mayst lere.' What this text offers under the label of 'meditation' is not any old moral discourse, but thoughts based on sacred biography, on religious narrative. And it is significant that among all the uses of meditation in the first and second senses, those that go beyond meditation or prayer in general or in the abstract, mostly refer to it in terms of joy, pleasure, the fervour of religious love; and for the single cited example that does suggest meditation on sin and hell, there are five that refer to meditations on the lives of Christ and of Mary, and their meaning. The repeated use of the term 'meditation' in the *Parson's Prologue* suggests preliminarily, then, that the Parson may have been at one time intended to 'knytte up' the 'feeste' with a work quite different in character and in tone, more fitting to the occasion, and certainly closer to Chaucer's known talents and tastes in religious subjects, than the piece we have.[12]

The argument that the Tale is so hopeless as art as not to be admissible as Chaucer's work, while not itself a hopeless argument, we have already generously abandoned. Let us go on to a related but different issue: that is, that the *Parson's Tale* simply *sounds* wrong in subject and point-of-view for the last place in the Tales. Chaucer had done last places in texts in a religious vein before; the ending of the *Troilus* is one. One remembers too the ending of the fourth book of the translation of Boethius: 'Goth now thanne, ye stronge men, ther as the heye wey of the greet ensaumple ledith yow. O nyce men! why nake ye your bakkes? . . . For the erthe overcomen yeveth the sterres.' Chaucer knew great religious utterances when he heard them. From the ending of the *Troilus* and the very opening of the *Canterbury Tales* we are prepared for a generous, complex tension in Chaucer's view of the realms of secular and divine; we are prepared, even, for a ceremonially sober and conservative closure to the *Tales*, a beckoning to the contemplation of higher things. What, then, is he doing with this endless, narrow, small-minded, inveterately enumerative, circumstantially punitive list of sinful acts?

It would argue a sorry ignorance of Catholic doctrine or of medieval culture to suggest that such a document had no place in Chaucer's world. But the *Parson's Tale* doesn't sound as if it belongs to the end of the *Canterbury Tales*; it forces on the other tales a sharp and almost grotesquely narrow confrontation – a bald, unrelieved confrontation, without appreciation, or pity or regret – that Professor Howard senses and accepts, but which some readers still find profoundly unChaucerian. It seems, as E. Talbot Donaldson says, 'wrong to read, as so many wish to do, the Parson's Tale as a reliable gloss on the rest of the *Canterbury Tales*'.[13] If, as has been argued, the very baldness of the *Parson's*

Tale signalizes Chaucer's explicit renunciation of art and even of literary language at this point, is it licit to yoke the piece retrospectively in any significant way with the literary art which it abandons? Would it not be more fitting rather to regard it as marking a trauma, a biographical or historical accident, something sudden, and rather pathetic?

I do not mean by expressing these speculations and doubts to assert facts that can't be proven. I mean only to suggest how speculative and doubtful it is to take so confidently the other position; and to raise a final question. Our experience of the Chaucer tradition, and its spirit, suggest that the new religious Chaucer should somehow be there, in the text; otherwise good critics and scholars, persons of talent and good will, would not have discovered him. Yet in this case the heavy weight of meaning that has been newly loaded upon the text suggests that a religious, almost puritanical Chaucer is less interesting as a discovery of twentieth-century critics than as their creation. I would almost call it a confection, that tells us perhaps more about the critics than it does about Chaucer. This reading of Chaucer involves the confident ignoring of so many of Chaucer's poetic and temperamental traits, the confident surmounting of so many factual or scholarly ifs and doubts, the ignoring of such palpable artistic embarrassments, that one is impelled to wonder – as one is even more easily impelled to wonder about the 'exegetical' reading – what in the culture of the second half of the twentieth century explains or responds to the discovery of a newly religious Chaucer.

It is a subject for an anthropologist or sociologist. Unfortunately no one has done a survey of the religious tendencies of medievalists. It is difficult to imagine any relationship whatever between what we are studying and the recent recrudescence of popular religion in America. I would guess, however, that an appreciable though small number of us have come to medieval studies as being congenial with our own prior religious sensibilities, and we can be expected to be especially appreciative of the religious dimension in any text. A few of us, I suspect, actually teach medieval literature as a pious exercise, and ask of ourselves and our students and colleagues more than an aesthetic appreciation of religious poetry. But even assuming that academics tend to be proper, moral folk, and would rather take the part of morality and religion than not, there must be something more in the air, something that prompted Ralph Baldwin to see the *Parson's Tale* as from the first the 'destination' of the *Canterbury Tales*, and when he reached that destination to evoke from him almost a lyric note:

> Chaucer and his pilgrims realize that they have jollied one another, and bandied about triviality, entertainment, and bawdry on the journey. But the ever-present, ever-prescient *memento mori* sets a date of death upon every action, and signs it for all eternity. The terms and finalities of a sacramental system made the beginning of the end a somewhat more obtrusive daily fact than it is today. There is its warning to 'learn to die daily,' with the omnipresence of the Four Last Things: Death, Judgment, Hell, Heaven. There is the terrible knowledge

that the soul is bound not by time but by state or condition, and the conviction
that 'a happy death is death in the state of grace, the death of the predestinate or
elect.' Finally, there is the realization that such a happy death is a special gift,
that one cannot presume upon the providence of God, and that of the person,
either living or moribund, has no right to the grace of final perseverance.

(p. 99)

Even Professor Kolve, one of the finest medieval scholars and critics of our
day, confronting the *Parson's Tale* at the conclusion of his book, speaks of the
sermon–treatise as having 'intellectual and moral beauty' sufficient to 'miti-
gate the shock' of the renunciation that it calls for, to make that renunciation
'acceptable and even welcome'.[14]

Whatever of Christian religious sentiment is operative here, it seems to me
to be mixed in these and many other critics and scholars with another piety, a
piety centred around the poet himself, and perhaps even around the study of
literature. One of the striking things, one of the most attractive things about
the 'religious' Chaucer is that he solves problems and provides answers about
Chaucer. An immensely, seductively important corollary of Baldwin's thesis
is that it virtually cleans up the mess – the problem of the structure – of the
traditional *Canterbury Tales*. It gives it, in his words, a new 'wholeness and
aesthetic pattern' (p. 15). 'If the Canterbury Tales is incomplete, it cannot
properly be called unfinished' (p. 110). Twenty years later the notion is so
congenial to Donald Howard that he can even play with it. The work is by its
nature unfinished, he says, but 'the idea ... is complete'.[15]

I cannot detail here how these views coincide with the apparent 'solving' of
other perennial problems, as whether Chaucer intended a return journey or
not (he didn't), as what the correct order of the Tales is, and as what was
Chaucer's relation to Dante. It fits with such growing hallucinations in recent
Chaucer criticism as that every vagrant turn or twitch in Chaucer's text must
be pregnant with deep meaning, or that the Canterbury pilgrims were real
people, whose psyches can be analysed with clinical complexity, and who can
be blamed for every infelicity in the text. It seems related to the growth of a
Chaucer Industry; to the entry of Chaucer into the class of literary superstars
like Homer and Shakespeare and Aristotle and Dante, of whom one does not
speak ill, in whom one does not find faults,[16] and whom one can invoke to
verify and support one's own innermost values. There is abroad in our time a
sort of Chaucer religion.

It is possible to view this Chaucer religion, with its newly discovered
symmetries and wholenesses and orthodoxies in Chaucer's texts, as having at
first been part of a late flowering of mid-century formalism.[17] Latterly, it
seems to be a part of a conservative movement that has been gathering itself
against the growing radicalism of intellectual life in the literary establishment.
Almost every other development in contemporary criticism tends to threaten
the integrity of the text, and the literary tradition: deconstruction, neo-
Marxist criticism, reader-response theory, feminist theory, neo-Freudianism,

hermeneutics, performance theory – all of these threaten to remake entirely the way we have understood, and thought understandable, the literary tradition itself. Perhaps the Chaucer religion has owed its continuing strength to its contributing in part to an attempted defence, a closing of ranks, in the face of a profound cultural threat. If so, there is much in it with which to sympathize. But it is worrisome too. For a scholarship that is also a religion, even if it be a religion of Literature or of Culture, is in danger of losing its status as scholarship.

These, of course, are only tentative speculations, and their subject may turn out to be as transient as many other moments in the Chaucer tradition; the puritanical Chaucer may already be undergoing considerable deconstruction. Meanwhile, we may continue to wonder with Pandarus what sort of enemy it is

> That so kan leye oure jolite on presse,
> And bringe oure lusty folk to holynesse!

NOTES

1 Derek Brewer, 'Images of Chaucer 1386–1900', in *Chaucer and Chaucerians*, ed. D. S. Brewer (London, 1966), pp. 258–60.

2 Brewer, 'Images', p. 269.

3 Thomas R. Lounsbury, *Studies in Chaucer*, 3 vols. (New York, 1892), vol. II, p. 508.

4 George Lyman Kittredge, *Chaucer and his Poetry* (Cambridge, Mass., 1915).

5 Florence Ridley, 'The State of Chaucer Studies', *Studies in the Age of Chaucer*, I (1979), p. 14.

6 Donald Howard, *The Idea of the Canterbury Tales* (Berkeley, 1976).

7 V. A. Kolve, *Chaucer and the Imagery of Narrative: The First Five Canterbury Tales* (Stanford, 1984), p. 369.

8 Alfred David, *The Strumpet Muse: Art and Morals in Chaucer's Poetry* (Bloomington, 1976).

9 Howard, *Idea of the Canterbury Tales*, p. 381.

10 Lee Patterson, 'The "Parson's Tale" and the Quitting of the "Canterbury Tales" ' *Traditio*, 34 (1978), pp. 376–9.

11 Lounsbury, *Studies*, vol. I, p. 206.

12 I am preparing a more detailed study of the use of the term 'meditation' to denote genre in Middle English. My preliminary impression is that among Middle English genres there is a reasonably clear distinction between works chiefly devoted to the inculcation of formal Christian doctrine and its practical application in daily life, and the meditation, which is more affective in character, approaching the nature of prayer. But in many works the two motives were combined. See, e.g., Peter Revell, *Fifteenth Century English Prayers and Meditations: A Descriptive list of Manuscripts in the British Library* (New York, 1975), pp. vii–viii; P. S. Jolliffe, *A Check-List of Middle English Prose Writings of Spiritual Guidance* (Toronto, 1974), pp. 29–30; John C. Hirsh, 'Prayer and Meditation in Late Medieval England', *Medium Aevum*, 48 (1979), pp. 55–66; C. A. Martin, 'Middle English Manuals of Religious Instruction', in *So Meny People Longages and Tonges* (*Essays presented to Angus McIntosh*), ed. Michael Benskin and M. L. Samuels (Edinburgh, 1981), p. 291.

13 E. Talbot Donaldson, *Speaking of Chaucer* (London, 1970), p. 172.

14 Kolve, *Chaucer and the Imagery of Narrative*, p. 370.
15 Howard, *Idea of the Canterbury Tales*, p. 385.
16 Kittredge's famous remark, that 'Chaucer always knew what he was about' (*Poetry of Chaucer*, p. 15), was defensible in 1915, amid readers relatively untutored in medieval convention. In terms of the biographies of most poets, however, it seems absurd.
17 An idea suggested by Professor Wendy Clein in discussion of the present essay.

18
A list of the published writings of Derek Brewer

TOSHIYUKI TAKAMIYA

The following list of the published writings of Professor Derek Brewer comprises his academic publications and excludes book reviews, except for a few significant ones, non-academic articles, poems, obituaries, and editorials (he was the editor of *The Cambridge Review*, 1981–6). The compiler wishes to express his gratitude to Mrs Brewer and Mr Takami Matsuda for their help at various stages.

1948　'Gawayn and the Green Chapel', *Notes and Queries*, 193 (1948), 13.

1951　'A History of English Studies in the University of Birmingham', *English and Germanic Studies*, 3 (1950–1), 1–32.

1952　'Form in the *Morte Darthur*', *Medium Aevum*, 21 (1952), 14–24. (Revised as 'the hoole book' in *Essays on Malory*, ed. J. A. W. Bennett, 1963, pp. 41–63.)
　　　'*Wanderer*, Lines 50–57', *Modern Language Notes*, 67 (1952), 398–9.
　　　'Brutus's Crime: A Footnote to *Julius Caesar*', *Review of English Studies*, 3 (1952), 51–4.

1953　*Chaucer*, 1953.
　　　'Sixteenth, Seventeenth and Eighteenth Century References to the Voyage of Ohthere', *Anglia*, 71 (1953), 202–11.

1954　'Chaucer's *Complaint of Mars*', *Notes and Queries*, NS, 1 (1954), 462–3.
　　　'Love and Marriage in Chaucer's Poetry', *Modern Language Review*, 49 (1954), 461–4.
　　　'Metaphor and Symbol in the Sixteenth Century: A Comment', *Essays in Criticism*, 4 (1954), 108–11.
　　　'Observations on a Fifteenth Century Manuscript', *Anglia*, 72 (1954), 390–9.

1955　'The Ideal of Feminine Beauty in Medieval Literature, Especially Harley Lyrics, Chaucer and Some Elizabethans', *Modern Language Review*, 50 (1955), 257–69.
　　　'*Measure for Measure*, I, i, 3–9', *Notes and Queries*, NS, 2 (1955), 425.
　　　'Lucretius and Bacon on Death', *Notes and Queries*, NS, 2 (1955), 509–10.

1956　'The Parlement of Foulys', *Essays in Criticism*, 6 (1956), 248.
　　　'The Augustinian and Possibly West Midland Origin of the *Ancrene Riwle*', *Notes and Queries*, NS, 3 (1956), 232–6.

1957   Sections on 'Chaucer', 'Fifteenth-Century Verse', and 'Fifteenth-Century Prose', in the *Supplement to the Cambridge Bibliography of English Literature*, 1957.
       'Dualism in the Poetry of W. H. Auden', *Hiroshima Studies in English Language and Literature*, 4 (1957), 1–14.

1958   *Proteus: Studies in English Literature*, 1958.
       'The Genre of the *Parlement of Foules*', *Modern Language Review*, 53 (1958), 321–6.
       'Graham Greene and a Doctrine of Opposites', *Essays and Studies in British and American Literature* (Tokyo), 6 (1958), 1–14.

1960   *The Parlement of Foulys*, ed. D. S. Brewer, 1960.
       Chaucer, 2nd revised edn, 1960.

1961   'English in the University: III. Language and Literature', with F. W. Bateson, *Essays in Criticism*, 11 (1961), 243–55.
       'The Study of English Literature outside England', *Venture* (Karachi) (1961).

1962   'English in the University: Language and Literature', with A. M. Pirkhofer and F. W. Bateson, *Essays in Criticism*, 12 (1962), 104–10.

1963   'Geoffrey Chaucer', *Encyclopaedia Britannica*, 14th edn, vol. 5 (1963), pp. 350–5. (An abridged Japanese translation by Shinsuke Ando in *Britannica International Encyclopedia*, vol. 13 (1974), pp. 446–50.)
       Chaucer in His Time, 1963.
       'the hoole book', *Essays on Malory*, ed. J. A. W. Bennett, 1963, pp. 41–63.

1964   'Children in Chaucer', *Review of English Literature*, 5 (1964), 52–60.

1965   'An Unpublished Late Alliterative Poem', *English Philological Studies*, 9 (1965), 84–8.

1966   'Courtesy and the *Gawain*-Poet', *Patterns of Love and Courtesy: Essays in Memory of C. S. Lewis*, ed. John Lawlor, 1966, pp. 54–85. (Reprinted in *Chaucer and his Contemporaries: Essays on Medieval Literature and Thought*, ed. Helaine Newstead, 1968.)
       Chaucer and Chaucerians: Critical Studies in Middle English Literature, ed. D. S. Brewer, 1966. (Contains 'The Relationship of Chaucer to the English and European Traditions', pp. 1–38 and 'Images of Chaucer 1386–1900', pp. 240–70.)

1967   'The *Gawain*-Poet: A General Appreciation of the Four Poems', *Essays in Criticism*, 17 (1967), 130–42.

1968   'The Fabliaux', *Companion to Chaucer Studies*, ed. Beryl Rowland, 1968, pp. 247–67.
       'Class Distinction in Chaucer', *Speculum*, 43 (1968), 290–305.
       The Morte Darthur: Parts Seven and Eight, ed. D. S. Brewer, 1968.

1969   *Geoffrey Chaucer. The Works 1532 with Supplementary Materials from the Editions of 1542, 1561, 1598 and 1602*, ed. D. S. Brewer, 1969.
       'The Criticism of Chaucer in the Twentieth Century', *Chaucer's Mind and Art*, ed. A. C. Cawley, 1969, pp. 3–28.

Troilus and Criseyde (abridged), ed. D. S. Brewer and L. Elisabeth Brewer, 1969.

1970 '*Troilus and Criseyde*', *Sphere History of Literature in the English Language*, vol. I: The Middle Ages, ed. W. F. Bolton, 1970, pp. 195–228.

'The Present Study of Malory', *Forum for Modern Language Studies*, 6 (1970), 83–97. (Reprinted in Arthurian Romance: Seven Essays, ed. D. D. R. Owen, 1970, pp. 83–97.)

'Malory Re-edited', *Medium Ævum*, 39 (1970), 35–9.

1971 '*The Reeve's Tale* and the King's Hall, Cambridge', *Chaucer Review*, 5 (1971), 311–17.

1972 'The Ages of Troilus, Criseyde and Pandarus', *Studies in English Literature*, English Number 1972, 3–13.

1973 'Honour in Chaucer', *Essays and Studies*, 26 (1973), 1–19.

Chaucer, 3rd edn, revised and enlarged, 1973.

'Notes toward a Theory of Medieval Comedy' and Translations of Selected Tales from F. Sacchetti the Fourteenth Century Italian Writer, *Medieval Comic Tales*, by Peter Rickard and Others, 1973.

1974 'Some Metonymic Relationships in Chaucer's Poetry', *Poetica*, 1 (1974), 1–20.

'Chaucer and Chrétien and Arthurian Romance', *Chaucer and Middle English Studies in Honour of Rossell Hope Robbins*, ed. Beryl Rowland, 1974, pp. 255–9.

'Some Observations on the Development of Literalism and Verbal Criticism', *Poetica*, 2 (1974), 71–95.

'Towards a Chaucerian Poetic', *Proceedings of the British Academy*, 60 (1974), 219–52. (Reprinted in *Middle English Literature: British Academy Gollancz Lectures*, selected and introduced by J. A. Burrow, 1989).

Cleanness: An Alliterative Tripartite Poem, ed. Israel Gollancz with new English translation by D. S. Brewer, 1974.

Writers and their Background: Geoffrey Chaucer, ed. D. S. Brewer, 1974. (Contains 'Gothic Chaucer', pp. 1–32.)

'Twf Rhyddiath Gyfiaith yn Ewrop' (i.e. 'The Growth of European Vernacular Prose' translated into Welsh, not published in English), *Y Traddodiad Rhyddiath*. Gol. G. Bowen, 1974.

1975 *The Thornton Manuscript (Lincoln Cathedral MS 91)*, with introductions by D. S. Brewer and A. E. B. Owen, 1975.

'Structures and Character-Types of Chaucer's Popular Comic Tales', *Estudios sobre los géneros literarios, I: Grecia clásica e Inglaterra*, ed. J. Coy and J. de Hoz, 1975, pp. 107–18.

'Shakespearian Comedy: Structure and Character-Types', *Estudios sobre los géneros literarios, I: Grecia clásica e Inglaterra*, ed. J. Coy and J. de Hoz, 1975, pp. 119–29.

1976   'The Interpretation of Dream, Folktale and Romance with Special
       Reference to *Sir Gawain and the Green Knight*', *Neuphilologische Mittei-
       lungen*, 77 (1976), 569–81.
       Publisher Printer and Book, the Caxton Quincentenary Address, 1976.

1977   'On the *Nun's Priest's Tale*', *Bulletin des Anglicistes Médiévistes*, 11 (1977),
       115.

1978   *Chaucer and his World*, 1978.
       Chaucer: The Critical Heritage, 2 vols., ed. D. S. Brewer, 1978.
       'The Nature of Romance', *Poetica*, 9 (1978), 9–48.
       'The Relevance of Medieval Studies in English', *The Rising Generation*,
       124 (1978), 302–6.

1979   'The Gospel and the Laws of Folktale', *Folklore*, 90 (1979), 37–52.
       '*The Lord of the Rings* as Romance', *J. R. R. Tolkien, Scholar and Storyteller:
       Essays in Memoriam*, ed. Mary Salu and Robert T. Farrell, 1979,
       pp. 248–64.
       'Guest Editorial', *Association for Literary and Linguistic Computing Bulletin*,
       7 (1979), 1–3.
       'The Arming of the Warrior in European Literature and Chaucer',
       *Chaucerian Problems and Perspectives: Essays Presented to Paul E. Beichner,
       C. S. C.*, ed. E. Vasta and Z. P. Thundy, 1979, pp. 221–43.
       'What is the *Nun's Priest's Tale* Really About?', *Trames* (*Travaux et
       Memoires de l'Université de Limoges*), 2 (1979), 9–25.
       'Furnivall and the Old Chaucer Society', *The Chaucer Newsletter*, 1
       (1979), 2–6.
       'The Fabliaux', *Companion to Chaucer Studies*, ed. Beryl Rowland, revised
       edn, 1979, pp. 296–325. (Reprinted from the first edn of 1968, with
       updated bibliography.)

1980   'The Traditional and Symbolic Story', *Medieval English Studies News-
       letter*, 2 (1980), 1–7.
       'The Battleground of Home', *Encounter*, 54 (1980), 52–61.
       *Symbolic Stories: Traditional Narratives of the Family Drama in English
       Literature*, 1980. (Reprinted with corrections, 1988.)
       'The Tutor: A Portrait', *C. S. Lewis at the Breakfast Table and Other
       Reminiscences*, ed. James T. Como, 1980, pp. 41–67.

1981   *Aspects of Malory*, ed. Toshiyuki Takamiya and Derek Brewer, 1981.
       (Contains 'Introduction', pp. 1–8: reprinted with updated biblio-
       graphy, 1986.)
       'Root's Account of the Text of *Troilus*', *Poetica*, 12 (1981 for 1979),
       36–44.
       'Observations on the Text of *Troilus*', *Medieval Studies for J. A. W.
       Bennett, aetatis suae LXX*, ed. P. L. Heyworth, 1981, pp. 121–38.
       'Malory: The Traditional Writer and the Archaic Mind', *Arthurian
       Literature I* (1981), pp. 94–120.
       'The Paston Letters', *Folio* (Winter, 1981), 16–23.
       'Medieval Literature, Folk Tale and Traditional Literature', *Dutch*

Quarterly Review of Anglo-American Letters, 11 (1981), 3–16.

1982 'Some Aspects of Style in Biblical Translation in English', *Essays on the English Bible and English Literature in Honour of Dr Tateo Kanda*, ed. Toshiki Yamamoto, 1982, pp. 1–17.

Tradition and Innovation in Chaucer, 1982. (Collection of Brewer's articles.)

'The Grain of the Text', *Acts of Interpretation: The Text in its Context 700–1600: Essays on Medieval and Renaissance Literature in Honor of E. Talbot Donaldson*, ed. Mary J. Carruthers and Elizabeth D. Kirk, 1982, pp. 119–27.

George MacDonald, *Phantastes*, with an introduction by Derek Brewer, 1982, pp. v–x.

1983 *English Gothic Literature*, 1983.

'The Presentation of the Character of Lancelot: Chrétien to Malory', *Arthurian Literature III*, [1983], pp. 26–52.

'The Advent of the Modern', *Studies in English Literature*, English Number 1983, 189–203. (A Japanese translation by Masao Kaiho in *Mita Hyoron* (Keio University), 829 (1982), 33–44.)

'Chaucer's Attitudes to Music', *Poetica*, 15 and 16 (1983), 128–35.

'Medieval European Literature', *The New Pelican Guide to English Literature*, ed. Boris Ford, vol. 1: Medieval Literature, Part Two: The European Literature, 1983, pp. 41–81.

Traditional Stories and Their Meanings, The English Association Presidential Address, 1983.

'Arithmetic and the Mentality of Chaucer', *Literature in Fourteenth-Century England: The J. A. W. Bennett Memorial Lectures, Perugia 1981–82*, ed. Piero Boitani and Anna Torti, 1983, pp. 155–64.

1984 *An Introduction to Chaucer*, 1984.

Chaucer: The Poet as Storyteller, 1984.

'Chaucer and Arithmetic', *Medieval Studies Conference Aachen 1983: Language and Literature*, ed. Wolf-Dietrich Bald and Horst Weinstock, 1984, pp. 111–19.

Childe Roland to the Dark Tower Came: An approach to English Studies, An Inaugural Lecture Delivered Before the University of Cambridge on 26 January 1984, 1984.

1985 [Introduction to Beardsley's *Morte Darthur*], 1985, pp. [vii–xxix]. (The present edition reprints in two-volume facsimile the small paper issue of the first edn of 1893–4 with the addition of a new introduction by Brewer, and is limited to 500 copies, of which the 150 copies for the Japanese market contain at the end of the second volume a Japanese translation by T. Takamiya of the new introduction.)

Arthur's Britain: The Land and the Legend, by Derek Brewer and Ernest Frankl, 1985.

'The International Medieval Popular Comic Tale in England', *The Popular Literature of Medieval England*, ed. T. J. Heffernan, Tennessee

Studies in Literature, 28 (1985), pp. 131–47.

'Middle English Romance and its Audiences', *Historical and Editorial Studies in Medieval and Early Modern English: Festschrift for Johan Gerritson*, ed. Mary-Jo Arn and Hanneke Wirtjes with Hans Jansen, 1985, pp. 37–47.

'The Reconstruction of Chaucer': The Presidential Address, *Studies in the Age of Chaucer, Proceedings, No. 1, 1984: Reconstructing Chaucer*, ed. Paul Strohm and Thomas J. Heffernan, 1985, pp. 3–19.

1986 'Malory's "Proving" of Sir Lancelot', *The Changing Face of Arthurian Romance: Essays on Arthurian Prose Romances in Memory of Cedric E. Pickford*, ed. Alison Adams, Armel H. Diverres, Karen Stern and Kenneth Varty, 1986, pp. 123–36.

'Chaucer's Poetic Style', *The Cambridge Chaucer Companion*, ed. Piero Boitani and Jill Mann, 1986, pp. 227–42.

'Welcome Address to the Manuscript Society', *Manuscripts*, 38 (1986), 292–5.

Henry James, *The Princess Casamassima*, with an introduction by Derek Brewer, a Penguin Novel, 1986.

1987 'Death in Malory's *Le Morte Darthur*', *Zeit, Tod und Ewigkeit in der Renaissance Literatur*, Band 3, Analecta Cartusiana, 117, 1987, pp. 44–57.

'The Reeve's Tale', *Chaucer's Frame Tales: The Physical and the Metaphysical*, ed. Jeorg O. Fichte, 1987, pp. 67–81.

Essay on *Troilus* in *Britain Abroad*, British Council Publications (detailed information not available).

1988 'The Other, the Self: Speculations Concerning an Aspect of Western Culture and Medieval Literature', *Medieval English Studies Presented to George Kane*, ed. Edward Donald Kennedy, Ronald Waldron and Joseph S. Wittig, 1988, pp. 317–27.

'Chaucer and the Bible', *Philologia Anglica: Essays Presented to Professor Yoshio Terasawa on the Occasion of his Sixtieth Birthday*, ed. Kinshiro Oshitari et al., 1988, pp. 270–84.

'Traditional Stories', *Studies in English Literature*, English Number 1988, 3–14.

'Orality and Literacy in Chaucer', *Mündlichkeit und Schriftlichkeit in englischen Mittelalter*, ed. Willi Erzgräber and Sabine Volk, 1988, pp. 85–119.

'Some Current Trends in Arthurian Scholarship and Criticism', *Arthurian Studies* (1988).

'Chaucer's Anti-Ricardian Poetry' in *The Living Middle Ages: Studies in Medieval English Literature and its Tradition*, A Festschrift for Karl-Heinz Göller on the Occasion of his Sixty-fifth Birthday, ed. U. Böller, M. Markus and R. Schöwerling, forthcoming.

Studies in Medieval English Romances, ed. Derek Brewer, 1988. (Includes the editor's 'Introduction: Escape from the Mimetic Fallacy'.)

Index